Sociology for Social Workers

Sociology for Social Workers

**Anne Llewellyn, Lorraine Agu and
David Mercer**
Faculty of Health, Leeds Metropolitan University

polity

First published in 2008 by Polity Press

Polity Press
65 Bridge Street
Cambridge CB2 1UR, UK

Polity Press
350 Main Street
Malden, MA 02148, USA

ISBN-13: 978-07456-3697-9
ISBN-13: 978-07456-3698-6 (pb)

A catalogue record for this book is available from the British Library.

Typeset in 10.5 on 13 pt Quadraat
by Servis Filmsetting Ltd, Manchester.
Printed and bound in Great Britain by MPG Books Ltd, Bodmin, Cornwall.

The publisher has used its best endeavours to ensure that the URLs for external websites referred to in this book are correct and active at the time of going to press. However, the publisher has no responsibility for the websites and can make no guarantee that a site will remain live or that the content is or will remain appropriate.

For further information on Polity, visit our website: www.polity.co.uk

This book is dedicated to Owen Parsons, a student on the BA (Hons) Social Work course at Leeds Metropolitan University (September 2004–July 2006)

Contents

Figures

Tables

Acknowledgements

We would like to thank the anonymous reviewers for their helpful and constructive feedback at various stages in the development of this book and Emma Longstaff for her enduring support, patience and advice. We would also like to extend our thanks to Professor Nick Frost for his support and helpful comments on draft manuscripts. Thanks also go to parents who have provided impromptu childcare at various times and to friends who have shown support and tolerance. We also thank various cohorts of social work students who we have tried various exercises out on and colleagues who have helped us to formulate ideas. Above all, we extend our gratitude to our respective partners, children and close friends for their love and support.

Introduction

Social work is a socially constructed phenomenon . . . defined by the economic, social and cultural conditions in which it takes place.

(Payne, 1991: 7)

This book is intended as a foundational text, introducing social work students to sociology and the ways that sociological theories and perspectives can contribute to our understanding of the history, role and purpose of social work within contemporary British society. It is important that social workers understand the social conditions and processes within which they operate and sociology offers theories to understand these processes and the nature of the social world that we inhabit. It can help us to understand the world that we are part of, through the exploration of how institutions are structured, how power is distributed and impacts on individuals, and how individuals interact and make sense of social situations. In their day-to-day work, social workers encounter some of the most vulnerable and marginalised people and groups in society, and sociology helps us to explore and explain the nature of inequality in society and the construction of disadvantage and advantage and helps to inform 'anti-oppressive practice' and 'anti-discriminatory practice'.

Sociological perspectives in social work are useful in understanding the role of social work in society by helping us to understand:

- how and why social work developed as a profession
- the purpose of social work in society and the role and function of social work
- the nature of social problems that social workers may encounter
- social divisions, inequality and discrimination and the contribution of sociological perspectives in the development of anti-oppressive practice.

Social work is a contested area and has changed and evolved in relation to the wider political, economic, policy and social context. There have been specific times in history where different theoretical perspectives have dominated the construction of social work knowledge (see Chapter 1). In contemporary social work education, there remain some courses where students are taught discrete areas of sociological theory within a single module, whereas other courses may subsume sociological perspectives within broader theoretical subject areas, such as the social sciences. However, the significance of a sociological understanding for social work is reflected by the QAA Benchmarks, which, alongside the GSCC and Department of Health (DH) requirements offer a prescribed curriculum for social work education and training. This is exemplified in the following social work benchmark statements, outlining requirements that social workers should have an understanding of:

- *The relevance of sociological perspectives to understanding societal and structural influences on human behaviour at individual, group and community levels.*
- *The social processes . . . that lead to marginalisation, isolation and exclusion and their impact on the demand for social work services.*
- *Explanations of the links between definitional processes contributing to social differences . . . to the problems of inequality and differential need faced by service users.*

(QAA Benchmark Statement for Social Policy and Social Work, 2000)

Sociology can help social workers to think critically, reflecting on the context of practice and challenging the processes that lead to disadvantage and oppression. Social work and the social context within which it operates are dynamic activities and processes, and therefore are constantly changing. The policies that are used as illustrations throughout this book demonstrate how sociology can help us to understand the social context of social work practice, and the individual and structural influence on and impact of social change.

The book is divided into twelve chapters, which focus on different social institutions, processes and user groups that social workers will encounter in their professional practice. However, many of the areas overlap, and you will see that issues are cross-referenced throughout the book. You will also find a number of exercises, discussion points and case studies that will help you to understand the theories and perspectives, but will also help you to apply these theories and perspectives to different areas of social work practice. Discussion points can be found at the end of each chapter, to summarise the debates and to help with your further exploration of sociology. In addition, you will find guidance for further reading to help you to explore some of the key theories in more depth. Some suggestions for useful web sources and journals can be found at the end of the book, although these are by no means definitive or exhaustive.

1

Sociology and Key Issues

This opening chapter outlines some of the key sociological themes which permeate the rest of the book. Key issues and themes in this chapter help us explore the nature of sociology and understand, analyse and critically reflect on the nature of social work practice.

The key issues that will be addressed in this chapter are:

- The nature of social work and how sociology can inform social work practice.
- The development of social work in the context of broader social, political and ideological changes.
- The nature of sociology identifying broad perspectives within the discipline.
- The relationship between sociological perspectives and social work theory and practice.
- An introduction to key themes which permeate throughout the text.

By the end of this chapter, you should be able to:

- Identify the reasons for studying sociology and ways that this can inform social work practice.
- Discuss the historical development of social work and the social processes that influenced this development.
- Identify the key social issues that are relevant in contemporary social work practice with a range of user groups.
- Identify sources of power and oppression that impact on service user groups.

In August 1861, Peter Barratt and James Bradley appeared in court in Chester. They were charged with the murder of George Burgess, a two-year-old boy. Barratt and Bradley were described as neglected and uneducated.

George Burgess had been playing on some waste ground while under the care of a child minder. Both his parents were working in the local mill. According to witnesses, George was dragged to a local stream, stripped and beaten. He was found dead the following day. Barratt and Bradley admitted the murder, and after a short prison sentence, were sent to a reformatory.

Wilson (2006) remarks that there are clear similarities between this case and the murder of Jamie Bulger in 1993. Barratt and Bradley, however, received a shorter sentence and the judge noted their circumstances.

What does this have to do with sociology? Sociology offers some important social theories, which provide explanations and critiques of human behaviour, social action and interaction and the institutions and structures of society. The fact that social workers are concerned with social change and problem-solving is precisely why sociological theories are so important to social workers. It follows that, if we are concerned with the relationship between the individual and society, then helping people to problem-solve will be connected with structures, institutions and systems within society. Cree (2000) discusses the historical relationship between sociology and social work where many social work courses have been based within sociology and social policy departments in universities.

Industrialisation refers to methods of production within manufacturing and agriculture. A region, nation or culture becomes more economically dependent on manufacturing than on traditional methods of farming.

Social work arose because of concerns about people being marginalised and impoverished as a result of industrialisation. As discussed below, the Victorian philanthropic tradition focused on changing society, and education, housing, health and employment were all key institutions for achieving social change. Mary Richmond formulated the precursor of modern social work assessment (Richmond, 1917), identifying social factors as well as psychological ones as key to understanding a given situation.

Thompson (2005) has argued that social work is sometimes viewed by society as a profession that mops up society's problems and deals with the failings of social policies in the areas of education, crime, health, housing and income maintenance. This relates to work with a variety of user groups who experience social policy changes and trends, e.g. work with the unemployed, the poor, the homeless, the mentally ill, or the disabled. This can be seen to reflect the early origins of social work where philanthropy was concerned with the 'fallout' from nineteenth- century economic and political conditions. It may be viewed as a little simplistic for the complexities of contemporary social work, in that it does not necessarily reflect the whole range of roles of the social worker, but it is a useful starting point for a discussion of the fact that social workers are often engaged with individuals, groups and communities who suffer some form of social disadvantage. The fact that the title Social Worker starts with Social is not coincidental

(Thompson, 2005). The nature of social work is fundamentally located in and influenced by social factors, processes and ideas in the following ways.

Many problems and disadvantages have their origin in social processes. For example, poverty and disadvantage result from processes of stratification. Societies are not just divided into two opposing parts, where you are either one thing or another, but are made up of a plurality of different groups and divisions.

- The solutions to individual problems may lie within wider social and community processes. The case study of Barratt and Bradley demonstrates societal concern about their lack of education and the failure of society and the local community to adequately provide for them.
- Individual behaviours and experiences do not operate in a vacuum, but are located within wider social contexts. As discussed below, risk is an important concept in contemporary societies, but wider social and structural processes influence individual decisions and behaviours. Furthermore, individual actions and experiences may be related to processes of interaction, and social action theories (see Chapter 2) will be explored throughout this book, to examine issues such as identity and stigma.
- Social work itself does not operate within a vacuum, but is located within the wider social organisation and is impacted on by social, economic and political factors and sets of dominant ideas.

These issues will be discussed throughout the book in relation to different user groups.

What is social work?

The social work profession promotes social change, problem solving in human relationships, and the empowerment and liberation of people to enhance well-being. Utilising theories of human behaviour and social systems, social work intervenes at points where people interact with their environments. Principles of human rights and social justice are fundamental to social work.

(IASSW (International Association of Schools of Social Work), 2001 – available at www.iassw-aiets.org/)

While the above definition of social work implies that there is an agreed definition of what social work is, the role and function of social work has always been contested, with social work being the subject of competing claims of definition and practice (Asquith et al., 2005). Many authors, social workers and commentators recognise that there are a range of activities, which are carried out by social workers, which may be either contradictory or complementary. These activities may be summarised as ones that include:

- counsellor or caseworker
- advocacy
- partnership
- assessment of risk and need
- care manager
- agent of social control (Asquith et al., 2005).

There may be conflicts, for example between the roles of advocacy and case management. On the one hand, the social worker may have a role in their supportive relationship with clients, facilitating access to services and empowering. On the other hand, they have a role within a bureaucratic organisation, with responsibilities in terms of policy, procedures and economic management. There may also be conflicts between the roles of protection and risk management and enablement and empowerment. These conflicting roles within social work are described in the following chapters.

Case study

Susie (28) is a white English mother of four children: Sara (10), Ryan (8), Kristy (5) and Rio (3). Sara and Ryan share the same biological father, with whom they have no contact, as he was violent towards Susie and their relationship ended. Kristy's father is unknown, whereas Rio's father has regular contact with Susie and the children and often stays at the family home.

Social services and other agencies have provided family support for long periods of the children's lives. Recently however, the children's school has reported increasing concerns to social services regarding the children's welfare. They note that the children often appear hungry and dirty. Sara has become quiet and withdrawn, Ryan is prone to aggressive outbursts and Kristy often falls asleep in class. Rio has a full-time place at a day nursery but usually only attends for two or three sessions per week. Although Social Services and other agencies are involved with the family and provide a package of family support, the family's social worker has noted that in the last few weeks Susie is appearing more lethargic and 'low' and she has concerns about her relationship with Rio's father.

- What social problems and issues can you identify here?
- What roles and activities might the social worker be involved in?

The conflict between the key tasks and roles of social work has been summarised in a report by Blewett et al. (2007), which highlights the constantly changing nature of social work. These contradictions impact directly on all areas of social work practice.

Social work therefore can be understood by the way in which practice operates within any given context. This suggests that the social work role is dependent upon the nature of social problems as they are identified, the perceived solutions to those problems and the societal and organisational context in which it is practised.

The IASSW definition of social work has been adopted as a working definition of social work by many countries, including the UK. While this may not adequately reflect the social control aspects of social work, it does highlight the fact that social work operates at the interface between the individual and their environment and highlights the relationship that social work has with individuals in their social context. Sociology helps us to understand these competing and contradictory discourses, as well as the nature of the society that we inhabit.

What is sociology?

Sociology is not a single discipline offering one set of theories, but is a complex range of theories offering explanations and understandings from different perspectives. No one theory is more valid than others, but all can contribute to our understanding of the social world.

Exercise

The social world

- How does the social world differ from the natural world?
- In small groups, discuss what you mean by the social world.
- Compare your list with other groups. Are there common elements? Is the social world made up of individuals and institutions? What is the relationship between these different elements?

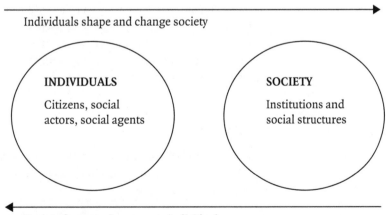

Figure 1.1 Diagrammatic representation of the relationship between individuals and social structures.

There are numerous examples of individuals influencing social structures and institutions both historically and in contemporary society, such as Elizabeth Fry's work to improve conditions in prisons in nineteenth-century Britain, or Octavia Hill's campaign to improve social housing. A more recent example is Esther Rantzen's establishment of Childline, providing a forum for children to discuss issues of concern, such as abuse and bullying, which has been significant, not only in the development of policies in relation to child abuse, but also in challenging the taboo of incest and childhood abuse. In the twenty-first century, the work of Sir Bob Geldof and Bono (among others) has been instrumental in raising awareness about Third World poverty, and the resulting Make Poverty History campaign has gathered momentum (www.makepovertyhistory.org/).

Exercise

Make a list of other individuals who have had influence over the nature of society or social institutions.

The institutions and structures of society also influence the lived experience of individuals within society. For example, the patriarchal organisation of society impacts on the nature of women's experiences, both within the home and within the paid labour market (see Chapters 5 and 8). *Institutional racism* within the Criminal Justice System has impacted on the experiences of black people in their encounters with the police, the judiciary and the prison system (see Chapters 4 and 6). Both the family and the education system have influence in the primary socialisation process (see Chapter 8), and in shaping people's expectations, beliefs and values.

Institutional racism a theory that racism exists within public bodies, organisations (institutions) such as the Police or Social Services.

Individuals also occupy social roles within society. From a functionalist perspective, these roles serve to maintain the smooth running of society, whilst Marxists see roles from a conflict perspective (See Chapter 2). People may occupy a number of different roles in terms of work, social relationships and positions in society.

Exercise

Make a list of the different roles that you occupy.
Is there any potential conflict between these roles?

Frequently we have to balance competing roles, based on our own priorities and those of the wider society to which we belong. In policy and managerial circles there has been much recent discussion about work–life balance, exploring ways in which individuals can more effectively balance competing roles, and how institutions and organisations can facilitate this. Strategies such as work smarter initiatives, encouraging a more efficient and effective use of work and travel time are of contemporary interest within many organisations (www.employersforwork-lifebalance.org.uk).

Thus sociology can help us to understand the relationship between individuals and institutions and the interdependent roles within social relationships. Sociology differs from biological and psychological theories in that it explores the relationship between the structures of society and the human actions and interactions that exist within it. Human life is seen as a higher form of life than animal life, and therefore behaviours cannot be predicted and explained purely through the natural sciences.

Sociology helps us to explain social relationships and individual interpretations of social situations. However, there are also clear interrelations between sociological theories and some psychological

Micro focuses on individuals and everyday life.

Macro concerned with broad social structures, ideas and institutions.

theories that explain human growth and development from *micro* and *macro* perspectives. In particular there are similarities between sociological perspectives and ecological theories. For example, Bronfenbrenner's (1979) ecological perspective on human development discusses the influence of the immediate micro world of the family and local community and the macro world of the national picture – policies, approaches and laws. This links to sociology and the theories are complementary rather than repetitive.

Political theory is also related to sociological perspectives. The 'macro' world that Bronfenbrenner describes impacts on society through the 'top down' effect of national policies, which are driven by political ideologies in a given period. Giddens (2006) discusses how political actions and behaviours have been of interest to sociologists. However, political trends are both 'top down' and 'bottom up'. For example, public demonstrations against the unpopular poll tax in the mid-1980s contributed to a revision of policy. The interaction between politics and society is therefore fundamental to sociological understanding.

It is important for social workers to have a broad knowledge of these different theories in order to help them explain and understand the social world that they and the people that they work with inhabit.

Why study sociology?

Giddens (2006) argues that there are three reasons for studying sociology:

1. It allows us to see the social world from other people's viewpoint. A much better understanding of someone's problems may be gained if we are able to understand them from the individual or

group's perspectives – sometimes referred to as putting oneself in the place of the other. This is particularly pertinent for social workers where in practice there is a need to move away from one's own value base and respect the views of other individuals, in order to respect diversity and operate in an anti-oppressive way.

Scenario

Richard, aged six, is in a school class of thirty children of mixed ability. He is constantly fidgeting about, talking to other children, making silly noises and apparently not listening. Teachers frequently need to manage Richard, removing him from the main group of children and discussing his behaviour with his parents.

From the teachers' perspective, Richard is seen as a disruptive influence and makes classroom management difficult. Despite numerous attempts to discipline Richard, his behaviour shows no sign of improvement.

If we listen to Richard, we can ascertain that he is bored. He does not find the work interesting and stimulating and does not see why he has to do it. He feels as though he has tried, but no matter how hard he tries, he does not seem to get praised by the teacher like the other children do. It seems unfair to him that he is constantly getting told off, when other children seem to behave in a similar way.

By listening to both perspectives, we can see that Richard is attention seeking – by being *naughty* he gets the attention that he craves. By listening to Richard's perspective, the teacher can adopt a different strategy, whereby Richard is given work that engages him more effectively and is positively rewarded in a meaningful way for the effort that he makes.

2. Sociology may help to provide practical help to people, by assessing the results and effectiveness of policy initiatives from different people's viewpoints.

Scenario

A local supermarket establishes an access bus service for older people in the neighbourhood, so that they can get out to do their shopping. Although initially the usage is high, it soon dwindles, and after a few weeks very few people continue to use the service. Seeing the lack of usage as evidence of a lack of need, the supermarket management decides to cancel the service, However, when older people are asked about the value of the service, they state that it is something that is needed and valued. Although the bus helps them to get to the shop in the first place, they feel that once they get to the shop they are still unable to be independent shoppers, as they encounter other obstacles, such as difficulty in carrying heavy baskets, manipulating trolleys or reaching products on high shelves, and they feel that staff are irritable and impatient with them if the shop is busy. An alternative solution to the accessibility problem would be to provide volunteers as shopping companions, educate and train staff to reduce *ageist* attitudes and to promote a culture of understanding, as well as providing the access bus service.

Ageism discrimination ◄ against people on the basis of their age.

3. Sociology can help to provide self-enlightenment as we explore the reasons for oppression, difference, diversity and social actions. The more we can understand our social situations and ourselves, the better able we are to influence our futures. In a profession like social work, where human interactions are an important part of the work, the ability to explore and reflect on our own values and meanings is paramount in establishing rapport with individuals. Equally the ability to reflect on the impact of our actions on the lives of others is a necessary component of anti-oppressive practice and emancipatory social work.

As stated in the National Occupational Standards for Social Work, a social worker should '*Have an awareness of own values, prejudices, ethical dilemmas and conflicts of interest and their implications for practice.*' (GSCC, 2002)

Is sociology common sense?

One common view of sociology is that it is just common sense and that you do not need theories in order to explain the social world. However, the examples above demonstrate that a greater understanding and analysis can be developed through sociological enquiry, and the theories that will be developed throughout this book will show how the world can be explained from different perspectives, to help to develop a richer understanding of our lives and those of the individuals that we come into contact with in practice.

> *The first wisdom of sociology is this: things are not what they seem.*
> (Berger, 1966 cited in Macionis and Plummer, 2005: 2)

Development of social work as a profession

By employing a descriptive definition of social work we could suggest that social work is simply what social workers do (Thompson, 2005) and that social work is what the agency or government policy requires it to do. However many of the activities performed by social workers, such as assessing needs and undertaking statutory responsibilities, overlap with other human services. Thompson (2000) suggests that by exploring the purpose of social work in society and by looking at its history, we can come to an understanding about what is meant by social work. It is therefore important to explore the historical development of social work and the legacy of this development, in order to understand the nature of the social issues that affect social work practice today.

All industrialised countries have developed responses to human needs, either through informal and voluntary means and/or through state-provided services. The emergence of social work as a distinct occupational activity can be seen as a statutory response to managing human needs largely in response to growing concerns about social problems and societal breakdown.

Whilst there has always been informal work done with individuals, families and communities, what we would now recognise as social work or social reform did not emerge in an organised manner until the late nineteenth century. It is of no coincidence that social work as an activity emerged during a period of rapid economic, political and social change. This period of mid to late Victorian Britain witnessed rapid societal change with industrialisation and *urbanisation* transforming work and family life. The negative effects of such changes have been well documented (Himmelweit, 1995) highlighting the downside of such social change in terms of unemployment, poverty, family break-up and ill health, prostitution, alcohol abuse and hooliganism and anti-social behaviour. These social problems, which were largely unseen in rural communities, had now become more highly visible in the towns and cities of a newly industrialised Britain.

Urbanisation growth of towns and cities. This particularly relates to economic changes in industry from the nineteenth century onwards. This has led to a vast growth in cities within modern societies. In the nineteenth century, manufacturing and production moved to large-scale factories in urban environments.j314

It is said that social work emerged in the space between the individual and the state at a period in time when there were growing concerns about the effects of deprivation on the vulnerable. Alongside this, there were concerns about the state of the nation as a whole, in terms of employability, social cohesion and the capacity of working-class men to fight and win wars, which led to widespread programmes of social reform.

A number of religious based charitable organisations (including Barnardo's, NSPCC and the Methodist National Children's Home) were established in the field of child welfare, and other individuals became involved in campaigns to improve care for the sick (Mary Seacole and Florence Nightingale) and in prison reform (Elizabeth Fry). These women largely carried out activities involving supervision, advice, and the giving of financial assistance, whereas men were engaged with the management and administration of the charities' work, highlighting a gender division in social work that persists today. (See www.gcal.ac.uk/heatherbank/index.htm for more detail about the founding mothers of social work.)

Normalisation process by which groups of people can be integrated into the usual and typical life of the majority of the community.

Moralisation process by which governing rules or behaviours are promoted as the common standards, in the interests of society.

The activity of early social work was characterised by individual intervention based on the principles of *normalisation* and *moralisation*. The first principle centred on the belief that vulnerable people should be encouraged to live a life that was as near to normal as was

Nineteenth-century Victorian mill. (Duncan Walker)

Less eligibility the principle that those reliant on state welfare should receive benefits or relief at a lower level than the lowest paid worker who maintains themselves–associated with 1834 Poor Law.

possible, taking into account the *less eligibility* criteria of the Poor Law (Fraser, 1984). This stated that people who received assistance through the Poor Law should be no better off than a lowest paid labourer. Moralisation was based on the belief that Christian values and morals of self-reliance, hard work and clean living should be promoted and from this emerged concepts of the deserving and undeserving poor.

Discussion points

The origins of social work are said to arise out of a concern for the welfare of individuals but also for the well-being of society. The term 'dangerous classes' was used to describe the lifestyle and habits of the poor, idle and feckless.

The language may have changed, but how far can contemporary social work be described as 'management and surveillance of the dangerous classes'?

The emergence of state social work in twentieth-century Britain

This period is characterised by the transition of social work from an essentially charitable activity to one which was administered by the state, as concerns grew that many of the activities by these reformers were being duplicated or carried out in an indiscriminate manner. In 1869 the Charitable Organisation Society (COS) was founded to act as an umbrella organisation to oversee and administer the work of these early social workers.

The creation of the COS has been viewed as the beginnings of state social work (Stedman Jones, 1976) and, as the twentieth century progressed, social work became increasingly *professionalised*, with work being carried out by the state or by voluntary organisations on behalf of the state. Social casework, with its belief that the individual is not only the cause, but also the source of the solution to their own problems, became the preferred way of working, leading to an emerging body of knowledge, as social workers sought theoretical paradigms to influence and validate their practices. The search for scientific methods led in 1903 to the first school of social work by the COS in the Department of Sociology in London University (Horner, 2006). Using casework as a method for operation, theories from psychiatry and psychology were influential.

Professionalism a form of work organisation for individuals in society, generally having regulations and a specific structure.

As social work progressed as a profession in the twentieth century, sociological perspectives became more prominent. Individualist explanations of social problems were challenged by sociological ones, which sought to understand the social and individual consequences of poverty, unemployment and other social changes.

Horner (2006) has argued that the history of the professionalisation of welfare and the care of the vulnerable has been significant in the development of an institutional approach to the containment and care of the vulnerable. The workhouse system of the 1834 Poor Law established a system of containment, which was mirrored by the incarceration of people who were seen as marginal or vulnerable within various forms of institutions: e.g. the asylum system in mental health practice (Pilgrim and Rogers, 2005); the containment of people with physical and/or learning disabilities in special institutions (Race, 2002); the institutionalisation of the care of older people in nursing homes and residential care (Means and Smith, 2003). Management of these 'social problems' within institutions became based on the dominant medical model, using scientific methods to manage people individually, and to control and contain what society saw as abnormal behaviour. This has left a legacy in health and social care, where the medical paradigm still dominates much health and social care provision and conflicts between medical and social models of care provision remain embedded in social policy provision for vulnerable groups.

Sociological perspectives can help us to understand the impact of institutionalisation of vulnerable groups, in the construction of stigma and societal responses to vulnerable groups, the marginality of the vulnerable and the losses of liberty and autonomy for those who are institutionalised. This is of major concern for the social work profession who seek to promote anti-oppressive practice and the empowerment of individuals. These issues will be explored in more depth throughout the book in relation to specific user groups.

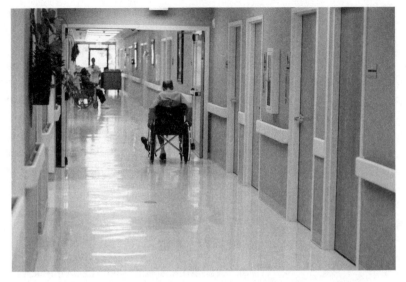

This shows institutionalised care, characterised by the long corridor, with multiple rooms leading from it.

The future of social work – key sociological themes and perspectives

As social work evolves in the twenty-first century the processes of change continue to affect the context and content of practice and continue to be affected by social, economic and political factors at a local, national and global level. Just as the processes of industrialisation and urbanisation were instrumental in the developments of nineteenth-century social work practice, changes in the global economy and the information and technology age have created new processes of social disadvantage and inequality and new contexts for the practice of social work on an international basis.

> Castells insists that information technologies represent a greater change in the history of technology than those associated with the industrial revolution.
>
> (Fitzpatrick, 2005: 95)

The media and information technology industry are important institutions of contemporary society with media discourses becoming increasingly important in the construction of dominant discourses in contemporary societies. Habermas (1989) was quite critical of classical sociological theorists (particularly Marx – see Chapter 2) for ignoring the importance of culture in society and viewed the media as an important institution in the creation of public attitudes and dominant cultural processes. An example of this can be viewed in the way that the media invigilated the grief response in the

Discourses concept used by Foucault to illustrate how language shapes our thinking. Foucault believed there is no such thing as absolute truth, but at any one moment in time a dominant 'way of seeing' exists, shaping our understanding.

aftermath of Princess Diana's death in 1997. Individuals, shocked by the news, were unsure how to react, and according to Walter (1999) looked to others to see how to respond appropriately. The media reporting of the grieving then became an important source of information, and the laying of flowers and signing of condolence books became more widespread. Merrin (1999) takes this further, arguing that Diana's death and funeral became a media event in itself. Drawing on the work of Nietzsche (1882) and Baudrillard (1994), he argues that the media has the capacity to create symbols and images. Thus he argues

> Media do not merely produce specific patterns of social organization, but more importantly, produce specific forms of consciousness and modes of knowledge which affect our experience and interpretation of the world.
>
> (Merrin, 1999: 42)

Giddens (2006) has examined the role of soap operas in contemporary society, and argues that they 'address universal properties of personal and emotional life' that people can identify with, and at times may help people to solve their own personal dilemmas. Parton and Franklin (1991) have argued that the media have been instrumental in the creation of moral panics in relation to child abuse and incest.

The televisual media and advances in phone and computer technology have created possibilities for the transmission of pictures and words around the world. One result of this increased interconnectedness has been the advent of global capitalism, with strong global economies being particularly advantaged through their ability to extend markets for their commodities.

> In the new century, social work is confronted with a global system in which the world's people are bound together in a complex web of economic relationships. People's lives are now linked to lives of distant others through the clothes that they wear, the energy that warms them and even the food that they eat.
>
> (Polack, 2004: 281)

Globalisation

Globalisation process of increasing global interconnectedness, whereby goods and services, capital flows, workers increasingly move around the world encouraged by trade and revolutions in communications and technology.

Studying the global world helps us to see our own society within the context of the wider world, helping us to realise that the perspective we may have about the way that society operates is only one perspective, and other societies may view things quite differently. Macionis and Plummer (2005) identify the following features of the global world:

1. The increased interconnectedness of countries and societies across the world. This is particularly related to technological advancements, with the increase in global tourism and travel

through advances in the aviation industry and advances in global informational technology. Thus the multi-national corporations have benefited through increased markets for profiteering. This global capitalism has led to new social divisions, inequalities and exploitations, as the new network and informational society has led to social polarisation, social inequality and social exclusion (Rowson, 2000).

Eurocentric the domination of white western European values and norms over other cultural perspectives.

2. A global perspective helps us to see that the problems experienced by Western industrialised countries are far more serious elsewhere in the world, and helps us to adopt a less *eurocentric* approach to social problems. For example, if we look at world poverty and life chances, there are gross disparities across the world, with many people in developing nations experiencing absolute poverty rather than relative deprivation (see Chapter 3) This abject poverty is starkly reflected in differential infant mortality rates, for example.

3. Global thinking also helps us to think more critically and to reflect on our own value systems. We learn more about ourselves through seeing the experiences of others.

Case study

Li arrived in the UK six months ago, with his pregnant wife, He is seeking asylum from a politically oppressive regime, where he was persecuted and tortured. Having worked in IT in his host country, he now takes on a number of menial jobs in order to earn a meagre income. He is frightened and upset by the hostility that he has experienced.

Discussion points

- How do you think global economics and politics impact upon this situation?
- How does this also relate to issues of social disadvantage and power?

This case study raises important issues that social workers face when working with vulnerable people, whether they be children, people from different ethnic and or cultural backgrounds, people with mental or physical health problems or disabilities, older people, or those who are seen as criminal offenders. There are common concepts that sociology can help us to understand and explain so that social work can be practised according to the values of social justice, empowerment and anti-oppressive practice.

- social disadvantage, discrimination and prejudice
- power and control
- citizenship and identity.

Table 1.1 Comparison of life expectancies, 2000–2005 and 2045–2050

	2000–2005			2045–2050	
Rank	Country or area	Life expectancy (years)	Rank	Country or area	Life expectancy (years)
A. Highest life expectancy at birth					
1.	Japan	81.9	1.	Japan	88.3
2.	China, Hong Kong SAR	81.5	2.	China, Hong Kong SAR	86.9
3.	Iceland	80.6	3.	Iceland	86.1
4.	Switzerland	80.4	4.	Switzerland	85.7
5.	Australia	80.2	5.	Sweden	85.5
6.	Sweden	80.1	6.	China, Macao SAR	85.4
7.	Italy	80.0	7.	Canada	85.3
8.	China, Macao SAR	80.0	8.	Italy	85.1
9.	Canada	79.9	9.	Australia	85.0
10.	Israel	79.6	10.	Norway	84.9
B. Lowest life expectancy at birth					
1.	Swaziland	32.9	1.	Swaziland	51.9
2.	Botswana	36.6	2.	Lesotho	52.9
3.	Lesotho	36.7	3.	Botswana	53.8
4.	Zimbabwe	37.2	4.	Zimbabwe	54.8
5.	Zambia	37.4	5.	Equatorial Guinea	55.1
6.	Central African Rep	39.4	6.	Sierra Leone	56.7
7.	Malawi	39.6	7.	Central African Rep	57.0
8.	Sierra Leone	40.6	8.	Angola	57.4
9.	Angola	40.7	9.	Zambia	57.5
10.	Mozambique	41.9	10.	Malawi	58.9
	WORLD	64.7		WORLD	74.7

Source:
Population Division of the Department of Economic and Social Affairs of the United Nations Secretariat (2005) (World Population Prospects: The 2004 Revision. Highlights. New York, United Nations)

Social disadvantage

Disadvantage results from social differentiation, which is a universal feature of human societies, but is not a static process. It often results in inequality and is not just about individuals being different from other individuals, but is also about a collective of individuals being viewed as different from other groups of individuals in society. Structural context is important as life chances and individual or collective actions are shaped by the social context within which they occur. People become categorised according to sociological labels, which in turn may affect social interactions and social experiences.

Problems are also *socially constructed*, where society establishes parameters of normality and abnormality and constructs categories of deviance and difference. This may be related to institutional practices in relation to welfare provision, and may reflect sources of power and authority within societies. The social construction of problems is not new, and we can see that the nature of social problems is specific to particular periods of time, social, political and economic processes. For example, in nineteenth-century Britain there were concerns about vagrancy and providing for vagrants, with people questioning why monies raised locally should be used to support those from other localities. The less eligibility principle and workhouse system of the Poor Law Amendment Act were designed in part to deal with these concerns (Jones, 1991). As the case study above demonstrates, we can see some similar attitudes to asylum seekers and refugees who have been displaced within the global economy through war, economic deprivation or political persecution.

Risk and consumerism are also related to patterns of social organisation and social disadvantage. Beck (1992) has argued that we live in a global risk society, with risks being related to environmental change and degradation, population growth and migration, new patterns of social consumption and lifestyle practices and threats of terrorism and illicit criminal activity, such as human trafficking and the drugs trade. However, the risks and threats are not equally distributed throughout societies, and thus patterns of social disadvantage may be exacerbated through the process of globalisation.

Social constructionism term used to describe theories, which considers how social phenomena develop in particular social contexts. This is related to the relationships between individuals and groups in society which shape identity and interaction.

Consumerism and the risk society

The concept of a 'risk society' has been formulated by sociologists such as Beck (1992) and Giddens (1991) and has particular resonance for social work as many aspects of practice involve the assessment and management of risk. A risk society is one which has been organised in response to risks.

> It is a society increasingly pre-occupied with the future (and also with safety) which generates notions of risk.
>
> (Giddens, 1997: 27)

There have always been risks or hazards in society, particularly ones produced by natural disasters such as hurricanes and tsunamis. More recent notions of risk tend to focus upon the processes of modernisation which produce 'man-made' risks or what Giddens (1991) refers to as 'manufactured risks'. Rather than controlling or removing traditional or natural risks associated with living, modernisation has resulted in the creation of new risks, which are global and have potentially more damaging effects. Manufactured

A UN helicopter responding to a natural disaster. A familiar picture from the late twentieth century and early twenty-first century, showing people who have been displaced through war or natural disaster, receiving aid or being evacuated. (William Walsh)

risks could be described as the by-products of nuclear power, industrial activity or global warming. They may also be felt more locally, such as social problems in the form of family breakdown, juvenile delinquency or alcohol misuse. Risk therefore is a routine feature of many aspects of life – crime, parenting, health, employment, and travel (Mythen, 2004).

The new technology and media era have also been associated with an increase in risk, with particular concerns about the effect of television and the internet on children. The internet has opened up new sources of information to people (Cheurprakobkit and Johnston, 2007) and, whilst much of this may be beneficial, it also means that children and young people have greater access to sources of pornography and violence. In addition, children may be more at risk from sexual predators who use the internet for the distribution of obscene images of children or as a medium for grooming (www.nspcc.org.uk). There has also been much criticism of the role of television in the increase of risk in relation to children's lifestyles and health, although authors such as Barker and Petley (2001) have argued that this reflects a moral panic.

> From television's inception, mass media critics have lined up to complain that banal programming, unrestrained marketing and perpetual violence were eroding children's literacy, while turning them into desensitized couch potatoes.
>
> (Cook, 2001, cited in Kline, 2005: 239)

Devastation caused by Hurricane Katrina in New Orleans, 2005.
The picture shows a house on the Bayou, totally destroyed and most
of it washed away. (D. S. Webb)

There have also been concerns about the relationship between obesity
and an increase in sedentary lifestyles (Wilfrey and Saelens, 2002) and
the role of television in promoting unhealthy eating through
advertising campaigns.

> the average child watches 10,000 television advertisements each year,
> 95% of which are for foods in one of four categories, sugared cereals,
> candy, fast foods and soft drinks.
>
> (Fairburn and Brownell, 2002: 436)

Since 9/11 and 7/7 there has been a fundamental shift in the way we
view and understand safety and danger, and thus the concept of the
risk society has important contemporary relevance.

Risk and social work

In social work the concept of risk is a familiar one and it could be said
that all social work practice either implicitly or explicitly involves
elements of risk. Risk is also inextricably linked to the blame culture
that exists within social work, and recent child deaths and murders or
attacks by people who have mental health conditions have focused
many aspects of professional practice around the assessment and
management of risk.

> The system we are in now is almost ready to treat every death as
> chargeable to someone's account, every accident as caused by someone's

criminal negligence, every sickness a threatened prosecution. Whose
fault? is the first question.

(Mary Douglas, 1992: 27)

In social work the risks may not be on a global scale but may be
identified as

- Risk to service users from other people, usually their own relatives
  (e.g. child abuse/elder abuse)
- Risks to users themselves, from their own behaviour (e.g. mental
  health, truanting from school)
- Risk to known or unknown others from service users (e.g. welfare
  professionals).

(Parsloe, 1999)

I felt a personal as well as a professional responsibility to get it right.
This all contributes to anxiety. The result is that if you make a wrong
decision, lots of people, particularly children will suffer.
(The words of a social worker, taken from SCIE 2005)

Social work is an unpredictable and uncertain activity and it is not
always possible to identify and prevent risks. There is also an
assumption that risks are always bad, which ignores the fact that risk-
taking is a part of life and development. Risks are not always associated
with harm, but could result in enrichment (for example a disabled
young person being able to live independently). This over-emphasis on
risk can lead to defensive and routinised practice in which service user
choices are further limited and restricted and social work practice
becomes risk-oriented as opposed to needs-led (Pritchard, 2001).
Although it may not always be possible to eliminate all risks, some
argue that undertaking a risk assessment is an important starting point
in identifying potential risks (Titterton, 2005)

A healthy culture begins with high-quality leadership by senior
managers willing to 'walk the talk' and who are anxious to understand
the issues facing frontline staff. It grows once people are willing to
analyse their individual practice and contemplate change. That in turn
requires management being willing to adopt, not a blame- free culture,
but a learning culture.

(Victoria Climbié Inquiry, 2003)

The values and principles of social work have changed from ones
which reflect paternalism and protection to ones that emphasise
rights and social justice. Marsh (2005) has argued that social justice
is an important principle that defines social work activity in the
twenty-first century and provides the basis for the profession to tackle
the international problems associated with population and
demographic change, poverty and inequality, violence and increasing
risks (Weiss, 2005).

Unlike some professions, the values, purpose and functions of social work seek to ensure that the profession adapts to the social and individual needs of a rapidly changing demographic, economic and social structure, and as such seeks to challenge traditional power relations and to empower individuals.

Power

Power is a pervasive element of social relations, and is thus an important concept for social workers to understand. It is not just about formal power exercised through political and economic systems, but is a central feature of all social relations and interactions. Context and actions are important to enable us to understand the manifestation of power. Power may be mediated through the following means:

- **Coercion** where one person makes another person do something that they may not necessarily want to do. For example, a person who is compulsorily detained in hospital under a mental health assessment.
- **Persuasion**, where an individual is persuaded to do something that they may not necessarily have chosen to do – e.g. a social worker may persuade a woman to report domestic violence.
- **Inducement**, where rewards are offered to people for behaving in a certain way. For example, the offering of financial rewards to 16–18 year olds to stay in full-time education.
- **Social sanctioning** (whereby an individual behaves in a certain way in order to achieve an anticipated reaction (e.g. feeling that you are being positively affirmed in a meeting).
- **Habituation**, where the individual is so used to behaving in a certain way that they act automatically without questioning their actions. An extreme example of habituation is where people have been brainwashed in order to behave as others wish them to. *Ideological hegemony* is also important here, as individuals may absorb the dominant views of society, even though it may not necessarily be in their best interests. For example, women may take on roles of caring, believing it to be their duty and role obligation (Dalley, 1988) (see Chapters 5 and 8).

Ideology a 'set of ideas' or a belief structure, but in practice ideologies reflect the thinking and interests of dominant groups in society. Hence feminists talk of 'patriarchal ideology' and Marxists talk of 'bourgeois ideology'.

Hegemony concept associated with Antonio Gramsci to explain how the upper class maintains power through the subtle use of ideas to win the consent of subordinated groups. Ordinary people are led to believe that the prevailing existing order is somehow natural and normal.

Exercise

1. Think of situations when you have felt powerful and powerless.
2. Where did the sources of power come from?
3. How was power manifested?
4. What examples of the use of power have you experienced within social work practice?

Oppression is clearly related to power and can be defined as a:

> *system of inter-related barriers and forces that reduce, immobilise and mould people who belong to a certain group in ways that effect their subordination to another group.*

(Kendall, 1992)

Oppressive actions limit opportunities for the oppressed group and also keep the group divided through the use of power to continue the oppressive ideology that characterises unequal relations in the social system. This oppressive ideology creates barriers to freedom, where the oppressed believe that the oppressor is right by virtue of their power, the oppressed fear risk-taking to achieve autonomy and there is an inclination to align with the more powerful group through conforming to the ideals of the oppressive group.

Thompson (1998) uses the concentric model shown as figure 1.2 to demonstrate how sources of oppression and discrimination occur at personal (P), cultural (C) and structural (S) levels. Using youth or young people as an illustration, one could consider discrimination and oppression on a personal (P) level when a neighbour regularly complains about young people and their friends, expressing derogatory comments about young people today; on a cultural (C) level, cultural practices e.g. signs in local shops which prohibit 3 or

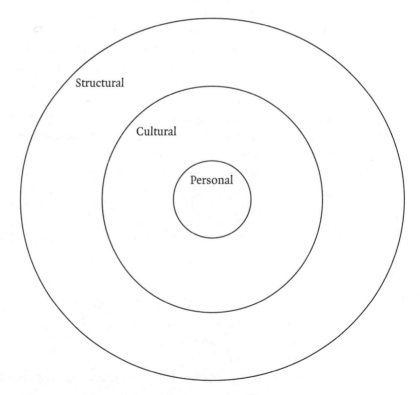

Figure 1.2 Adapted from Thompson (1998).

more school children entering the shop at the same time can be seen to discriminate against young people; while minimum wage legislation, legitimating differential pay based on age is an example of discrimination at a structural (S) level.

Foucault (1980) makes an important contribution to the understanding of how power operates within post-modern society. Foucault argues that the exercise of power has shifted from one based on the notion of sovereign power whereby an individual or group of individuals had ultimate authority over other individuals (e.g. King or Queen) to one based on disciplinary power, where individuals are persuaded to self-discipline through surveillance. In his work on prisons, he identified a particular way in which prisons were built. He used the term *panopticon* to denote a prison built around a central watchtower, so that inmates could be potentially observed at all times. Even if they were not actively being observed, the fact that there was the potential for being observed had the same effect.

Panopticon a prison model which was built on a central design, so that all could potentially be observed at all times (see fig. 1.3).

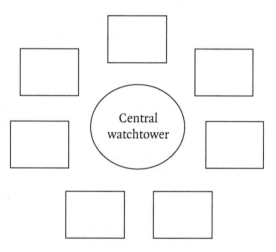

Figure 1.3 Model of the panopticon.

CCTV and speed cameras fulfill a similar function today, working on the principle of the control of behaviour through their presence and potential for operation, irrespective of whether they are actually operational at a given time.

Similarly, it is argued that professionals use surveillance in order to control the behaviour of the population. Armstrong (1995) discusses the contemporary practice of health surveillance, where health care professionals not only deal with the symptoms of illness, but also construct parameters of normality and abnormality and dissipate health information to individuals in order that they may control their own health. This can lead to a victim-blaming approach to illness, where responsibility is seen to reside within individuals, and ignores the structural features and processes that contribute to variants in ill health.

CCTV cameras, which are becoming a more common sight in towns and cities. The photograph shows four surveillance cameras mounted on the pole to oversee a construction site. (Stefan Witas)

Fook (2002) employs post-modern notions of understanding power as a way of developing empowering approaches to social work. She suggests that power is not finite, nor a commodity that can be given from one person or group to another. Regarding power as binary opposites (i.e. the powerful and powerless in which groups are mutually exclusive) does not recognise the concept of relative power, where marginalised groups may exercise power over other marginalised groups (e.g. in a patriarchal system, working-class men are able to exercise power over working-class women). Using Foucauldian ideas, Fook (ibid.) argues that power and disempowerment are processes and power is exercised not possessed. Also, power can be repressive and productive, good and bad, in that power can restrict and control but also provide identity and categorisations. Power is not always enforced downwards but can come from the bottom up, in that every person has the potential to exercise some power (ibid.).

Power and discipline may also be mediated through dominant institutions, which perpetuate ideologies, as well as shaping behaviours. In advanced capitalist societies, the media plays an important part in the development of dominant discourses and in structuring behaviour. For example, the media is an important source for health messages – we are constantly bombarded with health messages through magazines, the television and the newspapers. There is a significant body of research in relation to the role of the media in the construction of normative female body images, and the relationship of this to dieting practices and eating disorders. From a social work perspective, it could be argued that the way that social work practices have been reported, mainly in relation to negative incidents, has contributed to the poor image of social work amongst some people.

Conclusion

Due to the public and media perception of social work, work with the physical and sexual well-being, and the neglect of children, has become one of the defining characteristics of contemporary social work practice, but this reflects only some aspects of the role of social work. Social workers are involved in supporting and protecting a wide range of vulnerable people, including older people, those experiencing mental distress and people with disabilities both physical and learning.

Sociology has enabled us to understand the way in which personal troubles have become social issues and the National Association of Social Work in describing the history and achievements of social work in the USA suggests that the role of social work is to address people's needs within society and bring the nature of social problems to society's attention. The legacy of social work has been to bring to society's attention the nature of child labour, poverty, the abuse and neglect of older people, the sexual abuse of children, the incarceration of people with mental health problems, youth crime and institutionalisation of disabled people. This is not an exhaustive list of the contributions of social work to society but recognition that throughout social work's history there have been concerns with the social context and impact of problems. Hence this book will use a range of sociological perspectives to explore the social context and social construction of problems experienced by a range of service user groups.

Summary

- Social work developments and practice take place within the context of wider social processes and structures.
- Sociology helps us to make sense of the social world that we live in and the impact of institutions and actions on people.
- Sociology is a range of theoretical perspectives that help us to challenge the obvious and explore different ways of seeing the social world.
- Social workers work with a variety of service user groups, but there are common issues that affect these groups. Social disadvantage, power and oppression, risk and identity are all important concepts that social workers are involved with and that sociology can help us to understand and analyse.

Questions for discussion

- How can sociology help you to reflect on your reasons for coming into social work?
- Next time you are on placement, think about issues of power and disadvantage with respect to the service user group. Reflect on the ways that sociology can help us to explain sources of power, oppression and disadvantage.
- Read the extract below.

   Too much is generally expected of social workers. We load upon them unrealistic expectations and we then complain when they do not live up to them . . . There is confusion about the direction in which they are going and unease about what they should be doing and the way in which they are organised and deployed. When things go wrong the media have tended to blame them because it is assumed that their job is to care for people so as to prevent trouble arising. They operate uneasily on the frontier between what appear to be almost limitless needs on the one hand and an inadequate pool of resources to satisfy those needs on the other.

   (Barclay Report, 1982)

   These views were echoed in the review of social work undertaken by Blewett et al. on behalf of GSCC 2007.

- How does sociology helps us to make sense of these competing demands and social responses to social work?

Further reading

Giddens, A. (2006) *Sociology.* 5th edn. Cambridge: Polity. This is a really useful introductory sociology textbook, which covers a wide range of topics relevant to social work practice.

Horner, N. (2006) *What is Social Work? Context and Perspectives.* 2nd edn. Poole: Learning Matters. This is an accessible book, which explores the historical development of social work and the contemporary social context which impacts on social work practice. It provides a good introduction to the social and policy context with a range of service user groups.

McDonald, C. (2006) *Challenging Social Work: The Context of Practice.* Basingstoke: Palgrave Macmillan. This book provides a good critical discussion of the relationship between social change and social work practice. There is a particularly useful chapter on Global Social Work.

2

Key Sociological Theories

The key themes outlined at the end of the last chapter are closely linked to the development of sociological perspectives over the last two hundred years. This chapter explores the development of sociological theories from what are called 'the founding fathers' of sociology to more contemporary theories and ideas which help to explain and understand the social world of today.

Classical sociological theories can be broadly divided into two camps, structural theories and social action theories. Structural theories are concerned with the structures and institutions of society and pay little attention to individual actors and actions. On the other hand, social action theories take the premise that society can only be understood by studying those that make up that society and their actions, interpretations and interactions.

Recent sociological theories have challenged these classical theories and a more critical sociology has developed, which seeks to explain the social world from a plurality of perspectives and within the context of a rapidly changing society.

The key issues that will be discussed in this chapter are:

1. Structural theories, including consensus and conflict theories.
2. Social action theories, including social interactionism.
3. Critical sociology, including feminist and anti-racist perspectives.
4. The pluralist society and post-modern approaches.
5. Issues in relation to social identity, the body and consumerism.

By the end of this chapter, you should be able to:

- Discuss some key sociological theories.
- Distinguish between structural theories and social action theories.

- Understand the changing nature of sociology and explain how critical sociology can help us understand a plurality of viewpoints.
- Identify what is meant by a post-modern society.
- Explain the importance of identity to individuals and groups.

The founding fathers of sociology

Enlightenment a philosophical period of the eighteenth century based on notions of progress, reason and rationality, leading to an emphasis on human control and a decrease in religious dogma as a way of understanding the social world.

The discipline of sociology can be traced back to a historical period known as the Enlightenment, which signalled a shift in thinking and the way in which society was understood. Prior to the Enlightenment, religious teachings were the dominant set of ideas, which helped people to make sense of their worlds. However, during the Enlightenment, religious doctrine was increasingly replaced with critical and rational thinking. Human behaviour and society came to be understood in a more *objective* and systematic way. The discipline of sociology grew within this overall context, with attempts to objectively study human behaviour and society in a rational and scientific way.

Comte (1798–1857) coined the term 'sociology' and is viewed as the founding father of the discipline. Comte was concerned to explain the impact of rapid *industrialisation* and *urbanisation*, as well as the French Revolution, on individual lives. However, Comte took a particular perspective, i.e. that the rules and functioning of the social world could be explained objectively by observation of known facts in the same way that the natural sciences explained the physical world. This approach has been termed *positivism*. Thus Comte rejected religious explanations of society and sought to explain things more scientifically by *empirically* observing social phenomena. Comte explained the transition from religious doctrine to more rational and scientific sets of ideas in three stages:

Positivism the science of sociology, where only observable and measurable behaviours should be studied.

Empiricism a view on research, which emphasises factual enquiry through the collection of data based on facts and observation as opposed to reflection and theoretical enquiry.

1. Theological – Understanding of society is dominated by religious ideas and the belief in God's will.
2. Metaphysical – Society increasingly explained in natural rather than supernatural terms.
3. Positive stage – Society and social actors can be understood by the application of scientific principles and can therefore be explained objectively.

Classical sociological theories

Structural theories

Structural theories focus on the institutions and structures that shape society, which have remained relatively unchanged over time. It is seen as efficient and natural for society to be based on the divisions within these structures, and for structuralists these are widely and uncritically accepted. Individuals are seen as the product of the social structures rather than as free agents who shape their own destiny.

The process of industrialisation led to the development of institutions and structures to manage new practices. For example, rail and road networks were built to transport goods to enhance economic activity, particularly as the British Empire grew abroad. It also enabled vast areas of land to be 'managed' and administered. This is an example of a structure/framework, which has multiple aims in managing individuals and societal processes. Examples of structures within contemporary society are the system of law and order and health and social care organisations.

Exercise

- Identify an institution in contemporary UK.
- Is power/authority in this institution relatively unchanged over time?
- What influence does it have on the individual?

Functionalism dominated sociological thinking until the 1960s and stresses the importance of the 'functional fit' of the institutions that make up society and the importance of socialisation of society's norms and values in order to promote a consensus.

Durkheim (1858–1917) – structural-functionalist perspective. Durkheim was heavily influenced by Comte's views, and saw society as being made up of a set of inter-related components that could be objectively studied. This is known as the *functionalist* perspective, where society is not just about the interests and actions of individuals but is the sum of these inter-dependent parts. As a functionalist, Durkheim believed that in order for societies to maintain cohesion and stability, these components should operate in conjunction with each other. Durkheim was influenced by the French Revolution and as such was particularly interested in how social solidarity was achieved. He further argued that individuals are influenced by the structures and institutions of society to develop a *collective consciousness*. This collective consciousness is based on collective norms of society and promotes expectations for acceptable behaviour and places restraints on deviant behaviour.

Collective consciousness associated with Durkheim to mean shared moral values derived from religion or it could also stem from the education system.

Durkheim believed that societies were consensual, with shared belief and value systems and a moral cohesion. However, for him, this cohesion did not denote a static society, but one that is able to collectively adapt to change in order to maintain equilibrium. Equilibrium and the maintenance of the status quo are important concepts within the functionalist perspective, with individuals performing roles and functions in order to contribute to the collective whole. Like Comte, Durkheim believed that social facts can be studied in a scientific and objective way and this objectivity transcends individual behaviour. Some social facts he saw as normal and

Exercise

Consider these two scenarios:

A man is begging outside a supermarket. He is shabbily dressed, but seems clean and tidy. He respectfully asks passers by for money, explaining that he needs the train fare to get back to his hometown. He says that he has been ill and unable to work recently.

Down the road, a man is begging outside another supermarket. He is unkempt in appearance and appears drunk. He shouts abuse at passers by, when they do not acknowledge him or refuse to give him money.

Thinking about functional sociological perspectives:

- Which man is meeting standards of 'acceptable' behaviour in society and is more likely to receive support?
- Which man appears more excluded from societal norms, as he can be seen as 'not helping himself'?

Anomie a term used by Durkheim to describe a state of disorganisation in modern society that leaves individuals without structure or norms to follow. Durkheim used this term to describe the feelings of despair and helplessness that can lead to suicidal thoughts and tendencies.

necessary for a healthy society, whereas others he saw as unhealthy and pathological, creating disharmony and disequilibrium. A good example of his views can be seen in his study of suicide (1952, originally published in 1897). Durkheim studied rates of suicide and concluded that individuals were more likely to commit suicide if they were dislocated from the collective. This he termed *anomie*, a state of not belonging to the collective organisation.

Talcott Parsons (1902–1979) further contributed to the theory of structural functionalism through his theory of the social system. Parsons' contribution to sociological thinking is concerned with how the elements of society interlock to form a network of systems with shared values to provide a stable and coherent society. Within his theory, there are clearly defined roles and role expectations, which govern institutions and individuals. Parsons argues that societies function to contain deviance in order to maintain the smooth functioning of society. This is manifest in his theory of illness, which he sees as a deviant state. When individuals are ill they are unable to fulfil their normal roles and obligations and this can disrupt the equilibrium of society. Parsons (1951) argues that in order to contain this deviance, when individuals are ill they are assigned to a new role,

Sick role members of society who are ill are assigned a new and temporary role, which involves certain social obligations. This includes wanting to get well and working to manage their illness.

the *sick role*. This sick role allows the individual certain exemptions from normal roles, but also requires an obligation to get better as soon as possible, so that equilibrium can be restored. Thus when individuals are ill, they have the following exemptions and obligations:

1. They are exempt from normal social responsibilities (e.g. work roles).

2. They are exempt from responsibility for their illness, in that they cannot be expected to recover through their own free will.
3. They must be motivated to get better as soon as possible through the obligation to seek and comply with technically competent help (from medical personnel)

Although this ideal type model has been widely criticised (see e.g. Nettleton, 2006), it demonstrates Parsons' view of the social system and the organic nature of the whole system, based on collective values.

Within his systems approach, Parsons identifies four sub-systems (or institutions), which contribute to the maintenance of the whole and represent different structural elements of society:

1. The economic system, providing and distributing economic resources to individuals and institutions.
2. The political system, governing individuals and forming collective goals.
3. Kinships institutions, providing an important environment for socialisation into a shared value system of accepted norms and behaviours.
4. Community and cultural institutions (e.g. religious, education and mass media), integrating various elements of society as well as preventing social isolation and contributing to a collective consciousness.

Within functionalism, social rituals are important for promoting a sense of communal cohesion. Durkheim saw religion as an important social institution in this respect. He studied traditional, small-scale societies and argued that religious symbols were an important part of group cohesion, as they represent the shared values and ideals of that community. Thus collective rituals are important to reaffirm social cohesion and solidarity. For Durkheim, these collective rituals can be seen in religious worship, but also feature as an essential part of life transitions. Thus collective social rituals are part of social responses to births, marriages and deaths. Van Gennep (1960) has explored this in relation to funeral rituals, and argued that funeral rituals are an important rite of passage in the transitions of both the deceased and those who are bereaved. At the time of a death, the bereaved are separated from other living members of society in the acute stage of their grief, and the ritual of the funeral is important for their transition and re-incorporation into the social world of the living. Similarly, the funeral marks the ritual transition of the deceased from the world of the living and into the world of the dead. According to Van Gennep, social rites and rituals are important for the smooth running of society, as they offer a process by which individuals may effect transition into their new social role, and thus may maintain the equilibrium of society.

Social stratification term — used to describe and discuss the structure of groups within societies. It is normally applied to inequalities within society. In modern societies, this relates to how class divisions relate to wealth, power and lack of opportunities.

Functionalists also see *social stratification* as an important element of society, and in societies such as the industrialised West, where stratification is an important aspect of a complex division of labour, the stratified system is seen as a set of interdependent and cooperative groups. Power is derived from the fact that society places particular value on certain traits/attributes, and thus individuals who possess those traits are seen to have greater status. Thus, social inequality and relative disadvantage are necessary elements for the functioning of society. Whilst Parsons acknowledges that there may be some conflict between those who are advantaged and those who are relatively disadvantaged, this is kept in check by the pursuit of collective goals.

Professionalism

Functionalists argue that the professions serve an important function in the smooth operation of societies. While there are many theories of professionalism (Johnson, 1972), a commonly held definition of a profession is an occupational group that displays certain traits. For functionalists, not everyone can hold these traits, and therefore we place our trust in the professionals (e.g. doctors and lawyers) to use their expert knowledge for our benefit. However, it can also be argued that professionalism is concerned with the maintenance and regulation of the equilibrium of society.

The structural theories discussed so far emphasise consensus as the important element of inter-relationships and a stable society.

Exercise

Characteristics of a profession

- The creation and defence of a specialist body of knowledge, typically based on formal university qualifications.
- The establishment of control over a specialised client market and exclusion of competitor groups from that market.
- The establishment of control over professional work practice, responsibilities and obligations while resisting control from managerial or bureaucratic staff.

(Bilton et al, 2002: 426)

1. How far could social work be argued to be a professional group based on the above criteria?
2. Reflect on the National Occupational Standards for Social Work. Is the pursuit of professional status apparent within these standards?
3. How might the professional status of social workers conflict with their ability to promote anti-oppressive practice with service users?

However, there are also structural theories, which focus on conflict as the pervasive element that defines social organisation.

Conflict theory

Marxism

Marxist theory is based on the work of Karl Marx (1818–1883) who developed theories to explore the changing nature of industrial capitalism in the nineteenth century. In the nineteenth century there was a shift in the nature of economic and social relations, from a society based on feudal principles, to one that was based on the notion of waged labour. Marx saw society as divided into two distinct classes, based on the ownership of the means of production and the resulting commonality of interests and economic values. The first

Bourgeoisie the name Marx gave to the dominant class who own the means of production in capitalism and have an invested interest in preserving the capitalist status quo.

graph he defines as the *bourgeoisie*, a relatively small group who own the means of production (traditionally, factories, raw materials, tools) and who have control over the process of production. The second

Proletariat term used by Marxist theorists to describe the working class in capitalist societies.

group is the *proletariat*, who are a much larger group of workers, who do not own anything except their own labour power, which they sell to gain wages. Within capitalist society, Marx argues that the bourgeoisie are motivated by profit accumulation, and therefore

Surplus value a Marxist term referring to the extraction of profit, as wages are below which one sells the goods. Thus there is a gap between what the individual receives in wages and the production and sale of goods in capitalist society.

workers produce more than is actually required in order to create a *surplus value*. The bourgeoisie can make enough money to cover capital and labour costs from the sale of a percentage of the goods, and the remaining percentage is sold for profit. This relationship is based on exploitation of the workers, which is necessary for the accumulation of profit. For Marx, power was concentrated in the hands of the bourgeoisie, and social disadvantage resulted from the relations of economic production and the exploitation of the proletariat. In addition, Marx believed the proletariat became alienated from the processes of production through the fragmentation of tasks.

Like Durkheim, Marx believed that religion was an important institution of society, promoting social values and morals. The values and morals of society were created by human beings, but then projected onto the gods, and thus came to be seen as alien from human beings. Marx viewed religion as the *opiate of the masses*, as people accepted the sufferings and hardships of life as they pursued the promises and values of the afterlife, which were an important element of Protestantism. Thus, the social injustices and oppressions that were created through the capitalist organisation of society were justified through the social control of religion through doctrines such as *the meek shall inherit the Earth*.

The Marxist vision was that the relationship between the proletariat and the bourgeoisie was based on conflict, and that once the proletariat realised that the bourgeoisie would only ever make concessions to them within the existing capitalist structure, they would rise up and revolt against the system of production, regaining control for themselves. Thus Marx believed that societal change would occur through proletariat revolution rather than through the evolution of social processes. Within this theory the notion of *class-consciousness* is an important concept, whereby the different classes develop their own ideology (or set of ideas) that are collectively shared throughout the class. Thus Marx believed that the proletariat would develop their own ideologies and overthrow the ruling bourgeoisie in order to create a socialist society based on a fairer distribution of power and resources.

Class consciousness
Marxist theory relating to an awareness of one's own class position. This assumes shared values and common interests within classes, which can result in division and conflict between classes.

Since Marx developed his theory, other writers have built upon this in order to explain the increasing social divisions of modern society. It can be argued that, throughout the twentieth century, a society made up of two opposing classes has been replaced by a much more complex set of groups, although it remains dominated by a ruling elite. In particular, attention has been addressed to the development of an intermediary group of workers, known as welfare professionals, heralded by developments in the welfare state (these include social workers, teachers, doctors and nurses). Writers such as Navarro (1976) have argued that these welfare professionals serve the ruling elite by ameliorating the diswelfares created by the capitalist organisation, in order to protect the dominance of the establishment (ruling elite). Thus welfare is used as a concession to individuals, so that they believe that the state is providing for them, in order to divert attention from the structural factors which create the social divisions and exploitations. Thus the status quo of capitalist organisation is maintained.

Exercise

In recent years, a new form of welfare provision has focused on providing parenting classes and support, which often appears linked to social disadvantage, as Children's Centres are located in poorer areas. Parenting classes aim to offer direction to parents on the necessary 'skills' for parenting.

- How would a Marxist view the role of social workers in these classes?
- In what ways might they be seen as controlling parents?

Although some have argued that Marxism has not stood the test of time, as the predicted revolution has not occurred, Erik Olin Wright (1997) would argue that the theory retains contemporary relevance, in that society remains based on social divisions and continued exploitation. A good example of this is the use of sweatshop labour, particularly within the global South by multinationals, who pay minimal wages to workers in the pursuit of greater profits (Engler, 2006). Income and conditions can be seen as comparable here to those of western industrialised countries in the mid to late nineteenth century. Additionally, the Miners' Strike of the 1980s (which is so powerfully portrayed through films such as *Brassed Off* and *Billy Elliot*), demonstrated the nature of conflict between different classes within society.

Marxist theory may be useful for social workers to critically reflect on the social divisions and sources of oppression and alienation for the vulnerable groups that they often come into contact with and is a theory that has influenced the radical social work movement. Social work has always had a dichotomous relationship in relation to care and control, but the radical social work movement, influenced by Marxist sociological critiques of class relations, power and professionalism, challenged social work's contradictory relationship with the state. Radical critiques challenged social work's concern with individualistic and psychological explanations of social problems and demanded social workers work collectively with service users rather than being used as agents of state control.

Radical perspectives moved away from class analysis to incorporate feminist and anti-racist perspectives. More recently, there have been calls for social work to resist changes in role and function and to return to *emancipatory* ideals and values of social justice with the launch of the Social Work Manifesto in 2006 by a number of academics and practitioners.

Emancipation freedom or equality in a variety of contexts; in social work it is used to refer to practice that promotes freedom and liberty.

While it has been argued that social work in Britain today has lost direction, this idea is not new. Many have talked about social work being in crisis for over thirty years now. The starting point for this Manifesto, however, is that the 'crisis of social work' can no longer be tolerated. We need to find more effective ways of resisting the dominant trends within social work and map ways forward for a new engaged practice.

Managerialism process of controlling and structuring work, with power concentrated in the managers' hands.

Marketisation the provision of welfare based on market principles. Associated with welfare reforms in health and social care since 1980s.

The manifesto's suggested ways forward include a return to the values of social justice in challenging poverty and discrimination, an end to *managerialism* and *marketisation* of social care and greater alliances with service user groups, echoing some of the sentiments of the Case Con Manifesto of the early 1970s. However, there are limitations to the radical social work perspective, as social workers are employed by the state, and as such they may be faced with contradictory positions.

Exercise

- Think about your reasons for coming into the social work profession.
- How does this match with the debate about radical social work above?
- In small groups, discuss whether you think Marxist ideas are still relevant to understanding social disadvantage.

Social action theories

An opposing set of sociological theories have developed, which argue that society cannot be understood by objective measures, but that a true understanding of societies and the behaviour of individuals must be derived from an understanding of the individuals and their actions, not from the institutions and structures. These theories are collectively referred to as social action theories.

These theorists argue that the meaning and interpretations of individuals are important in determining our understanding of the social world. By simply observing someone's behaviour or interactions, we put our own interpretations on the meaning behind the behaviour or interaction. However, if we ask people about their subjective interpretation of events, interactions and behaviours we may get a different meaning, based on the experiences and understanding of individuals. Meanings and interpretations are based on *subjectivity* and social interactions are important within this tradition. Thus social actions theories are much more concerned with how individuals make sense of their social world within the broader structures and systems of society.

Subjectivity an emotional way of looking at things. This is contrasted with objective and factual based and scientific approaches.

Max Weber (1864–1920)

Max Weber is one of the early theorists within the social action tradition. He agreed with structuralists that institutions, classes and groups were important elements of society, but was also interested in the way in which individuals influenced and created the structural elements of society. Weber's fundamental view was that sociologists should seek to understand those that they study and not place their own interpretations on behaviours and interactions. In Weber's view, ideas and values have as much impact as economic conditions on social change.

Weber saw religion as being instrumental in the process of social change. Whereas both Durkheim and Marx saw religion as an essentially conservative institution, Weber, from his study of worldwide religions, believed that religious affiliations and movements often produced radical social transformations. For example, the Calvinists drove the development of industrial capitalism, a group who believed in Christianity, and in particular Protestantism. As such, they believed that human beings were carrying out God's work, and that material rewards gained through vocation were a sign of divine favour.

In contemporary society, there has been a rise in affiliation to the Catholic Church amongst Third World countries. This has been mirrored by a decline in the 'traditional' groups who made up the Catholic constituency. This in turn impacts upon communities and their social policies (e.g. in relation to HIV/AIDS and contraception).

This connects with Weber's views on religious affiliation leading to social transformation. However such transformations may be oppressive to certain groups.

Weber believed that religion provided moral guidance, and as such, there was a social control function. Therefore, sin and the concept of being rescued from sinfulness are important in terms of salvation and moralisation.

Exercise

Classical sociology and religion

- Identify the differences and commonalities in the view of religion between Marx, Durkheim and Weber.
- Would structuralists agree that religion had an important social control function?
- Look at two passages from the Old Testament – Leviticus 20: 13 and Esther 1: 16–22. How do these reflect the dominant ideologies of the nineteenth century?
- Think about contemporary debates in religion which reflect a dominant ideology.

Rational–legal authority a concept from Weber's theory of bureaucracy, where people are assigned positions on a rational basis, according to their skills and therefore authority is seen to be legitimate.

Weber also viewed power as being derived through *rational-legal authority* in modern society, where power and authority are seen as legitimate and therefore affect the way in which society is organised and structured. Weber's theory of bureaucracy is important here. For Weber, the most efficient way to organise large-scale organisations is through bureaucracy, based on hierarchical organisation. As such, bureaucracies provide a clear 'top-down' chain of command, with rules governing the way in which organisations are run (Weber, 1976). *Bureaucracy* is seen as the epitome of the expression of instrumental rational action, where the organisation's is divided up into a series of rational tasks and actions, with individuals being assigned to a place within the organisation based on their skills and abilities (there is some overlap with functionalist theory here).

Bureaucratisation method of work organisation characterised by regulation and a hierarchy of tasks. For Weber, bureaucratisation is a consequence of increasingly complex organisations in modern society. This leads to divisions of labour in which tasks are broken down on the basis of ability rather than personality and relationships.

Bureaucratisation is a rational process, as with technological advances, it provides the best way of organising complex tasks and functions. However, Weber was concerned with how organisations could wield unlimited power and therefore they need to be subject to political control. Weber's theory of organisation remains highly relevant today. Professionals in health and social care will often refer to organisations being 'too bureaucratic'. One of the key concerns for contemporary social work writers is that the running of social services organisations has become more important than the key tasks of social work itself. Writers refer to the '*new managerialism*' of social services (Healy, 2000; Adams et al., 2002). Here the emphasis is seen on procedures and methods with 'top down' authority and control becoming more important. Social services are now expected to meet certain targets (e.g. carrying out assessments), which is important as it supports ratings of performance.

Using Weber's theory, it could be argued that social services have become too preoccupied with the organisation of its functions, with control of resources and managing user and carer expectations creating inflexibility.

Exercise

- What elements of Weber's notion of bureaucracy are evident in social service departments?
- Can authority be seen as rational and legal?

Symbolic interactionism developed from the work of George Herbert Mead and explains human behaviour by understanding the meanings that lie behind actions.

Weber's notions of social action were more systematically developed through symbolic interactionism, which relates to a set of theories, often attributed to the work of **George Herbert Mead (1863–1931)**. Mead argued that the thing that sets humans apart from other forms of life is our ability to use language and to develop meaning through the use of language.

> It is through the acquisition of language that we become human and social beings: the words we speak situate us in our gender and our class. Through language, we come to know who we are.
>
> (Sarup, 1996: 47)

Language is a symbol, which allows individuals to express individuality and to see ourselves as others see us. Mead distinguished between the I and the Me, whereby the I refers to the individual who thinks and acts and the Me refers to the self as an object as viewed by others. The following quote illustrates this:

> It is the I that has the ideas, drives and impulses (such as the desire to walk out of a very boring class) while the Me takes into account the reaction of others (that wouldn't look good, the tutor has to mark your examination papers.

Putting oneself in the place of the other is an important concept within symbolic interactionism. Goffman (1968) explained the concept in the sense that the social world is like a stage play, with different actors playing out different roles. Relationships are interdependent in a similar way to the way that individuals perform their public roles. Behaviour is constructed and modified through the social reactions of others. Theories of symbolic interactionism are particularly relevant to social workers in enhancing their understanding of the behaviour of individuals, based on the way that they see the world and the competing interpretations of meanings.

Language and the use and meaning of language is important within symbolic interactionism and theorists within this tradition often focus on face-to-face interactions and the lived meaning of people's experiences. Language may also be an important symbolic identifier of identity, where the use of words and mannerisms denotes a sense of identity within a social group.

Bernstein's theory of socio-linguistics (1975) explores the relationship that individuals have to language, and how this is linked to social structures of society, in particular the class structure (see Chapter 3). He argued that the working classes are much more likely to use language in a way which signifies solidarity with their contemporaries, and that language is used in a prescriptive, rather than an expressive way. Thus, he argued, children from working-class backgrounds learn to use language in a way which reinforces cultural norms and differences. Children from middle-class families, however, have a different relationship with language, and are more likely to be encouraged to use language in an expressive way, using language as a way of explaining and exploring individual actions. Thus Bernstein argued that there is a restricted or elaborate code used in language (the elaborate code tends to be used more by middle classes and has greater universalistic meaning and understanding attached to it). The way that language is developed is an important cultural signifier and may contribute towards social stratification and the perception of others. For example, a classic study of doctor–patient encounters that was undertaken by Cartwright and O'Brien in 1976 concluded that people from the middle classes made better use of medical appointments, partly because they were able to share a common pattern of language with the doctor, and therefore were able to articulate their needs in a way that achieved the specific outcomes they desired.

Critique of classical theories

While these classical sociological theories are important for developing ways of exploring and understanding the social world, they have recently been subjected to a number of criticisms. Macionis and Plummer (2005) have levelled the following criticisms at these theories:

1. Theories have largely been developed by white heterosexual males, and therefore have limited value for explaining and understanding other viewpoints.
2. The views and understanding of other significant groups in society have been overlooked and under-represented (e.g. women,

minority ethnic groups, lesbians and gays, people with disabilities).

3. On occasions when different perspectives have been included, they have often been distorted by the white male heterosexual *hegemony*.

Giddens (1991) has argued that western industrialised countries witnessed a period of massive social and economic change in the twentieth century, which he called high modernity or late modernity, though some sociological writings describe this period as post-modernity to distinguish it from the period of modernity. The period of *modernity* was characterised by a process of modernisation through industrialisation, capitalism and urbanisation and the decline of traditional communities. This process of modernisation began in the 1890s and 1900s and was a time of massive technological development and change. The term *grand-narratives* was used to tell the story of the impact of this change on institutions and individuals.

Toennies' work on communities is useful for helping us to understand the impact of these changes on people's lives. In attempting to make sense of the changes associated with processes of modernity, Toennies (1963) used the terms *Gemeinschaft* and *Gesellschaft* to demonstrate the change in society. *Gemeinschaft* refers to the sense of community based on kinship networks, neighbourhoods and a shared purpose based on honour and virtue, whereas *Gesellschaft* refers to the impersonal urban communities associated with modernity and urbanisation, with a much greater emphasis on individualism and self-interest. He argued that modernity undermined the strong social fabric of society and the family unit by its focus on individualism and the pursuit of efficiency for profit maximisation in a capitalist society.

Modernity historical period from the end of the eighteenth century that saw great industrial and political change.

Grand-narrative a term associated with the period of modernity, where there is an overall theory that can explain the whole of society and historical developments.

Gemeinschaft a term used by Toennies to describe a community based on kinship networks, neighbourhoods and a shared purpose based on honour and virtue.

Gesellschaft a term used by Toennies to describe the urban communities associated with modernity and urbanisation, which are seen as individualist and impersonal.

> There is an implied antithesis between the past, when, so it is believed, the individual was integrated into a stable and harmonious community of kin, friends and neighbours, and the less palatable present when all too often it is possible to feel like a piece of human flotsam, cast adrift in a sea of apparently bewildering social changes and buffeted by impersonal and alien social forces.
>
> (Lee and Newby, 1983: 52)

The concept of post-modernity denotes a society, which is in some way different from this period of modernity. Society has become increasingly fragmented and there is a plurality of perspectives and meanings. Dahrendorf (1929–) has developed conflict theory, arguing that societies are made up of many different groups (*pluralism*) with different interests, and these groups are often in conflict, not just in economic terms, as Marx stated, but also through power and authority. Dahrendorf sees the conflict as one between the ruled and the unruled, those that have authority and those that do not.

Pluralism variety of different views and perspectives make up and contribute to a society or culture.

Lyotard (1984) has argued that the grand-narratives of modernity, which use all encompassing theory to try and explain the whole of society, are reductionist and no longer relevant. Instead, we need to understand the social world from local perspectives to fully understand the range of experiences and within this individual narratives are important sources of explanation. Therefore, for Lyotard, local takes precedence over universal in post-modernity.

Post-modernity view that society is in a different era from that of modernity (see Glossary). Generally dated from the 1960s.

In *post-modernity*, it has been argued that there has been a decline of locality as a basis for community. People live in impersonal urban environments, therefore trust is difficult as populations become increasingly mobile and there is pursuit of self-interest. Urban environments have been divested of community, as large supermarkets have moved to out of city environments, leading to competition and the decline in local and locally sourced shops in many areas. In addition, many people have moved into the leafy suburbs of societies, leading to marginalisation and residualisation of inner city dwellings. Currie (1989) has argued that fragmentation of communities results from an increase in transient populations, loss of stable employment and incomes, rising house prices and a resultant weakening of social cohesion. The result is the social exclusion of individuals and a breakdown of community cohesion, which places increasing strain on the family unit.

Secularism process whereby religious beliefs and practices no longer dominate in contemporary societies. This has been a gradual development, with religious institutions losing social significance over time.

Post-modern society is also seen to be an increasingly *secular society*. Although there is a lack of agreement amongst sociologists about the precise definition of secularisation (Giddens, 2006), it is generally agreed that organised religion is less significant than it was in modernity. While organised religion still plays a significant role in many people's lives, this may be in particular times of celebration or crisis. Hockey (1997) has identified the continuing role of the clergy

Figure 2.1 Cross and crescent. (Karen Moller)

and religion in many funeral ceremonies, whilst Davie (2000) has identified the importance of religious organisations and institutions during disasters such as the shooting of sixteen children and a teacher in Dunblane or the death of ninety-five football fans at Hillsborough. In addition, there has been an increase in *new religious movements* (Giddens, 2006) and within a pluralist society, a number of religions co-exist.

There is also an increasing sociological interest in spirituality (which may or may not be related to organised religion). Although there is no consensus on the definition of spirituality (Orchard, 2001), the one below encapsulates the key points and demonstrates the increased individualism and pluralistic nature of spiritual beliefs.

> *Spirituality is a personal search for meaning and purpose in life, which may or may not be related to religion. It entails connection to self-chosen and or religious beliefs, values and practices that give meaning to life, thereby inspiring and motivating individuals to achieve their optimal being.*

> (Tanyi, 2002: 506)

In recent years, there has been a growing interest in meeting the spiritual needs of individuals in health and social care settings, reflected in documents such as Department of Health (2003) *Meeting the Religious and Spiritual Needs of Patients* (www.dh.gov.uk.) and a growing body of literature exploring the role of practitioners in addressing spiritual needs (see e.g. Greenstreet, 2006).

Within new perspectives of critical sociology, there is an emphasis on hearing the multiple views and voices within society, including women, minority ethnic groups, older people, lesbians and gays, people with disabilities, children and youths. Critical sociology therefore rejects the use of grand narratives as there can be no single 'big story' to tell with this plurality of meanings, but instead there is a need for many different stories to explain the features of contemporary capitalist societies. In addition, whereas modernity focused on continuity and order, post-modernity is characterised by disorder and a constant state of change. Giddens

Runaway society the term used by Giddens to refer to the rapidly changing society of twentieth-century advanced capitalist societies.

(1991) used the term *runaway society* to denote this changing society and the process of rapid social change that distinguishes the post-modern period from the modern period. Giddens also argues that as society has become increasingly fragmented with the rejection of grand narratives, individuals now construct meanings about their social world through constant self-reflection on actions and

Self reflexivity people make sense of the social world through the constant reflection on their experiences and the knowledge of those personal experiences.

interactions within the social world – he terms this *self-reflexivity*. There are no universal truths, but an ever-changing set of truths and individual interpretations. Thus sociology has to adapt in order to explain this rapid social change and individuals' responses to it as well as offering different interpretations of the social world.

Feminist critiques of sociology

Male-stream a term coined within sociology to refer to the dominance of the male viewpoint and interests.

Feminist theories arose out of the invisibility of women and gender issues within sociology. The dominance of 'male-stream' sociology meant that women were ignored, both in terms of the subject of sociological study and analysis, and in developing and constructing sociological theory. In a critique of 'male-stream' sociology Abbott et al. (2005:4) provide the following:

1. Sociology has been mainly concerned with research on men and, by implication, with theories for man.
2. Research based on male subjects is generalised to the whole population.
3. Areas of concern for women are often overlooked and seen as unimportant.
4. When women are included in research they are presented in a distorted and sexist way.
5. Sex and gender are seldom seen as important explanatory variables.

Feminist sociology emerged out of the women's movement and in providing a brief overview of the development of the movement it could be said that it developed along a number of specific periods or 'waves'. The first-wave feminists were active in the nineteenth and twentieth centuries and fought for equal rights concerning property, voting and education and were typified by the suffragette movement in Britain. The second wave of feminism began after the Second World War and tended to focus upon the analysis of the family as a site of women's oppression. Recognising the changes and the diversity of experience within women's lives, the third-wave feminism suggests that:

> Feminism is not dead; in fact, it's on the rise again, but in a new form. We are the 20- and 30-something women who have always known a world with feminism in it. We are putting a new face on feminism. It's time to move away from the older feminism of the 1960s and 1970s and shape a new movement that speaks to women of today.
>
> www.3rdwwwave.com accessed 23 July 2007

Third-wave feminism refers to the body of feminist epistemology, which emerged in the 1980s following the apparent weaknesses of former feminist perspectives and challenges essentialist notions of womanhood with its bias towards white middle-class women.

Discussion points

- How do you think woman's lives have changed in the last fifty years?
- What do you think are the current concerns for women? Are these different from their mothers or grandmothers?
- How do you think feminist perspectives may have contributed to the above?

Anti-racist theory/black perspectives

Ethnicity the sharing of a
common cultural identity
or heritage.

Traditional and more recent perspectives within sociology have tended to ignore or minimise the significance of race, *ethnicity* and oppression within British society. Sociological interest in race emerged with significance in the 1960s following the aftermath of significant global changes in relation to race. The end of empire, mass migration to Britain, and the civil rights movements in the USA resulted in major social, economic and political changes, which had significant global impact but which also transformed the lives of black and white communities (Mason, 1995). Sociologists began to recognise that an analysis of race and ethnicity was central to an understanding of contemporary British society (Pilkington, 2003).

Mason (1995) describes the sociology of race as being concerned with social relations and the observation of actions at an individual and group level. This usually involves:

- Explaining what is meant by concepts of 'race' and ethnicity.
- Understanding racial and ethnic differences between people in terms of e.g. employment, housing.
- Explaining racism and discrimination.
- Understanding the interconnectedness of racism with other forms of discrimination and oppression.

However, black perspectives in sociology have challenged *eurocentric* traditions within the social sciences, which distort and misrepresent black peoples' experiences.

Despite its origins, race is a non-scientific concept in sociology (see Chapter 6) and many sociologists use the term to describe the socially constructed ways of categorising people on the basis of assumed biological differences. There are some sociologists (e.g. Miles, 1982) who prefer not to use the term at all, suggesting that its use gives the term validity and credence. However, there are others who believe that, whilst the term has no scientific meaning, the effects of racial categorisation are real and meaningful (Pilkington, 2003).

Black, however, is still a commonly used term to describe people of African, Caribbean and South Asian background, emphasising the unifying experiences of people who are subject to racism and discrimination in Britain. Similarly there is debate concerning meanings of *black perspectives*, though I tend to agree with Ahmed (1990) who suggests that the constant need for black writers to define black perspectives is not paralleled by the need for white writers to define a white perspective.

> White writers have not had to define a White perspective, as 'White' is accepted as the 'norm'. Definition of Black perspective needs to address this anomaly first . . . the factors that prescribe a Black perspective have a long history of subjugation and subordination. The circumstances that shape a Black perspective stem from the experience of racism and

powerlessness, both past and present. The motivation that energises a
Black perspective is rooted to the principle of racial equality and justice.

(Ahmed, 1990: 3).

Social identity

At the root of both feminist and black perspectives is the notion of
social identity, and how this is both interpreted by and experienced by
people. The concept of social identity has developed from the symbolic
interactionist school of thought. Identity is about a sense of belonging
to a social group, about the location of oneself within social
relationships and about a complex set of interactions with others.
Identity can either signify sameness or can differentiate individuals in
groups from other groups. The concept of community may be
important in terms of the construction of identity. Lee and Newby
(1983) use the term *communion* to define community, where locality is
far less important than the sense of identity and belonging and shared
value systems. Thus a geographically disparate group of individuals
such as the Countryside Alliance would be seen as a community. The
relationships can be between groups of individuals who are located
near to each other, or who are geographically distant and may not even
be in physical contact (e.g. internet communities).

Cohen (1985) argues that the desire to see oneself as different
from some people and having a common identity with others is
central to the concept of community. This is a phenomenological
perspective of community, focusing on the lived experiences of
individuals in constituting their social identity. However, some
individuals (for example, people who are homeless or people who
have enduring mental health problems) are dislocated from the
community within which they reside. Stigmatisation of individuals
may lead to marginalisation and social exclusion (see Chapter 12).

Clothing and bodily adornments may also be used as a way of
demonstrating identity and belonging to or identifying with a certain
group of individuals. Throughout history there are numerous
examples of the use of clothing, hairstyle and fashions as a way of
identifying with a particular group: teddy boys, mods, rockers,
skinheads and punk rockers, and more recently the *chav*, who wears
'Burberry' and bling. Thus a sense of belonging and identification
with other people is achieved through the cultural signifiers of
fashion and appearance. However, these can also lead to processes of
labelling by people outside the group, with the way someone presents
themselves being used as a judgement of character and purpose.
Savage and Warde (1993: 184) have argued that

judges, the police and social workers will use stereotypes based on
appearance and dress to label groups and link them with certain
characteristic kinds of behaviour.

For the individuals, the clothing that they choose to wear signifies belonging to a particular social group, with a set of shared understandings and value. However, others who are outside this group may misinterpret the meanings behind the symbols of identity, constructing their own meanings to differentiate themselves from the group. Thus a process of labelling may occur. This is demonstrated in photographs below and overleaf.

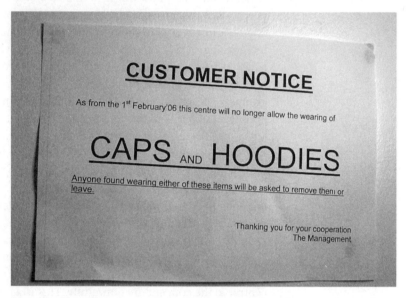

Sign in a local leisure centre, notifying users that they may not wear hoodies or baseball caps.

The youth in the photograph on page 49 may be using the hoody as a fashion statement, identifying himself with others within a group. However, as the sign from the leisure centre shows, the wearing of hoodies and baseball caps has come to be associated for many outside the group, with deviant and disruptive behaviour. Thus, two very different perspectives emerge with respect to this cultural signifier of clothing.

Fashion styles serve an important function of identifying a group's boundaries in relation both to its members and all outsiders, a function which has particular consequences for the group's continued existence (Hall and Jefferson, 1976: 53).

This also demonstrates how institutions may use clothing and other signifiers of cultural identity as a way of controlling individuals. School uniform, for example, whilst it denotes a sense of identity and belonging to the particular school, can also be used in a way that limits individuality and controls behaviour. The controversy about the banning of religious symbols and clothing in French schools exemplifies the way in which clothing and other symbols of cultural identity may be used by others and the impact that this has on personal identity.

Bored teen wearing a hoody. (Jami Garrison)

However, in contemporary western societies, clothing and jewellery continue to be used as an important way of making a statement about identity and belonging to a particular group or community. Boden (2006) explores the influence of popular culture on young people's identities and the influence of commercial sports, fashion and celebrity cultural icons. This popular culture helps to shape young people's identities, with the branded clothing market estimated to be worth £6 billion (see picture on next page).

Understanding symbols and meanings is particularly relevant for social workers. Failure to understand the symbolic value of language, actions and behaviours from the individual's own standpoint can lead to labelling and stereotyping and is incompatible with core social work principles of anti-oppressive practice and a respect for diversity.

Contemporary sociological theory has also focused on the body as a symbolic bearer of value. For theorists such as Shilling (1993) and Williams (2000) the body is not just a physical entity, but is also a way of portraying social identity or cultural belonging/heritage (Bourdieu, 1986). The body is shaped, constrained and invented by society, with

Although these four friends play for the same local team, on training nights, they demonstrate their allegiance to the professional club or international team they support.

ideas about the body corresponding to dominant social agendas (see Chapter 5). Shilling (1993) argues that in post-modernity, the body is a project, in a constant process of becoming, a canvas to be worked upon in order to constitute identity. The recent fashion trends of tattooing and body piercing are indicative of this phenomenon, where the practices are used as a way of portraying identity or belonging, or marking transitions in the life-course. Tattoos and piercings may be based on cultural and religious practices to denote life transitions and a sense of belonging to a particular cultural group, or may be much more individual, as a way of expressing personal identity and creativity.

Constructions of the body are important, with parameters of normality and abnormality being constructed through dominant social norms and mediated through professional ideologies. Thus the body becomes an important site of power and control. From a phenomenological point of view, the body is seen as the site for lived experience. From a symbolic interactionist perspective, body image is important as it impacts on the sense of self-identity or self-esteem, as well as social interactions with others. For example, someone who is seen as obese, may be stigmatised by society, leading to social judgements by others, with consequences in terms of e.g. employment, poor self-esteem and social interactions.

The body and interpretations of the body are thus shaped by the society within which we live. However, the body is not just the result

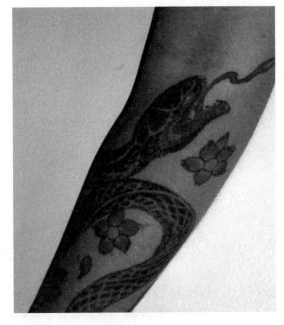

A young woman's tattoos on her lower arms.

of industrial production, but also the site for the marketing of products. Thus the body has become *commodified* in industrial capitalism, through, for example, the dieting and leisure industries. Consumerism and practices of consumption are important elements of advanced capitalist society (see Chapter 3), and the marketing and merchandising of products, which are used as cultural and symbolic signifiers of identity, has become big business. The example of football shirts is a good one to demonstrate this ← *commodification* process, with many teams changing the design of their shirts at the start of each new football season, and promoting the sale of replica shirts through official club merchandising outlets. This commodification process can be linked to developments in the global economy and how these reflect the priorities of the more powerful nations and exacerbate social divisions and differentials.

Commodification production of goods to be sold in the market as opposed to goods produced for subsistence. It is not just consumer products that become commodified, but also roles and tasks such as caring.

Exercise

Examine the data in Table 2.1.

- What does this tell us about the priorities of the global world?
- What are the implications of these priorities in terms of inequality, oppression and exploitation?

As a student social worker, it is important that you have an understanding of how we have progressed from the 'founding

Table 2.1 The world's priorities – Annual Expenditure

Basic education for all	$6bn
Cosmetics in the USA	$8bn
Water and sanitation for all	$9bn
Ice cream in Europe	$11bn
Reproductive health care for all women	$12bn
Perfumes in Europe and the USA	$12bn
Basic health and nutrition	$13bn
Pet foods in Europe and the USA	$17bn
Business entertainment in Japan	$35bn
Cigarettes in Europe	$50bn
Alcoholic drinks in Europe	$105bn
Military spending in the world	$789bn

Source:
Human Development Report, 1999

fathers' of sociology to the contemporary perspectives outlined in this last section and how they help to explain and analyse the social world.

Summary

This chapter has demonstrated a shift in sociological thinking, from traditional perspectives that explained modernity, to post-modern perspectives, explaining the complex and fragmented society that we now live in. New sociological perspectives help us to understand the changes that have occurred throughout the twentieth century and into the new millennium, and help us to critically reflect on the processes and structures that create divisions, inequalities and oppressions. They also help us to understand how people interact within societies and how interactions are interpreted and shape the way that we view the world and our place within it. As stated earlier, social work does not operate in a vacuum, but needs to understand these important social perspectives in order to critically reflect on their own practice and challenge the processes and impacts of multiple disadvantage.

Summary points

- The discipline of sociology is made up of a range of theoretical perspectives which help us to explain and analyse the social world.
- The founding fathers of sociology can be divided into two broad camps: structuralists, who emphasise the importance of institutions and structures in shaping people's lives, and social action theorists, who explore the social world through the eyes of individuals.

- Sociologists refer to the period of modernity as a period of rapid social change associated with industrialisation and urbanisation, where grand narratives were used to explain collective social experiences.
- According to sociologists, we are now experiencing a period of post-modernity, characterised by fragmentation and a plurality of perspectives.
- A critical sociology has developed which helps us to understand the many experiences of diverse groups and individuals in contemporary societies.

Questions for discussion

- Do you think stable structures are necessary for society to function?
- Reflect on the discussion of identity and social constructionism. What have been the major influences on the construction of your own identity?
- Using specific examples, think of ways that sociological theories can contribute to an understanding of social work practice.
- Can you identify sources of conflict and consensus in your social work role?

Further reading

Abbott, P., Wallace, C. and Tyler, M. (2005) An Introduction to Sociology: Feminist Perspectives. London: Routledge. This is a useful book for exploring a range of feminist perspectives and their contribution within the sociological debate. Although we have also included this in the gender chapter, we believe that it is important that feminist perspectives are seen as part of mainstream sociology.

Back, L. and Solomos J. (eds) (2008) Theories of Race and Racism: A Reader. 2nd edn. London: Routledge. This is a useful reader for students as it brings together comprehensive discussion of articles regarding the sociology of race. Although we have also included this in the race chapter, we believe that it is important that black perspectives are seen as part of mainstream sociology.

Giddens, A. (2006) Sociology. 5th edn. Cambridge: Polity. Giddens is one of the key contemporary writers in the discipline of sociology, and this revised edition provides a comprehensive exploration of contemporary debates in sociology. There is a very useful glossary of terms.

Haralambos, M. and Holborn, M. (2004) Sociology: Themes and Perspectives. 6th edn. London: Collins. This is a very accessible book, which introduces students to key contemporary sociological issues.

Macionis, J. and Plummer, K. (2005) *Sociology: A Global Introduction*. 3rd edn. London: Prentice Hall. This is a very readable book, which, as the name suggests, explores key sociological perspectives and areas of sociological enquiry in a global context.

Social Class, Poverty and Social Exclusion

Poverty, social exclusion and inequality are key factors that face the majority of users of social work. Therefore exploration of these concepts is crucial for social workers to understand the nature of the social problems that are faced by the recipients of social work interventions. Categories of domination and subordination are not static, but are dynamic processes, with movement over time, as groups may use their collective experience to resist the position of subordination. It is important for social workers to understand key theories of social stratification and processes of oppression and subordination, as the majority of the individuals and groups that they work with will be some of the most vulnerable and marginalised groups. Chris Jones (2002) suggests that throughout its history social work has remained a class-specific activity.

This chapter will explore these issues, principally in relation to the class system and income inequalities in contemporary Britain, discussing different theories that help us to understand both the structural context of inequality and the impact on individuals and their actions.

The key issues that will be explored in this chapter are:

- Different perspectives on how society is divided according to occupation and income.
- Definitions of poverty (including absolute poverty and relative deprivation).
- Explanations for the existence and persistence of poverty and disadvantage.
- The concept of social exclusion.
- The impact of these inequalities on individual lives.
- The implications for social work of working within a stratified society.

By the end of this chapter, you should be able to:

- Explain the nature of social divisions and social stratification in contemporary society.
- Identify the nature of poverty and discuss some of the causal explanations for the persistence of poverty.
- Distinguish between poverty and social exclusion.
- Identify the relationship between social disadvantage and ability to participate in the consumer society.
- Explain the nature of oppression.

Introduction

Modern societies are divided along a number of social divisions. One does not have to look very far to see that society is divided and differentiated. So what do we mean when we talk about social divisions? A simple definition would look at the division between the haves and the have-nots. Whilst this provides a useful starting point, it does not really help us to understand why some people have more than others and why some people struggle to make ends meet and satisfy even the most basic of human needs such as food, shelter and clothing.

Social stratification

Social stratification refers to processes within society, where individuals are classed in the hierarchical system, and incorporates ideas of power, inequality and difference. Social division and stratification often refer to

Hierarchy A system of ranking based upon superiority and subordination.

◄ a hierarchy of positions of inferiority and superiority in society, with a ranking of different individuals according to certain traits, criteria or subjective interpretation. Thus value judgements may be associated with positions in the hierarchy. Differences may be biological/natural or they may be social and cultural (Garrett, 2002). Social divisions can be described in terms of differences between groups and diversity within populations, derived from shared language, regional origin, nationality and national identity, physical condition or marital status. Difference therefore may be seen in positive terms, acknowledging the richness and diversity of experiences, social positions and beliefs and contributing to a pluralist and varied society.

Diversity refers to a 'difference claimed upon a shared collective experience which is specific and not necessarily associated with a subordinated or unequal subject position' (Williams, 1996:70). Divisions, however, are based on notions of power and oppression and can be defined as the

translation of the expression of a shared experience into a form of domination.

(Williams, 1996:70)

Social class

Social class is an important concept in the exploration of social stratification, and is a widely used concept. In everyday conversations, we hear people talking about working class, middle class and upper class as a way of identifying broad groups within society. But what do we mean by these different terms? Are they subjective definitions, representing our perception of where we sit vis-à-vis others, or do they reflect a more objective category of a system of stratification?

Exercise

1. How would you define your own class position?
2. What are your reasons for defining yourself in this way?
3. Do you think there is a consensus about the definition of social class?

Are the terms working class, middle class and upper class descriptive terms, based on assumptions about shared position and broadly similar lifestyles?

If we look at the classic comedy sketch by the Two Ronnies (Ronnie Corbett and Ronnie Barker) and John Cleese, three comedians of varying heights, they suggest class is associated with relative positions in a hierarchy of value and status.

Is this then what class is about? Is it about our location within a hierarchical system of social organisation, where people occupy a particular position relative to other groups? How then do we explain

Comedy sketch about social class.

how people come to be part of a certain class and how do we explain how people come to be seen as superior or inferior to others, or indeed how they may come to see themselves as superior or inferior? Is it about birth and heritage – e.g. members of a royal family are born into a system of privilege, or marry into such a system? This seems to reflect a fairly static view of society and a rather negative view that you are born into a particular group and there is little room for movement within the hierarchy. It also tells us little about the social construction of notions of value and privilege and social identity, and the way that structural processes and institutional practices may group individuals.

A more common way of exploring class divisions in society is based on the notion of work segregation and occupational grouping. A feature of modernity and post-modernity has been the increase in labour specificity, with greater specialisation of tasks and division of labour. Labour market segregation has its roots in the industrialisation process and shift to market capitalism of the late eighteenth century and has been a feature of labour market organisation ever since. With the drive towards efficiency and profit accumulation, the labour market has become increasingly segregated and specialised. Fordist and post-Fordist methods of work organisation saw production tasks being broken down into a number of component parts for the pursuit of increased efficiency (Thompson, 1998).

Fordism a form of industrial economy within advanced capitalist societies based on mass production associated with techniques and processes of Henry Ford in the manufacture of cars.

The labour market of contemporary industrialised societies is one that is based on horizontal and vertical segregations, reflecting differences in class, gender, ethnicity, age and disability (see Chapter 5). The social division of labour is related to other social divisions, with access to benefits and patterns of consumption being dependent on position within the social division of labour. Le Grand (1982) has shown how people higher up the social ladder have better access to health and educational welfare benefits, whilst classical studies by Titmuss (1958) and Sinfield (1978) have shown the relationship between labour market position and the benefit system, with those in secure and well paid employment having access to better levels of occupational and fiscal benefits in terms of e.g. pension provision and sickness and disability pay schemes. (See also Rose, 1981, for a feminist perspective on these theories.)

Although there are some disagreements amongst sociologists about the definition of class, there is some consensus that class is based on economic divisions and that people can be categorised on the basis of how they make their living or derive their income. Thus class is often associated with occupational status. However, class is not just about differential income levels, but also about ways of living associated with those incomes and shared value systems (there may be conscious and unconscious mediators of attitudes, lifestyles and behaviours).

It could be argued that the concept of class has three dimensions:

1. economic – wealth, income, occupation
2. political – status and power
3. cultural – values, beliefs and norms and lifestyles.

Measuring social class

The concept of social class may be either an objective or a subjective one, and has focused on the differentiation of either individuals or broader groupings within society. There have been several attempts to produce criteria for the objective measurement of social class, many of which use occupational categorisation to classify people. One of the earliest approaches to differentiating people according to class was the Registrar General's Classification (RGC), which divided people according to occupational position, and made broad assumptions about similarities within these groupings in terms of income, status and lifestyle. The Registrar General's Classification has been used for the compilation of statistical information, to help to develop policy. (See, for example, the Acheson Report, 1998, which explores the relationship between health status and wealth status.) Within the Registrar General's Classification, approximately 20,000 different occupations are grouped into five categories.

Registrar General's Classification of Social Class

Social class		
I	Professional and higher managerial	e.g. lawyers, doctors, bank managers
II	Intermediate managerial, administrative, professional	e.g. social workers, teachers, nurses
IIInm	Skilled non-manual	e.g. secretary, technician
IIIm	Skilled manual	e.g. electrician, bus-drivers
IV	Semi-skilled	e.g. postal workers, agricultural workers
V	Unskilled	e.g. window cleaner, labourer

Although this classification is widely used, sociologists have been very critical of it for a number of reasons. Assumptions are made about shared status, identity and lifestyle, which may be misleading. It tends to be rather descriptive and normative rather than theoretical and critical. People between different occupational groupings may have shared income levels, aspirations and lifestyles or the occupational groupings may hide differences. In addition, the degree of objectivity is questionable, as it seems to be a scale of relative standing in the community, based on subjective criteria of value, and makes assumptions about status and shared value systems. In the

1980s, the Conservative Government adopted the Standard Occupational Classification (SOC) for official statistical purposes. This system uses a nine category occupational scale for dividing the population. Whilst this system of classification may not address all the criticisms that have been levelled at the RGC classification, it does provide slightly less conflated categories of occupation. It does, however, still make assumptions about shared characteristics, lifestyle and income levels, and fails to explore the construction of differences and oppressions between the different classes.

Classical sociology and social class

The founding fathers of sociology viewed social class in terms of the relationship between different economic groups in society. For functionalists such as Parsons, stratification is both functional and necessary for the smooth running of society. They argue that not everyone can occupy an equal status and lifestyle, and that society is made up of a number of different roles and positions, which contribute to the smooth functioning of the whole system. This perspective has been widely criticised, principally for confusing cause and effect and assuming consensus. It tells us nothing about the way that social divisions are constructed and the oppressions and constructions of inferiority and superiority that are embedded within these constructions. Furthermore, it fails to acknowledge that social divisions are as likely to produce conflict as harmony (Dahrendorf, 1959). Most sociologists now agree that conflict theories offer the most plausible explanations for social stratification and inequalities are explained in terms of the relative power that different groups have.

Weberians see class in terms of economic resources, whereby class is related to market position, with the role of the labour market being crucial (Evans and Mills, 1998). However, they distinguish class from status, seeing status as being derived from more than just economic position, although this is clearly important. Neo-Weberians continue to use economic position and occupational role to explain social groupings, based on the assumption of a shared value system and lifestyle amongst people who have similar occupations and income levels. The Hope–Goldthorpe Scale, for example, acknowledges that people may be located within a stratification system based on their market position as well as the job they do. Thus class is associated with market situation as well as work situation. Hutton (1995) uses the concept of the 30:30:40 society to explain the fundamental changes in the class composition in modern Britain as a result of processes of global capitalism. The selected criteria, which he uses to explore the different groups, have parallels with the *dual labour market* model of employment, which sees the labour market being divided into two sectors, the primary and secondary sectors (see Chapter 5).

For Marxists, class is defined in terms of the relationship to means of production (see Chapter 2). Marxists view class as a relationship between two polar opposites, based on oppression and subordination and underpinned by conflict. Social status and position in society is related to economic position (Wright, 1978). Marx referred to the group who were outside the class system of the bourgeosie and the proletariat as the *lumpen proletariat, the surplus or relatively stagnant population* group characterised by a group of individuals who were largely excluded from the labour market and society in general. The following quote from Marx demonstrates the disregard that he had for this residual group, and the generally pejorative way in which they were classified.

> 'The lumpen-proletariat, this passive putrefaction of the lowest strata . . .'
>
> (Marx, 1848: 53, cited in Bovenkerk, 1984)

The underclass

Underclass group of highly deprived people who are seen as being at the bottom of the class divisions. They are seen as constituting a class in their own right. Commentators relate this to factors such as race and economic and political power.

The term, the *underclass*, as it is used today, emerged towards the end of the twentieth century as a way of referring to those who are located right at the bottom of the class structure, seeing them as a class that is distinct from the *respectable* working class. The term largely emanates from Charles Murray's work in the USA, in which he identified a group of marginalised and excluded individuals and groups, whose living standards were significantly lower than those of the rest of society. For Murray, there were three factors that united members of the underclass: illegitimacy, violent crime and drop-out from the labour market, related to an over-reliance on the welfare and benefits system. He primarily focused on members of minority ethnic groups, identifying a high rate of illegitimate births among young black females, a high rate of crime and long-term unemployment. Other commentators have argued that similar patterns of social organisation can be identified amongst black or immigrant groups throughout Europe who have limited access to secure employment, housing etc. and who may operate on the fringes of society within a black economy (see e.g. Giddens, 2006).

Murray has argued that there is an emerging underclass in Britain, with significant minorities being long-term unemployed, living in poor quality accommodation or having no permanent residency, and being dependent on state benefits for long periods. Although not exclusively related to ethnicity, there are a disproportionate number of blacks and Asians located within the underclass in Britain (see Chapter 6).

The benefits system is crucial to Murray's analysis, as he argues that benefits that are too easily accessible reduce incentives to work and create a class of individuals who are disaffected and dislocated from the labour market and the rest of society. From this perspective, the rise in teenage pregnancy is seen as being related to young girls getting pregnant in order to get council or social housing, and being reliant on the state benefit system for their income maintenance.

The underclass represents a form of social disintegration and the term has been used in the sense of a moral panic about the breakdown of society. Society is seen to be spatially segregated, with pockets of urban deprivation based on the existence of the underclass. Ghettoes and sink estates are seen as representative of this underclass and social disintegration with weak infrastructures, leading to poor educational facilities and inadequate health care facilities, reflecting the notion of the Inverse Care Law, where those with the greatest need are least well served by statutory sector services. These areas are also associated with run-down and marginalised housing and few local opportunities for meaningful employment. Crime may be a significant feature, with drugs, gangs and violent crime using guns, knives and other weapons being a concern for many (see Chapter 4).

New Labour's policies reflect some of this ideological perspective. For example the welfare for work policies are based on the notion of helping people to help themselves in the labour market, and reducing dependence on the benefit system (Prideaux, 2005).

Exercise

- Looking at the theories and scales above, how useful do you think it is to have a measure of social class?
- Is class still a useful concept for understanding people's position in society?

Because of the difficulties of measuring and determining social class, some sociologists have argued that class is no longer a useful concept for explaining the divisions of society, and that social stratification needs to be explored within the context of multiple variables such as age, gender, ethnicity, disability and sexuality as well as economic status (Crompton, 1998). Since the Second World War there have been changes in forms of production with a decline in the heavy manufacturing industries and an increase in service industries. In addition, there has been a fragmentation into part-time work, short-term contracts and less emphasis on a job for life. There has also been a decline in class politics, with a focus upon new social movements where individuals group together based on shared characteristics other than occupation (ibid.). Thus patterns of consumption are seen as important indicators of social groupings and collective identities.

Graffiti and defaced property, which may be a feature of areas of urban deprivation. (Galina Barskaya)

Patterns of consumption

In advanced capitalist societies, there is an emphasis on consumerism. This has led to a greater access to resources, with banks and credit companies offering people loans, a greater emphasis on credit arrangements and higher purchase arrangements, offering people greater access to lifestyle and consumer durables. Thus it is increasingly difficult to differentiate lifestyles on the basis of occupational group.

Consumerism is important when exploring the nature of divisions within contemporary Britain, yet ability to participate in the consumer market is related to income levels. Dunleavy (1986) coined the term **Consumption cleavages** ◄ *consumption cleavages* to explain people's positions within society. Divisions are based on the ability to participate in the consumer market and identity is increasingly being constructed through the consumption choices that we are able to make. In relation to needs and wants, preferences are revealed when people make choices in a consumer market.

The market is dominated by big brand names, with branded clothing, foodstuffs, consumer durables and leisure. Identities become constructed through choice of clothing, music, cultural and leisure pursuits. According to Social Trends (2000) shopping is the second most popular leisure activity in Britain (watching television being the first). Shopping is no longer a purely functional activity, but is a leisure pursuit, with the growth of more and more retail outlets in competition with each other (including home shopping, internet shopping and the TV channels which are purely devoted to shopping)

Consumption cleavages divisions in society are based on the ability to pay for goods rather than being derived from occupational income.

and the growth of the number of consumer durables that are available within the market.

Associated with this rise in consumption has been a concomitant rise in the credit industry, with a dramatic increase in the use of credit cards. Between 1991 and 2004 credit card transactions increased from £1 billion to £5.5 billion (Social Trends, 2006 www.statistics.gov.uk/socialtrends36/).

Managing consumption patterns and participation in the consumer market has led to a huge problem of debt in contemporary Britain.

- At the end of July 2006, the total UK personal debt was £1,237bn. Average household debt in the UK is approximately £7,463 (excluding mortgages) and £42,865 (including mortgages).
- Last year the Citizens Advice Bureau dealt with 1, 128,000 debt enquiries and almost half of the UK adult population is affected by money worries, leading to stress and anxiety, and a quarter of those who are in debt are receiving treatment from a GP for stress, anxiety and depression.

Source: Credit Action, www.creditaction.org.uk/debtstats.htm

Not surprisingly, the problem of debt affects those lower down the socio-economic scale disproportionately, although credit card spending, mortgages and borrowing are a wider feature of contemporary society.

Patterns of consumption are important, and discussion of the market and people's access to the market demonstrates stark inequalities in terms of the choices that people are able to make. An examination of the relationship between socio-economic status and housing tenures demonstrates these inequalities (see Social Trends, 2006).

Whether we choose to define class divisions according to class, or other scales of difference, the concept of social stratification is important, as it explores the divided society and the differences in power, status and income that different individuals and groups have. These differences also reflect different life chances and the ability to make lifestyle choices. Thus sociologists are interested in patterns of advantage and disadvantage and the processes that contribute to disadvantage and discrimination in society.

Exercise

- Look at the statistics for low income in 2006 Social Trends (available at www.statistics.gov.uk/socialtrends36/).
- What can you deduce about the sources of disadvantage from these statistics?
- In what ways does societal structure contribute to social disadvantage and social division?

Power

Power is important when exploring social divisions. Power is differentially distributed in society and may derive from one's position within the hierarchy of the social system. Related to the notion of power is ideology, the set of ideas which shape the structures and relationships of society. Gramsci (1971) refers to *ideological hegemony*, where there is a dominance of one set of beliefs over another, deriving from the power of the ruling elite. For example, in a capitalist society there is a dominant ideology of waged labour and capitalist modes of production. Those with power are able to perpetuate these sets of dominant beliefs. A single mother living in poverty on a marginalised council estate in an area of urban deprivation may not agree with the dominant set of values and beliefs which contribute to her disadvantaged situation, but lacks the resources to challenge the ideology or change her situation. In contrast, dominant groups use their different status as a way of protecting their privileged position within society.

Bourdieu (1988) explores notions of cultural reproduction in relation to the continuation of privilege: different actors and groups in society have power through their access to resources, which he terms capital. However, power is not just derived from economic capital, but also through social, cultural and symbolic capital. Social capital refers to the social networks and group membership that people may be able to utilise in their struggle for privilege; cultural capital refers to educational credentials and cultural goods (the value of which is constructed through social processes); and symbolic capital relates to the perceived legitimacy of all forms of capital. Through the possession of capital, Bourdieu argues that those who hold privileged positions are able to perpetuate that privilege as they are better placed to be able to mobilise their capital resources.

Parkin (1979) explores exclusionary practices that groups employ in order to limit membership to the group and therefore protect their position within society. For example, many occupational groups use a system of regulation to control entry of individuals into the training or educational programmes, based on academic achievement and the ability to present oneself in a particular way at interview. Thus, the occupational group may become a fairly **Homogenous** the same ◄ homogenous group of shared backgrounds and similar cultural and throughout, not diverse. social viewpoints. This may be perpetuated through promotion processes, which are influenced by implicit assumptions, such as the old school tie network.

Homogenous the same throughout, not diverse.

Meritocracy achieving high status or position in society is achieved through ability and effort, as opposed to, for example, inheritance.

Meritocracy

The concept of meritocracy is consistent with a consensus view on ◄ society in that a *meritocratic* society is one in which position or occupation is allocated on the basis of ability and merit, as opposed to one based on ascribed factors such as gender, race and class, or privilege or family connections. The extent to which Britain is a meritocratic society is an important aspect of sociological enquiry, particularly in relation to the analysis of the education system, the labour market and the distribution of income and wealth in society.

An education-based meritocracy is based on the premise that the system rewards children in terms of their educational attainment on the basis of their ability, rather than their social background, ethnicity or gender. Notions of meritocracy incorporate ideals of social efficiency, social mobility and social justice, which do not necessarily lead to equality of opportunity as differences in levels of ability and achievement are intended to keep people in their place (Young, 1958). The concept of meritocracy had been used in Britain and the US to justify differential outcomes based upon the basis of assumed differential abilities. Young adds that

> With an amazing battery of certificates and degrees at its disposal, education has put its seal of approval on a minority, and its seal of disapproval on the many who fail to shine from the time they are relegated to the bottom streams at the age of seven or before.
>
> (Guardian, 29 June 2001)

There is considerable evidence (Halsey et al., 1980, Swann Report 1985, Social Trends, 2006) to assert that ascribed factors significantly influence educational attainment at compulsory and post-compulsory levels, which later impact on an individual's life chances.

> While systems of distinction and discrimination have evolved, they continue to underpin and reproduce inequality, dramatically shaping the lives and opportunities of those they position.
>
> (Gillies, 2005: 836)

Education has become an increasingly important factor in determining which jobs people enter and in determining their social class position. Children from a higher social class have an increased chance of gaining higher-level qualifications than those from less advantaged classes (Shavit and Blossfeld, 1993), which in turn influences their future employment. Hobcraft's (1998) findings suggest that educational test scores during compulsory schooling are 'the most frequent and effective childhood predictor of adult outcomes' and that educational attainment is strongly linked to unemployment and social exclusion. It is accepted that whilst educational standards are rising there is persistent inequality in levels of attainment between children from higher social class groups and those from manual and unskilled backgrounds (DFES, 2004). Factors that influence educational achievement include poverty, parental interest and support (driven by parental experience of education), neighbourhood and the quality of schooling (Every Child Matters, 2003 – www.everychildmatters.gov.uk).

There has however been a significant improvement in the performance of girls compared with boys (DFES, 2006 – www.dfes.gov.uk) though this does not translate to higher education or income (NSO, 2006 – www.statistics.gov.uk). In relation to post-16 schooling, there has been significant emphasis via government policy on increasing the proportion of young people from lower social classes entering higher education. The resulting expansion of higher education has meant that the number of people entering higher education has risen from 0.6 million in 1970/1 to 2.4 million in 2003/4. (Social Trends, 2006 – www.statistics.gov.uk/ socialtrends36/). Yet participation rates for young people in manual social classes remains low compared to those from non-manual social classes, and students from minority ethnic groups (particularly those from students of Indian origin (ibid.).

For those young people who leave education without qualifications, the emerging interest amongst welfare agencies concerning the position of the young people who are not in education, employment or training reflects an awareness of the risks associated with a lack of qualifications and skills. A report by the Prince's Trust (2007) identifies the personal, social and economic costs of educational under-achievement and unemployment during a time of growing national prosperity (www.princes-trust.org.uk).

Case study

Despite being described by teachers as 'bright', Rochelle left school with no qualifications. Her father left her mother when she was born and her mother experienced difficulties with alcohol and drugs, resulting in Rochelle's removal from home due to neglect at the age of eight. From the age of thirteen Rochelle became bored and disillusioned with school and started to miss school at regular intervals. During her final year she attended a maximum of 36 days. Rochelle is now twenty, lives in a flat with her boyfriend and has ambitions to train as a beauty therapist. She hopes that a local salon will employ her as a trainee, although she has had no success to date. She is ambivalent about going back to college as she does not have the required GCSEs to start her chosen course but realises that this is the only way to achieve her ambition.

- Despite being described as 'bright' how can sociological theories help to explain Rochelle's underachievement?
- What do you understand by Young's comments regarding meritocracy and how do they relate to this case study?

Inequality

Inequality is an important concept in relation to social stratification. Inequality may be both material and symbolic, where individuals have differential access to material resources as well as to power and control. Thus within a socially stratified system, a group becomes superior or inferior to other groups. Disadvantage and vulnerability is often associated with poverty and social exclusion. For social workers, poverty and social exclusion are important concepts, as the people they work with may often suffer from the multiple disadvantages associated with processes of differentiation. Thus poverty, social exclusion and the underclass are concepts which have sociological relevance in the understanding of the position and experiences of the most disadvantaged within society.

Poverty

What do we mean when we talk about poverty and to what extent does it still exist in Britain and how is it defined and measured? It is important to have an understanding of different concepts of poverty, as the way that we define poverty is likely to have an impact on perceptions, measurement, identification, causes, attitudes and solutions. Different measurement scales are likely to reflect the values that we hold about acceptance of poverty. Sociologists have distinguished between absolute poverty and relative deprivation.

Absolute poverty

Rowntree's study of poverty in York in 1899 set the pattern for other studies of poverty and established an important concept of the poverty line, a level of income below which one is deemed to be in poverty. Rowntree defined poverty as the situation in which total earnings are insufficient to maintain the minimum necessities for the maintenance of physical efficiency (e.g. food, clothing, housing, heating, lighting, cooking utensils) – all of which should be purchased at the lowest prices and in quantities only necessary for maintenance of physical subsistence. A notion of deserving/undeserving underpins this theory, with moral undertones.

Exercise

- How far would you agree that a deserving/undeserving category of the poor exists within contemporary society?
- Are there groups of poor who are seen as more deserving than other groups?
- How is this reflected in public attitudes and charitable activity?

It was argued in the 1960s that poverty had largely disappeared from industrialised societies, based on the definition of absolute poverty (Abel-Smith and Townsend, 1965). There was a widespread view that a safety net of welfare provision, providing a subsistence level of provision for those who could not contribute to the social security insurance system, had eliminated poverty. However, the concept of relative deprivation was developed to explore the relationship between different individuals and groups in terms of their access to resources and consumption patterns.

Relative deprivation

Within the concept of relative deprivation, poverty is viewed in relative terms, where needs are not just physiologically determined, but also have a social and cultural dimension (Townsend, 1979). This is not fixed in terms of time or historical period, but is a dynamic process associated with the changing nature of societies and patterns of consumption. From this perspective, poverty is relative to the living standards and income of the rest of the population. In addition, poverty is not just about income and money, but must include non-materialist items like the ability to participate in society. People are seen to be poor if they are excluded from normal living standards. This concept broadens the notion of necessities of life and recognises that people have social roles as well as physical needs. One becomes an outsider if they lack resources for participation and are deprived of certain rights. Relative deprivation explores the whole issue of what we understand by resources. Inequality is not just related to money and material possessions, but is also about the ability to participate fully within a society.

Exercise

- What would you say are needs?
- Draw up a list of your ten most important needs.
- Do some needs have greater priority than others?
- Might someone in a different culture and environment have quite different ideas about what needs are?

There are also differences between what we need and what we want. For example, if the rest of your social group have the latest mobile phone technology, even though you may not need a new mobile phone, you may feel excluded from full participation in the group if everybody else is exchanging messages, games and music. Needs are therefore more basic or essential than wants – we may need things we do not necessarily want, such as immunisations to prevent the spread of infectious diseases. Needs and wants are also not necessarily objective categories, but classification of need may be based on dominant group interests who are better able to articulate those needs.

Although the concept of relative deprivation is seen as more inclusive and explanatory than the concept of absolute poverty, it has been subjected to a number of criticisms, in that it is difficult to make comparisons over times, the indices that are used may be quite selective and there is a failure to analyse the structural factors created by capitalist organisation and modes of production as explanations for positions of relative advantage and disadvantage (Alcock, 1997).

Explanations of poverty

Individual

This sees poverty as the result of one's own personal deficiencies and is known as the social pathological model (MacNicol, 1987). Various theories are subsumed under this umbrella term, the most common of which is the genetic theory, which sees behaviour and social activity as directly attributed to genetic make-up. Within this theory there is a belief that poverty can be linked with inheritance, intelligence and social class. Inherent within this definition is the notion that natural processes are at the root of disadvantage, as it is passed between the generations. The *eugenics* movement of the late nineteenth and early twentieth century reflected this social pathological view of poverty, with programmes of selective out-breeding operating throughout Europe and the USA to breed out undesirable and deviant characteristics, such as poverty. This theory fails to account for factors that are extrinsic to the individual which shape intelligence, access to labour market position and economic and wealth status.

Cultural

The cultural theory of poverty causation focuses on the roles of families and family sub-culture. Within this theory, it is argued that families who are poor have a certain belief system, totally different from the rest of society, and therefore children are socialised into poverty (Lewis, 1998). In the 1970s, the Secretary of State for Health and Social Services, Sir Keith Joseph argued that there was a cycle of deprivation, where deprivation is transmitted from one generation to the next. This is a good example of how poverty becomes viewed within the context of family behavioural patterns.

Within this perspective the solution rests on changing attitudes to break this cycle of deprivation. Some evidence of this approach can be seen to underpin some of the policies that have been introduced to tackle child poverty under the New Labour Government. Initiatives such as Sure Start, pre-school education for three- and four-year-olds

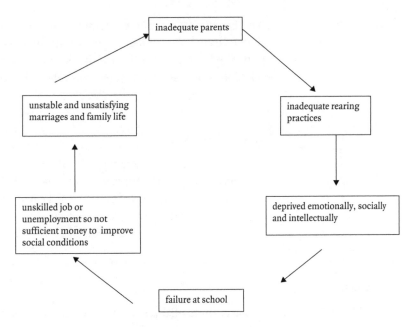

Figure 3.1 The cycle of deprivation.

and parent preparatory classes can all be seen within the context of this approach. In addition, social casework with families living in multiple deprivation are aimed at changing the values of parents.

While Sir Keith Joseph and Pierre Bourdieu may not be the most natural of bedfellows, there are some parallels here in the notion of intergenerational reproduction. However, the cycle of deprivation tends to *pathologise* individuals and families and ignores wider processes of structural disadvantage, which contribute to persistent and inter-generational poverty (see Holman, 1978, for a critique of this theory).

Pathologisation to attribute causes/ symptoms to a breakdown of the body or disease. Can be applied medically or socially.

Structural

The structures of society lead to poverty and the persistence of poverty. Inequalities in the labour market, economic policies and the relationship to labour market policies, unemployment, early retirement, redundancy and under-employment, as well as low wages, are all seen as causal factors in terms of poverty and relative deprivation. This then affects people's ability to participate in patterns of consumption, which is an important part of advanced capitalism. Certain groups are particularly susceptible to poverty, due to socially created dependencies:

- older people
- families with children
- low-paid wage earners
- unemployed
- sick or disabled

These social changes and the nature of contemporary capitalist societies have led sociologists and policy-makers to question the utility of poverty as an indicator of social disadvantage. Social exclusion is now seen as a better or preferred term than poverty, as it is more encompassing.

Social Exclusion

> Exclusion processes are dynamic and multidimensional in nature. They are linked not only to unemployment and/or to low income, but also to housing conditions, levels of education and opportunities, health discrimination, citizenship and integration in the local community.
>
> (European Social Policy White Paper, 1994: 37)

Exercise

- Think of a group who is excluded from society. What are the characteristics that define them as excluded?
- Compare your list with someone else who has identified a different excluded group. What are the common features of these groups?

Social exclusion can encompass a range of factors that limit one's ability to fully participate in society. Economic exclusion is one aspect, where an individual's ability to participate in the normal consumption patterns of society is inhibited, as discussed above. Levitas (1998) has argued that policy responses have often focused on integration through employment, reflecting a Durkheimian notion of integration. However, people may also be socially excluded through:

- legal exclusion, exclusion from voting or being able to participate in the democratic processes of the criminal justice system.
- failure of supply of social goods or services to individuals or a group of individuals. For example, failure to supply an adequate education system or health service will lead to social exclusion or a child who sees the education system as irrelevant to their needs may voluntarily exclude themselves from school, through truancy, leading to patterns of exclusion in other areas of life.

Social exclusion has become a significant feature of advanced capitalist society and is related to economic changes associated with global capitalism and concomitant changes of welfare regimes, with a greater emphasis on selectivity and targeting of statutory support services. There have also been demographic changes, with a higher level of unemployment and a greater longevity, leading to many more people living in retirement (see Chapter 10) which have contributed to social differentiation of incomes, as well as social judgements and social values being based on ability to participate in the labour market. Thus unemployment and old age may be stigmatised in a society that values economic participation. Spatial processes of segregation and separation (ghettoisation; travelling communities; refugees and asylum seekers; homeless and transient populations) have also led to patterns of social exclusion based on access to the labour market, legal inclusion and social and cultural inclusion. In a speech on 15 January 2007, Oliver Heald, Conservative Shadow Secretary of State for Constitutional Affairs at the time, said:

> We clearly have problems of social exclusion; the proportion of children in workless households is the highest in Europe, more than half the children in inner London are still living below the poverty line, more than 1.2 million young people are not in work or full-time education despite a growing economy, and 2.7 million people of working age are claiming incapacity benefits – three times more than the number who claim jobseeker's allowance.
>
> (15 January 2007, available at www.egovmonitor.com, accessed 23 July 2007)

Social exclusion and social inclusion are useful terms for understanding processes of social differentiation in societies, as they are related to the notion of rights. Human rights can be categorised as follows:

- Civil rights – basic freedoms under the law.
- Political rights – right to vote, to join and participate in political parties and to hold government accountable.

Isolated and displaced individuals on the streets of major towns and cities are an increasing reminder of the numbers of people who are socially excluded. (Dan Eckert)

- Social rights – rights to education, social welfare, social security etc.

Citizenship is related to notions of freedom to participate within society, through the political and civil processes as well as through social and economic processes. Thus the rights of citizenship are affected by inequalities in provision and quality of education, healthcare, housing, transport and other social amenities as well as

---

Exercise

A lost generation trapped on our forgotten estates

A five-year-old boy in a ripped coat and dirty trousers hammered on the front door of his council estate flat at 11 p.m. last Wednesday. 'Come on, you smackheads,' he shouted to his parents inside. 'I know what you're doing.'

By the boy's feet sat a plastic bag with bread and milk. The only shop open at that time is on the opposite side of a busy motorway, a fifteen-minute walk away. According to neighbours, it is a journey the child regularly makes on his own.

'Unless someone rescues that wee kiddie and gives him a second chance, he's doomed' said Jean, who has lived on the Clyde Court housing estate in Leeds for seventeen years. She is too scared of her neighbours to give her full name.

On an estate where deprivation and violence are commonplace, the boy's bleak, hopeless life is the norm and, if he takes his ambitions from those around him, his life chances are near to zero.

In a few years he could seek to emulate Steven Gedge, a twelve-year-old local boy recently arrested for the fifty-fifth time. He has already been given up for lost by his mother, his school and the local council.

Steven in turn has little to model his life on except the family living around the corner, three of whose four children are heroin addicts including the youngest, who had an abortion two years ago when she was eleven.

The only child in this family not using heroin is a sixteen-year-old girl who had a child last year with a local lad. The baby has never seen its father; he was arrested for drug dealing before his son's birth.

Two weeks ago, the local newsagent was robbed by a fourteen-year-old boy, high on drugs, wielding a butcher's knife and a plank of wood spiked with nails. The local church has barricaded its windows and surrounded itself with razor wire.

Looming at the heart of the estate is the residents' apex of fear; the sixteen-floor Clyde Court tower block where bloodied tissues lie in pools of urine and tinfoil stained with crack drifts around the stairwell like autumn leaves.

The block is a favourite with the local youths, who have stripped it of every piece of metal down to the lift call buttons. They attach used syringes with their needles exposed to the underside of the banisters, and throw shopping trollies from the roof heedless of anyone walking below.

Amelia Hill (2003) *The Observer*, Sunday 30 November 2003 © Guardian News and Media Limited 2003. Reprinted with permission.

by inequalities in ability to participate in economic life. In addition, as argued above, citizenship is related to the ability to participate in the consumer market. Furthermore, the rights of citizenship are related to freedoms from victimisation and abuse (Bochel et al., 2005). Thus racial victimisation, domestic violence, elder abuse and child abuse can all limit people's freedoms. Justice is related to freedom and citizenship within a democratic society.

- How could individual, cultural and structural explanations of poverty explain this boy's situation?
- What factors contribute to social exclusion on this estate?
- How can knowledge of these theories be useful in informing social work practice with people who experience widespread disadvantage?

Impact of poverty and social exclusion

Poverty is a key factor associated with children being looked after. Bebbington and Miles' research (1989) suggests that children living in poverty are 700 times more likely to come into local authority care. There is a persistent and widening gap between health and wealth. Those with the least economic resources in society have higher incidences of premature mortality and self-reported morbidity, limiting their activities of living. There is also a strong class gradient in terms of lifestyle behaviours. For example, there is a strong social class gradient in the prevalence of obesity, particularly amongst women, and there is a higher incidence of obesity in manual groups.

Exercise

Look at a government document about health inequality (e.g. Tackling Health Inequalities: A Programme for Action, 2003 – available at www.dh.gov.uk – or Report of the Measuring Inequalities in Health Working Group, 2003 – available at www.scotland.gov.uk.

   What evidence is there of the relationship between health status and poverty and disadvantage?

Poverty and material and social disadvantage and social exclusion remain important issues within the stratified society of contemporary western societies. However, policy responses and professional ideologies have largely failed to tackle the structural processes that contribute to these inequalities. The social pathological model has dominated policy decisions over time, and in many ways social work has failed to challenge the assumptions underpinning this approach. From the Poor Law to the notion of social problem groups, which have dominated social work practice since the 1960s, there has been an underlying assumption of the deserving/undeserving distinction, notions of individual moral deficiency and a pathologisation of the behavioural traits of individuals and groups. Thus social work has historically focused on tackling poverty at an individual level and neglecting the sources of the inequalities (Jones, 2002).

Emancipatory social work needs to acknowledge the structural and ideological factors that affect the continuation of poverty (and in recent years, the widening gaps between the haves and have-nots, with a greater number of individuals experiencing poverty). We would argue that persistence of poverty cannot solely be attributed to family traits. External factors which can limit people's opportunities and prevent people from climbing out of poverty must also change. Poverty must be located within the context of society in order to find the cause(s) which result from the inequalities within society.

It has previously been suggested that social workers have a good understanding of the impact of poverty on people's lives; however, Holman (1978) argues that while some workers understand how years on low income impacts on parenting, 'there is evidence that social work does not have a good record in understanding or combating family poverty'. Though social workers are required to take into account wider environmental factors, an understanding of poverty and social exclusion are not seen as central to assessment approaches in children and family work and other areas of practice. Increasing bureaucracy and managerialism within social work leaves practitioners as gatekeepers to resources as service users are expected to fit into more closely defined eligibility criteria. The social work role is marginalised in the social exclusion agenda to tackle poverty but instead social workers are expected to monitor, maintain and supervise those most damaged by poverty (Jones, 2002).

Conclusion

In order to promote anti-oppressive and anti-discriminatory practice, social workers must engage with the key theories and debates about social division and social differentiation. Not only do social workers need to understand the experiences and impact of divisions and oppression, but also the structural and institutional context. Social work can only be truly empowering if these structural contexts are challenged, otherwise the focus remains on individual adaptation within existing structures. As Weiss argues, an understanding of these issues can aid the social work profession in its

> dual commitment. . . . to social justice, understood as the need for the redistribution of resources for the benefit of those who have been deprived and to individual well-being.

> (Weiss, 2005: 108)

Summary points

- Society is divided according to occupation and income levels, with a hierarchy of positions.
- Social divisions in society lead to inequalities and are reproduced through systems of privilege, which favour the dominant classes of society.
- Poverty and social exclusion are related to systems of stratification and ability to buy goods in the consumer market is related to economic position.
- Processes of inclusion and exclusion reflect power and economic ability.
- Inequalities are experienced in many areas of life, including health status, access to housing and access to education.
- Social workers often work with people who are economically disadvantaged or socially excluded, but in the past there has been a tendency to focus efforts at an individual level.
- Understanding the structural and social causes of inequality and social exclusion can help social workers to work in a more empowering way.

Questions for discussion

- Think of your local area. What indicators are there of deprivation? Is there an identifiable gap between communities that you perceive as advantaged or disadvantaged?
- Is social class still a useful concept for understanding the divisions in society? How do sociological perspectives of social class differ from concepts of social exclusion?
- What do you think Jones means when he talks about social work being a class-specific activity?
- What can social workers do to help to alleviate the problems of social disadvantage?

Further reading

Best, S. (2005) *Understanding Social Divisions*. London: Sage. A comprehensive discussion of the nature of social divisions and the explanations for them.

Byrne, D. (1999) *Social Exclusion*. Buckingham: Open University Press. This book provides a good critical discussion of the concept of social exclusion, and has useful chapters on the underclass and Marxist analysis of reserve army of labour.

Crompton, R. (1998) *Class and Stratification: An Introduction to Current Debates*. 2nd edn. Cambridge: Polity. This book provides a comprehensive discussion of theories of class and stratification, with a particularly good chapter on class as a contested concept.

Payne, G. (ed.) (2000) *Social Divisions*. Basingstoke, Macmillan. This book provides a comprehensive discussion of the nature of division, class and stratification in Britain. There are chapters exploring the relationship between social categorisations and social divisions (gender, ethnicity, national identity, age and old age, childhood, sexuality, disability, health and community).

Roberts, K. (2001) *Class in Modern Britain*. Basingstoke, Palgrave. This book is an accessible introduction to theories and measurement of social class.

Sheppard, M. (2006) *Social Work and Social Exclusion: The Idea of Practice*. Aldershot: Ashgate. This book explores the role of social workers in tackling social exclusion and has important chapters on empowerment and coping.

4

Crime and Deviance

Terry Thomas*

Social workers come into regular contact with people whose behaviour may be described as criminal. This chapter considers how sociology can contribute to the social workers' understanding of that behaviour and the wider social context in which it takes place.

Key issues

The key issues that will be discussed in this chapter are:

- Classical sociological theories in relation to crime and deviance.
- Labelling theory and the social construction of deviance.
- Critical perspectives on crime and deviance, including feminist and anti-racist perspectives.
- The creation of moral panics and societal responses to deviant behaviour.
- The relationship between crime, deviance and labelling and social stratification.
- Social work takes place within a punitive and labelling framework, which conflicts with empowering practice.

By the end of this chapter, you should be able to:

- Demonstrate an understanding of the major sociological theories of crime and deviance.
- Demonstrate an understanding of labelling theory and its relevance in the construction of categories of deviance.
- Explain the sociological concept of the moral panic.
- Discuss the social response to deviant behaviour.
- Explain the relationship between crime and deviance and social disadvantage and divisions.

* Terry Thomas is Professor of Criminal Justice Studies at Leeds Metropolitan University.

Introduction

Youth Offending Teams (YOTS) multi-agency teams dealing with young offenders; created by the UK Crime and Disorder Act 1998. YOT teams' members can be from health, social care or other professional backgrounds.

Social workers in the UK are employed as members of multi-agency Youth Offending Teams (YOTs) to work directly with young offenders. They are also employed in Children's Services where a child or young person's behaviour may become criminal, the older that child gets. Social workers in child protection work will inevitably find that the adult perpetrators of child abuse they work with are going to have their behaviour described as criminal; some social workers may work directly with these adults in such settings as Sex Offender Treatment Programmes.

Sex Offender Treatment Programmes (SOTP) designed to treat people convicted and sentenced in the UK for sexual offences. SOTP often involve group work and have therapeutic elements.

Social workers with adults will engage with service users with learning disabilities or mental illnesses, who may well commit crime. The mentally disordered offender has become the *bête noire* of care in the community policies and the risk that such people pose to communities has become the subject of much inquiry and policy formulation. Our prisons are said to be over-represented with people who should be in a hospital environment rather than a penal one.

At one time probation officers were described as 'social workers to the courts', and their training was exactly the same as for all social workers. Since 1995, when a separate form of training was devised, probation work has dropped some of its associations with social work, but still retains an element of 'helping' offenders to rehabilitate their lives.

Criminology

The branch of sociology that covers criminal behaviour is usually described as criminology, which is a social science analysis of offending behaviour that seeks to stand back and understand that behaviour. It tries to avoid simplistic and superficial accounts and look at the wider and more in depth picture. Criminology sets the offender, and the offending behaviour, in the context of the social dynamics of their life and the communities they live in.

Over the years, the study of crime and criminals has been taken up by other disciplines, such as psychologists, biologists, legal philosophers and political scientists. Psychologists and biologists, for example, look for the explanations of criminal behaviour within the individuals themselves, rather than within social elements. Criminology can also be distinguished from criminal justice studies, which look at the workings of the criminal justice system, i.e. the police, prosecutors, courts, probation service, prisons and other agencies. It can also be distinguished from penal policy studies, which look at the application of punishment to our fellow citizens.

These other disciplines all contribute to our greater understanding of offending behaviour, but here we are looking only at the sociological analysis.

The study of criminals and criminal behaviour has evolved over the last 100 years. Here we take a brief look at the various 'schools of thought' and theoretical positions put forward to explain crime. Some of them have become dated and outmoded but most have a resonance and utility in our present-day understanding of criminal behaviour.

Classical criminology

Classical criminology the earliest philosophical ideas about crime (eighteenth to nineteenth centuries) which envisaged the offender as having 'made a mistake' in departing from collective social norms and who required punishment to correct their deviant behaviour.

In the eighteenth and nineteenth centuries crime and criminality were understood in terms of an individual's free choice to decide whatever behaviour they wanted to engage in. If that behaviour was considered criminal then a proportionate punishment might be applied to show them the error of their ways. The philosopher Jeremy Bentham was a key writer in developing these ideas. This 'classical school' of criminology was tied in with wider attempts to produce a clear and legitimate criminal justice system from an earlier rudimentary form that preceded it. The criminal was regarded as someone who knew what they were doing or had simply 'made a mistake' that required the application of punishment to correct them. Implicit in the 'classical school' was the simplistic notion that society had an agreed collective set of values or goals and there were no conflicting groups or aims (see Chapter 2).

The ideas of the 'classical school' are still around in theoretical thinking on crime. The American criminologist, Marcus Felson, has taken what he calls 'the rational choice perspective' to show how crime can emerge from everyday life. The implication is that crime is inevitable and constant unless we take steps toward crime reduction and prevention (Felson, 1998).

Routine activity theory a theory in which crime is seen to emerge from the routines of everyday life and is therefore almost inevitable and constant; leads to notions of crime prevention.

Felson's ideas have helped formulate the so-called 'routine activity theory' or 'rational choice theory' of crime. The motivation to commit crime is given as an ever-present factor that is triggered in everyday life by the availability of suitable 'targets'. In this way the theory posits three variables as leading to crime:

Rational choice theory choices made by potential offenders based on a rational calculation and decisions made within the constraints of time, ability and the information available.

- motivated offenders – usually young males;
- suitable targets – in the form of a person or property; and
- the absence of a capable 'guardian' against the crime.

The convergence of these three variables takes place in the routines of everyday life, and offers the opportunity for the criminal act. These routines include travelling to work or school, recreational activities, shopping etc. Sometimes the term 'opportunity crime' is used to describe this behaviour, and crime prevention policies seek to reduce the number of suitable targets and increase the presence of the capable 'guardian'.

Opportunity crime crime that emerges from situations that offer the opportunity to those inclined to take it.

In his study of street crime, Hallsworth demonstrates the degree of rationality and thought that goes into street robbery (or 'mugging'), including a thorough assessment of the 'suitable targets':

> they would know, for example, when specific individuals would congregate in areas amenable to robbery . . . know the time and days when they would have been paid . . . know that businessmen often stop outside tube stations to check for messages on their mobile phones.
>
> (Hallsworth, 2005: 113)

All of these activities are the stock-in-trade of the rational or calculating criminal and as Hallsworth concludes 'street crime . . . is an act by no means perpetrated by mindless or stupid people' (ibid.).

Since the 1980s there has been a renewed interest in the 'classical school' of criminology and rational choice theory. It has particularly been taken up by politicians of a right-wing persuasion and has been described as 'right realism'. In essence, the idea is that rational, calculating criminals who know what they are doing should be met by suitable sanctions (just deserts) that will stop them doing it. Fear is seen as the one factor that will stop people committing crime. Prison is the most severe (fearsome) penalty we have and therefore prison should be used more because 'prison works'.

Just deserts making punishment proportionate to the crime; builds on classical theories.

In the USA during the 1980s and 1990s the prison population rose inexorably and more prisons were built. At the same time crime went down, thus, for many, proving the case. A comparable rise in incarceration in the UK followed and by 2006 prison occupation reached its highest ever levels.

In political terms this hard-line 'law and order' approach in the UK grew in popularity throughout the 1980s and into the 1990s. Politicians started to intervene more directly with the criminal justice system. If three years in prison was seen as 'appropriate' for a given crime, why not make it four years or five years? Politicians could see that 'law and order' was a vote-winner and as the public grasped the idea the concept of 'popular punitivism' was formed to explain the new right-wing drift (Bottoms, 1995).

Popular punitivism a term coined in the mid-1990s to describe a swell of public opinion demanding ever more punitive (and disproportionate) sanctions against those convicted of crime; in practice politicians then pick up on this swell to ensure their own popularity.

For social work, this creates a tension between a political agenda focusing on punishment and the social work role of enablement and providing access to services and support.

Exercise

Discuss the following statement

> Jailing young people in ever larger number is not the answer to tackling youth crime.
>
> Ron Morgan, Guardian, 19/2/07

Note the contrast between the older architecture in the background and the newer building in the foreground, as the old Victorian prisons have been expanded to accommodate modern practices.
In recent years, prisons have become severely overcrowded, leading to the consideration of alternatives in sentencing policy.

Criminological positivism

Criminological positivism was the first attempt to go beyond classical criminology and study crime and criminals in a scientific way using the methods of the natural sciences.

◄ Criminological positivism simply means that scientific methods of enquiry used in the natural sciences have been brought to bear on the subject-matter of crime. Various theories are posited to explain why crime takes place and the social context in which it takes place. The criminal as rational actor thesis is replaced by the idea that criminality might be a social construction formed when social pressures act upon people to limit their ability to act in a law-abiding manner.

At the end of the nineteenth century the French sociologist Durkheim put forward the idea that crime took place in areas of social disorganisation, where the normal rules and regulations did not apply. A society with a clear social structure that everyone could subscribe to was a society with less crime. The opposite was a disorganised society that experienced what Durkheim called *anomie*. Without adequate social structure to act as a guide to behaviour, individuals were inclined to criminality (see chapter 2). Durkheim was clear that no society could be free of some criminal elements, but the presence of good education, recognised lines of authority and the emergence of a social structure that most people would want to be part of, was the starting-point for a reduction in crime.

Durkheim's ideas of *anomie* had been reflected in the work of those early social researchers who found crime amongst the 'dangerous classes' of the Victorian slums (see Chapter 1). In the 1920s the Chicago school brought a scientific framework of understanding to why certain parts of Chicago had more crime than other parts. Cities began to be studied as ecological systems that 'produced' crime in certain neighbourhoods. Today this might be seen as an obvious conventional wisdom that crime is, for example, higher in the inner cities (where the social structure may be more disorganised) and lower in other suburban areas. The Chicago school initiated this sort of urban geographical analysis. In particular, academics in 1920s Chicago noted the 'zone in transition' as an area prone to criminality. These zones were areas where industry expanded at the expense of housing, which became run down and marginalised. People moved out of these areas and only new immigrants, too poor to live anywhere else, would live there. Weakened families and communal ties equalled more 'social disorganisation' and therefore more possibilities for crime.

These ideas of 'zones in transition' have resonance with much more recent thinking on crime and disorganised areas. The so-called 'broken windows' thesis suggests that areas that are allowed to become run down because of broken windows, damaged property, graffiti etc. are likely to attract people who see it as signs of disorganisation and lack of regulation. In turn they bring their criminal or anti-social behaviour and take the area further down and past a 'tipping-point' from where it descends into an area of crime that people avoid. The policy answer is to make sure the 'tipping-point' is never reached and the area is maintained and not allowed to go down (Wilson and Kelling, 1982).

In recent years, there have been attempts to halt this urban decline through public and private investment. This, however, can also lead to greater social polarisation, as those living in the areas continue to be disadvantaged, while seeing first hand the privileged position of others, which may lead to greater opportunities for crime. Morgan (1996) discusses how urban decline has led to poor public transport and local infrastructures. This is generally not helped by public or private investment in single economic ventures.

In 2003 the UK government called on the 'broken window' thesis to support its interventions against anti-social behaviour:

> if a window is broken or a wall is covered in graffiti it can contribute to an environment in which crime takes hold, particularly if intervention is not prompt and effective. An abandoned car, left for days on end, soon becomes a burnt-out car; it is not long before more damage and vandalism takes place. Environmental decline, anti-social behaviour and crime go hand in hand and create a sense of helplessness that nothing can be done.

(Home Office, 2003: para. 1.8)

Exercise

Consider these two examples of investment.

1. The Government proposals for regional super-casinos to boost local economies. Whilst for many this has been hailed as a worthy enterprise, there has also been opposition from a number of groups. For example, Major Bill Cochrane from the Salvation Army has stated that

    Research from other countries shows that super-casinos can lead to a range of social problems, including increased debt, loss of employment, family breakdown and increased crime.

    (Reported by BBC News 24, 4 April 2006. Available at http://news. bbc.co.uk/1/hi/uk_politics/4876530.stm, accessed 23 July 2007.)

2. The Olympic Games, due to take place in 2012, have led to substantial public and private investment in the transport and local infrastructure in areas of East London, which have historically suffered from deprivation. The impact of this investment will go on long after 2012.

What might be the impact of this investment on:

- Community cohesion as a whole
- Local employment prospects
- Reduction in levels of crime?

Anti-Social Behaviour Order (ASBO) UK civil court order that seeks to restrain an individual from certain defined anti-social behaviour; breach of the ASBO leads to criminal sanctions.

The UK government has introduced a number of interventions to reduce what it has called 'anti-social behaviour', including the Anti-Social Behaviour Order (ASBO), the dispersal direction and the local curfew scheme.

What exactly constitutes anti-social behaviour has been a point of dispute. It has variously been called 'low level' crime, 'public nuisance' and 'youth annoyance'. The additional idea that it is behaviour which harasses and annoys particular individuals or groups of individuals introduces an element of subjectivity into the definition. Whereas the criminal law lays down a clear-cut line that, if transgressed, defines a criminal act, no such clear line exists for anti-social behaviour. Whilst some practitioners have welcomed this 'flexibility' others (especially lawyers) are concerned about this subjective departure.

The dispersal direction allows the police to disperse groups of youths gathering in public places if those groups present as 'threatening' (Anti-Social Behaviour Act 2003). The local curfew schemes declare designated public space as places that young people cannot enter at certain times unless accompanied by an adult. The ASBO is even more an intervention targeted on certain individuals. Youths or adults can be made the subject of an ASBO by the civil

An example of a building, which may once have been the pride of the community, now run-down and in disrepair, with broken and boarded-up windows. (Tomasz Szymanski)

courts (Crime and Disorder Act 1998), where the Order will list activities that the individual must desist from and may delineate a geographic area they must stay out of. Breach of these conditions means the individual can be brought before the criminal courts for suitable punishment.

The innovative feature of the ASBO is that it is made in the civil courts and not the criminal courts. It is made on 'application' by the local authority or police and is not a prosecution; its imposition is not a sentence of the civil courts and its existence results in no criminal record. It is only when breach of an ASBO takes place that the criminal courts take over with a prosecution, sentence and criminal record.

The critics point out that this could lead to a 'jurisdiction of difference' that effectively fast-tracks certain individuals into the criminal justice system and even into custodial settings for behaviour that is not necessarily criminal in the first place. In effect two youths of the same age, in the same city, could be acting in an identical manner on the same day, but one (on an ASBO) could be arrested, charged and imprisoned, while the other is not necessarily even committing an offence.

Case study

John is a fourteen-year-old boy who was given an ASBO for kicking footballs against the wall of a neighbour's house. He has been forbidden to kick a football in his local area. John's family complain to his youth worker that the nearest park is seen as a 'no go' area due to people using it to take drugs and ask where he can play football.

- How do you think the ASBO might have a negative impact on John?

Policies to clean areas up and never allow them to deteriorate or discourage the criminal element from moving in maintain an appearance of structure and regulation. The policy of 'zero tolerance' policing has also been supported by the 'broken windows' thesis, premised on the idea that if you ensure that all crimes, however minor, are dealt with seriously, you send out a message that deters the more serious crime. Some have argued that this has led to a demonisation and criminalisation of youth, although the evidence that youth crime has accelerated in recent years is contested. Indeed, misdemeanours that may previously have not attracted the attention of the penal system are now criminalised.

Strain theory

Another elaboration on the theories of social disorganisation and areas of disproportionate crime levels is that of Robert Merton's 'strain theory'. Merton was another 1930s American sociologist who examined criminality and, in particular, the way in which individuals could be frustrated or blocked in achieving their aspirations and ambitions in life. These aspirations and ambitions could be quite legitimate goals and indeed, often the same goals that everyone else had. But whereas others achieved through education, employment opportunities and application to the various steps necessary to get them, some people could not do this and as a result experienced a 'strain' in their attempts

Strain theory suggests crime is the result of individuals being 'blocked' in terms of mainstream society from reaching certain goals; under the consequent strain they seek deviant or criminal ways to reach those goals.

to reach the same goals. For some, the only way to get there was through illegitimate or criminal channels (Merton, 1938).

In today's consumer society Merton's ideas are even more pertinent. In a culture that celebrates material success, consumer goods, status and authority, the inability to achieve these goals places a strain on increasing numbers of people. Surrounded by media and advertising that pushes the consumer society, some may feel that only a deviant adaptation is going to get them there (see Chapter 1). Strain theory does not, of course, explain why some people, who do not experience 'strain', turn to crime.

Others have taken Merton's original thesis further to show how 'strain' theory can lead to other deviant adaptations. The 'blocked' individual may, for example, vent their frustration on others (using violence that appears random) or retreat from society in order to avoid the strain. The latter group may turn to drug dependency to 'forget' their position and effectively 'drop out' of society altogether (Agnew, 1992). The English criminologist Jock Young has described how rising crime rates have resulted from societies' tendency to exclude more of their members. Modern forms of communication can expound the virtues of the consumer society but not everyone can partake of it. The result is a class of people culturally included to share the values of the consumer society but structurally excluded and 'blocked' from joining in (Young, 1999).

Case study

Jodie, aged fifteen, lives on an inner-city council estate. She has a history of truancy and sees lots of people in her local community without work. Jodie and her friends have started to target students who live in the adjoining neighbourhood as they feel invaded by them. They resent the fact that the students have phones, i-Pods etc. and all the things that the local people do not have. The street robbery of 'soft' students gives direct access to some of these commodities.

- How would theories of social exclusion help us to explain Jodie's behaviour?
- Do social theories offer an excuse or an explanation for this behaviour?
- As a social worker, what strategies could you employ with Jodie?

Strain theory or status frustration has also been theorised as a cause of problems for young males trying to achieve an adult male status. If adult masculinity is perceived as involving independence, dominance, toughness and respect from your fellow citizens, the failure of young males to achieve these traits may cause them to look for deviant adaptations. This invariably involves a search for an ill-defined masculinity that gives adolescents a degree of self-autonomy (rather than independence), involves acts of violence (rather than dominance or toughness) and may involve the carrying of weapons (to invoke respect). Gang cultures may help support these deviant adaptations (Messerschmidt, 1993).

Hallsworth noted these particular 'masculine' traits in his study of young men who commit street crime; an adaptation 'forged out of a symbiosis between activities celebrated in the wider society and those condemned by it' (Hallsworth, 2005: 135):

> this vision of masculinity . . . reaches into the detail of life. It is there in the physical presentation of self to the world: it is evident in the clothes, in the language, in the walk, and in speech itself. It is evident in acts and deeds, in what is spoken about, and what is celebrated in speech.
>
> (ibid.: 136)

Deviant adaptations caused by strain theory are sometimes supported by gang cultures that maintain the deviant value systems and give approval to the resultant criminal behaviour. This role played by gangs has been particularly researched in the USA, where the influence of gangs appears to be stronger than in the UK. Work by Cohen (1954) outlined how gangs could give individuals status that they could not find elsewhere and enabled members to take pride in their deviant adaptations, such as being tough and 'hard'. The gang also allows members to use 'techniques of neutralisation' to justify and excuse their criminality (Matza, 1964).

In the UK the evolution of gangs has been less pronounced, and attention has been paid more to sub-cultures. Sub-cultures may not necessarily be overtly criminal but more symbolic and simply oppositional to the established order (Hall and Jefferson, 1976).

Bling in the fur, and stuff. (Jeremiah Deasey)

However, more recently, there has been an increased media reporting of violent crimes amongst youths, which may be related to gang culture. The IPPR Report of July 2007 reported that gang membership in Britain was much higher than in other European countries. (IPPR Report Institute of Public Policy Research (2007) Britain's Poorest Teenagers must be targeted by Government Youth Review, Available at www.ippr.org.uk/pressreleases/?id=2811, accessed 26 July 2007.)

Young people may be attracted to the idea of being in a gang, as it gives social identity and a sense of belonging to a social group. This identity may be reinforced through images of celebrities who portray a glamorous image, and are seen as cool.

How does this picture exemplify the statement above?

Labelling theory where one group categorises and classifies the deviant behaviour of another person or group; the stereotyped person or group has their identity reinforced, which in turn promotes the deviant behaviour that it is intended to prevent.

Deviance failure to conform to culturally expected norms of behaviour, which reflect the dominant values and rules of groups or society in a given period.

Moral panic a disproportionate and hostile reaction to a person or group defined as a threat to society; usually involves stereotypical media representations and demands for action that create a spiral of reactions.

◄ Labelling theory, deviancy amplification and moral panics

It is axiomatic that behaviour only becomes criminal when someone defines a particular act as criminal. Much has been said about the Labour government passing numerous laws between 1997 and 2006 which criminalised whole areas of behaviour that were previously not considered criminal. The repeal of a law equally de-criminalises areas of behaviour, no longer making them criminal acts (see Chapter 7).

Labelling theory looks at how the social response to crime is made and how certain behaviour comes to be considered deviant or criminal. Labelling theory also goes one step further, to suggest that the very imposition of social judgements on to certain individuals helps turn those individuals further into the paths of criminality that have been identified. The labelling becomes a self-fulfilling prophecy as the stigma, ostracism or exclusion attached to the social judgement, or label, only pushes the offender further in the direction of criminality. In simple terms, if you give a dog a bad name, it will become a bad dog.

In the USA, Becker outlined how the making of criminal law defines certain people as 'outsiders' and then the enforcement of those laws (the social response) enables the police, the courts and others to impose the deviant/criminal label on those people. The outcome is the creation of negative stereotypes on those considered as criminal (Becker, 1963). Once the label 'criminal' has been given to someone that person may well choose to simply organise their life around the label and adopt the new identity ascribed to them. In this way the self-fulfilling prophecy comes into play. The very act of labelling has had an adverse effect on the future behaviour of the person concerned. Adolescents who engage in crime or anti-social behaviour are particularly prone to the effects of labelling. Adolescents who are not caught and labelled often just grow out of crime as they get older. The labelled adolescent finds this harder to do, which is of particular concern as children as young as thirteen are being given ten-year ASBOs.

Labelling theory has contributed to such policies as 'diversion' from the courts and the criminal justice system. Interventions such as police cautioning, reprimands and final warnings seek to lower the degree of labelling by keeping offenders – especially first-time offenders – out of court and 'out of the system'. The short-fall in labelling theory is that it does not explain why the original criminal act took place.

Case study

Brian's parents divorced when he was twelve years old and he remained living with his mother. His mother later formed a new relationship with Ken who moved into the house when Brian was fourteen. When Brian was fifteen he had a huge argument with Ken. The argument took place at the same time of year that Brian's father had originally left his mother and memories came flooding back. In a fit of pique Brian took the family car and went for a midnight drive.

He was picked up by the police driving in circles in the car park of a nearby supermarket. A Youth Court placed Brian on a supervision order and he started reporting to the same social worker. The social worker assessed Brian as having minimal problems and the supervision was perfunctory. This changed following Brian's arrest for shoplifting along with some youths he had met at the YOTs team when he had been reporting. More reports and more court hearings followed and Brian's 'fear' of the court decreased.

- How can labelling theory be used to understand this chain of events?
- Does the social work role conflict with the punitive focus of the criminal justice system in this case?

Deviancy amplification

Deviancy amplification extends the ideas of labelling to demonstrate how social reactions to crime, in the way of policing, courts and penal policies generally, can lead to the furtherance of criminal careers. At its most simple, the prison system, with the goal of reducing crime and producing good citizens often does exactly the opposite. Offenders leave prison and return to crime more readily than before. Young used the term 'deviancy amplification' in his analysis of drug users in London during the 1960s. Much of this activity was low level and relatively harmless, but the press interest, followed by police crack-downs and court punitiveness, had a 'loop-back' effect. What had been a peripheral activity for some people now came to personify their identity against conformism and authority. The social response had given it more significance as a form of rebellion rather than restricting it (Young, 1971).

Today we might compare crack-downs on under-age drinking as having a similar unintended consequence. Thirty years ago such drinking was largely ignored and seen as an age-related rite of passage. Contemporary interventions see it as a major problem requiring appropriate policing, possible use of ID cards and severe sentences on those selling the alcohol. A rise in under-age drinking results as young people rebel against the crack-down and accord the activity more significance than before. Although many young people may enjoy drinking alcohol, A Report by the IPPR (2007) found that binge drinking among British adolescents is an increasing problem and hanging out on streets was more common for British youths than their European counterparts. Almost half of all fifteen-year-olds had been involved in some form of fighting or violence.

A familiar picture of young people enjoying a drink. (Sean Locke)

Deviance amplification therefore causes a loop-back effect, having exactly the opposite effect to that intended. For some people it is even a celebration of their identity and a source of status that they cannot find elsewhere. The current UK policies of publicising young people who are the subject of anti-social behaviour orders (ASBOs) with either newspaper reports of their activities or leaflets with their pictures on, are ostensibly designed to let communities know that action has been taken and that these people should be reported if in breach of their ASBO. The unintended consequence is an affirmation of their identity and the start of long-term criminal careers (see e.g. 'Thugs laugh at the ASBO, their "honour badge" ', *Daily Mail*, 4 November 2005).

As labelling and deviancy amplification cause problems and unintended consequences for individual offenders, so moral panics have similar influences on the wider public perceptions of crime. Integral to the moral panic is the way the media takes hold of a crime 'story' and reports it in such a way as to strike a chord with public concerns (Goode and Ben-Yehuda, 1994). The media reporting interacts with the social response to the crime – especially policing and court sentencing – to cause an escalating spiral of 'panic' to be present that requires someone to do something now before something else happens. At the heart of the 'moral panic' is a kernel of truth that 'something' has happened but that original truth can be lost in the distortions that accompany its reporting and the resultant social reaction can be overly hostile and disproportionate in its implementation.

Exercise

Consider the following quote:

> These . . . liquors, which to the shame of our Government, are to be so easily had, and in such quantities drunk, have changed the very nature of our people and they will if continued to be drunk destroy the very race . . .

1. When do you think this was written?
2. The quote is actually taken from Cadogan, E. (1937) *The Roots of Evil*. Cited in Hibbert, C. (1987) *The English: A Social History 1066–1945*. London: Collins.
3. Are there parallels here with the moral panics about under-age drinking in contemporary societies?

The term 'moral panic' was first popularised by Stan Cohen in his studies of the social reaction to fights between groups of young people in British seaside towns during the 1960s. These so-called 'battles' between 'mods' and 'rockers' were the subject of exaggerated reporting that caused disproportionate police responses and heavy sentencing, which in turn were the subject of widespread reporting which further escalated the whole 'panic'. The actual activities of the individuals concerned were so distorted as to become unrecognisable and the individuals themselves took on the symbolic role of the 'folk devil' that acted as a lightning rod for all contemporary concerns about young people (Cohen, 1972).

The 'moral panic' – and its 'folk devil' – can change frequently and as suddenly as it appears. Over the years the phenomena has struck 'single parent families', 'teenage mothers', 'football hooligans', 'muggers', 'dangerous dogs', 'paedophiles' and others. When two-year-old James Bulger was killed by two ten-year-old children it triggered concerns about the behaviour of young people, law and order, and appropriate responses to the extent that *The Times* newspaper commented 'Britain is in the grip of one of those moral panics that afflicts every nation periodically' (Editorial, *The Times*, 3 March 1993).

Exercise

- Take a daily newspaper. How do the headlines reflect crime?
- Are there particular crimes that are reported more than others? Do these crimes relate to particular groups?
- How does the media contribute to perceptions about crime and vulnerability?

Critical criminology is an attempt to broaden the analysis of crime to its context and to wider notions of social justice, and human rights as well as to the structural relations of production and distribution, reproduction and patriarchy.

Conflict theory accepts that there are not necessarily any collectively agreed norms in society and that to understand crime we have to understand the interests served by criminal law and the way power is used in society.

Left idealism a Marxist approach to crime and punishment analysing the processes of criminalisation and the social responses to crime.

Critical criminology

A new criminological school emerged in the 1960s that took a far more political analysis to the explanations for crime. Key aspects of 'strain' theory and 'labelling' theory were developed to look at the factors involved in determining when an act was judged to be deviant in the first place. This took the focus away from the individual engaged in crime and deviancy and looked at the social system that surrounds us.

   Conflict theories of deviance took 'strain' theory and 'labelling' theory forward by pointing out that these theories had presupposed a consensual set of values in society. Conflict theorists held that this was not necessarily so and that society was actually composed of numerous groups that interacted with each other and were often in conflict with each other. Many groups challenged the dominant societal values that they saw others as imposing upon them. Crime and criminalisation took on a new perspective, where the process of criminalisation was a form of social control by the more powerful groups in society and thus a way of maintaining the existing social order. The power to 'label' was critical in this interaction between groups, and not any sort of neutral application.

   In the 1970s sociologists of a left-wing persuasion used conflict theory to build a new criminology that explained crime in Marxist terms. A seminal book in the UK was called *The New Criminology* (Taylor et al., 1973) and this new perspective on crime would later be known as *left idealism*. The fusion of a Marxist analysis with criminological theories appeared to give a better explanation of what was going on in the field of crime and the social response to crime. This analysis was premised on the law being a mechanism drawn up and designed by the ruling class to perpetuate the capitalist economy and keep the working class in a subservient position. It followed, therefore, that:

- the ruling class define what is a criminal act based on their interests;
- the ruling class could break laws whenever they saw fit but the working class would be punished if they did so;
- criminal behaviour is a form of resistance to the oppression and excesses of capitalism;
- as long as capitalist societies promote inequality and class conflict, crime will always be present.

The mode of economic production therefore promotes crime as we experience it and is the basic explanation for criminal behaviour. The new criminology could see through the existing pictures of crime and criminality that we had been presented with and offered the structural injustices, inequalities and exploitation of the working class as the wider view. The critics responded that it was possibly too utopian in its outlook, seemingly dependent on a re-ordering of society before we could get to grips with crime and its realities for the victims of crime.

When it came to such sentencing theories as 'restorative justice', for example, left idealism would question the validity of trying to recognise 'wrongs' committed by juveniles against an individual or the community and then trying to correct that 'wrong' by suitable activities by – and communications with – that juvenile offender (see *sentencing theory* below). Not only did such an approach appear to ignore children's rights in its informal approach, but it also overlooked the wider 'wrongs' committed on the juvenile by the social disadvantages inherent in capitalist societies.

One of the methods used in 'restorative justice', for example, involved the bringing together of offender and victim in forms of mediation. Discussions were held to try and agree ways of putting 'right' the 'wrong' that had been committed. This could involve the young person from a low income family and a community with poor schools, poor housing and poor health facilities having to explain their criminal activity – and even apologise for it – to someone with none of these disadvantages and deprivations. Such an apology fits uncomfortably with proponents of left idealism.

Left idealism remains a strand in the schools of criminological thought, and its advocates argue that it can provide theories that can be used now to help groups struggling against oppression. In this way work on prisons, policing, 'mugging', violence against women, deaths in custody has been informed by left idealism (see e.g. Hall et al. 1978; Scraton, 1987).

In the mid-1980s a number of UK criminologists – including some who had been part of the 'new criminology' – reacted against 'left idealism' as being too utopian and too distant from the realities of crime experienced by many in the working class. In particular, criminologists based at Middlesex Polytechnic (later University)

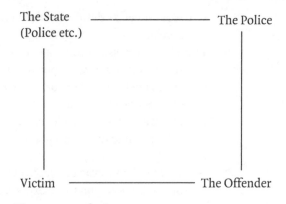

Figure 4.1 The square of crime.

Left realism a UK school of criminological thought emerging in the mid-1980s in reaction to the perceived utopianism of left idealism and the reactionary policies of conservative thinking on crime.

proposed a new *left realism* to take criminology forward (Lea and Young, 1984; Matthews and Young, 1986). The 'left realists' were not only parting company with the 'left idealists' but were also anxious to provide opposition to the rise of 'right realism' (see above) with its ideas of more severe sentences and greater use of incarceration as the appropriate punishment.

'Left realists' regarded themselves as taking crime more seriously than the 'left idealists' and providing a more complex analysis. This included the siting of crime more firmly in its social context. The

Square of crime a theoretical device created by the left realists made up of four sides stressing the interaction between the police and other agencies of social control the state: the public, the victim and the offender.

heuristic device of the *square of crime* was used to illustrate this social context (see fig. 4.1).

The 'left realists' criticised other theorists for focusing more on the social construction of crime rather than on the crime itself. Using the 'square of crime' the criminal act can be viewed from various perspectives and the varying different theoretical positions brought to bear:

> to control crime from a realist perspective involves intervention at each part of the square of crime: at the level of the factors which give rise to the putative offender (such as structural unemployment), the informal system (such as lack of public mobilisation), the victim (such as inadequate target hardening), and the formal system (such as ineffective policy).
>
> (Young, 1986: 41)

The victims of crime

The victims of crime have traditionally been the neglected players in the criminal justice system, but in recent years attempts have been made to rectify this position and the voice of the victim has been given more prominence. At a political level, the UK government has even talked of 're-balancing' the criminal justice system in favour of the victims of crime and the 'law-abiding' majority. One of the paradoxes of the victim's position is that the position can be quite an ambivalent one. The media construction of the victim is often that of the elderly and defenceless person or the very young – and equally defenceless – child. The reality of victims, however, is that many of them do not fit these ideal media portrayals.

Many victims of crime are young men who in other circumstances may well be the perpetrators of crime. This phenomenon was recognised some years ago when the Criminal Injuries Compensation Scheme was introduced in the 1960s. Victims of crime who had suffered 'criminal injuries' were able to apply for financial compensation from the state. In making an application, however, they had to declare any criminal convictions of their own. The existence of a criminal record meant the award made could be reduced as a penalty against the victim's life of crime. This system of reducing the level of compensation exists to this day.

The media portrayals of the ideal victim none the less persists and reinforces widespread 'fear of crime' amongst parents (for their children) and elderly people who are afraid to venture out at night. Policies and resources are then targeted at these groups to offer 'reassurance', and to tackle the 'fear' rather than the substance of crime.

Other measures to help victims of crime include compensation orders made in court. The Victim Fund and the Victim's Code of Practice (Domestic Violence, Crime and Victims Act 2004) provides special measures in courts to help victims (as witnesses) to give evidence when they are feeling vulnerable or intimidated. Probation officers and the Crown Prosecution Service now try to bring the victims views into pre-sentence reports and case preparation respectively and recent pilot schemes have looked at the practicality of bringing the victims' views directly into the court on cases of murder. Numerous voluntary groups now exist to help the victims of crime such as Victims Support, Women's Aid, Rape Crisis Centres, and Support After Murder and Manslaughter (SAMM).

A measure of how far the victim movement has moved forward over the last forty years can be noted in the killing of James Bulger in 1993. This high-profile case of children killing other children is often compared to the 1968 Mary Bell case where the circumstances were similar. The significant difference, however, is that reference to the 'Bulger case' refers to the victim and the 'Bell case' to the perpetrator; few can recall the names of Bell's victims and similarly with the Bulger perpetrators.

Criminologists have also noted how victims and their supporters have improved their position in actually defining crimes. When new activities start causing problems for a community, there is a need to define them and sometimes there is agreement on that definition and sometimes there is not. Criminologists refer to the concept of 'dominion' to reflect this struggle over who has the right to define what is going on.

The position of the man who has offended against children provides a case study. In the 1970s these men were seen as sad and rather pathetic individuals who were punished and released back into the community. In the 1990s, public opinion turned against such offenders – now more often referred to as paedophiles – and differences emerged about the best way to respond to them. The once pathetic individual now became the intelligent scheming man who manipulated children in a sophisticated manner. Practitioners such as doctors, social workers and others saw their behaviour as dysfunctional and needing to be treated while the general public saw it as an 'untreatable' affliction that required offenders to be incapacitated by long-term imprisonment. Women's groups saw it as a problem of masculinity. Yet other groups, including politicians, had to make judgements on the appropriate ways of achieving public protection and proportionate punishments. This whole struggle of definition is referred to as the problem of 'dominion'.

Crime and gender issues

Until the 1960s and 1970s, sociologists looking at crime invariably looked at male offenders and not at women offenders. Many of the sociologists of the time were male and most crime was committed by men. The study of female offenders was neglected or treated with indifference. At best they were seen as committing a limited number of crimes (e.g. shoplifting) often under the influence of hormonal imbalance (women's 'problems'). At worst the female offender was simply 'invisible'.

Carol Smart's book *Women, Crime and Criminology* (1977) is often cited as the first book to really identify this 'neglect' of female offending and to be critical of male-dominated criminology. Smart's work evolved from the Women's Movement of the 1960s and 1970s

---

Discussion points

How do constructions of masculinity and femininity impact on differential treatment of males and females?

Read the following extract:

Shifting the emphasis from the 1980s political rhetoric, which figured the single mother as the source of all national evil, we now have the loud, white, excessive, drunk, fat, vulgar, disgusting, hen-partying woman who exists to embody all the moral obsessions historically associated with the working class.

(Skeggs, 2005: 965)

- In what ways do you think this quote reflects a moral panic about changes in society?

Young woman being abducted.

and was an attempt to correct the 'distortions' that appeared to be taking place.

Women as victims of crime – especially violence and sexual offending – were studied far more. (See for example Dobash and Dobash's (1979) study of domestic violence against women (e.g.) and Cameron and Fraser's (1987) study of women as victims of murder and manslaughter.

Discussion points

- What is your immediate response to this picture?
- What does it say about violence towards women?

Why women committed less crime than men was put down to the additional socialisation and controls that are placed on women but not on men (Walklate, 1995). Although women appeared in the criminal courts far less than men, the fact that they appeared to be sentenced more harshly was studied. The conclusion was that women were sentenced 'twice'. Once for the offence and secondly for the fact that they were women and therefore 'deviants' from the law-abiding role they should take as good wives or mothers (Heidensohn, 1985).

The question of whether or not a fully fledged feminist criminology has ever appeared remains unanswered. Gender and crime has been a more fruitful way forward in many respects, with as much an emphasis on male offending and problems of masculinity (e.g. Messerschmidt, 1993).

The racialisation of crime

Sociologists have considered some of the following issues with regards to the relationship between race and crime: the explanations for the over-representation of black and ethnic minority groups in the criminal justice system; the explanations for African Caribbean people being more likely to be involved in the criminal justice system than other BME groups.

The following evidence demonstrates that Afro-Caribbean people are more likely to be stopped and searched by police, there are a higher proportion of arrests following these searches, and they receive harsher treatment in the courts and in sentencing procedures.

- Black people remain three times more likely to be arrested than white people.
- In June 2000, ethnic minorities accounted for 19 per cent of the male prison population (12% black, 3% Asian) and 25 per cent of the female prison population (19% black and 1% Asian).
- African Caribbean people are six times more likely to be stopped and searched than white people and Asians twice as likely.
- 13 per cent of black people were cautioned compared with 16 per cent of white people and 17 per cent of Asians.

(British Crime Survey, 2002/3 – www.homeoffice.gov.uk)

In seeking to explain these inequalities, sociologists and criminologists have claimed that crime has become racialised, in that this is not just an indication of inequalities in the criminal justice system, but reflects a reproduction and perpetuation of perceived racial differences (Keith, 1993). Institutional racism operates within the criminal justice system, where stereotypical beliefs about racial differences (based on phenotypical differences) become ingrained and mediated through the police, the courts and the penal institutions. Racial stereotypes are used to link black people with certain crimes (e.g. sex crimes, aggravated burglary and violent crimes) and serve to legitimate exclusionary practices.

> Black law breaking supplies the historic proof that blacks are
> incompatible with the standards of deviancy and civilization which the
> nation requires of its citizenry.
>
> (Gilroy, 1982: 215)

The use of stop and search has been a highly controversial aspect of policing as a result of the disproportionate amount of black men who were stopped in the 1980s and 1990s. The impact of the Macpherson Report in 1999 and an acceptance of institutional racism by the Metropolitan police led to a reduction in the use of stop and search. However in 2005, following the 7/7 bombings in London, stop and search increased by 14 per cent, with terrorism-related searches increasing by 9 per cent (Home Office, 2002).

The Centre for Crime and Justice Studies (2006) identifies socio-economic status as an explanatory factor for the over-representation of young African Caribbean males compared with other ethnic minority groups who are involved in the criminal justice system. The inquiry noted that there are strong links between black people being the victims of crimes as well as the perpetrators of crime due to their position in areas of social deprivation. Garside (2006) suggests that

> Some poor and disadvantaged people do commit crime because they are
> poor and disadvantaged. Some of them end up in our prisons and courts
> as a result. This does not mean that the poor and disadvantaged commit
> most crime. Nor does it mean that disadvantage is the cause of most
> crime. But some of the grossest victimisations are concentrated among
> the poorer members of society, and it is reasonable to conclude that the
> poor will often be perpetrators as well as victims.

The inter-relationship of crime, race and socioeconomic status is further highlighted by the position of black women in prison. African Caribbean women demonstrate a similar over-representation as for men and 15 per cent of the prison population are foreign nationals from under-developed countries, with many serving long sentences for the importation of drugs (Prison Reform Trust 2006 – www.prisonreformtrust.org.uk).

In spite of recruitment campaigns designed to attract black and minority applicants, the police service has only 3.5 per cent of officers from BME populations, compared with 4.4 per cent for prison officers and 10.9 per cent for probation staff. In 2001 there were no Law Lords or High Court Judges who were from an ethnic minority and only one per cent of circuit judges and 4.8 per cent magistrates are from ethnic minorities (Institute of Race Relations, 2004 – www.irrr.org.uk).

Sentencing theory

Contingent upon the various explanations for crime offered by sociology are the various theories of sentencing that are used by the courts. These different theories of sentencing have also evolved over the years and the different schools of thought identified. They were formalised and put into UK criminal law only as recently as 2003 by the Criminal Justice Act of that year (s.142). In essence they are:

- Retribution (also known as 'just deserts'): i.e. the imposition of a sentence to reflect the seriousness of the crime committed (the 'classical' school of criminology and the rational choice theory).
- Rehabilitation (also known as treatment or the 'welfare' model): i.e. recognising the deficits experienced by the offender and attempting to prevent the commission of future crimes (the 'strain' theory, 'labelling' etc.
- Restorative justice: i.e. recognising the 'wrong' committed against an individual or the community and endeavouring to correct that wrong with suitable activities and communication with the offender (an integrating of theories).
- Public protection: emphasising the social control and 'incapacitation' element of sentencing.

Incapacitation a punishment that removes the offenders ability to commit further crimes, e.g. imprisonment.

Social workers working with people likely to be sentenced will need to recognise these different theories of sentencing.

Discussion points

Successive Labour Governments have talked about being tough on crime and tough on the causes of crime:

How can the sociological discussion of sentencing theory help us to analyse the effectiveness of such a policy view?

A recurrent theme in contemporary sentencing is the idea of 'risk assessment'. Social workers and other practitioners are asked to assess the risk that individuals may pose in terms of further offending. This is clearly necessary for exercises in 'public protection' but is also a factor in rehabilitation and restorative justice.

The process of 'risk assessment' involves the weighing up of factors about an individual and their social circumstances and includes such factors as previous criminal record, psychological profiles, intelligence, use of drugs and alcohol, degree of self insight. The factors are usually divided into static factors and dynamic factors, which are liable to change and more amenable to change (see Grubin, 2004; Milner and Myers, 2007).

The 'risk assessment' seeks to inform sentencing decisions, parole decisions, and other decisions within the criminal justice system. This attempt to effectively predict the future has been assisted by various 'instruments' introduced to assist practitioners, including, for example, OASys for probation and prison officers

(Powis, 2002) and ASSET for workers with youth offenders (Baker, 2005).

Conclusion

In this chapter we have explored the main sociological contributions to understanding crime. In terms of crime reduction the big challenge is to take this understanding into appropriate policy changes. A series of sentencing theories have been formulated to reflect the different explanations. For the social worker the challenge is to locate his or her practice within this wider picture of how behaviour becomes classified as criminal and the subsequent social responses to that behaviour.

To bring the picture completely up to date we should make reference to the sociology of crime as it presents itself at the start of the twenty-first century. The growth of a politics of 'law and order' and the creation of what has become known as 'popular punitivism' has already been noted. David Garland has outlined a series of features that now characterise what he calls the contemporary 'culture of control'. According to Garland these features surround our current criminal justice policies and those who work for them. At the start of this chapter, for example, probation officers were referred to as coming from a tradition of being 'social workers to the court'. Now they are re-positioned so that:

> probation . . . (has) de-emphasised the social work ethos that used to dominate their work and instead present . . . as providers of inexpensive, community based punishments, oriented towards the monitoring of offenders and the management of risk.
>
> (Garland, 2001: 18)

The same might be said of social work itself as part of the wider community safety partnerships now seen as necessary to combat crime. The challenge for the social worker may be to resist pressures on them to limit themselves to the delivery of 'community based punishments' and to re-negotiate the space available to them to practise the values of the social work role.

> It is therefore fair to say that the relationship between social work and the criminal justice system is one of tension and flux . . .
>
> (Horner, 2006: 113)

Summary points

- There is no single sociological perspective on crime and deviance, but a range of viewpoints that help us to understand and analyse the nature of crime.
- The media are instrumental in constructing discourses around crime and deviance.

- An understanding of difference and diversity can help us to understand the context and experiences of people who commit crimes, as well as the victims of crime.
- Poverty and social exclusion are important variables in relation to crime and deviance.
- Social work has been marginalised in the area of crime and deviance, but has an important role to play in prevention as well as rehabilitation.

Questions for discussion

- Why do women commit less crime than men?
- Is it right to divert young offenders away from the criminal justice system on the grounds that it only exaggerates the problem?
- Why do some young men become street robbers to obtain money and possessions (e.g. mobile phones) when others use legitimate avenues to obtain the same things?
- How can we prevent some urban areas descending into areas of criminality and anti-social behaviour?
- Is there a role for social workers in the criminal justice system?

Further reading

Hale, C., Hayward, K., Wahidin, A. and Wincup, E. (eds) (2008) *Criminology*. 2nd edn. Oxford: Oxford University Press. Very useful for students of criminology coming to the subject for the first time and with contributions from a team of criminologists. The book looks at different forms of crime, and historical and contemporary understandings of crime and criminal justice. The book is accompanied by a website.

Hopkins-Burke, R. (2005) *An Introduction to Criminological Theory*. 2nd edn. Cullompton, Devon: Willan Publishing, An inter-disciplinary text coming to the subject from a psychological and biological angle as well as a sociological one.

Finer, C. and Ellis, M. (1998) *Crime and Social Exclusion*. Oxford, Blackwell. A good book for understanding the relationship between crime and social exclusion within a national and global context.

Jones, S. (2006) *Criminology*. 3rd edn. Oxford: Oxford University Press. Offers a clear exposition of all the criminological theories, following an historical path as to how these theories were developed. Particularly strong as a source of further reading.

Tierney, J. (2006) *Criminology: Theory and Context*. 2nd edn. London, Pearson Longman. An historical approach to criminology, using a broad range of data and examples providing evidence and grounding for its analysis and theory.

5

Gender

Social work is a feminised activity, in that women as qualified or unqualified workers perform the majority of social work and the majority of service users are women. Sociological insights into gender have been successful in developing feminist analyses of social work as a profession and campaigns against particular issues have had a major impact on social work practice undertaken with women (e.g. violence directed towards women and children). This is not to say that gender is not an unproblematic concept for social work, as there are many areas of practice which would benefit from a gendered analysis, particularly in the area of working with men and boys.

The key issues that will be explored in this chapter are:

- The contributions made by specific sociological theories regarding sex and gender in working with women, men and children within social work.
- The relationship between public and private spheres and roles.
- The employment of women and men in social work and social care.
- Feminist perspectives on prostitution and sex trafficking.
- Constructions of masculinity and femininity.

By the end of this chapter, you should be able to:

- Distinguish between the concepts of sex and gender.
- Explain the role of socialisation in the development of gender roles.
- Discuss the relationship between the public and private domains of home and work in relation to gendered roles.
- Discuss the gendered nature of the labour market.
- Describe the evidence in relation to changing gendered identities.

Gender

What do we mean when we talk about gender? What is the difference between sex and gender? Oakley (1974) has argued that there is an important distinction between sex and *gender*: sex refers to basic biological differences between men and women, such as genitalia and reproductive systems; gender on the other hand refers to the socially and culturally specific traits and behaviours between men and women. These may be actual differences, or they may be *normative* differences – the way in which men and women are expected to behave. Thus, when we talk about sexual differences, we are distinguishing between males and females, whilst when we discuss gender differences we distinguish between notions of masculinity and femininity. Much sociological debate has focused on whether these gender differences are the product of nature or nurture (biologically determined or the product of *socialization*).

Gender a cultural term reflecting social attributes associated with being male or female.

Normative a system of rules or expectations, which are common to the majority and become the expected ways of behaving.

Biological explanations of gender difference

Many popular conceptions of behavioural traits of men and women (and girls and boys) have been based on notions of innate difference related to genetic composition and biological make-up. Beliefs about boys being more naturally aggressive and girls being more naturally caring have a surprisingly long history. The Greek philosopher Aristotle wrote in the period 285–322 BC that women are

> 'more compassionate . . . more envious, more querulous, more slanderous, and more contentious' whereas men are '. . . more disposed to give assistance in danger' and 'more courageous'.
>
> (Cited in Miles, 1989: 700)

Can we really say that there are objective and observable differences between males and females based on biological differences, or do the different behavioural traits represent a socialisation process related to social and cultural norms, environments and the differential nurturing of boys and girls? Psychologists have argued that there are variations in ability between boys and girls, such as the fact that boys have superior spatial ability (the ability to see how objects would appear at different angles and how they would relate to each other in a given space) and that boys have superior mathematical ability. However, the findings from the psychological tests of the 1960s and 1970s that produced these conclusions have been the subject of much debate and criticism.

Socialisation the process of learning how to behave in a way that is appropriate for an individual's particular culture. This process is governed by certain standards and values about behaviour and roles within society.

Exercise

- List the traits that you think are most associated with males and females.
- Is there a clear distinction?

The socialisation of gender

Sociologists have drawn attention to the role of nurture and socialisation in the construction of masculinity and femininity, leading to a social construction of gendered characteristics. The family and education systems serve as institutions for the primary socialisation of children, providing the environmental and social context for the development of *normative* gendered traits. Thus boys may be encouraged not to display emotion (big boys don't cry), to develop practical skills and to stand up for themselves. Girls on the other hand may be encouraged to be more emotionally expressive, to be involved in cooking and cleaning and to be more passive. This *socialisation* may be either a deliberate manipulation of behaviour, or may be done unconsciously, the stereotypical behaviours being so firmly entrenched in society.

Exercise

- Look at ways in which children may learn about gendered roles.
- Watch the adverts that frequently appear between children's television programmes.
- How do they reflect social constructions of difference between boys and girls play patterns and behaviours?

'If you make me clean my room, won't it encourage the stereotype of the female as subservient housemaid?' (© 2003 by Randy Glasbergen. www.glasbergen.com)

Feminist theory and gender

Alsop, Fitzsimons and Lennon (2002) argue that feminist analyses of the social construction of gender can be broadly divided into two strands: materialist theories and discursive theories. Materialist approaches emphasise objective categories and the nature of macro power in constructing women's disadvantaged position. Discursive theories, on the other hand, emphasise subjective experience and how women attach meaning to social labels. Language and culture are important in understanding experiences, whilst power is seen to operate at the micro level, rather than through the structures of society. Thus discursive theories emphasise women's different experiences and how roles may be contradictory, complex and fluid.

Materialist theories

Materialist theories emerged in the 1970s and 1980s and stress the importance of structural processes and how they impact on men and women's lives. From this perspective, men and women are fitted into different roles and pathways, and the social relations of family, work and sexuality are important for understanding the systems of power, exploitation and oppression that frame women's experiences. There are two different strands to material theories: Marxist theories, which stress the importance of capitalist relations of production in the construction of gender divisions (Barrett and McIntosh, 1982) and patriarchy, which explores the nature of power and oppressive gendered practices which may or may not be related to processes of capitalist production (Millett, 1977).

Patriarchy male domination of a system or network, leading to the oppression of women.

Social anthropology the study of human society and behaviour. Modern social anthropology is concerned with the interface between different cultures and societies.

Matriarchy a system, network or structure where women dominate.

Patriarchy is a useful concept in understanding the different political strands of feminism. Meade et al. (1988) have argued from a social anthropological perspective that the patriarchal society is not just associated with industrial capitalism, but also with agrarian and hunter-gatherer societies. Although there are examples of matriarchal societies, patriarchy is the dominant form of social organisation globally. Patriarchy is a system which controls women and constitutes their inferiority and inequality within society and becomes embedded in the institutional practices of the society.

It is not possible here to do justice to the broad range of feminist thought, but it is useful to provide an overview of a number of key perspectives, which have been influential within sociology. The categories below could represent ideal types, but ideal types rarely exist and as women have multiple identities, sociologists may not always fit neatly into a single category of being e.g. a black feminist, but they may also share Marxist or radical ways of thinking (Dominelli, 1997).

Liberal feminism

Liberal approaches to feminism tend to focus upon issues of women's discrimination in society and view equality of opportunity as a way of addressing inequality. Hence the sources of women's inequality reside with the law and policies and differences in the socialisation of males and females. Consequently changes to the law, via equal opportunity legislation such as Equal Pay Act or the Sex Discrimination Act, and changes to the socialisation of boys and girls and the expectations placed upon them, would serve to reduce the inequalities between men and women. Liberal feminists hence see an end to women's inequality within the existing social frameworks and without significant structural change, and thus reflect a functionalist view of society.

Marxist feminism

Marxist feminists recognise the inadequacy of Marxist theory in explaining the exploitation and subordination of women through capitalist relations of production. Marxist feminists argue that traditional Marxist theory was gender-blind and failed to recognise the specificity of women's oppression (Abbott et al., 2005). They wish to retain aspects of Marxist theory, but seek to offer an explanation of the centrality of women's experiences in the labour market, either in low paid or unpaid work (as housewives) for the benefit and maintenance of capitalism. They see the domination of class relations as central to the definition of women's oppression.

Radical feminism

Radical feminists view the dominance of patriarchy or the rule of men as being responsible for women's oppression. Patriarchal relations are seen as permeating all forms of oppression and men are seen as the main enemy in this respect. Some radical feminists view men and women as separate sex classes, which causes antagonism and friction (Firestone, 1971) and only by overthrowing patriarchy can women and children become truly emancipated. Some radical feminists would argue that separatism (either by the avoidance of heterosexual relationships or by artificial insemination) is the only way that women can be removed from the oppressive relationships associated with childbearing (Dominelli, 1997). Radical feminists have been particularly influential in developing an understanding of women's sexual exploitation and campaigning against male violence towards women and the pornographic exploitation of women (Dworkin, 1981).

Socialist feminism

Socialist feminism recognises the inter-relationship between patriarchy and capitalism in oppressing both men and women. This is

Dual systems theory a feminist theory that recognises that both the public world and the domestic world impact on the oppression of women.

sometimes referred to as *dual systems theory*, as it seeks to provide an explanation of women's oppression by retaining the materialist aspects of a Marxist analysis, whilst incorporating a radical feminist emphasis on patriarchy (Abbott et al., 2005). Socialist feminists hence seek to engage men in feminist struggles through either reform in housework or childcare or by promoting anti-sexist social relations in tackling male violence towards women (see Dominelli, 1997). They seek to appreciate the diversity and commonality of women's experiences.

While there are different political strands of materialist approaches, they share the common view that gendered relations operate within and are influenced by the structures of society, such as paid work, the private domain of the household and sexuality and sexual relations (Walby, 1990).

Discursive theories

More recent feminist theories have challenged the notion of a common notion of sisterhood and a common experience for women. Giddens' (1991) concept of the runaway society is useful here (see Chapter 2), arguing that the world is rapidly changing, and people's experiences within this changing society are dynamic and varied. Post-modernist feminists (Nicholson, 1990) are concerned therefore with women's diverse and changing experiences, and how the meanings that women attach to their experiences are shaped by structures and ideologies. Black feminists have also challenged the concept of sisterhood and questioned the term of womanhood as a uniting concept (Mohanty, 1992). Similarly, feminists within the disability movement have critiqued mainstream feminism for failing to account for disabled women's experiences (Lonsdale, 1990), whilst gerontologists have been critical of feminism's neglect of older women's experiences (Arber and Ginn, 1995).

Black feminism

Although black feminism is defined here under a single umbrella, it is important to recognise the range of black feminist thought that exists and appreciate that black feminists may also align themselves with radical, Marxist or other forms of feminist thought. The roots of modern black feminist thought arose out of the civil rights movement in the United States and the women's movement in 1970s and gained particular momentum in the 1980s. Black feminists have challenged the assumed sisterhood that exists between black and white feminists and the assumed universality of women's experiences, but argue that much white feminist thought has tended to minimise the experiences of black women (Hill Collins, 2000). Bell Hooks (1986) also challenges forms of racism within the construction of feminist knowledge, which expects black women to write from the heart about their experiences and white women to write from the head.

Black feminists argue that racism and sexism are inextricably linked in causing women's oppression and do not see men as necessarily the main enemy, but recognise the oppression of black men in particular and suggest that black women and men should work together to fight racism (Lorde, 1984). Black feminists have also challenged the white feminists' critique of family as the location of patriarchal power, but instead recognise the significance of familial relations as a potential haven of support in a hostile and racist society (Hill Collins, 2000). The pressure that is sometimes placed on black and minority ethnic women to leave violent relationships without consideration of the significance of a move outside their neighbourhood on wider family and community support systems highlights an example of ethnocentric social work practice (Hooks, 1991).

Due to the impact of racism, many black women are part of the working class, and black feminists argue that elimination of oppression on the basis of race, sex and class would lead to freedom for all women (Hill Collins, 2000).

Post-modern feminism

Feminism is a political activity and could be said to be at odds with post-modernism, which has often been described as apolitical. However there has recently emerged a body of thought which is described as post-modern feminism. Some of the tensions between feminism and post-modernism concern the challenges that post-modernism makes to feminism in challenging the grand theories (e.g. patriarchy, race and class), which seek to explain women's oppression. It also questions unitary concepts such as woman, femininity, emphasising multiple identities that individuals possess. This raises the question that if individuals can no longer be defined as being women, are they able to unify around common concerns which are central to the varying strands of feminist thought.

> This approach runs the risk of encouraging fragmentation of social entities through collective action or the isolation of the self.
>
> (Dominelli, 1997: 39)

Nevertheless, post-modernist perspectives focus on women's subjective accounts of meaning and the analysis of ideology and discourses are important in these subjective experiences. The ideology of gendered roles is based on a set of ideas, which reflect the interests of those who are dominant economically. These ideas then become a framework to guide the actions of others, and thus shape the experiences of men and women. The ideology of gendered roles can be seen in societal attitudes to women who do not want to have children, or who leave the marital home and their children. Furthermore, women who commit crimes against children are viewed as particularly deviant and invoke a hostile reaction from the public, as well as achieving notoriety for their crimes. For example, the public reaction to Myra Hindley or Beverly Allott or Maxine Carr reflects this outrage that women should harm children (this is not to say that men who commit crimes against children are not also seen as deviant and invoke feelings of horror, but that it is disproportionate). The notion of the female nurturing role is also reflected in child settlement policies following divorce, with the female often being favoured.

Feminists argue that these gendered differences are a specific outcome of power relations and the patriarchal oppression of women, which is derived from the distinction between the public and private spheres of society (the public sphere being the labour market, political and economic systems, whilst the private sphere is the home and the ideologically structured notion of the family – see Chapter 8). Thus roles become socially constructed to provide within these separate spheres of society, reflecting the construction of a male breadwinner society under industrial capitalism. The skills and attributes associated with masculinity become more highly valued, with greater status and wealth being associated with masculine roles.

Sociological perspectives on masculinity

A gendered analysis of sociological theory and perspectives has focused upon women's experiences and the causes of women's subordination. However more recent theory on gender has begun to incorporate theories on masculinity and male experiences (Mac and Ghaill, 1996). Sociological perspectives on the construction of maleness and masculinity are particularly relevant for a social work practice, which has often struggled to engage with men and boys.

The influence of the women's movement has been partly responsible for the rise of the men's movement in Britain in the late 1970s. The early movement was pro-feminist as men aligned themselves with women in challenging women's oppression, articulated and supported by academic sociological knowledge (Hearn, 1996).

The 1990s witnessed a growth in the sociology of masculinity, and some perspectives, rather than being pro-feminist, blame feminism for the *demasculinisation* of men as traditional roles for men have been challenged (Cavanagh and Cree, 1996).

There are four themes that are central to the theories about masculinities:

1. Masculine identities are historically and culturally situated.
2. Multiple masculinities exist.

3. There are dominant hegemonic and subordinate forms of masculinities.
4. Masculinities are actively constructed in social settings.

Functionalist perspectives on masculinity regard male roles in terms of the benefits for the individual and society. Gilmore (1990) for example identifies three features of masculinity:

1. Man as impregnator who takes the initiative in courtship and relationships.
2. Man as provider, which relates to the concept of male breadwinner.
3. Man as protector, from other men.

Men who conform to societal expectations of masculinity tend to be rewarded with high status whilst non-conformers may receive ridicule or negative sanctions. Such fixed notions of masculinity are problematic, as many women work hard as contributors or sole providers to the family income (see Chapter 8), and male violence towards women challenges notions of men as protectors.

Sociological insights into sex and gender explore ways in which cultural differences between men and women interact with biological ones. Connell (1995) emphasises the plurality of masculinity and recognises the emergence and decline of different masculinities. Hegemonic masculinity represents the dominant forms of masculinity, which exist within society. In British society this may be represented by white, heterosexual, able-bodied forms of masculinity and is subject to challenge by women or black and gay men. Sexuality is integral to constructions of masculinity and while men may benefit from dominant forms of masculinity in society, masculinity is not fixed and contradictions exist.

The body and gender

In addition to socialisation processes, notions of appropriate femininity and masculinity are constructed through normative perspectives of the ideal body. The body is not only a site of physicality, but is also a socially constructed phenomenon, depicting symbolic value, based on notions of the good and bad body type. Foucault (1979a) has argued that constructions of the body are developed through discourses, representing dominant ideologies and constituting processes of social control. There is a long history of the relationship between the female body and constructions of identity, value and social control (Ehrenreich and English, 1978). Showalter (1987) has demonstrated how the institution of psychiatry has been instrumental in controlling perceived female *deviance*. This demonstrates how normative social roles are constructed and reinforced through the dominant institutions of society.

In the contemporary western world, slenderness is seen as the attractive ideal, and ideas of normality and social worth are constructed through the thin ideal (Williams and Germov, 1999). The second wave of feminism of the 1960s saw this thin ideal being more firmly embraced, and the super-fit, slender female was seen as indicative of women's strength and control – a woman who could control her eating habits had personal control, and was thus valued in a society of plenty. Since the 1970s we have seen a commodification of female body image, with the fashion, cosmetic and dietary industries

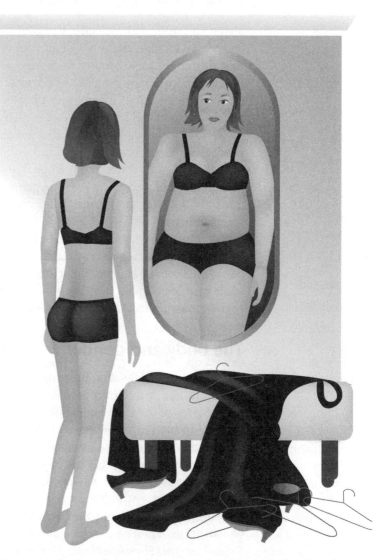

This picture depicts the way that someone with an eating disorder may have a distorted image of their own body. (Julie Ridge)

particularly promoting the slender body as the norm of attractiveness and beauty.

O'Connor (2006) undertook an analysis of 14–17-year-olds in Ireland to explore how they made sense of their selves and their lives. The following extract is taken from one of the females in the study group.

> Fashion! Looks! Labels! . . . The fact of the matter is that no-one is happy with the way they look and to be popular and cool you have to be pretty thin.
>
> (O'Connor, 2006: 119)

O'Connor concludes that boys in his study group were more likely to demonstrate authority in a number of subject areas, whilst girls confined their areas of authority to fashion and appearance. While generalisations cannot be made on the basis of a small sample, this does reflect gendered differences in construction of self, and the importance of the body as a symbolic bearer of value.

A number of studies have linked body dissatisfaction to increased dieting and disordered eating (Polivy and Herman, 2002; Stice, 2002) However, for some individuals the social construction of the idealised body and construction of self can have deleterious consequences for psychological and physical health. Although there is a growing incidence of eating disorders among boys and men (National Institute for Mental Health, 2001 – available at www.nimhe.csip.org.uk), these are still disorders that disproportionately affect women.

Case study

Emily is fifteen and lives with her parents and two brothers, who are both at university. Emily remembers being teased by classmates at school, as well as by her brothers because she started to develop breasts at the age of eight. She became increasingly conscious of her body, and was reluctant to engage in swimming or PE activities because of the ridicule that she encountered. Emily started to diet in an attempt to control her body development and by the age of thirteen only weighed 5 stone 8 lbs. Emily's class teacher became increasingly concerned about her concentration in class, and her parents started to notice her lethargy and were concerned about her relationship with food. The GP diagnosed anorexia nervosa and referred Emily for treatment. Although her weight has been as low as 4 stone 9 lbs, she is now responding to treatment and currently weighs 6 stone 5 lbs.

- What social factors might have contributed to Emily's eating disorder?
- How can sociology help us to understand the social context of Emily's problems?
- How might a social worker have been involved in this case?

Social disadvantage and inequality

The domestic division of labour and the paid labour market

The notion of the division between work in the home and work in the paid labour market is relatively new. During the rise of industrial capitalism, there were relatively good opportunities for paid employment outside the home for women, although the jobs tended to be of lower status and less well paid, reflecting constructions of masculinity and femininity. However, the rise of industrial capitalism led to an emerging division of labour, with men working outside of the home and women providing unpaid work within the home, with responsibility for the maintenance of a future healthy working and fighting force (the national efficiency argument – children are tomorrow's future, and therefore need to be provided for and maintained in order to safeguard the future of the nation's economic position and national security). Ironically, middle-class women tended to employ single women to do the household chores, leaving them free to participate in other forms of unpaid work, namely charitable activity and voluntary work. Nevertheless, the model of the male breadwinner/female home-maker society became well established by the beginning of the twentieth century. The home-maker role came to be known as the housewife role, and the scientific discipline of domestic science emerged to give some credence to home-making roles. Female employment remained relatively steady at approximately 33 per cent between 1901 and 1951, compared with 84–91 per cent for men (Hakim, 1996).

The unpaid domestic work model for women has become fairly well embedded in kinship and community relationships, as well as being perpetuated through social policies. For example, the Beveridge blueprint for social security, which formed the basis for post-Second World War income protection policies, was based on assumptions about male full-time working patterns and female dependence within a marriage. Feminists such as Callender (1992) have demonstrated how women have been disadvantaged with respect to unemployment policy, both in terms of public provision through contributory benefits and in the sphere of work-related fringe benefits. The male breadwinner model of social security also fails to take account of the unequal distribution of resources within the household (Pascall, 1997).

The second wave of feminism succeeded in identifying unpaid work as a concept, and this has resulted in campaigns to identify domestic work within public accounting systems (Himmelweit, 1995). Some feminists and policy-makers, with the aim of acknowledging the contribution of women's domestic role to the functioning of the capitalist economy, promoted the notion of the family wage (Barrett and McIntosh, 1982). However, other feminists have been critical of this, arguing that it reinforces women's subordinate position within the division of labour.

A significant shift has occurred in the labour market in the post-Second World War period, with increasing numbers of women taking on paid employment outside the private sphere of the home. However, gendered inequalities within the labour market reflect social constructions of stereotypical gendered roles. Dex (1985) explored the value and sex-role stereotypes in relation to labour market employment, and concluded that work roles reflecting traditional male stereotypical traits were more highly valued than those that reflected femininity and therefore attracted higher status and remuneration. Logical thought and rationality, strength, drive, focus and aggression typify gendered roles associated with masculinity, whilst the skills of nurturing and caring come to be seen as inherent qualities of females and thus are less valued.

The labour market

The domestic division of labour and socialisation of gendered roles is transposed to the paid division of labour. Rose (1981) argues that the domestic division of labour and the contribution that it makes to the creation of sexual divisions within the labour market and in welfare provision can be attributed to the patriarchal ideology on which the domestic division of labour is premised. This is further reflected in the division of labour by gender, which is segregated both vertically and horizontally. *Horizontal segregation* occurs when men and women are generally employed in separate spheres of the labour market, while *vertical segregation* occurs within the same occupation, with men predominantly occupying the higher-grade posts, whilst women are concentrated in the lower grades. This accounts for the disparities between men and women's pay.

Horizontal segregation the division of the employment market into 'men's work' and 'women's work'. The origins are usually historical, but even today there is usually a pay and status differential between jobs done primarily by men and jobs done primarily by women.

Vertical segregation the division of the workplace into top and bottom jobs divided by a 'glass ceiling'. For example, such segregation keeps women at the bottom or lower levels of organizations.

Dual labour market theory theory associated with Barron and Norris that sees the labour market divided between secure well-paid jobs in the primary sector and those in insecure low-paid jobs in the secondary sector.

Exercise

Look at the following report:
 Equal Opportunities Commission(2006) *Sex and power: who runs Britain?* (available at www.eoc.org.uk).

- What examples of horizontal and vertical segregation can you identify?

The dual labour market theory by Barron and Norris (1976) argues that the labour market can be divided into two related but separate sectors. The primary sector is characterised by high pay, job security and promotional opportunities, whilst the secondary sector is characterised by semi- or unskilled work, relatively low pay and job security and lack of a career path. Barron and Norris argue that men are usually employed in both sectors whereas women tend to be largely employed in the secondary sector. This theory describes the situation facing many women who, due to the combined responsibilities of caring and working outside of the home, are more likely than men to gain part-time and more flexible employment.

Beechey's reserve army of labour thesis (1986) provides a Marxist feminist explanation of disadvantage in the workplace, where the cyclical nature of production under capitalist economies results in periods of boom and bust. At times of boom more workers are required and women represent a flexible source of labour. In this instance women represent a reserve army of labour and their concentration in low paid, less organised and unionised employment is an attractive source of employment for employers.

Reserve army of labour a Marxist and a feminist term used to describe sections of the society who are employed when the economy is buoyant or doing well.

There are many professional women, however, who are employed by the state, as in social work, and though they may be subject to public expenditure cuts, they are generally protected from cycles of boom and bust.

Men have a particular place within social work, and feminine occupations like social work construct and maintain particular forms of masculinity (Hearn, 1996). *Hegemonic* forms of masculinity are replaced by more liberal forms, which allow men to accelerate in terms of management and leadership positions within social work. There may be different representations of masculinity depending upon the location and position of men within social work. In some areas of social work, men are significantly under represented (e.g. child-care and work with older people), while in other areas, the proportion of men increases (e.g. probation and mental health) and in management positions men proliferate. These different positions may impact upon the way in which masculinities are represented. Considering the impact of managerialism within social work, it may be hard to relate *liberal* forms of masculinity to contemporary social work.

Exercise

- Examine the data shown in Table 5.1.
- What evidence is there of vertical and horizontal segregation?
- How useful are theories of gender socialisation to explain these data?

There are some groups of women who are particularly disadvantaged in the sexual division of labour. The combination of sexist and ageist

Table 5.1 Staff of Scottish social work services, 2005

| | Numbers and WTEs by client group and gender | | | | | |
	males	females	total	males %	females %	WTE %
children	1,741	6,495	8,236	21.1	78.9	17.0
adults (community care)	4,083	31,348	35,435	11.5	88.5	61.3
older people	897	6,767	7,664	11.7	88.3	14.2
people with physical disabilities	149	370	519	28.7	71.3	0.9
people with mental health problems	64	213	277	23.1	76.9	0.5
people with learning disabilities	1,279	3,333	4,615	27.7	72.2	8.8
adults (not separately identified)	1,694	20,665	22,360	7.6	92.4	37.0
offenders	693	1,164	1,857	37.3	62.7	4.0
generic provision	960	3,728	4,691	20.5	79.5	9.6
management/administration	941	2,653	3,594	26.2	73.8	7.7
unknown	60	135	195	30.8	69.2	0.4
Total	**8,478**	**45,523**	**54,008**	**15.7**	**84.3**	**100.0**

Source:
Scottish Executive, 2006. available at www.scotland.gov.uk/publications/2006

assumptions and practices means that older women may come up against the 'glass ceiling', whereby promotion prospects are denied to them (either consciously or unconsciously) (Arber and Ginn, 1995).

The increase in female employment in the paid labour market has led sociologists to question whether the male breadwinner/female home-maker role is still relevant for contemporary industrialised societies. Young and Wilmott's (1973) classic study in the East End of London looked at the changing nature of the family and gendered roles within the family. They used the term the *symmetrical family* to explain the family where both parents worked in paid labour market and shared the household duties and tasks. However, despite changes in labour market participation, many argue that women continue to perform a disproportionate number of the household duties, and where men participate, this too is selective, based on gendered assumptions of masculinity and femininity.

Symmetrical family a family where there is a more equitable division of domestic labour between men and women.

Despite some women having the resources to challenge traditional gendered roles in the domestic division of labour (Benjamin and Sullivan, 1999), the reality for many is that they take on roles in the paid labour market in addition to their roles in the home. Finch (1983) identified a triple burden of the housewife role; paid work, unpaid work and contributing to men's paid work, by acting as a receptionist or book-keeper. Castells (1997) elaborated on this, stating that women may do a quadruple shift of paid work, home-making, child-rearing and the night shift for the husband.

Table 5.2 Attitudes to household chores, 2000–2001, UK

Housework
Average time per day spent on household chores (excluding shopping and childcare)

Women	Men
Nearly 3 hours	1 hour and 40 minutes

Women spend more time than men looking after children and men spend more time than women at work or studying (4 hours 20 minutes per day compared to 2 hours 30 minutes per day on average)

Source:
UK Time Use Survey, Office for National Statistics (2005)

Caring

Since the 1960s, the social care agenda has been dominated by the concept of community care and Finch and Groves (1983) have argued that community care has come to be seen as care by women due to the gendered division of labour. Underpinning the notions of community care are assumptions that people within a locality or local social system will provide care for each other in times of hardship. The notion of a locality as a community (Lee and Newby, 1983) is flawed as a premise for community care, as it assumes that people will care for each other by virtue of being in the same locality. Equally, the idea that community is defined by a set of social relationships is inadequate as a premise for community care, as notions of care are constructed through particular ideologies.

Sex role stereotyping and construction of gendered roles are significant in an analysis of caring. Cree (2000) makes a useful distinction between care and caring. Care generally refers to support provided by agencies in a domiciliary or institutional setting. Caring refers to a support role fulfilled by a relative or friend, which is generally unpaid. Someone who lives with the person may provide caring or there may be a varying amount of support provided by a number of people.

Graham (1983) argues that in order to understand the ideas which underpin caring and the gendered nature of caring, we need to distinguish between caring about and caring for. Caring for is concerned with tending to someone's needs. Caring about is concerned with emotional attachment. Both men and women are capable of both types of care, but Dalley (1988) argues that caring about and caring for coalesce in motherhood, which is seen as an integral part of women's nature and role. Caring is seen as part of the essentially passive nature of women – an innate or socialised characteristic as discussed above.

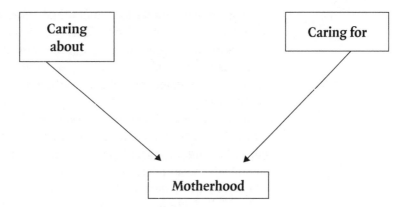

Figure 5.1 The ideology of caring.

Feminists such as Pascall (1997) have been critical of the assumptions underlying the ideology of caring, arguing that there are consequences for women such as their subordination in the domestic sphere, which is bound up with the assumptions about their caring function. At the basis of assumptions about family care and the domestic division of labour is the notion of the nuclear family, although family units are structured around many different forms, with the nuclear family only accounting for just over one quarter of all family types (see Chapter 8).

> *The nuclear, individualistic family is the reality for relatively few, but the model for the many.*
>
> (Dalley, 1988: 16)

The premise of family care (either for dependent children or for other family members in need of care) is based around normative expectations of gendered roles within the domestic division of labour. This is an ideological construct, which becomes translated into social policies and may be internalised by women themselves. Women invest large amounts of time in maintaining the family, but also invest more emotional energy in the family unit (Duncombe and Marsden, 1993).

This is not to suggest that men are not involved with caring. Indeed, there are ideological assumptions in relation to male caring. Men may be expected to take responsibility for care, but not to provide the care themselves necessarily (a man who provides care is seen as untypical). Spousal caring is becoming more common, but daughters and daughter-in-laws are far more likely than sons and son-in-laws to give up paid employment or reduce working hours to provide informal care. Thus the ideological constructs are translated into social policies – male carers are seen as heroically coping and tend to be offered more support from statutory care providers than female carers, who often remain invisible (Blaxter, 1976).

Women may have feelings of duty and obligation to care, even though caring is context- and relationship-bound. There may be feelings of burden and frustration or resentment and the increased acknowledgement of practices such as domiciliary elder abuse (see Chapter 10) fundamentally challenge the assumptions underpinning the ideology of caring.

In the 1970s feminists began to critique the issue that caring was 'private' and part of the family. Rather it was argued that women fulfilled caring responsibilities. This reflects the sexual division of labour, which was postulated by feminist theorists in the 1970s (Oakley, 1974). Women traditionally have been employed in low-paid and unskilled jobs and caring reflects this, as a low status and low-paid activity. This feminist critique of caring is exemplified in the work of Finch and Groves (1983), who discussed how women were keeping the new community care policies going. As women support the family, and community care relies on the family, then they are most likely to be in a caring role. Caring is often an isolated and stressful activity, that can lead to physical health problems and financial difficulties. Studies have shown that carers themselves are at risk of developing physical and mental health problems (McKinlay, 1995).

Case study

The duty team refers fifty-eight-year-old Joan to you, who lives with her eighty-year-old mother who has Alzheimer's. Joan has rung social services 'in desperation', saying she has not slept properly for months. Joan says she does not really see anyone else, apart from the neighbours, as her mother 'is an embarrassment'. She used to work as a teacher, but now cannot leave her mother on her own. She is also worried about finances, as she has used most of her savings to keep her and her mother afloat.

- What are the principal stresses for Joan?
- How could sociological theory help you to understand Joan's situation?

Feminist perspectives on caring have been criticised for a number of reasons. Abrams (1978) discusses the positives of caring for both individuals and society, where caring is seen as a reciprocal activity. In return for support in childhood, family members repay a 'debt of gratitude'. Caring is not necessarily a burden, but experiences vary and are linked to a range of psychological, sociological and environmental factors. Finch and Mason (1993) discuss how there is an element of obligation to caring, but that this is by no means universal. People from working-class communities may be more likely to take on a caring role than their middle-class counterparts.

The feminist critique of caring also loses sight of other groups that provide care. The 2001 Census showed that while the majority of carers were still women, 42 per cent were men. This is particularly the case among carers who are seventy years or over.

The commodification of care

Although informal care has always been important, policy changes in health and social care since the 1980s have strengthened the role of informal care within a mixed economy of welfare (Evers et al., 1994). Payments such as Invalid Care Allowance (1975) were introduced to support carers, and carers have become central providers of care. Rather than being the expert providers of care, health and social care professionals are increasingly working in partnership with carers. There have even been calls for a ban on the term *informal care* as it fails to give sufficient credit to the work that carers do.

Care is increasingly being commodified, with a policy shift from payments to carers to payments to care users. The social model of disability and the disability movement have been particularly influential here (see Chapter 11). Thus individuals become empowered to pay for their own packages of care, which fundamentally shifts the relationship between the family, the market and the state and challenges processes of medicalisation, professionalisation and bureaucratisation. In terms of caring, there is a breakdown of the boundaries between the gift relationship (Cheal, 1988) where care is provided within the context of a personal relationship and the market economy and care becomes a commodity. However, whilst the nature of caring in the informal sector may be changing, caring still remains a gendered activity, with women providing much of the care within the mixed economy of welfare (Ungerson, 1997).

Exercise

More than 1 million people are employed in the care workforce in Britain – over 750,000 in social care and nearly 350,000 in childcare. They are mostly women (88 per cent), especially in childcare, and, apart from social workers, they have below average levels of qualifications. With the increase in the levels of qualifications of school leavers, the pool of young women with low levels of qualifications is likely to shrink, implying more competition between those occupations which draw on this pool of recruits. As the qualification requirements within the sector rise, new competition for recruitment is introduced, particularly with the health and education sectors.

(Simon et al., 2003)

- What are the implications of this for the future of social care provision in Britain?
- What impact might the commodification of care have on women's paid employment and the value that is attached to caring?

In conclusion, there is now a body of literature and research on caring and the needs of carers. While feminist perspectives have been criticised, there appears to be a correlation between caring and women. Interestingly, there are issues about caring tasks. Clarke (2001) discuss how women are likely to carry out more personal care tasks than men. Certainly, caring represents a significant issue for women and the roots of this can clearly be seen in sociological debates around gender and gendered roles.

Risk and exploitation

There are risks associated with gendered roles and societal expectations and feminists have argued that patriarchal oppression causes risks for women in terms of economic and sexual exploitation. The economic relations of society and the sexual division of labour has led to a feminisation of poverty (Scott, 1984), whilst oppressive practices within the domestic sphere may lead to domestic violence, which is a risk for a significant number of women within the institutions of marriage and the family.

A central feature of the risk society is an increase in individualisation as traditional supportive forms such as the family, community and fixed gender roles are reconstructed via new forms of socialisation (Beck, 1992). As men and women break free from traditional roles regarding constructions of masculinity and femininity, they are faced with not only new opportunities but also new risks. Women are no longer dependent upon men for economic support, but for many women economic freedom may also bring about financial hardship (Social Exclusion Report, 1999). Women may also be disempowered and denied the rights of citizenship through domestic violence.

- One in four women and one in six men will be a victim of domestic violence in their lifetime.
- On average two women per week are killed by a male partner or former partner and thirty men per year are killed.
- There are more repeat victims than in any other crime.
- Domestic violence is the largest cause of morbidity worldwide for women aged 19–44.

(Home Office, 2007)

Most feminist theories of domestic violence emphasise patriarchal power relations that exist within society and heterosexual relationships and reject individualistic explanations which highlight the pathological behaviour of the aggressor. There has been a significant shift in the law and social work practice, which recognises the risks posed to children where domestic violence persists. While a shift in policy and practice is a welcome aspect of child protection, these changes are borne out of a concern for the welfare of children as opposed to a concern for women.

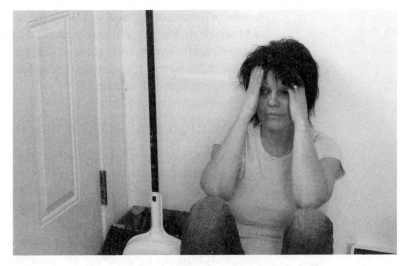

Domestic violence is often hidden, but this staged picture demonstrates some of the psychological effects on women.

The notion of patriarchal violence has led to questions about men's position in social work, which faces several contradictions in relation to men's roles as workers in a 'caring' profession and men as service users. Following a series of abuses by social workers, significantly in residential care homes for children, the role of men in caring professions has been questioned. Feminist social workers have challenged the failure of many public enquiries to consider the gendered nature of the abuse. However some (Pease and Pringle, 2001) have argued that men should not be employed in childcare work because of the risk posed by male abusers. Pease and Pringle (2001) recognise that women may also act as perpetrators of violence towards children but conclude that men perpetrate the overwhelming majority of sexual abuse. Explanations of male sexual violence towards children draw upon psychological as well as sociological theories and social psychologists discuss the role of the peer group in rape-supportive cultures in which such violence is accepted and socially endorsed. Theories of socialisation may also explain male violence in terms of power and subordination in personal and social relations. Connell's (1995) concept of hegemonic masculinities in which masculinity is in part expressed through sexual desire, may explain why men as opposed to women are more likely to engage in abusive sexual relations (Pringle, 2001). Yet Pringle reminds us that the majority of men and boys do not commit sexual violence towards children.

> Imperious sexual desire plays an important role and is strongly linked to a sense of personal adequacy and success; numerous conflicts and uncertainties over dependency and personal adequacy remain which may be viewed by satisfaction of sexual desire
>
> (Pease and Pringle, 2001: 45)

The control of men's violence and their role in the caring professions is one which challenges personal, interpersonal and structural gendered relations within society and takes place in and beyond social work. Pease and Pringle (2001) provides a model for anti sexist practice for male social workers.

Prostitution and sex trafficking

The regulation and exploitation of women's sexual behaviour is seen as a key feature of the patriarchal domination of women. The word prostitute generally refers to a woman over the age of consent who willingly exchanges sexual services for money. While legal in Britain, many activities associated with prostitution remain illegal. Prostitution is heavily stigmatised and prostitutes continue to receive harassment from the police and wider community. Prostitution is illegal in some countries, including much of the USA. In Iraq, dozens of women suspected of prostitution have been beheaded (Matter of the Inquiry into the Legality of the Use of Force by the United Kingdom against Iraq, 2002). Criminalisation does not put an end to its activity but leaves women vulnerable and at risk of further victimisation and exploitation.

Feminists have long debated whether the role of prostitution represents a form of control and subordination or whether prostitution is a legitimate form of work in a wider sex industry which requires state regulation and protection. The term 'sex worker' emphasises the employment aspect of the role and puts prostitutes alongside other women who experience low pay and poor status in a segregated labour market. Dworkin (1981) claims:

> When men use women in prostitution, they are expressing a pure hatred for the female body. It is as pure as anything on this earth ever is or ever has been. It is a contempt so deep, so deep, that a whole human life is reduced to a few sexual orifices, and he can do anything he wants.

Some feminists argue for the redefining of prostitution as sex work, emphasising the need for the empowerment and protection of women through better rights, police protection and

> the designation of prostitution as a special human rights issue, a violation in itself, emphasises the distinction between prostitution and other forms of female or low-status labour. . . however exploitative they are. It thus reinforces the marginal, and therefore vulnerable, position of the women and men involved in prostitution. By dismissing the entire sex industry as abusive, it also obscures the particular problems and violations of international norms within the industry which are of concern to sex workers.
>
> (Bindman and Doezema, 1997)

Exercise: what's wrong with prostitution?

During the 2006 football World Cup Final in Germany, it was estimated that over 40,000 women would be trafficked for prostitution. Germany legalised prostitution in 2002 and Berlin has over 8,000 registered prostitutes.

1. What is the difference between someone who has chosen to be a prostitute and someone who is forced into it?
2. What difference does it make for the man who pays a woman for sex whether the prostitute he has sex with is there by choice or force? Should it make a difference?
3. What is your reaction to all of this? Is prostitution fair?
4. What bearing does sex trafficking have on the nature of protection?

Some feminists view globalisation as providing opportunities for women in providing a global platform in which to articulate women's political agenda through increased communication and the presence of global institutions such as the EU and UN. Biemann (2002) however, argues that globalisation through an expanding global sex trade and the migration of women into low paid domestic service has led to the feminisation of migration. Trafficking is a form of globalised slavery and is closely linked with prostitution. Reports estimate that between two million and five million men, women and children are trafficked each year (International Labour Organisation, 2005) and approximately 80 per cent of those trafficked are women and children and up to 50 per cent are minors (US Department of State, Trafficking in Persons Report, 2005). The majority of trafficked people come from the poorest parts of the world including, Africa, Asia and Eastern Europe. Following arms and drugs trafficking, human trafficking is the third largest source of income for organised crime (UN Office on Drugs and Crime, 2000). There was no specific law or penalty in Britain which deals with trafficking and other laws tended to be used to prosecute offenders. In 2005, two Albanian men became the first people to be prosecuted for human trafficking under the Sexual Offences Act, 2003. Now under the Asylum and Immigration Act, 2004, traffickers can face up to fourteen years in prison for trafficking for forced labour or organ removal.

Changing identities

There have been changes in roles and behaviours, with traditional female and male identities being challenged. Annandale (1998) identifies a change in lifestyle, with females adopting more of the health damaging behaviour that has traditionally been associated with males. For example, in terms of alcohol consumption, there has been a narrowing of the gap between teenage boys and girls (Alcohol Concern, 2006).

This change in female behaviour and lifestyle practices has led some commentators to suggest that there is a moral panic about the nature of femininity and the role of girls in society. Barron and Lacombe (2005), for example, have suggested that there has been a rise in aggressive and anti-social behaviour in girls, while others have pointed to a rise in mortality and morbidity from cirrhosis and other alcohol-related disorders amongst women as a result of changed drinking practices (Alcohol Concern, 2004).

Table 5.3 Percentage of young adolescents drinking more than once a week

	Boys	Girls
1990	15	12
2005	17	16

Adapted from Alcohol Concern (2006)

Exercise

What period would you guess that the following headlines are from?

she doesn't really care whether she gets married or not, so long as she can earn a comfortable living and have a good time . . .

[she] crawls home at three or four in the morning, a haggard, weary-eyed creature
(cited in Jackson and Tinkler, 2007)

These quotes are actually taken from the 1920s (*Girls Weekly*, 24 January 1990)

- How far do these concerns reflect changing gender roles or the nature of adolescent transition?

Jackson and Tinkler (2007) have argued that the moral panic of ladette culture has been exaggerated, and the changes in lifestyle behaviours have a rather longer history than many commentators suggest. It has also been suggested that there is a crisis in masculinity as a result of changes in the economy, social structures and household composition.

The 'demasculinising' effects of poverty and of economic and social change may be eroding men's traditional roles as providers and limiting the availability of alternative, meaningful roles for men in families and communities. Men may consequently seek affirmation of their masculinity in other ways; through irresponsible sexual behaviour or domestic violence for example.

(Cleaver, 2001)

This crisis is not universal but confined to particular groups of men. The decline of manufacturing has primarily hit working-class men, with unemployed, unskilled and unmarried men having higher mortality and illness rates than other groups of men. In non-traditional employment areas such as social work, men may not necessarily conform to constructions of hegemonic masculinity, though they do benefit from being located in a female-dominated profession (Hearn and Parkin, 2001). A study carried out by JRF in 2001 explored 'the "laddish" attributes commonly associated with white working-class masculinity and whether they have become a disadvantage in the new labour markets' (www.jrf.org.uk). It found that young men's views of masculinity in some ways conformed to the notion of a 'lad' but also emphasised domestic conformity. Attitudes, behaviours and definitions of masculinity were varied, changing and complex but the 'traditional' notions of masculinity dominated as opposed to a 'new version of masculinity which might be more in tune with the requirements of a service-based economy' (ibid.).

Links have been made to masculinity and young men's perception of themselves and this may have effects on their mental well-being. Suicide is the most common form of death for men aged thirty-five and under in England, having doubled in the last twenty years. Males in lower socio-economic groups, gay and bisexual men are more likely to commit suicide than heterosexual and middle-class men.

> conversely, new roles and expectations of young men in society may lead to loss of self-esteem if they are unable to live up to expectations. They may then be vulnerable to suicide if they lack appropriate supportive social networks or are not able to communicate their concerns
>
> (McClure, 2001: 3)

This study concluded that those young men who held stereotyped perceptions of masculinity were less likely to express their feelings and seek help with their problems. This was reinforced by agency's responses to them; they felt that there was little point in targeting this group. Rather than a preference to see male workers, the study identified that men did not want to be viewed as weak or vulnerable by other men, challenging notions of 'role modelling' as promoted by some texts. Rather than talking through difficulties men preferred to 'escape the stress' through the use of alcohol, use 'inner strength' to protect themselves or 'talk it out with a friend'. Differences in emotional expression were mostly related to the significant differences between gay and straight men.

Significant gender differences have been noted by the way in which men respond to loss and bereavement. Thompson (1998) has argued that models of grief and bereavement have been constructed around normative constructions of femininity and masculinity, with men being expected to be strong and supportive of others. Thus men may be disenfranchised through societal expectations that they will not be emotionally expressive (Martin and Doka, 2000) There are numerous examples of how the media invigilates these societal expectations, with men being portrayed as strong and in control (Walter et al., 1995).

Working with men as service users

There has traditionally been a reluctance by feminist social workers to address working with men, as they have given priority to working with women (Cavanagh and Cree, 1996). It is argued that men-blindness in feminist social work runs the risk of reinforcing traditional stereotypes about women's roles and behaviour as well as leaving men to challenge male power and masculinity in areas such as violence towards women and children.

Social work has been criticised for failing to engage with men, either as service users in their own right or as fathers of children and other relatives. A conference by the Family Rights Group in 2005 highlighted the systematic failure of health and social care services to engage fathers and father-figures through failing to listen to fathers' concerns, negating the role of fathers in assessments and through inadequate provision of support. A SCIE Research briefing (2005) discusses the specific issues raised for fathers who are caring for disabled children.

There are some understandable reasons as to why social workers are reluctant to engage with men. Female service users may be perceived as less threatening and intimidating than male service users, as men carry the threat of violence even when it is not transferred into action (Cree, 2000). However, engaging and working effectively with fathers and other men who affect the wellbeing of children and families is now firmly emphasised in policy frameworks as a strategic requirement for all children's services and a number of projects have been set up in social work with such a remit.

Hearn's (2001) research on male violence towards women is significant in terms of the minimal contact the men had with social service departments and other agencies. When contact is made, the focus is not directed at stopping the violent behaviour as other problems are addressed. He recommends that agencies including the police, probation services, health and social services address men's power and their oppression of others through development of specific policies and practices. In addition, agencies should address men's experiences of their personal problems and their avoidance of agency contact. He further suggests that the challenge for those male-dominated agencies is how to renounce violence and not collude with it. Cavanagh and Cree (1996) have developed a useful code of practice for females working with men in social work.

Exercise: working with men

1. What are the issues for female social workers in engaging with men?
2. What role can male workers play in working with men?
3. How we do influence future attitudes of boys to fatherhood and working with children?
4. How would sociological theories explain this?

Social justice and empowering social work

Dominelli (1997) uses the phrase 'feminist sociological social work' to refer to 'the sociological insights into women's condition provided by both black and white feminists'. This is an attempt to recognise the diversity of thought that exists within feminist sociology and also to firmly locate feminist social work practice as concerned with challenging and eradicating racism as well as other forms of oppression which women experience.

> Feminist social work is a form of social work practice, which takes gendered inequality and its elimination as the starting point for working, whether as individuals or groups within organisations and seeks to promote women's well being as women define it.
>
> (Dominelli, 2002)

Insights from sociological perspectives on gender relations within society are valuable in not only developing feminist social work practice with women, but are particularly relevant in developing an understanding of gender relations in working with all men, women, girls and boys in all areas of social work practice.

Summary points

- Social work is a feminised activity.
- Feminism is not a single theory, but a range of theoretical perspectives, which help us to understand the position of women in society.
- Sex and gender are differentiated. Whilst sex refers to fixed biological entities, gender relates to social processes and experiences that influence men and women's lives.
- Feminist theories have traditionally focused on women's oppressions. More recently, there has been a growing body of theory exploring the nature of masculinity, which has helped to inform contemporary debates in social work about working with men and boys.

Questions for discussion

- How can theories of gender relations contribute to your understanding of social work practice?
- What evidence is there that the differences between the genders are narrowing?
- Think about the roles in your household. Who does what? Are there distinctive gendered roles?
- What are the dominant ways that men and women are depicted in society?
- On your next placement, look at the gendered roles in the department. How far do these reflect segregated roles in the workforce?

Further reading

Abbott, P., Wallace, C. and Tyler, M. (2005) *An Introduction to Sociology: Feminist Perspectives*. London: Routledge. This is a useful book for exploring a range of feminist perspectives and their contribution within the sociological debate.

Dalley, G. (1988) *Ideologies of Caring*. Basingstoke: Macmillan. Although rather old now, this is a classic text in the analysis of the construction of caring and the relationship to gendered roles and expectations that underpin the politics of care.

Dominelli, L. (2002) *Feminist Social Work: Theory and Practice*. Basingstoke: Palgrave Macmillan.

6

Race and Ethnicity

It has long been accepted within sociology that there is no scientific basis for the concept of race but the social, economic and political effects of processes of racial categorisation of people remain real. However, as debates regarding scientific racism appear to re-emerge with every generation, this chapter will explore some of the key sociological theories, which explain the phenomena of race, ethnicity and racism in Britain and the implications for social work practice.

The key issues that will be explored in this chapter are:

- Definitions of race and ethnicity and the legacy of scientific racism.
- Explanations of discrimination on the basis of racial and ethnic categorisation.
- Social work's relationship with race and ethnicity.
- Contemporary issues within the context of social work practice with BME service users.

By the end of this chapter, you should be able to:

- Explain the differences between the terms 'race' and 'ethnicity'.
- Discuss issues of discrimination, disadvantage and oppression related to ethnic categorisation.
- Explain what is meant by the terms 'institutionalised racism' and 'internalised oppression.
- Understand the impact of immigration on social and psychological well being.
- Discuss the role of social workers in working with BME service users in an anti-oppressive way.

Defining race and the myth of scientific racism

Race, ethnicity and racism are highly sensitive and controversial issues within British society and this is particularly true within the professional arena of social work.

> Race and ethnicity are not 'natural' categories, even though both concepts are often represented as if they were. Their boundaries are not fixed, nor is their membership uncontested. Race and ethnic groups, like nations, are imagined communities. People are socially defined as belonging to particular ethnic or racial groups, either in terms of definitions employed by others, or definitions, which members of particular ethnic groups develop for them. They are ideological entities, made and changed in struggle. They are discursive formations, signalling a language through which differences accorded social significance may be named and explained. But what is of importance for us as social researchers studying race and ethnicity is that such ideas also carry with them material consequences for those who are included within, or excluded from, them.
>
> (Bulmer and Solomos, 1998: 822)

The sociology of race is concerned with the causes and consequences of the socially constructed division of social groups according to their so-called racial origins. The idea of a scientific basis to race emerged in the mid 1700s with the view that human beings could be separated

Phenotypical differences ◄ into distinct racial groups based upon biological and *phenotypical*
the physical manifestation of genetic differences, e.g. skin colour, hair type. characteristics (the expression of genes – skin /eye colour, hair type). The races, which were identified, included Caucasian, African and Mongoloid and within those groups emerged a hierarchy with white European males being placed at the top and others placed below on a scale of differences marked by skin colour and skull size and shape. This period in history known as the Enlightenment reflected a time of a growing interest in rationalisation whereby differences in people could be articulated and measured (see Chapter 2). Differences in behaviour, intelligence, morality and godliness were attributed to physiological differences and Africans were viewed as amoral and less intelligent and human than Caucasians. There were similar comparisons being drawn in the area of criminality, prostitution and differences in skin, eyes, ears and skull size were seen as a causal link for any behaviours that were defined as immoral (Nott and Gliddon, 1854 in Haralambos, 2004).

It is widely believed that racism as an ideology developed at the end of the sixteenth century and was used to justify the slave trade between Africa, Europe and America. The racism that was associated with notions of Britishness and superiority was used to promulgate colonial expansion into Africa and Asia. The ideology epitomised by Rudyard's Kipling's poem 'White Man's Burden' was used to justify European domination and control in colonised countries whereby civilised white people, under the guise of paternalism could take responsibility for the economic and legal governance of uncivilised communities that were unable to rule themselves.

Ideologies of racial superiority were extended beyond colour to include all immigrants to Britain in the nineteenth century. There is evidence of Irish settlement in Britain as early as the twelfth century, though mass immigration did not occur until prior to, during and after the Great Famine of 1846 when approximately 1.5 million people emigrated. In terms of scientific racism, Irish people were viewed as being marginally superior to Africans (Irish people were sometimes referred to as White Negroes) and concerns were raised regarding the over-breeding of the Irish and the threat to Anglo-Saxon community and culture (Douglas, 2002).

Eugenics belief that those with poor-quality genes should be restricted from reproduction. In the early twentieth century, it was widespread practice across United States and Western Europe.

Scientific racism validated the aspirations of the *eugenics movement* in Western Europe and the US in the early twentieth century. It promoted the use of science to control breeding in order to increase desirable characteristics and remove inferior ones, with the primary aim of creating a pure race. This pure race consisted of white, able bodied, heterosexual human beings.

The scientific basis of race differences has been refuted and any differences in genetic make-up between people do not reflect the so-called racial groups. Jones (1993) states that modern genetics shows that there are no separate groups within humans and that genetic differences between people are individual as opposed to being based upon any ideas of nationality or 'race'.

However, despite this discrediting of the scientific basis of race, the debates concerning the so-called biological differences between people continue. A controversy has been in the area of intelligence differences between racial groups. This first arose in the 1950s (Eysenck, 1971) and later through the work of Herrnstein and Murray (1994) in which it was claimed that black people score consistently less on IQ tests than whites. In 2006, a university lecturer, Frank Ellis, wrote a controversial article claiming that black students were intellectually inferior to their white counterparts. This edited article, which appeared in a university student union publication, again fuelled a debate concerning the scientific basis of race and demonstrates the continued power and significance of discourses surrounding race within contemporary British society. So whilst there is no biological basis for the concept of race, the social and political aspects of racial categorisation persist and the area of race and ethnicity has emerged to be a significant aspect of sociological inquiry. Most sociologists now prefer to use the term 'race' to mean a socially constructed way of categorising people on the basis of assumed biological differences recognising its flawed origins.

Discussion points

From the 1940s to 1960s many British colonies were granted independence and the Commonwealth headed by Queen Elizabeth II now represents the interests of former British colonies.

- Though Britain has few existing colonies, how far does the ideology and racism of imperialism reflect contemporary discourses concerning race and ethnicity?
- What issues may be raised by the continued existence of the Commonwealth Games, which is based on this notion of British colonies?

Explaining ethnicity

The legacy of scientific racism has meant that in common usage the term race is used to refer to physical or visible differences between people, and ethnicity and ethnic group is associated with cultural differences (Fenton, 1999). Though they are conceptually different, there are times when the terms race and ethnicity tend to be used interchangeably, particularly in relation to research and social work practice. Some sociologists prefer to employ the concept of ethnicity as opposed to 'race', in an attempt to dismiss notions of biological determinism and recognise the centrality of social constructionism (see Chapter 2).

Theories of ethnicity and ethnic relations have re-emerged in sociology following ethnic conflicts in Europe and Africa. Ethnicity can be described as the identification of individuals with particular ethnic groups. An ethnic group can be defined as 'a group whose members identify with each other, usually on the basis of a presumed common genealogy or ancestry' (Smith, 1986). Ethnic groups are also usually united by common cultural, behavioural, linguistic or religious practices, which may or may not be associated with common descent. The last census of 2001 changed its classifications of ethnicity to include the category 'mixed' instead of 'other', representing the significant growth in numbers of people from mixed ethnic backgrounds.

Diaspora is used to describe the dispersion of people from their homeland. It is usually used to mean a forced dispersion of a religious or ethnic group, but it can refer to the situation of any group dispersed, forcibly or voluntarily, throughout the world.

Identification of membership of a particular ethnic group is based upon an understanding (by self or others) of a sense of shared history or belonging, real or imagined. Pilkington (2003) identifies processes of ethnic group formation in his discussion of a black or African American ethnic identity, which unified culturally and nationally diverse groups of people from West Africa through the processes of enslavement and *diaspora*.

Table 6.1 Classifications used in 2001 Census for England and Wales

England and Wales	%
Those who say they are white	
White British	87.5
White Irish	1.2
White other	2.6
Those who say they are Asian	
Indian	2
Pakistani	1.4
Bangladeshi	0.5
Other Asian	0.5
Those who say they are black	
Caribbean	1.1
African	0.9
Other Black	0.2
Those who say they are mixed race	
White/Black Caribbean	0.5
White/Asian	0.4
Other mixed	0.3
Other ethnicities	
Chinese	0.4
Other ethnic groups	0.4

Source:
2001 Census: www.statistics.gov.uk/census

Exercise

Identifying ethnicity

- How would you describe your ethnicity?
- Do you belong to an ethnic group?
- How is your ethnicity characterised?

Ethnicity and ethnic groups are both fluid and changing concepts and boundaries between groups are not fixed, as they appear with the risk that cultural distinctiveness can be exaggerated (Pilkington, 2003). The idea of groups can imply a static category, whereas viewing ethnicity as social classifications within relationships avoids *essentialism* and recognises the fluidity that exists between ethnicities. Ethnicity can thus be understood as a relative or relational social process, involving the shifting of boundaries and identity which people draw around themselves in their social lives (Fenton, 1999).

Discourses regarding ethnicity usually involve constructions of ethnic majority and ethnic minority, a form of dualism in which differences are exaggerated. Within discussion of ethnicity it is often assumed that reference is being made to ethnic minority groups. There is an assumption of homogeneity with the so-called ethnic majority and that it is not worthy of analysis.

> Perhaps one reason that conversations about race are so often doomed to frustration is that the notion of whiteness as 'race' is almost never implicated . . . Exnomination permits whites to entertain the notion that race lives 'over there' on the other side of the tracks, in black bodies and inner city neighbourhoods, in a dark netherworld where whites are not involved.
>
> (Williams, 1996)

Thus whiteness and majorities are assumed to be natural and the norm, whereas blackness and minorities reflects difference and diversity. White people can therefore operate from a position where their way of being is normal while other ways of being are, at best, exotic and at worst, wrong. This can lead to a danger of *ethnocentrism* whereby one judges other groups or societies by the standards that apply in one's own society. Ethnocentrism can also refer to the way that lifestyles, experiences, values and norms of one group in a society are assumed to be common to everyone. This has been one of

---

Exercise

Who are they?

What do you think of them?

What do you think of them? Go to the airport any day and look at them arriving on the flights?

They pour out of the planes.

They don't exactly bring a lot of money into our economy – half of them are penniless, old people coming to visit their sons or daughters or wives and children coming to join their husbands who've been working here for years. Have you got near to them?

They must really stink. According to statistics they only take a bath once a fortnight, their economy is in a mess, they can't make money, they have no jobs at home, so they come over here to mess up our economy and take our jobs.

And why is there so much unemployment in their own country?

Because they're a lazy lot who don't want to work well let them be warned, they won't be allowed to live on social security here.

- To whom do you think the article is referring and why?
- It is actually an extract from an Australian newspaper concerning British immigration to Australia.
- Does the article reflect discourses regarding race and migration in Britain today?

the criticisms of social work practice with black users that will be explored later in this chapter. Sociologists have fallen into the trap of assuming white homogeneity and it is only recently that the construction of whiteness has become an aspect of discourse of ethnicity within sociology. In particular, sociology has been accused of ignoring the racialisation of Irish people and the experiences of Irish communities as a minority ethnic group (Hickman, 1995).

Sociological approaches to understanding race and ethnicity

Functionalism

Integrationist approaches to race focus upon black people and immigration and point to the problems of immigration in terms of securing employment, gaining appropriate education and training and obtaining housing. Once people have adjusted to living in Britain and have *assimilated* within British society, problems of unemployment and exclusion and differences between groups should disappear.

Assimilation the process whereby minorities adopt and blend into the dominant culture of the host nation. This was a feature of 1960s race relations policies.

Functionalist perspectives .on race have tended to explain racism and discrimination in relation to integration and assimilation by the migrant communities into the host society (Best, 2005). In his analysis of American society in the 1950s and 1960s, Parsons viewed the discrimination faced by black Americans based upon shared values, which viewed black skin colour as inferior, and was used as justification for the summation of black American people. He saw the existence of such racism as failure by black American communities and white American society to successfully include black people in the dominant culture and value system (Best, 2005). In order to successfully integrate into the host community, migrants are required to adopt the dominant cultural value systems. Since resistance to inclusion can take place on both sides, Parsons favoured state intervention in the form of anti-discriminatory legislation to assist this process.

Merton (1938) also saw the common value system as important in understanding racism. He developed a theory regarding prejudice and discrimination, which suggested that there are four main types of relationship between prejudice and discrimination. Merton concluded that prejudice does not necessarily lead to discrimination and that people may discriminate for a variety of reasons, e.g. material gain (see Table 6.2).

- The bigot is a racist person who is prejudiced and does discriminate.
- The timid bigot is also a racist, in that this person is prejudiced but does not discriminate, possibly because s/he believes it to be wrong or fears the consequences of discrimination.

- The fair-weather liberal is a person who is not prejudiced but who does discriminate, possibly due to the advantages of indirect forms of discrimination.
- The all-weather liberal is not a racist, is not prejudiced and does not discriminate.

Table 6.2 Merton's typology of personalities

Personality Type	Prejudice	Discrimination
Bigot	+	+
Timid bigot	+	−
Fair-weather liberal	−	+
All-weather liberal	−	−

Source:
Merton's typology of personalities' in *Understanding Social Divisions* by Shaun Best, 2005:155, Sage Publications, 2005. Reprinted with permission.

Some of the main criticisms of functionalist theories focus upon the premise that racism and discrimination would disappear as communities become more integrated within society and its failure to explain the persistence of racism and inequality in almost all aspects of social and economic life. Functionalism also assumes a consensus amongst the host society and ignores the differences and hostilities that exist within white communities. It assumes that there is a consensus of the superiority of white English or American culture, blames BME communities for the inequality they experience and their apparent failure to integrate successfully into host communities and gain full citizenship.

Singh (1992) provides a discussion of social work's recent history of working with black and ethnic minority communities. Acknowledging the significant strides made within social work in recognising and meeting the needs of BME individuals and groups, the book does not necessarily represent a successful progression of social work through the last twenty years. Instead, it provides a discussion of social work, which at times has an uncomfortable and controversial history with regard to race and ethnicity and recognises that at any one time poor and ineffective practice can be found alongside creative and empowering practice with black service users.

Social work values, centred on notions of equality and treating people the same, have led to accusations of colour blindness in which social workers not wanting to discriminate or recognise difference, found themselves ignoring specific cultural and religious needs of black service users and instead provided inappropriate services or provided no service at all. The emphasis within social work and other welfare agencies was one of assimilationist and integrationist practices, in which particular cultural needs were ignored or minimised – a one-size-fits-all approach. It was assumed that if immigrant communities learnt the language and adopted the customs and norms of British society, then they would be integrated into the host community and would overcome some of the specific issues faced with regard to education, housing and employment.

A colour-blind approach could be seen in relation to the placement needs of black children in the public care system. A critical attack on social work practice with black children was provided by the Black and in Care Report (1985). The report identified over-representation of black children in care, the lack of recognition of children's religious, cultural and linguistic needs, proportionally longer time spent in care compared to white counterparts and the placement of black children with white foster carers. The overwhelming message was that black children were being denied their blackness and were being failed by the state as corporate parents.

Marxist and neo-Marxist perspectives

Traditional Marxist approaches to understanding race and ethnicity tend to regard race as being largely irrelevant and assert that discrimination and oppression experienced by black and minority ethnic groups is a product of capitalism. The bourgeoisie generate racism to justify exploitation and the under-development of the Third World. Hence the eradication of capitalism will lead to the removal of racism. Traditional Marxists see racism as a key element in the creation of false consciousness, which draws divisions between black and white workers, in order to explain working-class racism

The Birmingham Centre for Contemporary Cultural Studies (CCCS) included in their ranks notable writers, such as Solomos, Findlay, Jones and Gilroy; in their collection of essays entitled *The Empire Strikes Back* in 1982, they agreed with some aspects of Cox's views, but provided a neo-Marxist critique on race. They regarded traditional theories as being too simplistic and economically reductionist, in which everything is reduced and explained by the capitalist economic system. There is also some evidence to suggest that racism predates capitalism (CCCS). They therefore regarded race and racism, not through evolutionary terms, but as a series of different events; 'struggles, breaks and discontinuities' in which black people do not simply submit to racism, but resist and challenge it.

Solomos et al. (1982) in the CCCS recognised what they described as the concept of *New Racism*, which expressed superiority and inferiority through cultural differences rather than biological ones. Cultural superiority emphasised difference in which black culture, values and beliefs were regarded as inferior to those of white British communities. Rather than focusing purely on capitalism as creating racism, neo-Marxist sociologists such as Miles (1989) consider the ways in which class and race interact in some form of causal dependency to create racialised factions within classes.

Miles (ibid.) regards race as a social construct, and argues that racialisation occurs in any situation where racial meanings are attached to any situation. Miles separates out the concept of race from the ideas associated with race. He describes race as a 'socially imagined', arbitrary term in which only particular physical features are ascribed to race. However, while Miles recognises the significance of race as a social construct, racism tends to be subsumed under class exploitation.

Weberian and neo-Weberian approaches

Within Weberian theories of race and racism, race is regarded as a separate class. The term *race relations* is used in an attempt to construct a theoretical framework for the analysis of race and racism.

Race relations term used to describe how different cultural groups interact within society.

For Weber, inequality in power and advantage takes three forms: class, status and party. Class inequality relates to inequality produced as a result of the capitalist economy, where black people tend to be concentrated in low-paid, low-skilled, non-unionised work, as well as having a disproportionate presence among the unemployed. Status refers to qualities and human attributes and in this instance race is linked to status and race inequality, which forms a part of status inequality. Finally in relation to party, ethnic groups tend to be politically marginalised.

For Weberians BME groups occupy a weak market position and in combination of class, party and status, black people constitute a separate class or *underclass* (Rex and Tomlinson, 1979). The underclass thesis was initially coined by Weberians (and later hijacked by new right ideology) and is characterised by an inability to improve their situation due to discriminatory employment laws and practices (see Chapter 3). It explains how exclusionary practices (by employers, trade unions, colleagues etc) result in situations whereby BME communities are given differential rewards on the basis of their race and ethnicity and hence people of BME backgrounds tend to be located in the secondary market. Similar processes operate in relation to access to health, welfare and housing.

Social closure employed by Weber to describe the action of social groups, who restrict entry and exclude benefit to those outside the group in order to maximise their own advantage. This exclusion prevents other social groups from positive life chances.

The concept of *social closure* is used to explain the exclusionary practices within occupations whereby BME workers face exclusion or restricted entry to certain occupations or professions. Carter (2003) suggests that concentration of BME groups in particular areas of employment is associated with boundary markers such as gender and ethnicity, as opposed to the more objective elements of skill and qualification.

Interviews in Hackney conducted by Koutrolikou (2005) highlight aspects of the Weberian concept of social closure as poor minority groups compete over limited resources and often shifting boundaries as groups redefine their identities.

The underclass thesis does not account for the social mobility that exists within some black communities and assumes consensus and homogeneity within class and occupational groupings. The concept of race is used in an uncritical way, minimising the significance of race as a social construct. These perspectives have been questioned for their tendency to focus upon individual or personal racism and as such reduce racism to the individual actions of those who exclude or discriminate, for example, employers in the labour market or teachers in education.

Post-modernist perspectives

Post-modern critiques of traditional approaches to the understanding of race, ethnicity and racism tend to suggest that discourses around race arise out of the need to see the world in terms of binary opposites (black/white, majority/minority). They view concepts such as race and black ethnicity as totalising concepts, which are too rigid and inflexible and seek to emphasise sameness and commonality within complex and diverse peoples (Rattansi, 1992; Hall, 1992; Anthias and Yuval Davies, 1998). They regard such concepts as linguistic categorisations and challenge the essentialist notions that are expressed by other theories. *Essentialism* is used to refer to the 'essential essence' of people and the ways in which complex and multiple identities are reduced to a single attribute such as race or ethnicity. Hall (1996) employs the term '*new ethnicities*' to challenge notions of blackness or black identity as a fixed category, in which he recognises the plurality of ethnic identities that exist with non-white communities. All groups are ethnically differentiated (white and non-white) thus weakening the emphasis on difference between black and white. As discussed earlier in the chapter, ethnicity is not an absolute concept and new ethnicities emerge as reflected by state recognition through inclusion of the category of 'mixed' in the 2001 Census.

There is a shift away from the concept of black to represent all non-white groups, as there is no essential black subject in whom all black people share common histories, interests and lifestyles. Totalising labels such as Black or Asian tend to suppress the diversity and difference that exist within BME communities, as some minority groups struggle to represent themselves (Rattansi 1992). An example of this within popular culture could be seen as British born, second-generation Muslim women choosing to wear the veil as an expression of their religious and cultural identity.

Anthias and Yuval-Davis (1998) argue that multiple identities based upon gender, race and class should be understood in terms of the context in which they are constructed. Different social processes, based upon the social divisions of race, class and gender, interrelate to create specific social outcomes for people, thus resulting in situations in which people with multiple and contradictory identities

Essentialism the way in which groups become defined as homogenous on the basis of predefined characteristics or dispositions.

New ethnicities a post-modern term used to refer to changing ethnic identities (see Stuart Hall).

Veiled woman. (Hasan Shaheed)

are located in positions of subordination in different social and economic contexts. For example, BME women occupy spaces of subordination within the family, work, and in sexuality and although white working-class men may be subordinate through class, they still may be seen as dominant (Best, 2005).

The particular experiences of Irish discrimination in Britain provide an illustration of the construction of racial categories and visibility/invisibility of particular ethnic groups. Assumptions regarding white homogeneity have meant that Irish people are often classified with the native population or with other white minorities and as a result Irish people often remain invisible.

The ethnic category of 'Irish' was only added to the Census in 2001, however there is much evidence to indicate that Irish people as an ethnic group experience systematic discrimination and exclusion throughout society. But the absence of census data results in a lack of research evidence to support claims for services to meet specific needs and furthers the denial or minimisation of the individual and cultural needs of Irish people.

The CRE Report, 'The Irish in Britain' (1997) indicates that Irish people are discriminated against and disadvantaged in employment, housing, education, and the criminal justice system and in access to health and social care services. Irish people are twice as likely to be unemployed and more likely to be involved in manual, unskilled and personal service employment. High proportions of Irish men are unskilled workers and are employed in the building industry, where employment patterns are often erratic (CRE, 1997). The report 'Room to Roam' (2004) provides a comprehensive research into the experiences of Irish travellers and identifies the specific needs of traveller children and their difficulties concerning access to education. Irish people make up the largest single group sleeping rough in Britain's cities, and are more than twice as likely to be admitted to hospital with a diagnosis of mental illness as the indigenous population. Since the troubles in the North of Ireland, Irish people have been subject to police harassment and it is considered that stop and search has gone far beyond the powers under the Prevention of Terrorism Act and reflects widespread anti-Irish attitudes in the British police force.

Explanations of the racialisation of specific ethnic groups are complex and are illustrated by the experiences of Irish people and more recent economic migrants to Britain. However the hostility that is directed towards migrants from Eastern Europe contrasts sharply with that directed towards migrants from Australia or the USA.

Hence post-modern perspectives within sociology, in rejecting totalising constructions of black and black identity, recognise

This Englishness has been associated with national identity at football matches, and at times has been seen as perpetuating racist attitudes. (Simon Askham)

difference and diversity within BME communities. However the representation of difference may in fact promote nationalism and fundamentalism, as people may feel threatened in losing their cultural distinctiveness. This can be seen from some groups who wish to assert Englishness following devolution in the UK.

Malik (1996) is critical of these perspectives, suggesting that post-modernism is apolitical and defeatist in its approach to promoting strategies to eradicate racism, that it is associated with an acceptance of the status quo in a fragmented and disunited world. The relevance of post-modern perspectives has also been challenged in terms of its effectiveness for social work practice.

> Without wishing to minimise the importance of ideas such as those of Foucault, I think it is wise to bear in mind these were not developed in social work or even in a field akin to social work but in the context of purely academic disciplines whose practitioners are not required to make decisions about how to respond to problems in the real world.
>
> (Beckett, 2006:79)

There are however some writers within social work education such as Fook (2002) and Healey (2005) who are successfully combining aspects of post-modern ideas and concepts in their understanding of social work theory and practice.

Racism, islamophobia and inter ethnic conflict

The roots of anti-Muslim attitudes can be traced to Christian writers prior to the Crusades of medieval Europe. Said (1997) discusses the origins of islamophobia in his analysis of discourses regarding orientals, which emerged in the nineteenth century. Orientalism for Said represents the western world's relationship with and representation of the Orient, which is characterised by racist attitudes, beliefs and images of people from the eastern world.

With more than 1.6 million UK Muslims (2.7% of the population), Islam is now this country's second largest faith after Christianity (Census, 2001). Muslims and Islam have been seen as a particular threat to the values of Christianity and Britishness and this was further amplified by events such as 9/11 in the US in 2001, the international war on terror and the 7/7 bombings in Britain in 2005. Islamophobia has now become a recognised form of racism in Britain and in other parts of the world. The Pew Centre (2006) in an examination of Muslim attitudes across thirteen countries stated that 'Muslim opinions about the West and its people have worsened over the past year and by overwhelming margins.'

The Parekh Report (2000) on the future of multi-ethnic Britain stated that 'Recently Muslims have emerged as the principal focus of racist

Cartoons of Muslims in newspapers led to widespread
demonstrations by Muslims throughout Europe. (Chris Schmidt)

antagonisms based on cultural differences.' The report entitled
Islamophobia: A challenge to us all by the Runnymede Trust (1997) is an
illustration of the extent of the racism towards Muslims in Britain
(www.runnymedetrust.org).

   The report discusses the history of Muslims in Britain, current
issues faced by Muslims of all generations and the role and
responsibility of the media in reinforcing islamophobia. It also
highlights violence and racial *harassment* towards those perceived as
Muslim and systematic social exclusion in all areas of life from
employment to politics. Polarising attitudes regarding this can be
seen by an ICM/ *Observer* opinion poll in Britain in which 71 per cent
of those polled felt 'That immigrants should embrace the British way
of life', this had been 59 per cent before the attack. The numerous
recommendations made within this report incorporated the three
central concepts of cohesion, equality and difference to be addressed

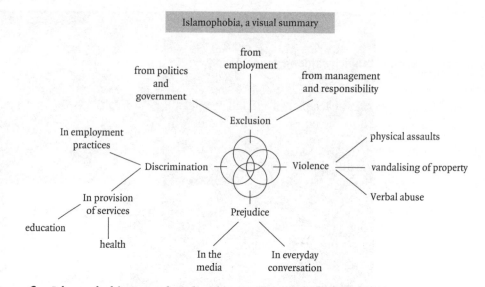

Figure 6.1 Islamophobia Reproduced with permission of the Runnymede Trust.

by organisations and services such as education, the police and health and social care.

Malik (2005) expresses some caution regarding recent discourses of racism resulting in the concept of islamophobia being used widely and in an uncritical manner. On one hand islamophobia may be referred to as the fear and hatred of Muslims, and on the other hand, it may be used to describe legitimate acts, such as criticism of Islam. Malik discusses underachievement and poverty among Pakistani and Bangladeshi communities and while acknowledging the pervasiveness of anti-Muslim attitudes amongst individuals and in organisational practices, he cites the causes of long term disadvantage among specific ethnic minority populations as being due to a myriad of factors including class, race and religion.

There is some evidence to suggest that hostilities exist within black and minority ethnic communities. The tensions that existed were highlighted in Birmingham in 2006 with the death of an African Caribbean man by Asian men following allegations of an assault against an African Caribbean girl. One local resident said

> You'd have to walk miles to find a black-run business in Lozells, even some of the businesses selling Caribbean food like yam, they've been taken over by Asians, forcing African Caribbeans to spend their money with Asian businesses.

In challenging attitudes and assumptions regarding race Milner's research (1975) into the development of racial attitudes in young children is useful. It identified that in many children an appreciation of racial differences starts from around the age of three years old, and that by five years old children reproduce versions of the stereotypical social roles of black and white people.

Exercise

Attitudes to race and ethnicity among young people

Reasons why people are 'disliked':
Afghans . . . because they hijack planes and kill people
People in Iraq . . . did horrible non-forgivable actions

Dislike of difference:
Coloured people . . . are different to us
Asians are different

Too many incomers:
Pakistan . . . are invading our country
Asylum seekers . . . there's too many of them

Preferential treatment:
They do nothing for our country and get free housing, food and they have their own
    country
Refugees get more than us

Discussion points

- How can you account for the views expressed above?
- What are the implications for working with young people in social work?
- Is racism the prerogative of white people?

The Channel 4 film *Who You Callin' a Nigger?* Presented by Darcus Howe
(2004) provides an interesting and provocative discussion of issues
concerning inter–racial conflict.

Race, racism and social work

The changing context of race in Britain was characterised by marked
civil unrest in a number of English cities in the 1980s leading to policy
initiatives challenging racial inequality. The subsequent Scarman
Report (1982) highlighted that racial discrimination existed in the
police force on individual levels (a few bad apples) as opposed to at
an institutional level. He said that 'the direction and policies of
the Metropolitan Police are not racist'. He recognised that some
officers were 'ill considered, immature and racially prejudiced' but
made it clear that institutionalised racism itself was not a problem.
The solution, therefore, was centred on more recruitment of black
officers and better race awareness training.

Anti-racist initiatives were also reflected in social work education
and practice. Many social work organisations engaged with what
was known at the time as Race Awareness Training (RAT) for their

staff. This was intended to educate white staff about the nature of multiculturalism in society and to challenge conscious and unconscious racist beliefs and attitudes. This training received mixed responses and was sometimes referred to tokenistically as 'steel band saris and samosas'.

> by focusing on the superficial manifestations of culture, multiculturalism failed to address the continuing hierarchies of power and legitimacy that existed among different centres of cultural authority.
>
> (Donald and Rattansi, 1992)

Such approaches were criticised for focusing upon individual workers' personal prejudices, attitudes and beliefs rather than on the institutional practices and structural inequality that led to differential treatment for BME communities.

Some organisations took on a more radical approach to addressing racism within service delivery and RAT training with Anti-Racist Training (ART), which was intended to go beyond consciousness-raising. Instead it attempted to identify ways of working and engaging with BME communities and service users to address specific areas of inclusion and exclusion. The response for some black communities to the lack or denial of appropriate services was via self-help with the organisation and provision of their own services. The growth of the black voluntary and community sector was particularly evident in the area of mental heath and childcare. Though voluntary organisations have often struggled to maintain their independence and funding, organisations such as the Muslim Women's Helpline (www.mwhl.org) reflect the awareness of needs within black communities as well as understanding of the processes of discrimination (Chouhan and Lusane 2004).

The appointment of black staff under Section 11 of the 1966 Local Government Act to work specifically with BME communities was common not only in social work but in other areas of the welfare state. Gilroy (1997) suggests that black workers' position in state institutions leads to contradictions in terms of both class and race; as a part of a middle-class profession, black workers found themselves performing local state functions with the poor and powerless. The stress of managing competing and contradictory identities resulted in black social workers espousing 'a black cultural nationalism' particularly in relation to the placement needs of black children (Gilroy, 1997). The demand for same race placements, whereby black children would be placed only with black carers as opposed to being trans-racially placed in foster or adoptive families was seen as an understandable response to poor practice within childcare. However, this was criticised by Gilroy for being misplaced, as the black community was too small and fragmented to respond in that way.

The assumption that the inclusion of more black people in positions of power would lead to an end to racism within social work fails to consider the role of organisational structures and systems in maintaining the status quo and therefore in perpetuating systems of discrimination. Anti-racist initiatives targeted social work education as well as service delivery. The Central Council for the Education and Training of Social Work (CCETSW) implemented an anti-racist policy, a Black Perspectives Committee and a steering group, which looked at specific ways of educating students and qualified practitioners re anti-racist practice. The Diploma in Social Work (DIPSW), which was introduced in 1991, required qualifying students to specifically demonstrate knowledge of race and racism and evidence of their ability to combat racism in their practice (The Rules and Requirements for the Diploma in Social Work, 1991). The promotion of anti-discriminatory practice was seen as a key part of social practice, but race and racism was the only specific form of discrimination identified, representing a victory for the anti-racist campaign within social work. It may be viewed that the current GSCC's Code of Conduct, which states that social care workers must not discriminate against service users, is a watering down of social work's commitment to actively combating racism (GSCC, 2002).

Social work has been accused of racist practices in pathologising black culture, lifestyles and practises. Stereotyping of Asian households constructed notions of family life based upon the control and oppression of women and children, whereas African Caribbean families were regarded as fatherless, punitive and lacking warmth. Owusu-Bempah (1993) suggests that the differentiation between Asian and African Caribbean families could be construed as an attempt to respond to cultural difference, though it could also reflect the dominant discourses regarding race and ethnicity within social work.

Social control within social work could be seen in relation to mental health provision, in which specific experiences of black people within mental health and psychiatry led to accusations of insensitive and racist practice by social workers and other professionals.

> The pathologisation of the black community, and of cultural differences in particular, is taken a step further by the racialisation of schizophrenia that British psychiatry has achieved in its institutional practice. This only leads to psychiatry being used, once again, as a powerful medium for articulating ideas about race rather than about mental illness.
>
> (Sashidharan, 1989: 15)

Internalised oppression self-hatred or self-loathing, turning on one's self the negative attitudes of the oppressor.

◄ The concept of *internalised oppression* (Fanon, 1952) is a useful one in understanding some of the impact on black service users of racism and domination within social work and society. Internalised oppression refers to ways in which oppressed groups through processes of domination and learning accept and articulate some of the values and attitudes of the oppressor. Internalised oppression can be expressed (consciously or unconsciously) in a number of ways and can include hatred, self-loathing and wishing to be white. The personal impact of this is brought home powerfully by the 'Black and In Care' video, which includes footage of black children scrubbing themselves with bleach to rid themselves of their black skin. Skin-lightening creams have been on sale in Western countries since the 1950s. Rather than seeing this as a part of black pathology, it should be understood as a normal aspect of how people may respond to processes of oppression and discrimination (Lipsky, 1987). Freire (1972) discusses how oppressed groups need to unlearn the dominant ideologies in order to achieve liberation.

> Only as they discover themselves to be 'hosts' to the oppressor can they contribute to the midwifery of their liberating pedagogy. As long as they live in the duality where to be is to be like, and to be like is to be like the oppressor, this contribution is impossible.

What was emerging in social work was practice in which BME service users found themselves over-represented in the more controlling aspects of welfare such as child protection, school exclusions and in the compulsory use of mental health legislation, and under-represented in the more supportive, non-compulsory aspects of welfare such as family support, family therapy and counselling (Dominelli, 1998).

Race and adoption practice

In the late 1990s social work witnessed a backlash from politicians and other commentators (particularly in the media) against anti-racist and other equality initiatives in social work. Social work, through a number of high profile cases, usually involving the placement for adoption and fostering of black children, led to accusations of dogmatism and putting political correctness before the needs of children. In a case which attracted massive media attention, Norfolk Social Services removed a black child from a white foster family, which drew criticism from Paul Boateng, the Home Office Minister at the time.

> It is unacceptable for a child to be deprived of loving parents solely on the grounds that the child and adoptive parents do not share the same racial and cultural background. We must not let dogma get in the way. We have to put children first.
>
> (BBC interview, 18 November 1998)

In a different case, concerning inter-country adoption, the government and the courts took a rather different view. The case of a white couple, Alan and Judith Kilshaw (Guardian, 9 April 2001) led to their notoriety after they bought black American twin girls for £8000. The girls were subsequently removed by social workers and returned by the courts to the USA.

Sociological understandings concerning race and ethnicity provide a framework for analysing discourses that exist within social work practice, yet the complexities and contradictions involved in providing social work are highlighted through the example of child placement. A study by the National Children's Home (2004) summarises some of the issues concerning the recruitment of BME adoptive families and highlighted a number of practice issues, including a shortage of all minority ethnic adopters and in particular, a need for black, black mixed-parentage and mixed-relationship adopters. The impact of racism, though, has affected people's willingness to approach agencies.

While minority ethnic children comprise 18 per cent of all the children looked after in the UK and 22 per cent of children on the National Adoption Register, they represent only 13 per cent of those adopted. Some minority ethnic groups have very young age structures. There may be few minority ethnic adults living in the community and thus a very limited pool of potential adopters. There is a need for agencies to understand the demographics of their areas. The report suggests that social workers need to give greater consideration to how adopters would help a child understand their heritage, culture and form a positive sense of self and asks whether a black or a white family is a perfect match for a black mixed-parentage child. Minority ethnic communities tend to be characterised by large family sizes, poverty, poor housing and myths and stereotypes around adoption are still prevalent in minority ethnic communities, despite all the advertising and publicity. The recruitment of more minority ethnic social work staff is a factor in gaining more applicants from BME communities (NCH 2004 – www.nch.org.uk).

There are far-reaching benefits for children from making concerted efforts to recruit more black adoptive families. (Kevin Russ)

Case study

'Same race' placements

Joel is a healthy five-year-old of mixed Irish and African background. Joel had a difficult start to life, experiencing physical abuse and neglect. Joel is an active boy who enjoys all sports. He needs to build his trust with adults and benefits from having clear behavioural boundaries. Joel needs one or two parents, preferably with no other children or with children much older than him.

- As a social worker what sort of family do you consider suitable for Joel?
- List the advantages and disadvantages of 'same race' and trans racial placements.
- Does it matter if the prospective carers are black or white and wish to adopt from a different ethnic background? What others factors affect 'matching' such as class and background?
- How can sociological theories regarding 'essentialism' and race and ethnicity inform adoption practice?

Social work with asylum seekers

While we have seen the nature of racism change during the past fifty years, Sivanandan (2001) discusses a new type of racism. This takes a different form from other forms of racism, in that rather than being based on skin colour, racism originates from being identified formally or informally as an asylum seeker. As in any discourse the language associated within this *new racism* is significant. People who fled Nazi Germany during and after the Second World War and Idi Amin's Uganda in the 1970s were described as refugees, affording people the status of having to seek refuge. Contemporary discourses use the term asylum seekers, which could indicate that they are genuine or fake or more commonly asylum seekers may be described as 'real or bogus'. The majority of people seeking refuge in 2001 (Refugee Council) came from Iraq, Zimbabwe, Afghanistan and Somalia, areas which have witnessed brutal wars and oppressive regimes, which seems to have little relationship to the anti-immigration argument. The very nature of this form of racism has been successfully deployed by the British National Party, who gained a number of seats in the local elections of May 2006.

In spite of demands for social workers to refuse to engage in what has sometimes been described as racist asylum policies and practices (Community Care 2004) social workers (particularly in the area of work with children) increasingly find themselves involved in work with refugees and asylum seekers. Debates concerning asylum have become a significant feature of discourses regarding race, ethnicity and nationality in Britain and Europe in the 1990s and early twenty-first century. Social workers have unwittingly found themselves working with and against the state in order to meet the needs of families and individuals who are seeking a place of safety.

The relationship between social work and asylum is an uncomfortable one and one which produces tensions and dilemmas within its own ranks. Social workers may find themselves working with unaccompanied children in need and disabled people who require assessments under community care legislation or people who present with the effects of trauma and mental distress. Workers often feel unprepared for such work with little attention being paid to the issues faced by asylum seekers on qualifying and post-qualifying programmes of education. Beth Humphries discusses the implications for contemporary social work with its emphasis on regulation and identification and assessment to resist calls to collude with oppressive and dehumanising immigration controls.

> Talks of anti-racist and anti-oppressive practice in social work are a nonsense, a self-deception and a hypocrisy. White social workers continue to accept without a murmur of protest their allocated role in the hounding and harassment and the impoverishment of some of the most vulnerable people in the planet.
>
> (Humphries, 2004: 39)

While these may appear harsh words, which may also implicate black and other minority workers, such accusations are not new for social workers, whose humanist values appear to be at odds with the care and control functions they perform on behalf of the local and national state. The dichotomous role of social work is apparent in areas such as asylum, mental health and child protection and social work has struggled to engage in anti-oppressive practices in what appear to be oppressive situations.

Risk, race and child protection

Discourses concerning child protection with BME families in Britain have concentrated on a number of issues, including the possible over-representation of black children in care populations. Professionals have been accused of misunderstanding and having stereotypical views of practices concerning BME families, resulting in an apparent failure of the child protection system to prevent and protect BME children from harm.

Questions as to whether BME children are over-represented in the public care system are difficult to assess, as there is a paucity of research in this area and there are no general statistics about how many BME families are referred to Social Services Departments in any year. The few studies that exist (Brandon et al., 1999; Thorburn 1995) tend to be quite small (looking at two or three local authorities). However, what is indicated is that BME families tend to be referred to SSD for different reasons than white families. In March 2002,

17–18 per cent of families on the Child Protection Register were from BME backgrounds.

The death of Victoria Climbié and the subsequent inquiry has been one of the defining features of British childcare practice in recent years, and followed a number of controversial child deaths concerning BME children in the 1980s (Jasmine Beckford, Kimberly Carlisle). While Lord Laming never accused the local authority of racist practice, the fact that Victoria was an African child had a racialising impact on the case and Part 5 of the Report addresses issues of working with diversity (2003).

Victoria's counsel suggested that

> Race can affect the way people conduct themselves in other ways. Fear of being accused of racism can stop people acting when otherwise they would. Fear of being thought unsympathetic to someone of the same race can change responses.

(Part Five Paragraph 16.7)

The report stressed that, while cultural factors must be considered, the overall objective is one of child safety and that Victoria should have been treated as a child like any other child and her needs and rights should have been recognised.

Exercise

> There is some evidence to suggest that one of the consequences of an exclusive focus on 'culture' in work with black children and families is [that] it leaves black and ethnic minority children in potentially dangerous situations, because the assessment has failed to address a child's fundamental care and protection needs.
>
> (Race Equality Unit, part 5, paragraph 16)

Lord Laming states:

> Several times during this Inquiry I found myself wondering whether a failure by a particular professional to take action to protect Victoria may have been partly due to that professional losing sight of the fact that her needs were the same as those of any other seven-year-old girl, from whatever cultural background.
>
> (part 5, paragraph 16.2)

The above quotes from the Laming Report indicate that, while the professionals involved were not accused of racist practice, professional ideologies regarding the construction of Victoria as a black African child permeated the case.

- How may attitudes and assumptions regarding race and culture affect professional responses in such situations?

Chand and Keay (2003) examined some of the research concerning BME families and suggested some ways of improving practice. These include monitoring referral rates to SSD based upon ethnic composition, challenging practices which suggest control measures rather than supportive ones as fewer BME tend to be referred to child guidance units. There is also a need to challenge myths, stereotypes and workers' values and work in partnership with voluntary organisations, which may have a more successful history in working with BME families. Social workers have to recognise and balance the fears of being accused of over-intervention in black families with the risks of failing to protect children from abuse and harm.

Conclusion

The majority of social workers enter the profession with the intention of enabling service users to improve the quality of their lives. Yet the effects of racial and ethnic categorisation has resulted in a social work profession which has struggled to find effective ways of working to address the inequality experienced by many black and ethnic minority communities. While some minority ethnic communities have responded through the provision of their own services and forms of support, such provision is uncertain and it is only through a consistent commitment to understand and challenge the systems that perpetuate individual and organisational forms of discrimination that racial discrimination and oppression will be eradicated. The understanding and application of sociological theories regarding race and ethnicity allows social workers to understand the shifting nature of racism within society and provides a framework in which to provide a challenge to professional and institutional practices which marginalise the shifting population of minority ethnic groups.

Summary points

- While race and ethnicity are social constructs, the effects of categorisation for black and ethnic minority communities are real.
- Constructions regarding race are complex and extend beyond a simple black/white dichotomy.
- Changing sociological perspectives in understanding racial and ethnic categorisations help to understand the emergence of 'new ethnicities' and multiple identities.
- Sociological theories can enable social workers to understand the differential experiences of some BME communities within social work practice.

Questions for discussion

- Explain why sociologists prefer to use the term 'ethnicity' as opposed to 'race' to refer to people's experiences.

- What evidence is there to suggest that institutions like the police or social services are institutionally racist?
- How can social workers challenge racist practice?
- How can sociological explanations enable you to understand discourses concerning asylum and immigration?

Further reading

Despite the significance of race and ethnic categorisation there are few accessible texts within sociology and particularly within social work which focus exclusively on understanding race and ethnicity and which discuss the implications for practice.

Back, L. and Solomos, J., eds (2008) *Theories of Race and Racism: A Reader*. 2nd edn. London: Routledge. This is a useful reader for students as it brings together comprehensive discussion of articles regarding the sociology of race.

Dominelli, L. (1997) *Anti-Racist Social Work. British Association of Social Workers (BASW) Practical Social Work*

Though over ten years old this book is one of the few to provide an examination of how social work can perpetuate racial inequality and offers constructive ideas to develop anti-racist practice.

Donald, J. and Rattansi, A. (1992) *Race, Culture and Difference*. London: Routledge. A collection of essays from major writers on the subjects of race and ethnicity, using contemporary sociological theory to examine formulations of race and difference.

Parekh, Bhikhu (2000) *The Future of Multi-Ethnic Britain*. London: Profile Books.

7

Sexuality

Talking about sex is still something that makes some professionals uncomfortable. Yet, sexuality and sexual expression can often be an issue for user and carer groups with whom social workers engage (Hicks, 2005; Green, 2005). The difficulties for professionals in discussing sexuality reflect wider attitudes in society about sexuality, sexual activity and sexual orientation. It is interesting to note that it is only more recently that general sociological texts have incorporated a specific section on the sociology of sexuality. Giddens (2006) argued that one of the reasons we study sociology is so we can be 'enlightened' about issues such as difference and diversity. This is certainly important when we look at notions of 'normal' and 'abnormal' in relation to sexuality. This chapter will explore how the study of sexuality has developed and more recently how critical sociological perspectives have developed. A post-modern critique has challenged the notion that sexuality is fixed (Wilton, 2000; Weeks, 2003).

The key issues that will be explored in this chapter are:

- Definitions of sexuality and historical perspectives on sexuality.
- Classical sociological theories; how did the founding fathers view sexuality?
- Social constructionism and deviant sexualities; the development of critical perspectives on sociology and sexuality.
- Contemporary perspectives and debates; e.g. the lesbian and gay movement and the impact of homophobia.
- Sexuality and the social work role; the impact of social disadvantage, power and risk on working with a range of sexual issues with service users and carers.

By the end of this chapter you should be able to:

- Explain what is meant by the terms sex, sexuality and sexual orientation.
- Discuss the ways that deviant sexual identities are constructed in societies.
- Explain the relationship between oppression, social control and sexual identities.
- Explain the impact of homophobia on the experiences of lesbian and gay people.
- Demonstrate an understanding of the role of the lesbian and gay movement in promoting diversity.
- Explain the role of social workers in working with issues of sexuality and sexual identity with a range of service users.

Defining sexuality

Many writers discuss how talking about sex is a highly sensitive and taboo area (e.g. Jackson and Rahman, 1997). This perhaps explains why health and social care professionals may find it difficult to discuss sex with their patients/service users. It is also inevitably affected by what we think about sex ourselves. Is it possible to define sexuality? Hogan (1980: 1299) defines sexuality as 'a quality of being human, all that we are, encompassing the most intimate feelings and deepest longings of the heart to find meaningful relationships'. This quote illustrates how difficult it is to define sexuality, as definitions are inherently subjective and shaped by our own values and opinions. In this quote, sex is clearly linked to expressing emotions and feelings, although other definitions stress the physical act. In many cultures, for example, sexual activity has been linked to reproduction. A singular definition of sexuality would imply that there is one common sexual identity, but sexual expression and activity is variable and the way that sexuality is expressed is affected by the cultural and social norms of a given period. Herdt (1981) argues that what constitutes a sexual act cannot be defined without looking at cultural and social norms, a view shared by the majority of contemporary sociologists (e.g. Giddens, 2006).

As sexual behaviour began to be more carefully studied in the nineteenth century, beliefs around 'normal' and 'abnormal' sexual behaviour began to develop. For Foucault (1979a) this stemmed from sexuality being classified and defined as part of a 'discourse of sexuality'. This has heavily influenced how an individual's sexual preferences, activity and orientation are expressed. His ideas around language and discourse shaping how sexuality is viewed are important when we think about helping professionals to talk about sex to service users and carers. How are our interactions shaped by what is perceived as 'normal' sexuality? For example, do we see disabled people engaging in sexual activity as abnormal? How do we think professional power shapes such situations? What is clear is that communicating about and discussing sexual issues is often difficult.

Discussion points

- What is your immediate reaction to talking about sexuality and sexual issues?
- How do you think this would affect your interactions with service users and carers?
- Do you think as a professional you have power and control in discussing sexual matters with service users?

The medicalisation of sexuality

Throughout history, people have been required to conform to certain patterns of sexual behaviour and expression. Certain sexual behaviours may be seen as deviant or shocking in one culture and not in another. However, sociologists have argued that in the last two centuries, there have been significant changes to our contemporary view of sexuality in western society. To understand why this has occurred, we need to look at the relationship between science and sexuality.

Foucault (1979a) saw the nineteenth century as the starting-point for *discourses* on sexuality. Prior to this period, sexuality and sexual expression were connected closely with religious morality. Notions of 'normal' and 'abnormal' sexuality had not been clearly defined, as religious beliefs and social order governed sexual behaviour. Weeks (2003) discusses how Christian religions established a conflict between the mind and the body where sex was concerned. Tomlin (2002) in her analysis of Samuel Pepys (a seventeenth-century diarist) points to his puritanical upbringing clashing with the (at the time) permissible sexual pleasures of the newly restored monarchy. While sexual activity existed outside marriage, this tended to be limited to certain groups. For example, some wealthy men engaged in sexual relationships outside marriage, but for the vast majority of the population (and particularly women) sexual expression was part of marriage and reproduction and adultery was a sin, with moral and social consequences. It can therefore be argued that social constructs around sexuality existed during this period.

Sociologists see the rise of science and medicine in the nineteenth century as leading to a debate about normal and abnormal sexual behaviour. In this period, sexual behaviour began to be classified according to a predominantly biological and *medicalised* notion of sexuality. Jackson and Rahman (1997) see classification as leading to labelling according to natural and unnatural sexuality. This had huge social implications in the nineteenth century, and still has implications for contemporary society.

The emphasis on sexuality and biological process is known as *essentialism*. An essentialist perspective sees sexuality as biological, fixed and given. Macionis and Plummer (2005) argue that biological factors historically have taken precedence over social and cultural constructs in theorising sexuality. For Foucault (1979a), the scientific discourse around sexuality led to social control, where science defined sexuality in terms of normal and abnormal sexuality, which then permeated throughout society, leading to cultural and social norms around permissible sexual identity and activity. Foucault's analysis is referred to as 'biopower', the core principle being that the science of sexuality became associated with power and control. In the late nineteenth and early twentieth centuries this had profound implications for certain groups in society.

Discussion points

- In today's society, do you think there are the same ideas about 'normal' and 'abnormal' sexual behaviour?
- Do you think our sexual identity is pre-determined by biology?

Women and essentialism

For women, the medicalisation of sexuality led to a discourse about 'good' and 'bad' sexual behaviour. 'Good' sexual behaviour was related to modesty and chastity, while 'bad' sexual behaviour was seen as provocative and amoral. Because of these definitions, sexuality and gender has become a focus for feminist debate and discussion. For feminist commentators such as Rich (1980) and Shersey (1973) women's natural sexuality was controlled and defined by male scientists. Men were seen as sexually active, whereas women were passive within the sexual process. The sexual function for women was to reproduce and run the family. Sexual violence within marriage was also hidden, with sexual violence often being seen as the result of women being provocative and 'asking for it'. Related to this is that male sexuality is seen as uncontrollable, a view which, it is argued, is still prevalent in how rape cases are processed in contemporary society (Lees, 1993; Brown et al., 1993).

Biological and religious perspectives are both concerned with the control of women's sexuality. Biological factors provide the classification and justification for what is normal and abnormal. Women who were seen as having 'unnatural' sexual desires became the focus of psychological and psychiatric intervention. In the nineteenth and early twentieth centuries, women who were seen as having 'unnatural' sexual desires or men who were seen as deviant because of homosexual identification were the subject of study by sexologists and psychiatrists. The novel by Sebastian Faulks, *Human Traces* (2005), features a number of female characters who are referred for assessment and medical intervention due to 'hysterical' and sexualised behaviour. Nymphomania was the medical term given to women who were seen as having 'unhealthy' sexual desires or fixations. The condition was also seen to affect women's genitals, and in some cases led to clitoridectomies (castration of the clitoris). Goldberg (1999) discusses how women were subjected to a range of treatments to cure abnormal sexual desires. So, here we see a clear link between abnormal sexual behaviour and mental health treatments. White (2002) discusses how gynaecology defined sexual and reproductive problems in a medical framework. In particular, problems in these areas were seen as a result of a rejection of femininity.

Wilton (2000) discusses how both Islamic and Christian fundamentalist religious perspectives impact on women's sexuality and sexual practices. For example, right-wing Christian groups are against abortion and sex outside marriage. Islamic fundamentalists see women's sexuality as related solely to monogamous heterosexual marriage, although in some Islamic cultures men are able to marry several times.

This reflects the dual sexual role of women, as 'madonnas' or 'whores'. Women who stepped outside conventional sexual roles were outcasts, but still 'used' by men. For example, prostitutes operated on the periphery of society, often subject to danger and physical and emotional violence. Women who had illegitimate children found themselves socially disgraced or at worst incarcerated in asylums, reflecting male power and control over sex and sexual relations (Goldberg, 1999). For feminist commentators, such as Jackson and Rahman (1997), sociological debate on sexuality is inextricably linked with gender issues.

Discussion points

- What are your views on how women's sexual behaviour was treated in the nineteenth and early twentieth century?
- Thinking sociologically, do you think women's sexual identity is still 'controlled' by men?

Sexuality and the body

The biological emphasis of sexuality leads to an emphasis on reproduction and connects with issues around the 'sociology of the body'. Turner (1992) argued that the institutions of medicine, law and religion are involved in regulating the body, particularly in relation to birth and death. Thus sanctions can be placed on families in order to control them, e.g. the relationship between the benefit system and the number of children in the family in an attempt to contain population growth in China. Equally, positive rewards can be accrued by families who conform to ideal types through legal, economic and status privileges – e.g. financial benefits for families through the tax system.

Nettleton (2006) discusses the correlation between the control of female sexuality and the control of reproduction and the impact of new reproductive technologies. However, control of reproduction and reproductive capacity is influenced by the cultural and social norms of the time and access to the resources is not equal. Dillon (2004) discusses how the practice of lesbian parents of obtaining sperm from donors has led to calls for restrictions from certain groups (e.g. American right-wing religious organisations). Additionally, lesbian women who have the economic means may be more able to use donor services.

The sociology of the body is therefore important in terms of examining the link between sexuality and reproduction. It also follows that social constructs shape how the body is 'used' in this process. Femininity is constructed around the notion of desirability constructed within patriarchal ideologies, so that women can attract a suitable mate for procreative purposes (see Chapter 5). In terms of healthy bodies, sexual attractiveness and desirability is also closely connected to body image, which is heavily influenced by societal norms. Being overweight, for example, is generally seen as sexually unattractive (although this has not always been the case). Magazines, TV and books are dominated by discussions about how to 'sell' yourself as a sexual product. This commodification is wide ranging in terms of staying young and desirable. The impact of consumer culture on the body and sexuality is therefore highly important (Featherstone, 1991).

Gender and sexuality are closely inter-related. It therefore follows that there will be social and cultural constructs concerning what men in particular are looking for in their 'mate'. For example, how do we think sexual attractiveness is rated if you are an overweight person with mental health problems? How does this affect perceived reproductive potential? If a person is not perceived as sexually desirable or having reproductive capacity, how does this affect the way that sexual behaviour and identity are viewed?

Exercise

Have a look at a health and beauty/lifestyle magazine.

- Make a list of all the types of health and beauty advice that is given in one edition. Bring to your next class and discuss with a colleague.
- How does this connect with the sociology of body and being sexually attractive and able to reproduce?

Essentialism and sexual identity

The development of a science of sexuality is also seen as damaging to those who were not heterosexual, as a binary expression of sexuality was conceptualised within a medical framework. Heterosexuality was conceptualised as normal behaviour, whilst homosexuality was seen as abnormal. However, studies such as those by Kinsey et al. (1948 and 1953) and the work of sexologists such as Havelock Ellis (1946) showed that there is no fixed pattern of sexuality or sexual expression, but sexuality is variable and fluid. Kinsey's study of sexual behaviour in America indicated a wide range of difference in sexual expression (Kinsey, 1948 and 1943). His work was ground-breaking at the time, as it indicated that sex and sexual expression was far from being simply about reproduction, nor was it fixed between a heterosexual and homosexual identity. Sexual expression, however, was often hidden. This reflects the work of contemporary sociologists who have argued that sexual eroticism became taboo in capitalist society (Weeks, 2003).

While not ignoring biological perspectives, the focus of these studies was on how sexual behaviours were expressed and how this impacted upon sexual development. However, to a degree, this led to the development of a biomedical model of sexual orientation. For example, Havelock Ellis discussed homosexuals as 'inverts'. The discourse of this time was therefore concerned with definitions of abnormal and normal behaviour. The language of sex itself can be seen to have led to misconceptions. Havelock Ellis's writings led to other theorists using these perspectives to support medical treatments and cures for sexual orientation, although Wilton (2000) argues that this was not his intention.

In the nineteenth and twentieth centuries, sexologists, psychologists and psychiatrists were concerned with looking at sexual behaviours that were considered outside 'the norm'. Sexual behaviours that were not heterosexual were seen within a 'deviant' framework. One of the most well-known figures is Sigmund Freud. There has been much debate about the writings of Freud and whether he saw homosexuality as arrested development, particularly in relation to the Oedipal complex. However, twentieth-century doctors used his ideas as a method to look at how a child had not developed a heterosexual identity because of problems with parents, leading to a medicalisation of homosexuality. Until 1973, the American Psychiatric Association defined homosexuality as a mental disorder.

It has been argued that Freud's work has been misinterpreted in this area (see for example, Davies and Neal, 1996). However, many of Freud's followers (e.g. Melanie Klein) saw homosexuality as a disturbed form of sexual expression. Psychoanalysis can be seen as partly responsible for labelling lesbians and gay men as deviant, and historically led to interventions based on 'curing' people from homosexuality. More recently, it has been argued that Freud did not see homosexuality as a deviation. Gay and lesbian psychologists such as Isay (1989) have reframed Freud's initial thoughts on

Psychoanalysis the treatment and study of psychological problems and disorders, developed initially by Sigmund Freud.

◄ homosexuality to demonstrate that psychoanalysis can be a positive tool to support people who have issues with a lesbian or gay identity.

However, psychoanalytical ideas informed a medicalised approach to 'forbidden' forms of sexual activity, including homosexuality. Norton (1992) discusses how, pre-eighteenth century, homosexuality was simply seen as not existing in western societies. With a medicalised approach came a political and legal framework with laws against sodomy across Europe. Therefore, if an individual went against the prevailing norm, the punishment was harsh. It is also important to note that anthropological studies have shown that in some cultures, homosexuality was an accepted behaviour (Wilton, 2000).

E. M. Forster in his posthumous novel *Maurice* discusses medical intervention concerning homosexuality and its effect on his principal character in the early twentieth century (Forster, 1971). It is telling that Forster did not feel able to publish this novel while he was alive, because he himself had kept his sexuality hidden. This illustrates that until relatively recently, lesbian and gay identities were kept hidden. Oscar Wilde is an example of someone whose sexual preferences became the subject of public disgrace, leading to a prison sentence at the turn of the twentieth century. Indeed, even in the later part of the twentieth century, public figures and celebrities who were homosexual still struggled with a lesbian and gay identity. The popular entertainer Kenneth Williams records the dilemmas associated with his sexual orientation in his diaries, published posthumously in 1995.

Discussion points

- Do you think that heterosexuality is the cultural norm?
- Can you think of a current celebrity who is lesbian or gay? How did they deal with 'coming out'?
- How might the biomedical model affect social work practice with people who are lesbian or gay?

Issues for social work

There is evidence that lesbians and gay men are over-represented within the mental health system (Tew, 2005). The idea that a lesbian and gay identity is 'abnormal' has led to some people with a same-sex orientation seeking support from mental health services. Lesbians and gay men are also more likely to experience issues with alcohol misuse (Herbert 1994) and Paul (et al., 2006) suggests that lesbians and gay men are more likely to commit suicide or attempt suicide. It is only relatively recently that the biomedical model has been challenged and therapeutic approaches advocated. However, it should not be assumed that changes in how sexual orientation is viewed in contemporary society mean there are no identity issues for lesbians and gay men. Attitudes, culture, values and religion can all impact upon the mental health of lesbians and gay men.

Classical sociological theories and sexuality

Classical sociological theories located sexual roles within a discourse about the family (Foucault, 1979). Men and women had clearly defined sexual roles, related to biological processes of reproduction. Functionalists, such as Talcott Parsons (1951) and Murdock (1949) saw sexual roles as necessary in the socialisation of children and for stable family environments. Gender and sexuality are closely linked, as the function of the family was also a basis for the sexual division of labour between men and women (Haralambos and Holborn, 2004). Wilton (2000) sees the link between sexuality and family as inherent within social policies, which are still relevant today.

Bilton et al. (2002) also point to stable families being needed for capitalism to function. For Marx, sexual relationships provided the basis for the reproduction of the labour force. Engels (1902) developed Marxian perspectives concerning sex and the family. Engels saw society as responsible for regulating sexual behaviour (sexual behaviour was naturally promiscuous). Engels saw the monogamous nuclear family developing as private property and state structures developed. Men needed to protect their property and their inheritance and monogamous marriage provided a clear 'blood' line enabling this transmission of property. Women 'sold' their sexual and reproductive services in order to be provided with material stability. Engels saw communism as providing a solution to women 'selling' themselves, and can be seen to have recognised that gender roles were heavily associated with sexual behaviour. Marxist feminist perspectives further examined the link between gender, sex and family (e.g. Benston, 1972). Gramsci (1971) discusses how industrialists, such as the Ford Company, were concerned with the sexual affairs of their employees in order to have a stable workforce.

The scientific classification of sexuality served to treat as well as reinforce cultural and social norms. From this perspective, sex and sexual activity is socially controlled and has a structural function to enable stable families to contribute towards a stable society (Foucault, 1979).

Discussion points

- Think about a TV programme or a magazine article.
- Do you think sexual relationships are still seen as predominantly taking place within families?
- How does this reflect social norms?

Social constructionism and deviant sexualities

A critical sociology of sexuality has developed which has challenged biological perspectives. While not disputing that biological factors are important, contemporary perspectives would see social and cultural norms as regulating and shaping how sexuality is expressed. Issues of power and control are important here, as there are particular issues for groups who are socially disadvantaged. This makes it important that health and social care professionals engage with sexual issues, as there may well be structural issues that are oppressive and inhibit expression of sexual identity for service users or carers. Our personal values need examination, as social and cultural constructs can be seen to lead to sexual stereotypes. For example, do we see learning disabled people having sexual relationships as 'abnormal'?

Firstly, there are some broad themes that shape social constructionism and sexuality. Expression of sexual identity is connected to the dominant 'discourse of sexuality'. The fact that sexual identity has been closely linked to the family is seen as socially constructed and linked to power and control. Connell (1987 and 1995a and b) discusses the predominance of male-dominated heterosexuality, which he refers to as 'hegemonic masculinity'. At the top of the tree are white, heterosexual men, while at the bottom are lesbian women (subordinated femininities). This relates to the earlier discussion about how gender roles relate to sexual activity. Because men are more powerful, their sexual behaviour is regulated in a different way from women.

Factors such as race, disability and class further shape power relations in sexual relationships. For example, in the early years of the twentieth century, there was a general pre-occupation about over-population and poverty, which can be seen to have informed the development of the *eugenics* movement (see Chapter 6). Wilson (2006) refers to a letter written by the author D. H. Lawrence concerning potential genocide of certain groups in society (a view echoed by other authors and intellectuals of the time) to alleviate this issue. In a given period, sexual behaviour may need to be regulated and controlled for a variety of reasons. Social constructs shape how sexual activity is expressed and this in turn is related to issues of power, control and disadvantage. Weeks (2003) defines a number of ways in which social and historical constructs impact upon sexuality and sexual identity, which can be related to sexual orientation in the following ways:

- Family/kinship – the experiences of 'coming out' to family.
- Economic and social organisation – across the world lesbian and gay people tend to congregate in large urban centres, where they are better able to work and lead their chosen lifestyle. Sometimes, gay ghettoes develop (e.g. Soho/San Francisco), resulting in a perception of 'safety in numbers'.
- Social regulation– it is only recently that legislation has been repealed which disallowed the teaching of lesbian and gay lifestyles within UK schools. Lesbian and gay organisations such as Stonewall have been concerned with changing structural positions towards lesbians and gay people. For example, the recent Civil Partnership Act 2005 (www.opsi.gov.uk/ACTS) is the product of many years campaigning for the rights of lesbian and gay people to marry.
- Political interventions – sometimes, governments intervene to promote the sexual norm. The rise of the new right led to the promotion of a traditional agenda of family and heterosexual marriage. Within institutions, such as the armed forces, there has until recently been politically sanctioned intervention regarding sexual orientation.
- Identity and resistance – lesbian and gay people's identity is shaped by their interaction with the world around them. Adverse reactions, bullying, hate crimes and rejection by families may affect the psychosocial development of lesbians and gay men. Goffman (1961) identified the importance of stigma and labelling on health and wellbeing (Chapter 11).

If we accept that society regulates our behaviour, then we begin to see the problems that arise when our identity does not 'fit'. This identity crisis for lesbians and gay men has become known as *internalised homophobia*, which may manifest in institutions as *institutionalised homophobia*.

Internalised homophobia homosexual men or women may self-loathe or self-hate, due to sexual identity.

Homophobia

Homophobia can be defined as a fear or aversion to lesbians and gay men. As sociological thinking on sexuality has developed, so has the debate on the impact of internalised homophobia. The way that our sexuality can be perceived as regulated can have a powerful and detrimental effect on lesbians and gay men. There are many studies and articles detailing the impact of homophobia upon the development of a lesbian and gay identity (e.g. Wilton, 2000; Brown, 1998). Comstock's (1991) study showed that violence towards gay men, in particular, was seen as more socially acceptable than violence towards other groups. It is particularly interesting that violent homophobic attitudes appear in institutions where hegemonic masculinity is at its most dominant.

There is a clear connection between internalised and institutional homophobia. For example, the media has both reinforced and challenged homophobia. The recent film *Brokeback Mountain* was portrayed widely in the media as ground-breaking in detailing a love story between two gay cowboys. Both male stars in the film were seen as taking a career risk in playing homosexual characters. Therefore, while Hollywood was dealing with the impact of institutional homophobia, there appears to be a risk for actors in portraying gay characters or in being openly gay.

Exercise

- Look at the following list of societal structures
    political organisations e.g. MPs
    security organisations e.g. army/police
    religious organisations e.g. parish priest
    media organisations e.g. TV actor
- Thinking about internalised and institutional homophobia, how might this affect lesbians and gay men within these structures?
- Can you think of a recent case or example where this has been highlighted?

There is evidence to suggest that health and social care professionals generally are influenced by cultural norms and beliefs in relation to homosexuality. The NHS has recognised this in the recent production of training standards for staff on sexual orientation (Cree and O Corra, 2006). This report discusses research showing how homophobic attitudes have affected how lesbians, gay men, bisexual and transgender people have been treated in the NHS. Recent research is quoted to show that a third of gay men, a quarter of bisexual men and 40 per cent of lesbian women experience a negative response from mental health professionals on disclosing their sexual identity (King and McKeown, 2003).

Homophobia is also evident within social services and social work. Hicks (2005) draws attention to the fact that homophobic attitudes have often been addressed within the generic framework of anti discriminatory practice, although this is insufficient. Brown (1998) has looked at how a lesbian and gay identity has been perceived within social work theory, whilst Price (1997) looks at how lesbian and gay issues are not appropriately addressed in social work education. There is also a range of research looking at homophobic attitudes within particular service user and carer groups (Manthorpe, 2003; Hicks, 2006; Green, 2005).

Discussion points

How do you think homophobic attitudes might relate to social work practice with the following:

- carers of older people?
- lesbian and gay adopters/foster carers?
- young people in care?
- people with mental health problems?

Generally, lesbians and gay men have begun to challenge homophobic attitudes within society. This has been in response to both the development of a lesbian and gay movement, but also because of the impact of HIV/AIDS on lesbian and gay communities.

Discussion points

Without looking at the next section, what other groups in current British society might be affected by social and cultural constructs in relation to sexuality?

Sexuality and older people

There are social and cultural taboos around sexual activity and older people. Older people are often seen as asexual, devoid of sexual feelings and needs.

> Sexuality in old age is a subject which is enveloped with secrecy and half-knowledge and referred to in society in general with embarrassment and by joking allusions, that is if it is not dismissed altogether, the old so patently being 'past it'.

> (Pickard, 1995: 268)

Older women may be particularly disadvantaged here, as we live in a society that constructs images around the symbolic value of the body.

Women who are past the age of reproductive ability are seen as past it, and therefore their sexuality may not be acknowledged by society. Men are able to father children throughout the adult life course, although motility of the sperm and erectile performance may diminish this capacity. Therefore, there is less evidence of men being viewed as asexual, although there is social pressure not to acknowledge this. Older men who are open about sexual activity may be viewed as dirty old men, with social sanctions placed on them to conform to dominant ideals. Television programmes, literature and other forms of popular culture often perpetuate the negative image of older people as sexually inactive beings.

Exercise

- Next time you are in a card shop, look at the birthday cards aimed at older people.
- How many of them depict pejorative images of older people's capacity for sexual activity or for having a sexually attractive body?

Older people may be further disadvantaged in achieving a fulfilling sexual and or emotionally intimate relationship through bereavement of a partner. The opportunities for meeting new partners may be limited, due to societal taboos and a focus on youth in the field of dating. The consequences of the social image of asexuality in old age can have far-reaching consequences. If physical changes are impacting on sexual ability, older people may feel embarrassed to seek help, thus being denied the possibility of a fulfilling physical relationship. Although physical changes in later life may make it necessary to make adjustments in order to participate in sexual intercourse, a loving and intimate relationship can be a positive experience and any difficulties can be faced together within the context of a mature and trusting relationship.

Case study

On 20 September 2006, BBC news reported that a 95-year-old man had been arrested for kerb-crawling. In view of his age, police let him off with a reprimand (http://news.bbc.co.uk/1/hi/england/dorset/5366354.stm, accessed 21 September 2006).

- Do you think that it is right that he should be treated any differently to any other man because of his age?
- Sociologically, what does this suggest about views/beliefs about older people's sexual capacity?
- Why do you think that this might have been deemed newsworthy?

Understanding the sexual needs of older people is essential to assessment and person-centred care. There are research and anecdotal examples of older people in acute care and long-term care sectors being denied the possibility of an intimate relationship, either within an existing relationship or through the development of a new relationship (Roach, 2004). An understanding of the importance of sexuality and intimate relationships can help social workers and care managers to address this.

Social workers also need to be aware that there is an even greater taboo around lesbian and gay older people. Manthorpe (2003) discusses how lesbian carers are more likely to have problems accessing services. Quam (1997) discusses a case example of a lesbian couple whose relatives sought to separate them at a time of illness. This highlights the need for social work to be sensitive to family and sexuality issues in work with lesbian and gay older people.

Sexuality and disability

Notions of deviancy and abnormality have been applied to disabled people developing a sexual identity. As with older people, disabled people are often seen as asexual. Bonnie (2004) points to how disabled teenagers and adults can often be dressed in babyish or androgynous clothing. Alternatively, disabled people can be seen as sexually threatening. At the beginning of the twentieth century, one of the primary reasons for an asylum model of care for people with learning disabilities was to control sexual relationships between people with learning disabilities (Race, 2002). Social and cultural constructs also manifest themselves in a fear of abnormality in relation to disability (Barnes, 1991). Field (1993) describes the dual oppression of being disabled and a lesbian. These can be extended to stereotypes around disability and sexual activity, which may be perpetuated by portrayals of disabled people as asexual in popular culture.

> many people assume we are asexual, often in order to hide embarrassment about the seemingly incongruous idea that such 'abnormal' people can have 'normal' feelings and relationships
>
> (Morris, 2004:80)

There are also particular issues related to women with disabilities and reproduction. Bonnie (2004) discusses how historically disabled people have been sterilised (particularly women) and access to sexual health and contraceptive advice may be hampered by the inability of family to see disabled children/teenagers as sexual beings. However, as a recent report has shown, parents with a learning disability are more likely to have their children taken into care and not to have had access to a range of support services (Baring Report). Sheldon (2004) highlights the debate about prenatal screening and foetal abnormalities. From a feminist perspective, this is giving women control of their bodies and a choice about abortion, but for disabled writers prenatal screening can be seen as a new form of eugenics. There are therefore particular issues about disabled women's sexuality both in terms of attitudes towards reproduction and concerning parenting support.

Nettleton (2006) discusses the impact of chronic health conditions on the development and maintenance of sexual relationships. Again, professionals are seen as poor in discussing the impact of health problems on sexual relationships. For example, Multiple Sclerosis may lead to erectile problems for men and the use of catheters can affect sex for both men and women.

Williams (2006) highlights the need to support people with learning disabilities concerning sexual relationships and sexual identity, which is often hampered by professional attitudes towards discussion of sexual issues with people with learning disability (Grant et al., 2005). Sexual identity and disability appears to be something generally that professionals struggle with, and appears to be the legacy of asylum care and a denial about the sexual needs and feelings of learning disabled people. Shakespeare et al. (1996) relate this to societal attitudes towards the body and the fear of disability. Social workers need to be aware of stereotypes in their work with disabled people. For example, Lipton (2004) discusses the impact of chronic illness on lesbians and gay men. Social workers need to be aware of how 'layers' of oppression may interact with service users where sexual identity and disability may be inter-related.

Sexuality, children and young people

Issues of sexual identity are particularly relevant to social work with children and young people. Sexual development in children and young people is a complex area. Robinson (2005) discusses how assumptions are made about the sexual identity of children and young people, and this can particularly be the case where sexual orientation is concerned. Green (2005) examines the importance of gender in responding to issues about sexuality and sexual abuse within residential childcare services. In addition, professionals need to be sensitive concerning issues of sexual orientation for looked-after children (Thomas, 2005). Social workers need to be particularly sensitive to how an emerging sexual identity can be compromised by abuse and exploitation, which can often be a particular issue for looked after children. Children may also need empowering to deal with sexual issues (Green, 2005).

Sexual identity can affect children and young people in their interaction with peers. A number of studies have explored the impact of homophobia on bullying in schools (Rivers, 1995) and links have been made between developing sexual orientation and bullying. Stonewall, for example, found that in a survey of 300 secondary schools, 82 per cent of teachers were aware of pupils who had experienced verbal homophobic bullying and 26 per cent of teachers were aware of physical incidents of homophobic bullying (Citizenship 21/Stonewall, 2001). Stonewall also points out that homophobic bullying can lead to truancy and self-harm. There is evidence to suggest that homophobic bullying and problems within families can lead to young people entering care. The Albert Kennedy Trust in Manchester was formed in 1990 following the death of a 16-year-old teenager who had run away from a children's home and was fleeing homophobic attackers. It specifically exists to counter homophobic attitudes and address issues such as addiction, homelessness and mental health problems that lesbian and gay men may experience. The trust works closely with social services to protect young people who are at risk. Its website details some moving testimonials of young people that the organisation has placed in safe supportive environments because of bullying and harassment.

Exercise

- Have a look at the Albert Kennedy Trust website – **www.akt.org.uk**
- How would you support young people in this position?

Offering support can be vital to positive practice. Trotter (2000) sees social workers as being in a good position to help young people with issues of sexual identity. Social workers can give support, avoid pathologising 'deviant' behaviour and offer an accepting and affirming approach to the sexual development of children and young people.

Moral panics and sexual activity

Moral panics can act as a great lever for changes in societal attitudes, as well as leading to repressive measures by political and social organisations in society. For example, asylum care for people with learning disabilities arose from a moral panic about poverty and over-population. There was a concern that people with learning disabilities would affect genetics and reproduction at this time (Race, 2002). This can be seen as a response to a concern about sexual activity, class and population and resulted in repressive measures.

Weeks (2003) discusses moral panics as 'flurries of social anxiety' (p. 101) that arise when groups challenge the general social values and norms. He further discusses how they usually occur when the boundaries of 'normal' behaviour are loose and flexible. AIDS/HIV occurred at a time when changes in attitudes towards lesbians and gay people were evident by the early 1980s. Homosexuality had been de-criminalised and lesbians and gay men had become more visible. However, the identification of AIDS/HIV was seen as a punishment or curse for the sexually promiscuous behaviour of gay men. This connects to Goffman's work around stigma, where some conditions can have negative moral attributes. This can lead to active discrimination against those with the particular condition (Scambler, 1997).

Certainly, at this time, there was a very hostile reaction to gay men, which was given impetus by the outbreak of HIV/AIDS in the early 1980s. Religious and moral groups talked about a 'gay plague' and this approach reinforced the attitude that homosexuality was abnormal and deviant. A moral panic can be seen to have resulted from fears that the spread of HIV/AIDS was going to become endemic. In terms of the media in general, reactions were mixed. Some celebrities and political figures were supportive of the needs of people with HIV/AIDS. Ultimately, the 'moral panic' led to some changes in approaches and attitudes towards people with HIV/AIDS. Thus HIV/AIDS was an important issue for social work practice and also was important in galvanising the lesbian and gay movement.

Many social work departments received specific funding in the 1980s for work with people with HIV/AIDS. Social services staff needed particular training in this area and there continue to be specific posts in this area in many local authorities. It is also important to recognise that HIV/AIDS is an issue for social work practice with a range of user and carer groups and cultures. For example, Joseph (2005) discusses issues around HIV/AIDS in work with men in India.

Discussion points

- How might HIV/AIDS have reinforced homophobic attitudes?
- How might social constructs affect social work practice with people who have HIV/AIDS.

The emergence of the lesbian and gay movement

The social constructs concerning sexuality have been increasingly challenged in the last thirty years, particularly in relation to 'deviant' or 'abnormal' sexualities. In the late 1960s, homosexuality was de-criminalised and a few years later homosexuality was officially de-classified as a mental disorder. These changes were reflected within wider societal shifts connected with gender roles, sexual identity and behaviour. Lesbians and gay men began to develop a more visible and collective identity. The attack by police on the Stonewall Bar in New York in 1969 saw a fight back at police brutality. One of the key civil rights organisations for lesbians and gay men in the UK, Stonewall, is named after this incident. Lesbians were also organising themselves politically as part of the feminist movement, separately from gay men. Gay pride marches and lesbian and gay organisations developed throughout the 1970s and 1980s.

This picture demonstrates the open expression of homosexual identity. Rainbow colours may be worn as a symbol of gay pride. (Eric Hood)

This political mobilisation of lesbians and gay men can be seen as a resistance to sexual regulation and classification. Weeks (2003) talks about 'cultures of resistance' taking place throughout history in response to moral codes and regulations. Political and social movements, such as the lesbian and gay movement, are part of the campaign to recognise a more pluralist society and challenge the fixed and biological perceptions of sexuality.

This challenge certainly led to social anxiety in the 1980s. There was a re-assertion of heterosexual 'family' values by political, social and religious institutions. For example, the Conservative administration introduced legislation prohibiting the promotion of same-sex relationships and lifestyles within education. Margaret Thatcher, Prime Minister at this time, disputed homosexual rights in a conference speech. There was a wider concern about sexual activity and behaviour that has led to ongoing contemporary debate about sexuality generally. However, the lesbian and gay movement has led to significant political, social and economic changes:

- Legislation concerning teaching about same-sex relationships in schools has been repealed.
- Many state institutions have changed working practices towards people with same-sex orientation (e.g. the army).
- The Civil Partnership Act 2005 entitled same-sex couples to legal and property rights.
- The age of consent for same-sex relationships has been lowered.

The above reflects how the lesbian and gay movements have campaigned for citizenship rights, which can be seen to challenge social exclusion and disadvantage (Richardson, 1998).

Academically, there have been challenges to structuralist and medicalised perspectives on sexual orientation. Queer theory rejects fixed identities of sexuality and offers new perspectives on sex and gender (e.g. Butler, 1990; Warner, 1993). Jackson and Rahman (1997) see queer studies as deconstructing the relationship between sex, gender and desire. Therefore, rather than a fixed (and heterosexual) notion of sexual identity, sexuality is fluid and diverse. However, this is seen as being expressed within minority groups, and has not changed a majority heterosexual culture. Wilton (2000) also discusses how some sections of the lesbian and gay community see essentialist perspectives as valuable, particularly in relation to the search for the 'gay gene' as a basis for equality.

It is also important to relate the lesbian and gay movement to social disadvantage, class and social exclusion. The movement has campaigned for citizenship rights and there have been significant changes for many lesbians and gay men. However, social workers often work with those people who have been marginalised and excluded. It is therefore important that you are aware of your own values and attitudes in relation to sexuality and the support services available.

Discussion points

- Before reading this section, were you aware of any lesbian and gay organisations?
- Make a note here of what you need to research.
- Do you think that society has more positive attitudes to lesbians and gay men?
- What is your evidence for this view?

Risk and empowerment

We cannot assume that because of being 'signed up' to social work values and ethics, social workers are aware of issues of sexuality and sexual orientation. Studies highlight a range of attitudes towards working with sexual issues in different user and carer groups. Service users and carers may also have issues about sexual development and identity due to poor relationship experiences, abuse, physical or mental health problems or exploitation. The concluding section examines empowering practice in social work in relation to sexuality.

It would appear that a variety of user and carer groups find it difficult to talk about sexual issues with professionals. For example, in mental health services, some lesbians and gay men do not disclose their sexual orientation to health providers for fear of being stigmatised (Harris Interactive, 2002). Other mental health studies have echoed this view (Golding, 1997). This may be a particular issue for people who are socially disadvantaged, as Davis (1994) notes that lesbians and gay men are more likely to seek support from the private sector with mental health issues. Income may therefore be an important factor in terms of accessing support.

Social constructs about deviant and abnormal sexualities also influence how we view sexual issues with older people and people with disabilities. It is therefore essential that social workers engage with issues described in this chapter and training and input from users and carers is an important issue here. For example, people with learning disabilities have been involved in some degree programmes (Race, 2002) and more generally, Hicks (2005) talks about a more explicit discussion about sexuality within the overarching framework of anti-oppressive practice.

Discussion points

- What do you think your training needs are in relation to sexual issues and social work practice?
- How might these be addressed?

Empowering social work practice is concerned with supporting people who are marginalised and excluded and sexual identity or sexual issues can contribute to social exclusion. As a social worker, you can support users and carers by your approach but also by your knowledge base. For example, Manthorpe (2003) highlights the issues lesbian carers may have in accessing appropriate services. This may be related to fear of professional reactions, family issues or lack of awareness of what is available. Recently, organisations such as the Alzheimer's Disease Society and Age Concern have started to recognise the needs of older lesbians and gay men and Age Concern produces a number of fact sheets detailing the issues for older lesbians and gay men. A conference held by the organisation in 2002 recognised the need to be aware of the particular needs of lesbians and gay men (Age Concern, 2002). This is one example of how knowing what is available in local communities can counteract exclusion (Ben Ari, 2001).

Social workers frequently work with users and carers where risk is a key issue and issues of power affect the way in which risk is 'managed'. A negative example of this is forbidding or controlling sexual relationships between people with learning disabilities. In a general discussion of sex and disability, Oliver and Sapey (2006) highlight that workers may need to facilitate sexual activity for disabled people, by, for example, putting a person in bed in with another person. Social workers engaging with the social model of disability (see Chapter 11) may need to support service users to take positive risks around sex.

Conclusion

Sexuality is an important issue for all of us. Sexual identity and behaviour has historically been linked predominantly with heterosexuality, located within monogamous marriage and related to issues of gender and reproduction. Abnormal or deviant sexual behaviour has been classified with significant consequences for many societal groups. A sound knowledge of critical sociological perspectives on sexuality can help social workers understand how social constructionism has challenged essentialist perspectives on sexuality, and can inform positive practice with a range of user and carer groups. Social workers also need to be aware that the over-arching framework of anti-oppressive practice is often inadequate for understanding the full impact of sexual identity issues.

Summary points

- Sexuality was classified into 'abnormal' and 'normal' definitions in the nineteenth century, which had significant consequences for groups in society who were considered a 'threat' to dominant social and cultural norms.
- Social and cultural norms concerning sexuality have particularly affected disabled people, older people, women and lesbians and gay men.
- People with a same-sex identity can experience structural oppression and internalised homophobia.
- Social movements have been instrumental in promoting the interests and civil liberties of lesbian and gay people.
- An understanding of sexuality and sexual identities is an important aspect of empowering social work practice.

Questions for discussion

- How do you think we become sexual beings?
- Do you think that there are still certain groups in society, where the discussion of sexual issues is a moral taboo.

- In contemporary society, which forms of sexual behaviour and expression are permitted and which are regulated?
- What issues would need to be discussed on a training day looking at empowering social work practice in relation to sexuality?

Further reading

Brown, H. C. (1998) *Social Work and Sexuality: Working with Lesbians and Gay Men*. Basingstoke: Palgrave. This text provides a sound introduction to lesbian and gay issues in social work and the need for empowering practice.

Shakespeare, T., Gillespie-Sells, K. and Davies, D. (1996) *The Sexual Politics of Disability: Untold Desires*. London: Cassell. Provides a detailed exploration of the way in which sex and disability is perceived within society and how this relates to the social model of disability.

Weeks, J. (2003) *Sexuality*. Routledge: London. Provides comprehensive discussion of the development of the sociology of sexuality. This is effectively linked to contemporary societal issues regarding sexual morality and behaviour.

Family and Change

This chapter explores one of the social sub-systems that Parsons describes as a necessary element of society, the family. The family forms a normative basis for government policy, as well as historically representing elements of continuity and change. The complexity of definitions will be explored to help to understand social structures, before going on to look at the nature of the sub-system and the relationship to welfare policy and social work practice. The family is a central location for much social work practice, not just in relation to children, but also older people, people with disabilities and people with mental health problems. Sociologists are interested not only in the structure of the family, but also in function and purpose and the relationship with other institutions and structures of society. Much sociological analysis of the family is gendered, and has particularly focused on the role of women. This chapter therefore seeks to explore the nature and function of the family.

Key issues

The key issues that will be explored in this chapter are:

- Definitions of the family and explanations and debates about the function of families within the social system.
- The structure, composition and size of families, exploring notions of continuity and change in the nature of the family in modernity and post-modernity.
- Notions of the *problem family* or *dysfunctional family* and the implications of this for social work practice.
- The role of social work in relation to family intervention and social control.

By the end of this chapter, you should be able to:

- Describe different family types.
- Discuss the nature of family and the roles of family.
- Discuss the relationship between disadvantage, oppression and family life.
- Explain what is meant by the term 'dysfunctional family units'.
- Discuss the nature of risk within the family.
- Explain the importance of sociological understanding for informing social work practice with a variety of family types.

What is meant by the family?

It could be argued that, broadly speaking, our location within some form of family structure is a general feature of human societies, although the constitution, structure and size of these formations will vary across and within societies and over time.

Exercise

- Write down who you would class as a member of your family.
- Compare your list with other people.
- Are there any differences?

Definitions of the family

The family is

> a social institution found in all societies, that unites individuals into cooperative groups that oversee the bearing and raising of children.
> (Macionis and Plummer, 2005: 462)

Most definitions of family are based on the notion of kinship, blood ties, marriage or adoption that joins individuals into a family group. However, the concept of family may be used in a broader way, to incorporate the notion of a set of shared values. Institutions may then use this to inculcate the notion of a collective set of beliefs and ethics – e.g. the church family or family of workers. A family is

> a grouping that consists of two or more individuals who define themselves as a family, and who over time assume those obligations to one another that are generally considered an essential component of family systems.
> (National Association of Social Workers, quoted in Vosler, 1996: 13)

Phenomenology to study and observe behaviour, in order to understand its meaning.

This definition of the family is what is termed a *phenomenological* definition. It is based on people's lived experiences and the meanings that they themselves attach to the concept of family. It also allows for a dynamic view of family life, seeing the family unit not as something that is fixed and static, but as something that changes over time to reflect changing social circumstances and sets of ideas.

Therefore, when sociologists talk about the family, they are increasingly looking beyond different living arrangements, and seeking to explore the multiple levels of meaning that the family has in post-modern society, as well as explanations for changes in the nature and structure of families and the social construction of particular family forms as normal or problematic (Lewis, 1998).

There is a difference between household and family. However, many definitions of the family conflate the two to construct a normative definition, the conjugal nuclear family, based on the monogamous marriage of heterosexual partners, with one or more dependent children. It has been argued that this normative construction of the nuclear family addressed the needs of modernity and the industrialising society (Lewis, 1998). In pre-industrial times, the family would be concerned with functions such as education and work. However, industrialisation saw the transference of these functions to specialist institutions (e.g. schooling system and factory system of capitalist production). Thus, the family took on different specialist functions, namely the socialisation of children and the stabilisation of adult personalities (Parsons, 1951).

You may find that some people conceptualise the family as a small group of people who are bound together by marriage and blood ties and who live under the same roof – usually a small group of individuals, including adult(s) with or without dependent children. For others, the family is a wider social grouping than this, including people who are related through marriage or blood ties, but who do not necessarily live under the same roof. The former is known as the *nuclear family* and the latter is known as the *extended family*.

Nuclear family the nuclear family is based on the notion of a man and woman living in a monogamous marriage with dependent children.

Extended family a family form that includes members outside the immediate parent and child relationship such as grandparents.

Some people may have conceptualised the family in a different way, seeing the family in a broader context of groups of people who have a mutual obligation to each other, who may or may not necessarily live under the same roof. This is known as the *family of choice*, where two or more individuals assume mutual obligation to one another, not necessarily on the basis of marriage, blood ties or kinship ties. Therefore the family may be made up of groups of friends or a communion of individuals, such as members of a church or other religious/spiritual organisation. From this phenomenological perspective, family becomes associated with a sense of identity or belonging and forms the basis of existential questions such as *who am I?* Perhaps this can be most clearly evidenced by accounts of individuals who have been adopted and as they grow older, may seek to find or find out about their biological parents in order to understand their historical and genetic location within society. There is a growing interest in genealogy and ancestry,

The archetypal nuclear family, which forms the normative basis of many policy interventions. (Sean Locke)

linking the past with the present. Thus, family is not just about living arrangements, but constitutes an important part of social identity.

The numbers of children within the nuclear family type has decreased over time, with the average number being just over two, compared to an average of six in the late Victorian period (Edgell, 2006). There are a number of reasons for this. Firstly, the increased availability of contraception has given women (in particular) more choice and control about the numbers of children they will have and when to have these children (if at all). Other accompanying changes have been the rise in female employment outside the home, leading to a rise in the average age of first pregnancy, as more women may choose to pursue a career before starting a family. In advanced capitalist societies, there has also been a dramatic decline in the infant mortality rate over the twentieth and twenty-first centuries, meaning that couples may make a conscious choice to have fewer children, with a normative expectation that the vast majority will survive (of course, this pattern is not true globally, with vast differences in infant mortality rates between developed and under-developed countries).

Extended family

This is a wider grouping of individuals, including members of kinship networks who are related through blood ties or marriage. Extended families may be extended vertically and/or horizontally. Vertical extension includes grandparents and great grandparents, whereas horizontal extension includes aunties, uncles and cousins. Thus the extended family can be a complex grouping of individuals – the concept of the family tree with multiple branches and sub-branches, united by a central trunk.

The extended family (or some form of it) may reside under one roof. However, there may also be what is referred to as a modified extended family, where there is a series of separate nuclear families, who may not have much physical contact, but who may come together for a shared purpose – e.g. a celebration, such as a christening or golden wedding.

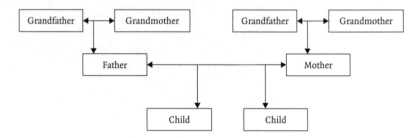

Figure 8.1 Family tree (vertical extension).

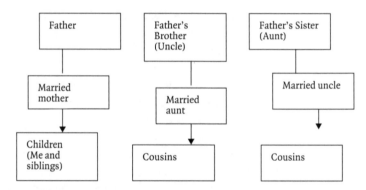

Figure 8.2 Family tree (horizontal extension).

Historians are not in entire agreement about the extent to which there has been a decline in the significance of the extended family type in modernity and post-modernity. Some historians have argued that there has been an exaggeration of the extent of the extended family type historically, portraying a halcyon vision of a lost sense of values. Others, however, have argued that the processes of modernity have led to increasing geographical mobility, leading to a greater physical segregation of families (Abercrombie et al., 1988). In addition, there have been ideological changes, with young people being encouraged to move away from the nuclear family at particular times of life course transition (e.g. many school leavers being encouraged to move away from the parental home to pursue a college or university education or married couples moving away from parental homes to set up their own homes). This is reflected in the historical concept of the dowry and the bottom drawer concept of the acquisition of consumer durables in order to help people with this transition. This second example demonstrates the associated changes of individualism and consumerism, as individuals are encouraged to be independent and self-determinate, entering the world of the housing market (through either the property-owning democracy or access to the private rented sector predominantly, although some may also occupy public sector or social housing).

There is some evidence that geographical mobility is decreasing, as the rise in house prices makes it increasingly difficult for first-time buyers to get a foothold in the housing market and rising rents in the private sector make it difficult to afford independent living. In addition to the changes in the housing market, the introduction of student loans and tuition fees have led to changes in the higher education sector, with a growing number of people electing to study at further or higher education institutions that are local so that they can stay in the parental home. Further and higher education institutions have contributed to this, through funding arrangements for home students. Also changes in the benefit system for 16 to 21-year-olds under the 1986 Social Security Act impacted on younger people's potential for independent living, unless they could demonstrate the means for self-sufficiency.

Although there may be some cultural and ethnic variations in family size and structure, it is important not to make stereotypical assumptions. In particular, there is an enduring myth that black and Asian ethnic minority populations may have a higher representation in extended family types than white populations. However, it is not true that all minority ethnic groups live in extended families. This is particularly relevant in terms of family care policies, where the enduring myth of the *they look after their own* philosophy may lead to dependent members within minority ethnic households not receiving the care that they require. In addition, Ahmad and Walker (1997) have concluded from their research in Bradford, that if care is provided informally within the household, rather than it being provided by a network of extended family providers, it is more often provided by one person, usually a daughter or daughter-in-law.

Case study

Mrs Patel is an 84-year-old Asian lady, who has diabetes and arthritis. She is finding it increasingly difficult to get out, although she can walk a short distance with the aid of a zimmer frame. She has lived on her own since her husband died five years ago. She has four children, who pop in when they can, and her daughter helps with her shopping once a week. Mrs Patel misses her independence and feels isolated from her community and cultural background.

- What problems might this lady face?
- How can the social worker use sociological knowledge of the family to improve the quality of life for this lady?

Changing family structures

Cohabitation Living together in a sexual relationship without having undergone a wedding ceremony.

← Cohabitation

There has been a rise in the numbers of people cohabiting and dependent children living with cohabiting parents. However, the degree to which this reflects a decline in the institution of marriage and a change in the constitution of the family is questionable. Whilst this may reflect a *secularisation* of society, with a reduction in the importance of the church and organised religion in structuring the norms and values of society, it has also been found that many couples who cohabit, do go on to marry, and cohabitation is a prelude to or deferment of marriage rather than a rejection of it (Lewis, 1998).

Reconstituted families where one or both partners have been divorced or separated and are now in a new relationship taking some or all of the children from the previous relationship with them.

← Reconstituted family

A rise in the divorce rate and other demographic changes mean that an increasing number of families are living in what are termed reconstituted units. Changes in legislation have been significant in allowing people to divorce, and since the 1960s there has been a dramatic rise in the number of divorces, with the number of divorces quadrupling since 1969. (Social Trends, 2006 – www.statistics.gov.uk/ socialtrends36/.) Some concern has been raised about the effect on children, although it is generally accepted that children derive more benefit from being cared for within a happy environment (see Chapter 9). One area of concern about divorce has been the adversarial nature of the family legal system, which may contribute to acrimonious relationships, which has the potential to affect both the divorcing couple and any dependent children. The rising divorce rate has also caused some concern to policy-makers and politicians, as well as sociologists, with some concerns that divorce is too readily available and that may discourage people from trying to work through problems together (Abercrombie et al., 1988). Relate and other such organisations have had an important role in helping people to solve problems, and may represent an ideological shift. The breakdown of traditional support and mutual benefit systems and the concomitant rise in individualism has resulted in a growth in the welfarist approach to problem-solving and problem management.

Same-sex relationships

Civil partnerships and family units based on arrangements other than heterosexual monogamy are being increasingly recognised (see Chapter 7). There is a growing acknowledgement of the conjugal and emotional rights of same-sex partnerships, linked in part to a growing acceptance of homosexuality and the challenge to homophobic attitudes. The Adoption Law (2002) seems to

Table 8.1 Dependent children: by family type, 2004, UK

	Thousands	Percentages
Married couple family	8,585	66
Co-habiting couple family	1,412	11
Lone-mother family	2,829	22
Lone-father family	254	2
All dependent children in families	13,080	100

Source:
Office for National Statistics, 2005

acknowledge the diverse nature of family form and gives rights to lesbian and gay couples to foster and adopt. However, although this is a legal right, local authority priorities may continue to favour the normative monogamous conjugal nuclear family. Thus there have been major and significant changes in the nature of the family and family structure. Despite these changes, the majority of children (two-thirds) continue to be brought up within a household with both parents.

As can be seen from the figures shown in Table 8.1, the majority of children still reside in a married couple family, but a growing percentage are living in lone parent families, with the vast majority of these being headed by the mother. There are a number of reasons for the rise in lone-parent families, such as the rise in the divorce rate, in widowhood and in the number of women choosing to have a child when not in a stable relationship. Nevertheless, ideological perspectives of family remain rooted in stereotypical notions of the nuclear family, despite the plurality of family types within

'Never mind what Susie's mother said. Two-parent families are *not* a cult!' (© 2001 by Randy Glasbergen. www.glasbergen.com)

contemporary Britain. Normative interpretations of family are the cornerstone of community care policies, which have become a dominant form of health and social care policies since the 1990s.

Summary of changes in family structure

1. Families have become smaller, as the birth rate has fallen.
2. The divorce rate has risen markedly since the 1960s.
3. A growing percentage of births are occurring outside marriage.
4. The number of lone-parent families has increased, many of which are headed by a woman.
5. A significant proportion of children in lone parent households lose contact with the absent parent.
6. There has been a significant rise in the numbers of children living in step-families and reconstituted families.

While the family remains an important institution in societies, not everyone lives in a family setting. As argued above, people may choose to live in a family of choice, a small community, such as those formed by New Age Travellers (Hetherington, 2000).

The role of the family

What we can conclude from the above discussion is that we live in many different ways, but the family continues to serve an important societal function in the reproduction of social and economic functions, which are required for the maintenance of stability and social order. This can be related to the function of the family as a unit of reproduction, reflecting a socialised concept of the family as the ideal place for the rearing of children. Historically, we can see how society has sanctioned this function of the normal married family. For example, prior to the 1959 Mental Health Act, women who gave birth outside the institution of marriage were often incarcerated in the asylums of the mental health system (Pilgrim and Rogers, 2005).

> Strong families build the social cohesion of our nation and its communities. Families are primarily institutions of social control and social welfare.
>
> (Levitas, 1998: 28)

From a functionalist perspective, Parsons (1955) viewed the family as having two important functions:

1. The primary socialisation of children.
2. Personality stabilisation for adult members.

Primary socialisation is concerned with the teaching and learning of social values and cultural norms.

Exercise

List the things that families may do in order to teach their children about social norms and values.

You may have included the following in your list: eating and nutrition; speaking and language; clothing; religious and cultural practices; sleep patterns; inter-personal relationships; respect for others and discipline; health-related practices – for instance, dental care or personal hygiene – as well as illness behaviours (the socialisation of responses to illness and help-seeking behaviours – see Chapter 11). This notion of primary socialisation and the dominant norms and values of society reflects Foucault's (1979) notion of disciplinary power (see Chapter 1) in which individuals self-regulate their behaviours and actions, but these are reinforced through professional ideologies.

Discussion points

There has been considerable debate in recent years about whether parents should be allowed to smack their children.

1. What are the arguments for and against smacking?
2. Is social work intervention justified if a parent smacks their child?
3. How would this reflect Foucault's notion of disciplinary power and the role of the social worker in policing the dominant set of ideas?
4. Consider your own position in this debate.

Personality stabilisation

This is concerned with the emotional assistance of adult family members and reflects an ideological and normative construct of the ideal family type. Durkheim's (1952) study of suicide concludes that the family (amongst other forms of social organisation) can help to create a sense of belonging and identity. Those who are outside this form of supportive unit are described as in a state of *anomie* and are more likely to commit suicide. Within the discourses of the normative family unit, marriage is seen as an important adjunct to the stable family unit.

> *Marriage between adult men and women is the arrangement through which adult personalities are supported and kept healthy.*
>
> (Giddens, 2006: 175)

Marriage reflects a set of traditions, values and beliefs within a society, and throughout the world we can identify different types of marital organisation. Polygamous marriages relate to marriages of more than two partners: polyandry involves one woman and several men, whilst polygyny is where a man has more than one wife. These types of marriages often exist in societies where there is a marked difference in the numbers of men and women (Macionis and Plummer, 2005). Monogamy refers to a marriage between one man and one woman and is the legally accepted type of marriage in the UK (Murdock, 1949). Usually, partners choose marriage through their own free will, but some cultural practices favour arranged marriages, where parents of individuals will choose partners for them.

Polygamy a type of marriage involving three or more people.

Polyandry the marriage of one woman to two or more men.

Polygyny the marriage of one man to two or more women.

Monogamy system of marriage between a man and a woman.

Family roles are also important, and the family is seen as an important economic unit of society. For adult members of the family unit there may be joint roles or segregated roles, depending on arrangements within the domestic division of labour (see Chapter 5). Elliott (1996) argues that, although there may be many different forms of family unit in contemporary western societies, the gendered roles within the family remain relatively stable. Despite a growing number of women in paid employment outside of the home, there has generally been little change in the division of labour within the family unit, reflecting continuing patriarchal ideologies and the notion of the male breadwinner society (Equal Opportunities Commission, 2006).

Marxist perspectives

Marxists have argued that stable families are needed for capitalism to function. Labour power is produced and reproduced within the family, through reproduction, maintenance of health, education and the socialisation of dominant value and ideological systems. Engels (1902) developed a Marxian analysis, arguing that the private domain of the nuclear family and the dominance of monogamous marriage developed as a result of private ownership of property. Married men were able to protect their property through the production of heirs and women traded their sexual and reproductive functions to their husbands, in return for material protection. Marxist feminists have further argued that women contribute to the capitalist economy through their unpaid

---

Exercise

- Next time you are watching commercial television, make a note of the adverts.
- How many of the adverts are aimed at family units of production?
- How far do these adverts reflect normative family roles?

labour in the domestic sphere (Oakley, 1974) and as a reserve army of labour to be employed in the secondary sector of the dual labour market. From a Marxist perspective, the family also contributes to the capitalist economy through patterns of consumption.

Feminist perspectives

Egalitarianism a philosophy associated with the promotion of equal opportunities in society.

Feminist perspectives of the family have been important for challenging notions of *egalitarianism* and harmony within the family, seeing families as a potential source of disharmony and unequal power relations.

Three important themes emerge from feminist writings on households/families.

1. Domestic division of labour. Although some households may reflect a unit with shared roles and responsibilities, the trend remains one of segregated roles between adult members of families, with a disproportionate burden of housework, childcare and family care falling on women (Equal Opportunities Commission, 2006).
2. Unequal power relationships in families. The incidence of domestic violence and family abuse exposes the myth of the family unit as one of stability and harmony (see Chapters 5, 9 and 10).
3. Emotional labour and ideologies of caring. There is a social construction of the notion of caring, based on gendered roles and socialisation processes (see Chapter 5). Ideologies of caring are reinforced through social policies in relation to the family, with child settlement policies/procedures often favouring the woman and maternity care and maternity leave being structured around norms of female care (Central Statistical Office, 1995).

Black perspectives

Black theorists have been critical of mainstream sociology in relation to the family, pointing to the implicit racism that is embedded in the *eurocentric* approach that is largely adopted. Through constructions of the normative family, alternative family forms come to be seen as deviant and alien (Elliott, 1996). In addition to this, the focus on the family as a unit of oppression (particularly for women) ignores the positive elements that the family provides within the context of wider community hostility (Bhavnani and Coulson, 1986) and diverts attention away from other structural and institutional processes that contribute to black women's continued oppression (Thorogood, 1987).

Post-modernity

Post-modernist theorists take *pluralism* and the notion of continuous change and instability as their starting point, and argue that traditional notions of the family are inadequate for an understanding of the many family types that co-exist in contemporary societies (Cheal, 1998). Morgan (1996) has suggested that the concept of *doing family* is more useful in understanding the nature of diverse forms of contemporary family lives. Families need to be understood in terms of their fluidity, and as a set of relationships built around common purposes. For Morgan, analysis of what goes on in families is important, in terms of intimate connections, the routine of everyday activities, and the connection between history and current lives.

Beck and Beck-Gernsheim (1995) suggest that our age is characterised by much more complex series of negotiation. Marriage is now entered into voluntarily (in the main) rather than for economic reasons, and the nature of roles has changed, not least because an increasing number of women have entered the paid labour market. Therefore, family life is not just about the negotiation of roles within the private sphere, such as domestic roles, sexual relations and childcare, but also about negotiating paid work and economic inequality. Thus family lives are seen as more chaotic and the 'battle of the sexes' is the 'central drama of our times'. This has resulted in an increased breakdown of relationships and all the issues that are related to this.

Denzin (1987) launched a scathing attack on the American family in post-modernity, arguing that the traditional model of the family is no longer applicable to many people's circumstances. He defines the modern family as 'a single parent family, headed by a teenage mother, who may be drawn to drug abuse and alcoholism' (Denzin, 1987: 33). He further suggests that the family is far less significant in terms of child care, with the institutionalisation of day care provision. Thus the state and statutory providers have become increasingly important in terms of the primary socialisation of children and children's development. This could be reflected in government policies about extended schools and wrap-around care (Every Child Matters – see Chapter 9).

Denzin also points to the role of television in many children's lives, and in the development and perpetuation of cultural myths. Widgery (1991), for example, suggested that by the time a child living in California is five, they will have seen 2,000 deaths on television, but are unlikely to have experienced bereavement first hand. Cline (1995) also suggests that the television deaths that a child views are often fantastical and bear little resemblance to most people's reality. Denzin concludes that in post-modernity a child is 'cared for by the television set, in conjunction with the day-care center' (Denzin, 1987: 33). Thus it is argued that the nature of family life is in chaos as day-care providers are unable to provide children with the emotional guidance that they require as there is more limited emotional investment (Leavitt and Power, 1989).

Discussion points

1. How useful do you think Denzin's argument is in explaining contemporary family life?
2. How far does this reflect a victim-blaming approach and ignore the structural context within which social change occurs?

Social disadvantage, risk and moral panics

The discussion above clearly identifies a number of concerns about the stability of the family unit and the extent to which the decline in traditional family forms has contributed to the breakdown in social cohesion. Rather than providing stability and serving the functions of the wider society, families have increasingly been blamed for the problems of society. Children are seen to be vulnerable to the damaging effects of poor parenting (Furedi, 2002), with a number of childhood health problems being viewed as a consequence of parental action. One in five children is considered to have a mental health problem (National Service Framework for Children, Young People and Maternity Services, 2004), and Hehir (2005) has argued that nurturing, socialisation and early stimulation may be viewed as contributory factors. Family breakdown in particular is associated with the rise in mental health problems in children (Bramlett and Blumberg, 2007).

One consequence of the rise in lone parent families is poverty and social exclusion, with a significant proportion of lone parent families living in poverty. People may find themselves in a benefit trap, where loss of benefits and extra costs in, for example, childcare are not offset by their wage levels (Hill, 1996). There may also be stigma attached to lone-parent families, particularly in a society that

Conjugal family a nuclear family of adult partners and their children in which the married relationship is strong and ties to external members are on a voluntary basis rather than on duty or loyalty.

◄ constructs a normative definition of the *conjugal nuclear family*. However, it could be argued that the rise in lone-parent families in recent years makes it a more visible form of family unit, and reduces some of the stigmatisation.

The rise in lone-parent families has led to much discussion about absent parents, and Bradshaw and Millar (1991) have argued that a significant minority of children in lone-parent families lose contact with the absent parent. The Fathers for Justice pressure group has highlighted some of these issues, claiming that the rights of absent

Case study

You go to see Kim, seventeen, who is pregnant and lives on a local housing estate. Her mother has significant health problems and feels unable to help Kim when the baby is born. The father of the baby wants nothing to do with Kim or the baby. Kim is anxious and seems unsure about her role as a mother. She is worried about whether she will keep her job and is not sure if she has any entitlement to benefits. She doesn't seem to know where to go for support.

- How can sociology help us to understand the problems that Kim experiences?
- What would be the social work role in this situation?
- What services might help Kim?

fathers have been rather overlooked in recent history, although this may be starting to change. Chawla-Duggan (2006) reports on a project which uses father development workers to support early years learning, acknowledging the important role that fathers have to play, and how their involvement 'is associated with better educational, social and emotional outcomes for children' (DFES, 2004).

Wentzel (1994) argues that, irrespective of social background, children academically achieve more if their parents are involved in their education. While historically the notion of parental blame has been gendered, with mothers particularly being implicated, more recently attention has turned to the role of fathers. A survey by the Save the Children Fund found that at the age of seven, boys lagged behind girls by an average of 7 per cent in reading ability. Amid these fears, the charity launched a campaign to encourage fathers to read with their sons.

Case study

The Save the Children Fund has enlisted the support of footballer John Barnes to promote the message that boys need to have positive male role models to encourage them to take an interest in books.

- What are the implications of this for boys in households with absent fathers?

In addition to family violence, the family may perpetuate social problems and social disadvantage. Social exclusion and poverty are often related to income levels of the adult partners within the household, and thus the entire family unit experiences the impact of income and material deprivation.

Food is the only place I find I can tighten up. So it's food . . . You've got to balance nutrition with a large amount of food which will keep them not hungry. I'd like to be able to afford to give them more nuts and I'd like them to be able to eat fresh fruit whenever they wanted. But the good food has to be limited. Terrible isn't it . . .

(Extract from an interview with a mother, Graham, 1987)

Distribution of resources within the family may not always be equal, with some evidence that women will often go without when resources are scarce, in order to ensure that children and male partners are provided for (Goode et al., 1994). Lifestyle practices and risks are inculcated within the family. As previously discussed, the family is a unit for primary socialisation, but that socialisation may involve learning of poor lifestyle choices, e.g. in relation to diet and leisure, with implications for health status.

The rising divorce rate has caused grounds for concern, with questions being asked about the nature of family life in post-modernity and some form of moral panic about the breakdown of the family as a sub-system in the whole system, leading to concerns about the breakdown of society and traditional values. However, the remarriage rate remains high, and it is difficult therefore to draw conclusions that the institution of marriage has significantly reduced in popularity as a form of social organisation. The remarriage rate, however, has implications for family structure in contemporary society, as an increasing number of children live with a biological parent and a step-parent and may also live with step-siblings or half siblings. Ten per cent of all families in the UK with dependent children are step-families (Office for National Statistics, 2005). Children and adults may spend time in two different reconstituted family arrangements, constantly having to negotiate boundaries and their place within the family unit.

In addition, there have been moral panics associated with the rise in teenage mothers, with some social commentators seeing this within the context of pursuit of social housing. (See e.g. Charles Murray's discussion of the *underclass* in Chapter 3.) The reality, however, is much more complex than this, with the rise in teenage motherhood being related to a number of different factors (Phoenix, 1991; Smith-Battle, 2000). It is also a misrepresentation to see all teenage mothers as a drain on society and the welfare system. The majority live within their parents' home and continue to be supported emotionally, functionally and financially by their family.

Nevertheless, the notion of the family unit as a stable unit which has a positive influence over the smooth functioning of society has come under increasing criticism, with a growing concern about the family as a dysfunctional unit, both for society as a whole, and for the individual members of the family. The term *dysfunctional family* is one that has been used by sociologists and policy-makers. Although social workers may well find themselves working with such families, the language of dysfunctional does not fit easily with social work values and principles of anti-oppressive practice. Labelling a family as dysfunctional, or a problem family, tends to pathologise the members of that family and it is a negative and disempowering term.

Dysfunctional family a term used in society to refer to families that are not operating according to society's expectations and are seen to disrupt social cohesion and the smooth organisation of society.

A family is seen to be dysfunctional when there is constant conflict, misbehaviour and/or abuse. This may be by one or more members of the family, but may lead to accommodation of these behaviours by other family members. Dysfunctional behaviour becomes reinforced within the family unit, with a cycle of behaviours emerging. The common elements to the dysfunctional family are:

- under-functioning by adult members of the family unit
- little guidance and few boundaries for behaviour
- children being left to fend for themselves
- inconsistency and violation of basic boundaries of behaviour
- difficulties in controlling own behaviour or reacting to the behaviour of others. Thus there may be an undercurrent of violence and violent response to behaviours.
- a model of family violence.

Dysfunctionality of the family breeds hatred and conflict, which is then reflected in wider society (Vogel and Bell, 1968). Thus social problems and anxieties about the moral values of a society become rooted in the dysfunctional family.

Case study

Jim is thirty-six and has been unemployed for the majority of his adult life. He is married to Chris who has worked in the past, but was sacked for poor time-keeping. They have three children, Nathan (16), Jamie (14) and Tonya (8) . Both Nathan and Jamie have been in trouble with the police on a number of occasions for petty theft, fighting and vandalism. Neither have been to school for the past three months and Tonya is now also starting to truant. Jim and Chris can often be found in the local pub, and don't seem to be bothered about what the children are doing. They occasionally scream at the children, if they have had a visit from the police or school welfare officer, but have no consistent way of managing the children's behaviour.

1. What elements of this case study would suggest that this is a dysfunctional family?
2. What strategies might you employ in working with this family?

In recent years there have been attempts to reverse processes of disadvantage and family intervention has been seen as important in building community solidarity and a collective consciousness (see

Chapter 2). Urban regeneration programmes, such as dockland developments to attempt to rebuild communities and work with families have been used as a way of uniting communities and promoting a sense of social cohesion.

Case study

The Families in Focus project in Camden is a community-based pilot project, using both interventionist and preventative strategies to work with children and young people. Through this, they gain the trust of families and are able to provide intense support to address some of the problems that the local residents experience. An important aspect of this project is that it is based in a small locality and builds on the strengths of local residents and empowers them to make decisions and changes to their lives. Community-based officers work with local residents and help them to regain a sense of community and social cohesion (Wigfall, 2006).

- How does this case study reflect the importance of family in relation to wider social stability?

Policing the family

The changing nature of the family and the move away from the normative *conjugal* family model, has led some commentators to argue that the family is in crisis or decline. However, the family remains a central feature of government policy and welfare intervention. Since 1989 all governments have focused on family values as a cornerstone of policy and ideology, reflecting a functionalist perspective of the role of the sub-system in social stability. Thus the family is not just a private institution, but is located within a political environment and dominant set of ideas. Margaret Thatcher talked about the need to return to Victorian values, by which she meant the primacy of family as a unit of caring, as well as notions of self-sufficiency, thrift and economic support within the family. John Major had a 'back to basics' ideology, with a need to return to the basic values of family life, similar to the beliefs of Thatcher. These ideological views of the values underpinning family life have continued under the Blair administration and are reflected in health and social care policies (e.g. Our Health, Our Care, Our Say, 2006) and the Blairite vision for tackling social exclusion (see Chapter 3).

Until the late nineteenth century, the family unit was seen as a private domain, but throughout the twentieth and twenty-first century there has been increased state involvement in family policy and family development. State care of children in the early 1960s and 1970s was largely in residential homes, which were small and mirrored family

Expectant mothers are the focus for interventionist policies by welfare professionals, as disciplinary power is used to control behaviours in the interest of the unborn child (see Chapter 1). (Kirill Zdorov)

units. In the 1980s, social work intervention with families demonstrated a preference for family-based care (e.g. foster care, as opposed to residential care). There were lots of initiatives to close down residential homes (based on the notion that they were not good for children, due to the impact of institutionalisation and concerns about residential home abuse, which was highlighted through various scandals).

Donzelot (1980) has argued that family policy has increasingly focused on 'policing of the family', with the family being seen as a site for normalisation and moralisation. He argues that the patriarchal domination of the private family unit by the father has been replaced by a patriarchal surveillance of the family through state intervention. Social workers, the education system, psychiatry and philanthropy are all seen as agents of the state, responsible for the surveillance and protection of families, and thus contribute to the perpetuation of the dominant set of social values and morals. However, Donzelot also provides a critique of Marxist and feminist perspectives on the family, arguing that the state policies and professional interventions have shaped family roles in very different ways for mothers from different social backgrounds.

Donzelot's notion of the policing of the family continues under New Labour through reform programmes such as Work for Welfare and Sure Start. Originally New Labour's family policy was concerned with getting mothers back into paid employment in order to reduce family (and in particular) child poverty. However, the Sure Start programme has shifted emphasis more directly towards child development and the institutionalisation of children's welfare. As Toynbee (2004) argues

> It is child development that matters above all. So a whole new profession is born – the pedagogue, combining nurturing and teaching; all childcare, state or private, must be led by someone with a relevant degree, moving away from low-paid, untrained 16- and 17-year-old childcare assistants who themselves failed at school. Giving every child the same jump start in life is the prime goal and the research is absolutely conclusive.

The establishment of the Child Support Agency (CSA) in 1993 can be seen as an example of government intervention in the family, requiring biological fathers to provide for children, even if they are not residing with them. While some would argue that this recognises father's responsibilities and can lead to a greater recognition of father's rights, others have argued that this can lead to impoverishment in reconstituted families (see e.g. Finch, 2004)

Current family policy continues to emphasise the role of professional intervention in the family, with a primary focus on safeguarding children (see also Chapter 9). The announcement of £1bn in the extended schools programme (Every Child Matters, 2007 – www.everychildmatters.gov.uk), the focus on helping teenage parents and young families to fulfil their potential and the Law Society proposals to give financial rights to cohabiting couples who split up (www.lawsociety.org.uk), similar to those enjoyed by married couples, are all examples of this greater intervention and welfarist approach to family care. Indeed, the recent change in the title of the government department responsible for family policy to Department for Children, Schools and Families (www.dfes.gov.uk) reflects the welfare partnerships in relation to children and families.

Discussion points

- How far does this reflect increased state intervention and a shift away from Parson's notion of the family as a sub-system of society?
- How would Foucault's notion of disciplinary power (see Chapter 1) help us to explain the increased state intervention and policing of the family?

Although many commentators have argued that the Sure Start programme has been a success (and indeed the Government is extending the numbers of programme areas), Ormerod (2005) has argued that for certain disadvantaged groups the effect of the programme has been detrimental. He argues that less disadvantaged families may be better placed to take advantage of Sure Start initiatives, thus leading to inequalities of opportunity and exacerbating social divisions. He points to evidence from evaluations of the Head Start programme in the USA (upon which Sure Start is modelled), which show that white families are more likely to benefit from these community interventions than black families. Thus the welfarist approach to community improvement reflects not only the gendered nature of disadvantage, but also class and ethnic divisions.

Conclusion

This chapter has explored the institution of family and its central place within the ideological and policy context of society. There are both continuities and change in the nature and structure of the family. Cree (2000) has argued that there is an institutionalisation of practice in relation to the family, but much social work practice remains structured around an outdated model of the family and fails to reflect the experiences of many service users. This is an important issue for social workers to address in their role as advocates and in looking at ways to empower some of the most vulnerable people of society.

Summary points

- Families have changed, but the majority of children still live in two-parent families.
- Social workers may work with people who are marginalised and may be outside a family system e.g. mental health service users.
- An understanding of sociological perspectives on the family helps us to look at our own values and acknowledge that people may not have the same networks of support.
- Family has become idealised and is often seen as a safe and secure place. However, abuse and disadvantage occur in some families. This may lead to moral dilemmas and tensions for social workers in practice.
- Caring is an important function of the family and in community care policies, but is structured around a particular notion of family formation and family roles.

Questions for discussion

- Is the family still the best place to bring up children? Justify your response to this question.
- There is evidence to suggest that your own experience of family affects how you perceive the nature of family life. How can sociological perspectives on the family help you to understand the diverse nature of family life?

- To what extent does the professional role with families adopt a surveillance or supportive function? Are the two necessarily mutually exclusive?
- Government policy reflects a commitment to the promotion of safer communities. What evidence is there that the community and family contribute to the stability of society or that there is a breakdown in the structure and function of these sub-systems?

Further reading

Allen, G. (ed.) (1999) *The Sociology of the Family*. Oxford: Blackwell. This edited book covers a range of issues that are pertinent to family life. There are useful chapters on the changing nature of family, as well as on family roles.

Donzelot, J. (1980) *The Policing of Families*. London: John Hopkins Press. This is a classical study of the historical development of state intervention in family life, and the role of welfare systems in the social control of families.

Morgan, D. (1996) *Family Connections: An Introduction to Family Studies*. Cambridge: Polity. This book provides an analysis of the family in contemporary society, and has a particularly useful focus on roles within the family.

Silva, E.B. and Smart, C. (eds) (1999) *The New Family?* London: Sage. This is useful for a feminist analysis of the family.

9

Childhood

Practice with children and their families has consistently been a dominant and controversial aspect of social work practice for the past fifty years, but the concept of childhood as a distinct social category is a relatively new one. The sociology of childhood is a fast-growing body of sociological knowledge and an understanding of key concepts and theories is an important aspect of understanding the nature of social work practice with children and young people.

The key issues that will be explored in this chapter are:

- The definition and concept of childhood.
- The social construction of childhood as a social category.
- Social disadvantage in relation to the category of childhood.
- Risk and childhood.
- The particular issues that face children who are seeking asylum.
- The importance of sociological understanding in informing social work practice with children in contemporary society.

By the end of this chapter, you should be able to:

- Identify childhood as a distinct social category and a form of social division that exists within society.
- Consider the differential childhood experiences that exist within contemporary British society.
- Explore sociological theories of childhood with a view to understanding the changing social meanings of childhood in our society.
- Discuss the modern child as a focus of state social concern and its relevance for contemporary social work practice.

Childhood as an area of sociological enquiry

While modern sociology has explored and developed theories concerning social divisions such as class, gender, race and the family, the period of existence known as childhood has until the past twenty years or so been largely ignored as a concern for sociological enquiry. Corsaro (2005) views the marginalisation of children within sociology as an extension of the marginalisation of children within society as a whole. This is a marginalisation that takes place within the social and academic worlds occupied and dominated by adults.

More recently there has been a growth in the sociological interest of the lives of children, which has arisen as a part of sociology's concern with minority and marginalised groups within society. Hence sociology's rediscovery of childhood is a part of a wider phenomenon of the sociological study of the biographies and experiences of excluded minority groups such as disabled people and gay and lesbians and older people in our society.

Sociology's interest in children has reflected a wider societal concern for the current and future lives of children within our society. The rise of the children's rights movement and the concerns of the state through its social and legislative policies reflect the state's interest in the children who will become its future adults.

The emergence of childhood

Early sociological and historical interest in the study of childhood is characterised by an analysis of the emergence of childhood as a distinct social role in society. The work of Aries (1962) has been influential in gaining an understanding that conceptions of childhood have varied over time and childhood is culturally and historically specific. Childhood as a social role and category separate from adulthood began to emerge in the late eighteenth century. Concerns about the moral and physical welfare of children led to numerous legislative controls and regulation. This recognition of childhood and the acknowledgement of their welfare and rights was highlighted by specific pieces of legislation and policy, primarily concerned with the protection of children from abuse. In addition, laws were passed to prevent children from working in factories, accompanied by a framework for the education of children and the recognition of the need for specific interventions for juvenile delinquency (Hendrick, 1992).

Hendrick (ibid.) suggests that this period was significant as children were no longer wage-earners, but were school pupils. Nevertheless, class divisions in childhood remained firmly embedded. While many welfare initiatives offered genuine protection for children, they also demonstrated increasing state control and regulation over children's lives. Working-class children particularly came under increasing scrutiny from the state and its agencies (see Chapter 1) and out of these reforms emerged the early activities of modern social work.

Through the state's focus upon improving the lives of working-class children, there appeared to emerge a consensus of the notion of what constitutes an ideal or natural childhood. A childhood that is good and beneficial for children, families and society as a whole or, as Hendrick (1992) states, 'a maturing bourgeois domestic ideal' which constructed children as vulnerable, innocent and in need of protection by adults.

What is childhood?

There is no single, agreed definition of childhood as its meaning changes in relation to the social context in which it was created. The questions about what is childhood and when it begins and ends may seem straightforward, but they involve challenging 'taken for granted' assumptions about childhood and exploring a range of differing theories and perspectives across the social sciences.

It may here be worthwhile distinguishing between the notion of being a child and the concept of childhood itself. In biological terms a child is someone who is biologically immature or has not yet reached puberty. In legal terms a child may be defined as a minor, someone who does not exercise specific legal rights and responsibilities by virtue of their age. Being a child can be seen as a biological and physical state characterised by certain physiological and psychological stages (see Freud and Piaget). Wyness (2006) suggests that childhood is an abstract set of ideas or conceptions, and children are the grounded physical manifestations of childhood. The ideas that we hold about the nature of childhood are said to define children's lives and the relationship they have with others in society whether they be real or imagined. The perspective that although children exist, childhood is socially constructed will be discussed later in this chapter.

The term childhood implies a period of existence, which is fixed, and essentialist; fixed suggests that there is an assumed consensus that childhood begins and ends at particular ages and that this is unchanging and that this period called childhood can be viewed over different historical periods. In this sense, it could be argued that the stages of childhood are the same in twenty-first-century Britain as they were in Victorian Britain. When sociologists refer to the notion of something being essentialist, it is suggested that there are particularly defining characteristics or traits associated with it.

Exercise

Defining features of childhood

- Make a list of ten of the essential features and characteristics associated with childhood.
- Compare with a fellow student or colleague.
- How many do you share in common? Are these features or traits common to all children and to all societies?

This may have proved a more challenging exercise than first thought, as one realises that many of the traits associated with childhood tend to be culturally specific and tend to describe one's own experience of childhood, our perception of our children's childhood or what we hope or wish childhood was like. What might have emerged from your own discussions are images of different childhoods based upon different childhood experiences rather than a period of life, which is characterised by common distinguishing features.

Some insight into understanding childhood can be gained through comparative studies, which demonstrate the way in which different societies develop different conceptions of childhood, adding further weight to the argument that childhood is socially constructed. Benedict (1955) compared complex industrial societies like Britain and the USA with rural and less industrialised parts of Africa and Asia. In describing the characteristics of childhood she identifies three main areas of difference:

1. Levels of responsibility or lack of responsibility.
2. Levels of dominance or submission to adults.
3. Difference in sex roles.

What determines childhood and what distinguishes childhood from other stages such as adulthood is an interesting and challenging question and alludes to the perspective that childhood is neither natural nor essential and the distinction of adulthood from childhood is predominantly a false one.

Several definitions of childhood tend to define it in negative terms, i.e. a child can be defined as a young human or someone who has not reached puberty or adulthood, the period between infancy and adolescence. Hence some of the defining characteristics of childhood are described by the absence of something as opposed to common unifying traits. It could be argued that these definitions tend to define adulthood rather than childhood, as they imply that adulthood signifies the period in which human beings are recognised and acquire status and standing in society.

Walther in Gittens (1997) describes childhood as

The invention of adults reflects adult needs and adult fears quite as much as it signifies the absence of adulthood. In the course of history children have been glorified, patronised, ignored or held in contempt depending upon the cultural assumptions of adults.

For an adult reading the above statement this may seem like an attack on the power and authority that adults have over children. However, for sociologists and for social workers and other practitioners who work with children, what becomes evident in understanding the history and discourses concerning childhood is that it is almost impossible to avoid adult interpretations, adult concerns and adults' constructions of those histories and experiences.

The social construction of childhood

The view that childhood is a social construct is relatively new and there exists a range of sociological theories, which attempt to explain the nature of childhood in society. Aries (1962) and Denzin (1987) have been particularly influential in developing theories that suggest that childhood is socially constructed. Aries (1962) examined literary and artistic representations of children and put forward the theory that childhood did not exist in medieval society, and it only emerged around the fifteenth century. By examining the depiction of children in art and literature, Aries believed that prior to the fifteenth century children were viewed as miniature adults who wore similar clothes to adults, were treated like adults, worked in factories or on the land and did not engage in playful activities. He concluded that there was no distinct period known as childhood, with little separation between the adult and child world.

Aries was eager to assert that while childhood was not recognised, it did not mean that children were not liked or cared for. He believed that children were nurtured until around the age of seven and they were then deemed ready to join the adult world. He draws a distinction between the lack of concern for the physical and mental wellbeing of children in medieval society compared with the obsessions regarding the moral, physical, educational and sexual problems of the modern child.

Though accepted as significant in the study of childhood, Aries' work has been criticised and undermined, with critics accusing him of flawed methodology through his reliance on artistic and literary representations of children, which can be unrepresentative and unreliable (Hendrick, 1992). This evidence can be taken out of context and the images and writings about children may be in fact be prescriptions about what or how children may be viewed as opposed to how they were viewed and treated in practice. While methodologically flawed, Aries' work is accepted as significant for the way he proposed the idea of childhood as a developmental notion and its significance within the family and social context.

Jenks (2005) viewed childhood as neither natural nor universal, but the distinction between adulthood and childhood was a false one. Hanson (in Best, 2005) views the construction of childhood as one in which childhood is seen as a route to adulthood (an incomplete adult) and one in which children are constructed as vulnerable and hence in need of protection. Childhood and adulthood are seen as binary terms and thus are defined in opposition to one another. For example adulthood can be defined as the possession of certain rights, responsibilities, work, voting and so on, and childhood defined by the absence of these factors.

Perspectives on childhood and theories of socialisation

Functionalism

Traditional sociological theories of childhood tend to focus on the role of socialisation within society as a way of preparing future citizens. These predominantly functionalist theories regarding the role of socialisation have dominated much of sociological thinking in understanding children and childhood. Functionalist perspectives identify childhood as a distinct stage from adulthood, emphasising the role of socialisation and suggesting that childhood plays a preparatory function in becoming an adult. Socialisation as performed by society's institutions of the family and school play an essential role whereby children absorb the values, standards and norms of the society in which they live.

Most theories (Parsons and Bales, 1955) emphasise the early socialisation, which takes place in the family, in which children are passively moulded into hopefully responsible members of society (see Chapter 8). This view offers a rather deterministic view on childhood in which children are passive recipients in the process and play no role in shaping their future or creating the society of which they are a part. The active participants in the process are adults, whether they are parents in the family or other adults in the form of teachers, religious leaders or social workers.

Functionalist models tend to describe the process of socialisation rather than focus upon how and why children become integrated into society. Within this approach Talcott Parsons viewed children in two ways: either as a threat or as a potential benefit to society, depending upon how successfully they were socialised into being responsible citizens (Parsons and Bales, 1955). However socialisation is not a one-way process and these theories have been challenged for being overly deterministic and ignoring the part that children play in

To many people, this image of a child smoking crosses the line between appropriate adult and child behaviour. (Alexander Hafemann)

society. Children may actively resist attempts to incorporate themselves into the dominant culture and create counter-cultures.

Social action theories

Interpretive sociology a theoretical approach closely associated with phenomenology and the sociological perspective of interactionism that explains social life through the interpretation of the meanings that lie behind the behaviour of individuals.

Interpretive sociologists, on the other hand, view socialisation as an interactive process and stress the role played by individuals in shaping society. Emphasis is placed on the roles individuals play in which roles are created, resisted and acted upon. Socialisation is seen as a more complex process in which children are free to make choices although those choices may be constrained (Cree, 2000). The social institutions of the family, school and health and social care play a powerful role in regulating childhood. An analysis of the power in society is important and of interest to sociologists in the question of how society socialises children. Questions about who socialises society, how society works and who exercises power and in whose interests are also relevant (ibid.).

Radical perspectives

Radical perspectives, including Marxist, feminist and anti-racist perspectives may view socialisation as the transmission of capitalist, patriarchal and racist values and ideology. As far as children are concerned, the welfare state represents a process of state socialisation in which public space is created for children in the form of nurseries and schools. Children are thus socialised into adopting dominant values and beliefs. Mackie (1987) states that the main purposes of gender socialisation are in the interests of patriarchy and to maintain the inequality between men and women. Hence socialisation is important in reproducing inequality and power within society in relation to gender, race and class as well as other forms of social division.

Discussion points

Childhood – the waiting room for adulthood

- How are children socialised to become adults?
- What roles do institutions such as the family and schools play in preparing children for adulthood?
- Are children passive recipients in the process and in what ways are children social actors who shape their own lives?

Childhood as a social division

Societal concerns and sociological interest in the experiences of children in society have led some sociologists (Corsaro, 2005) to recognise the existence of childhood as a social division. Best (2005) goes a step further in recognising the concept of childhood as a *state-sponsored* social division. He suggests that the period of childhood is something that is not biological or naturally occurring, but a period of life which is socially constructed. To a certain extent it is constructed by the modern state through legislation and social policies and instructions of the criminal justice system, the education system and health and social welfare services.

The importance and significance that is attributed to the state of childhood is one that does not necessarily reflect the status and value of children in society. What emerges is a rather contradictory and dichotomous position where the activities of the state through legislation and social policies and state institutions could be argued to be more concerned with promoting adults' concerns and interests and those of society as a whole, which may not be consistent with the interests, wishes and needs of all children in our society. The recognition of the needs and rights of children and the compatibility with the rights and needs of adults is a common ethical and professional dilemma that challenges practitioners in the field of social work. This can be seen in relation to the Every Child Matters policy agenda, in which plans to extend the school working day may be of benefit to the state, employers, and possibly working parents, but may have different implications for children who could be looked after in day care from 7.30 a.m. to 6.00 p.m. If childhood is a structural division there are also further intra-structural divisions within the category of child, and the diversity of childhood experiences in Britain challenges the notion that childhood is a fixed entity.

> *childhood is a variable of social analysis. It can never be entirely divorced from other variables such as class, gender, or ethnicity. Comparative and cross-cultural analysis reveals a variety of childhoods rather than single and universal phenomena.*
>
> (James and Prout, 1990: 8)

The child population in Britain has been in decline since the 1970s and, while there were approximately 12.1 million children in Britain in 2001 (Social Focus in Brief: Children, 2002 – www.statistics.gov.uk), the child population varies regionally and across ethnic groups. The child population is greater in the North of Ireland compared with South West England and ethnic minority population are relatively younger than the majority white group. One in three children are from an ethnic minority group and this trend is set to continue with a decline in birth rate among white middle-class families and an increase in accompanied and unaccompanied children seeking asylum (ibid.). Children of mixed parentage represent the fastest growing ethnic category and are the fourth category after white, Pakistani and Indian. Fifty per cent of the mixed population in the UK is under sixteen years of age (Census, 2001).

Of particular significance for social work is a picture within British society of not one childhood, but many different childhoods characterised not by innocence, or images represented in Enid Blyton books, but one characterised by differences and diversity in relation to class, ethnicity, migration status and wealth.

The state, through the activities of social workers and other occupations, is concerned with intervention and regulation of childhood and evidence suggests that social workers are more likely to be involved in work with children and families from specific socio-economic groups and ethnic backgrounds (IPPR Report, 2006 – www.ippr.org.uk). There is no national research evidence concerning referral rates of minority ethnic families to social services departments, however, the significance of race and ethnic categorisation is an important factor in working with black and ethnic minority children and families.

The concept of childhood as a single entity is not reflected by the diversity of experience of children in contemporary British society. The 2001 Census highlights differential childhood experiences regarding family structure, ethnicity, poverty and housing. The problems associated with defining and understanding poverty have been discussed in Chapter 3. Child poverty can be measured by the

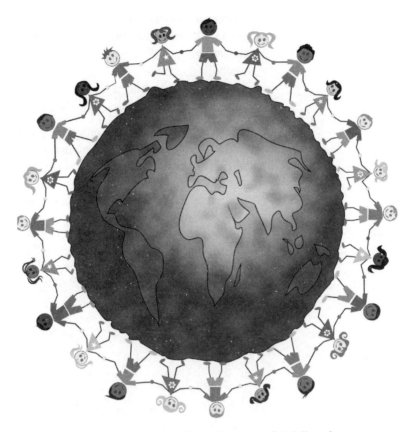

The symbolic representation of the diversity of childhood across the globe.

number of children living in households with less than 60 per cent of median income. Despite Tony Blair's intention that 'our historic aim will be for ours to be the first generation to end child poverty' (Beveridge Lecture, 1999), as well as specific attempts by Labour governments to reduce child poverty, the numbers of children living in such households remains at 2.4 million or 3.4 million (after housing costs are taken into consideration) (CPAG, 2006 – www.cpag.org.uk).

Poverty has particular relevance for health and social care practice as

> disproportionate numbers of working class, black and lone parent families attract the gaze of state agencies and are exposed to state-directed family interventions.
>
> (Goldson, 1997: 24)

Babies born to poorer families are more likely to be born prematurely and to be of low birth weight. They are more likely to experience health problems in later life, including a greater risk of respiratory infection, gastro-enteritis, dental caries and tuberculosis. Children from poorer households are at increased risk of experiencing accidents in the home, including fires.

> *In overcrowded homes, chip pans, knives, pills and bleach are more*
> *likely to be in reach of children . . . parents on income support . . can*
> *not afford a fireguard . . . a stair gate . . . or a playpen.*
>
> (Holman, 1978)

Poverty affects children's self-esteem, their ability to participate in children's social activities and can have a long-term legacy. Children raised in poverty are, as adults, more likely to be unemployed, in low-paid employment, are more likely to live in social housing, have a greater risk of alcohol and drug abuse and involvement with criminal activities (CPAG, 2006 – www.cpag.org.uk).

Children from poorer backgrounds are unlikely to receive the services they require. In addition, despite what we know about the correlation between poverty and the likelihood of experiencing care, there are no longitudinal studies of the effects of poverty on parents' ability to parent and their experiences while their children are looked after. Social workers and other professionals need to consider the impact poverty has on the lives of service users and social work assessments.

There is tension between those who wish to protect children from the adult world and those who see the best protection for children as recognising children as independent beings and treating them with the same rights as adults. Firestone (1971) regards childhood as an institution of oppression, stating that 'for women and children to become fully human they need to be liberated from childhood'.

Goldson (1997) argues that the structural relationship between adults and children is characterised by power and dependency. This is presented as natural and good for social order. Within this relationship adults are mature, rational and strong and provide and protect, whereas children are immature, irrational, receive, consume and are in need of protection. On this view, age is seen as a fundamental determinant in the distribution of rights, power and participation. He goes on to discuss how the social, economic and political position of childhood in capitalist societies is based upon exclusion and marginality. Childhood is characterised not just by interpersonal dependency but also by structured dependency.

The notion that children do not belong in the public space is an important consideration in the maintenance of boundaries between the child and adult worlds. Lee (2001) discusses how throughout the nineteenth and twentieth centuries children were gradually removed from the streets and the workplace, through education and early social work and the concept of a 'child out of place' is used to refer to children who do not conform to middle-class, western ideals that children are dependent and require adult supervision particularly in public places. Later in this chapter we see that there are legal restrictions placed upon children's work. However, children who care for parents and other family members provide a challenge for social workers in identifying and responding to their needs but also challenges our understanding of childhood and the space and roles that they occupy.

Children as carers

The concepts of both formal and informal caring have been studied within sociology, primarily in respect to women (see Chapter 5), yet children have cared for relatives for centuries. However, it was not until the 1980s that the extent and nature of the informal care provided by children was identified through research. The issues that young carers face highlight the strengths and abilities that many children possess, rather than emphasising their vulnerability and lack of responsibility. The issues facing children who care (young carers) for parents or siblings has remained relatively hidden in social work practice, though the consequences of caring can have a major impact on their experiences of childhood and later life.

The 2001 Census identified over 175,000 young carers in Britain and there are a further three million children in the UK who have a family member with a disability. Approximately a quarter of a million young people in the UK live with a parent who is misusing a Class A drug and 920,000 young people in the UK are children of alcoholic parents. It is most likely that the official statistics for young carers reflects an under-representation of the numbers of children involved (NCH, 2005 – www.nch.org.uk).

Although many young carers are hidden from education, health and social services, NCH (2005) identifies some of the factors that can identify that a child is a young carer. These include under-achievement at school, suffering depression or tiredness, school absence, inability to take part in extra-curricular activities and a parent who often misses appointments. The largest survey to date of young carers in the UK has been conducted by Dreaden and Becker on behalf of the Children's Society (Young Carers' Report, 2004).

Dreaden and Becker (2004) found that the amount of time spent caring ranged between ten and twenty hours a week, with a small minority of children working over fifty hours, leading to significant implications for schooling and educational difficulties. Caring can be a very long-term commitment for many children, and can start at an early age. One-fifth of young carers and their families receive no other support except for their contact with a specialist young carers' project and most often social services support is the most common external service received.

The experiences of young carers challenge our ideas of an appropriate childhood. Children may be seen as in need of care and protection, particularly when it is judged that the roles of parents and children have been reversed. Children as carers can be assessed under the Carers Recognition Act (1995) and under Section 17 of the

Children Act 1989 as a *child in need*. In relation to involvement with social workers, children are more likely to be assessed if they are living with a lone parent or if they are caring for an adult with drug or alcohol problems (Young Carers Report, 2004). Such a referral to social services may reflect potential child protection concerns and the risk of being accommodated by social workers can represent a real fear for young carers and their relatives and prevent them from seeking support.

Case study

Ravinder is twelve and lives with his mother and younger sister, Kuldeep. His mother has suffered from severe depression for ten years and Ravinder has provided care for his mother and sister. Lately his mother has been having difficulty sleeping at night and most days she stays in bed until 11 a.m. A typical school day for Ravinder involves him waking at 6 a.m. to get himself and Kuldeep ready for school. He takes Kuldeep to school and usually arrives at his own school late. On their return from school Ravinder does some housework and prepares the family meal. Ravinder loves his mother and appears very protective towards her. He says that he is her best friend.

- What impact may Ravinder's caring responsibilities have on his personal wellbeing, education and social life?
- What responsibilities do you consider appropriate for children to assume?
- How does this compare with your and your fellow students' experiences?
- As a social worker what do you consider to be the individual needs of each member of this family?

Legislative constructions of childhood: children's rights and social work practice

The age at which children can assume responsibility for their actions is highly contested and is linked to our ideas and perception of childhood. If children are perceived as being innocent, shy and immature, then they will assume very little responsibility for their actions. On the other hand, if children are deemed to be capable, rational and confident, then it could be said that they are responsible for their own actions. Levels of childhood responsibility are linked to debates around children's rights and are of particular relevance for practitioners working with children, particularly in social work, education and health.

The following exercise highlights the different ages at which children are afforded certain adult rights and choices and reflects the lack of clarity that exists in legislation defining and governing childhood.

Exercise

Childhood and the age of responsibility

1. What age can a child have a bank account?
2. What is the compulsory age for school attendance?
3. What is the age of criminal responsibility in (a) Scotland (b) England and Wales?
4. What age can children be given an Anti-Social Behaviour Order?
5. What is the sexual age of consent for (a) heterosexual (b) same-sex relationships?
6. What age can children work?
7. What age can children buy cigarettes?
8. What age can children enter the armed forces?
9. What age can children learn to drive a car?
10. What age can children marry without parental consent?

One of the most controversial areas in which children are expected to assume legal responsibilities for their actions is in the area of criminality. Following the death of James Bulger in 1993 and the release of his killers in 2000, there has been debate regarding the age of criminal responsibility in Britain. There are many who believe that the age of criminality is set too low in Britain, in comparison with other European countries. A report for the Centre for Crime and Justice Studies by Allen (2006) calls for the age to be raised from ten to fourteen, as too many children are prosecuted and criminalised. It calls for greater emphasis on the educational, social and mental health needs of children and suggests care proceedings should be used for younger offenders. The report recommends the phasing out of the use of prison for fifteen and sixteen-year-olds and the use of restorative justice (see Chapter 4).

> The minimum age of criminal responsibility differs widely owing to history and culture. The modern approach would be to consider whether a child can live up to the moral and psychological components of criminal responsibility; that is, whether a child, by virtue of her or his individual discernment and understanding, can be held responsible for essentially antisocial behaviour. If the age of criminal responsibility is fixed too low or if there is no lower age limit at all, the notion of criminal responsibility would become meaningless. In general, there is a close relationship between the notion of responsibility for delinquent or criminal behaviour and other social rights and responsibilities (such as marital status, civil majority, etc.).
>
> (United Nations Standard Minimum Rules for the Administration of Juvenile Justice (the Beijing Rules), 1985)

However, at the time of writing it is unlikely that the age will change, as the age of responsibility is not set in isolation but reflects society's history and construction of childhood and is linked to other aspects of rights and responsibilities for children.

The issue of children's rights is a contentious debate amongst politicians, policy-makers, parents, children and welfare practitioners. British childcare policy is centred on notions that children are vulnerable, and need support and protection and these principles are embodied in legislation and policy (Children Act, 1989; Every Child Matters, 2004; Children Act, 2004). Situations where children are abused, neglected, not listened to, not trusted and not believed has led to a growing realisation that adults do not always protect children, nor make decisions that are in their best interests. The perception that children are possessed by adults, are dependent upon adults and thus in need of their protection is slowly changing to one that recognises that while children have needs, they have the right to have their needs met (Lansdown, 2001). The adoption by Britain of the UN and European Charter of Children's Rights reflects this change and a view that children are capable of becoming self-determining agents with the ability to make their own informed choices is a central feature of the Children's Rights movement. The United Nations Charter defines a child as *every human being under the age of 18* unless the legal age of majority in a country is lower. The main principles are:

- All rights apply to all children without exception or discrimination of any kind (article 2).
- The best interests of the child must be a primary consideration in all actions concerning children (article 3).
- States have an obligation to ensure that as much as possible every child's survival and development is promoted (article 6).
- Children's views must be taken into account in all matters affecting them (article 12).

However, while Britain has ratified both policies, the earlier discussion on the differential childhood experiences suggest that Britain has a long way to go in fully realising these principles in practice. Article 12 poses a particular challenge for adults in working with children as to what age and how far children are able to make decisions for themselves. However, Revans (2007) reports on a project where seven local authorities are working with looked-after children and involving them in care decisions in order to improve the quality of their lives. Under the Children Act (2004) the first Children's Commissioner was appointed in Britain.

> The Commissioner's remit is to promote awareness of views and interests of children. He is expected to raise the profile of the issues that affect and concern children in England, and promote awareness and understanding of their views and interests among all sectors of society, both public and private.

(Every Child Matters, 2004)

There are many issues in social care and health practice in which children's rights to self-determination are crucial. Social workers may find themselves in a hospital setting, working with children suffering with long-term or acute conditions where consent to treatment is both a legal and an ethical issue. There are occasions where a social worker is the lone practitioner who is advocating on behalf of child who does not wish to consent to treatment.

Exercise

Children and consent

You are a hospital social worker.
Max, aged fifteen, has been diagnosed with terminal cancer and after several long spells in hospital has told you that he no longer wishes to continue with his 'treatment'.

- What do you consider are the main issues in enabling Max to make a decision about his treatment?
- What other areas within social work practice may involve a child's capacity to give consent?

The concept of 'Gillick competence' or 'Fraser Test' is the benchmark by which professionals have to ascertain the ability of children to provide consent.

> In 1985, the House of Lords held that a child under 16 could give valid consent to health care treatment without parental knowledge or agreement provided the child had sufficient competence (intelligence and understanding) to give consent.

A person who has reached the age of sixteen years should be regarded as competent to give consent, unless there is evidence to the contrary. Competence should be assessed in the same way as it is in adults. The rules were revised by the Department of Health in 2001, stating that 'Gillick' or 'Fraser' test is about a child's capacity to consent and not about what other people consider right. It recognises that it is good practice to involve families of sixteen and seventeen-year-olds in the decision-making process unless the young person specifically requests that this should not happen. It also states that attempts should be made to persuade the young person to confide in their families, but stresses that confidentiality should be maintained unless there is a risk of harm.

The rights of children to make decisions about their lives and also to participate in adult arenas challenge notions of childhood and children's rightful place. The UN Charter has ensured that children's rights are now a global concern. Lee (2001) suggests that the UN

Charter represents an abstract set of principles without any practicable applications, and makes several promises of providing global spaces for all children. Rather than extending the rights of children across the world, he suggests that such a charter creates more ambiguity regarding the position of children and their relationship with adults throughout the world.

Children seeking asylum

The effects of globalisation on the lives of children can be witnessed through children who seek asylum, as women and children are over represented in the numbers of people who are illegally trafficked and represent a significant proportion of migrant labour (UNICEF, 2006). Amnesty International suggests that half the world's refugee population are said to be children (www.amnesty.org).

Social work with asylum-seeking children and their families is a rapidly growing area of practice and one in which many socials workers feel ill-prepared, though this may change as it becomes a more common aspect of social work practice. In 2001 it was estimated that there were 23,000 asylum-seeking children who were in contact with social work agencies and 6,000 unaccompanied minors . (Community Care, 2007). There are different legal responsibilities for social services depending upon whether children seeking asylum are accompanied or unaccompanied. An unaccompanied asylum-seeking child is a person who, at the time of making the asylum application:

- is, or (if there is no proof) appears to be, under eighteen;
- is applying for asylum in his or her own right;
- has no adult relative or guardian to turn to in this country.
        (Home Office, Immigration and Nationality Directorate, 2002)

> However, the concept of family is a problematic one concerning asylum as little is done by immigration officials to check the relationships of the adults who accompany children. So whilst adults may accompany children, it is not clear whether the adults have responsibility for them.
> (Grady, 2004)

Despite the children's rights agenda, British childcare policy continues to be based primarily upon principles of welfare and protection for children, but there is genuine concern that these values are not afforded to all children, particularly in relation to children's immigration status.

> The social work response to unaccompanied refugee children offers a good gauge to reflect on how much our professional value base and practice has been compromised by resource-led thinking and the prejudices with which we become stained through the creeping influence of the wider political agenda – both on a local and national level.
> (Chester, 2003)

There are concerns that the government's responses to accompanied and unaccompanied children contravene the UN Charter on Rights of the Child. Grady (2004) states that the British government is able to prevent children from legally seeking support from social services as the Nationality, Immigration and Asylum Act 2002 states that families who seek support from the Secretary of State via the National Asylum Support Service (NASS) are not eligible for support from social services under the Children Act as a child in need. NASS's primary function is one of housing and financial support and as an agency is not in a position to offer support and protection to asylum-seeking children.

The Audit Commission Report, *Another Country* (2000), concluded that as result of their experiences of separation, loss and social dislocation, many unaccompanied children have multiple needs and that though children may present as being mature and capable, due to the circumstances they have experienced, this may hide post-traumatic stress disorder and other mental heath conditions.

Childhood, risk and moral panics

The ideas associated with a risk society (Beck, 1992) is one which permeates contemporary sociological thought and current welfare practice in terms of the assessment and management of risk and nowhere is this more evident than in the area of social work practice with children and their families. Within social work with children, risk is strongly associated with the potential for harm and is defined in relation to physical, emotional and sexual harm and neglect. The risks of harm for children by their parents are highlighted by the NSPCC (2004), which suggests that:

- Seven per cent of children experience serious physical abuse at the hands of their parents or carers during childhood.
- One per cent of children experience sexual abuse by a parent or carer and another three per cent by another relative during childhood.
- Six per cent of children experience serious absence of care at home during childhood.
- Sixteen per cent of children experience serious maltreatment by parents, of whom one-third experience more than one type of maltreatment.

(www.nspcc.org.uk)

The rather narrow focus of safeguarding children from harm as enshrined in child protection law and policy in England and Wales fails to recognise child protection as a global concern. According to UNICEF, child protection refers to the prevention of and response to violence, exploitation and abuse against children – including commercial sexual exploitation, trafficking, child labour and harmful traditional practices, such as female genital mutilation/cutting and child marriage (2006). Welfare organisations in the UK have at times failed to respond to the needs and safety of children who are subject to forms of child abuse that go beyond *eurocentric* norms and definitions.

However the risks associated with modern childhood appear to be more extensive. There are major concerns regarding the risk associated with food and obesity, 'stranger danger', road traffic accidents, alcohol and drug use, mental heath problems, mobile phone use, and use of the internet. Modern childhood appears to be full of risks and this was echoed recently by a letter published in a national newspaper by over one hundred academics, child welfare professionals, and children's authors who were concerned about the state of modern childhood and requesting an urgent debate fearing the loss of childhood.

Sir

As professionals and academics from a range of backgrounds, we are deeply concerned at the escalating incidence of childhood depression and children's behavioural and developmental conditions. We believe this is largely due to a lack of understanding, on the part of both politicians and the general public, of the realities and subtleties of child development.

Since children's brains are still developing, they cannot adjust – as full-grown adults can – to the effects of ever more rapid technological and cultural change. They still need what developing human beings have always needed, including real food (as opposed to processed 'junk'), real play (as opposed to sedentary, screen-based entertainment), first-hand experience of the world they live in and regular interaction with the real-life significant adults in their lives.

They also need time. In a fast-moving hyper-competitive culture, today's children are expected to cope with an ever-earlier start to formal schoolwork and an overly academic test-driven primary curriculum. They are pushed by market forces to act and dress like mini-adults and exposed via the electronic media to material which would have been considered unsuitable for children even in the very recent past.

Our society rightly takes great pains to protect children from physical harm, but seems to have lost sight of their emotional and social needs. However, it's now clear that the mental health of an unacceptable number of children is being unnecessarily compromised, and that this is almost certainly a key factor in the rise of substance abuse, violence and self-harm amongst our young people.

This is a complex socio-cultural problem to which there is no simple solution, but a sensible first step would be to encourage parents and policy-makers to start talking about ways of improving children's well-being. We therefore propose as a matter of urgency that public debate be initiated on child-rearing in the 21st century. This issue should be central to public policy-making in coming decades.'

(Daily Telegraph, 12 September 2006)

Two children enjoying themselves on a trampoline. However, concerns about the risks associated with trampolines have been widely expressed, reflecting the debates about protection and risk.

Emphasis on risk management and safeguarding children is reflected in the 2007 Staying Safe Consultation (www.everychildmatters.gov.uk), which focuses on multi-disciplinary activity to safeguard children, aiming to:

- Raise awareness of the importance of safeguarding children and young people.
- Promote better understanding of safeguarding issues, encouraging a change in behaviour towards children and young people, and their safety and welfare.
- Ensure work in this area is coherent, and effectively coordinated across government, by outlining existing work in this area.
- Reinforce existing activity by proposing new actions to plug gaps and improve linkages.

It appears that every generation has concerns regarding the physical, sexual and moral welfare of its children and young people and moral panics regarding the nature of childhood are not new or unusual. This can be reflected by previous concerns over 'Mods and Rockers', child criminals following the tragic death of James Bulger, the 'Soham murders' and the depiction of young people as 'hoodies'. The latest concern over the impending death of childhood reflects Cohen's description of moral panics as

> A condition, episode, person or group of persons emerges to become defined as a threat to societal values and interests, it is presented in a stylized and stereotypical fashion by the mass media, the moral barriers are manned by editors, bishops, politicians and other right-thinking

people; socially accredited experts pronounce their diagnosis and solutions; ways of coping are evolved or (more often) resorted to; the condition then disappears, submerges or deteriorates and become more visible.

(Cohen, 1972: 9)

I do not wish to be cynical or negate the genuinely expressed concerns, but to highlight the fact that concerns regarding how much time children and young people spend on the internet tend to trivialise some of the major hazards that some children face as they struggle to overcome the impact of poverty, discrimination and abuse.

A contemporary image of children enjoying themselves in a playground. (Marzanna Syncer)

> **Exercise**
>
> **Has childhood changed for the better or worse?**
>
> This discussion could take place in the form of a debate whereby the group is divided into two and asked to present an argument in the style of an Oxford Motion.

Conclusion

An understanding of the social construction of childhood provides a useful framework in which to understand and articulate some of the issues and debates that concern social work when working with children and their families. The view that adults do not always know or act in the best interests of children, and the recognition that children have rights as well as needs, challenges the dominance of the welfarist approach in social work. Many adults, including parents, social workers, police officers and teachers, share the resistance to the recognition of children's rights. In social work, empowering children does not mean that they are able to do anything they want without consideration of their competence, but that child-centred practice means involving children of all ages in the matters and decisions that affect them. As Lansdown (2001) says, 'a commitment to respecting children's rights does not mean abandoning their welfare'.

Summary points

- Childhood is not a unitary concept but a diverse range of childhoods is experienced within society.
- Childhood is socially constructed and is shaped by adult and children alike.
- Sociological perspectives are relevant in understanding contemporary debates concerning the nature of childhood in society.
- Social work with children and families is characterised by poverty and social exclusion.
- Recognition of the rights of children, and a willingness to work in partnership with them and their families is essential for child-centred practice.

Questions for discussion

- Frones (1994) suggests that childhood has become more individualised, as children become consumers in their own right, with their own books, magazines, television programmes and games. Could this be seen as children acquiring greater rights and adult status or does such individualisation represent a greater division and separation between the states of being an adult and being a child?

- Are children free and innocent or are they now blighted with adult responsibilities and concerns?
- What evidence is there to suggest that childhood is a global concept?
- How can sociological perspectives of childhood enable social workers to promote the empowerment of children?

Further reading

Corsaro, W. (2005) *The Sociology of Childhood*. London: Sage. This book provides an overview of key social theories of childhood incorporating historical and contemporary perspectives.

James, A. and Prout, A. (2007) *Constructing and Reconstructing Childhood: Contemporary Issues in the Sociological Study of Childhood*. 2nd edn. London: Routledge. This 2nd edition is a useful book for students seeking a discussion of a wide range of contemporary issues regarding the construction of childhood in a global context.

Foley, P., Roche, J. and Tucker, S. (2001) *Children in Society*. Buckingham: Open University Press. Using children's rights and social inclusion as key themes, this book addresses a comprehensive range of issues concerning policy and practice in working with children across a range of different settings.

Lee, N. (2001) *Childhood and Society: Growing up in an Age of Uncertainty*. Buckingham: Open University Press. Using the ideas that the separation between adult and child worlds has become more fragmented, this book provides an interesting analysis of how children are growing up in an age of uncertainty. Contributions from scholars and professionals include an exploration of issues concerning children's rights to street children.

Parton, N. (2006) *Safeguarding Children: Early Intervention and Surveillance in a Late Modern Society*. London: Palgrave. Incorporating contemporary social theory this book examines latest developments in social work policy and practice.

10

Old Age

Older people make up a diverse group of individuals, with many different social, economic and cultural circumstances. However, a significant minority of older people make up one of the most disadvantaged and excluded groups in advanced capitalist societies. Thus social workers may encounter older people who are particularly vulnerable and who have specific care needs. Furthermore, social work practice operates within a social context of ageism and discrimination, where older people may be subject to stereotypical views and direct and indirect discrimination. Phillipson, 1998, discusses how social work with older people is a 'Cinderella' service, with work often carried out by unqualified staff. This in itself may be connected with social constructs linked to ageing. Social work with older people may also take place against a number of organisational constraints that hinder the promotion of positive practice.

This chapter will address the following key issues:

- Social definitions and context of ageing in contemporary Britain.
- Ageism and stereotypes of older people.
- Discriminatory practices in relation to older people, which relate to anti-oppressive practice and the role of social work.
- Social disadvantage, disempowerment and social exclusion of older people.
- Factors that promote positive images and experiences of older age.
- Contemporary issues in social work practice with older people.

By the end of this chapter you should be able to:

- Identify the social construction of old age as a distinct category of adulthood.
- Explain what is meant by chronological age.

- Critically explore the concept of chronological age as a basis for service provision.
- Demonstrate an understanding of the concepts of ageism and age discrimination.
- Explain the sources of disadvantage and oppression for older people.
- Demonstrate an understanding of positive ageing and the role of social work in the empowerment of older people.

There have always been older people in societies, but in the twentieth and twenty-first centuries they have become more visible (Wilson, 2000). The population is ageing and we are in a period of unprecedented change, with significant demographic transitions occurring. Not only are people living longer, but the birth rate is also declining, leading to a shift in the balance of the population and the ratio of economically active to non-economically active (Wilson, 2000). Lower fertility rates and the increase in divorce has led to a change in the structure and size of families, which has led to an increase in solo living in older age, as well as having implications for informal care for older people. In addition to this, the so-called baby-boomers of the 1940s are now entering a stage of older age, further increasing the relative size of this group.

While many older people live comfortable and fulfilled lives, there are a significant proportion who are impoverished, experiencing poor health or who are subject to various forms of institutional and domiciliary abuse. Social exclusion is an issue for a significant minority of older people, leading to vulnerability and poor quality of life. Whilst ageing itself does not necessarily result in poor health, there is a greater likelihood of deteriorating health and increased need for assistance with social care needs.

What is old age?

Traditional approaches to understanding phases in the life-course have focused on transitions between different life stages. One of the most frequently used definitions of old age is based on the notion of chronology, which views old age as a particular phase in the chronological life cycle, characterised by transition from independent

Chronological age a measure of age, related to number of years since a person was born. ← adulthood through retirement (Victor, 2005). *Chronological age* 'refers to the number of years that have elapsed since a person's birth' (Rybash et al., 1995: 13) and orders people according to historical experience. This is frequently the basis for institutional categorisation. Older age in western societies is therefore seen as a distinct phase of life, partly because of early research, which viewed older age as an event that could be objectively measured and observed.

However, this fails to take account of the social construction of this life stage, particularly within the capitalist division of labour. Old age as a distinct phase is associated with the introduction of pensions in the early twentieth century, following concerns about the productivity of the older age group and the increasing poverty amongst this age group. The introduction of fixed retirement ages and eligibility criteria was introduced in the 1908 Pensions Act (Hill, 1996) and was further developed by Beveridge in his blueprint for social security in 1942. Beveridge established the pension age at sixty-five for men and sixty for women, based on the premise of monogamous marriage and a male-breadwinner society (see Chapter 8), and the assumption that, as people aged, they were no longer as productive to society and so the pension was seen as an alternative source of income to work. The pension age was set at 60 for women, based on *patriarchal* assumptions (see Chapter 5) and the generalised assumption that on average, women marry men two years older than themselves, and therefore the differentials allow married couples to retire at the same time. The pension age for men and women has subsequently been equalised, and the age of eligibility for state pension is under increasing scrutiny because of demographic changes and projections (Baldwin and Falkingham, 1994).

However, based on the notion of chronological age, there are evident demographic and population changes. In 1995 there were less than 9 million people in Britain over the age of 65. This figure is projected to rise to over 14 million by the year 2030 (Debate of the Age, 1998).

Table 10.1 Population projections by age groups

Age	1994	2001	2011	2021	2031
All 65+ (millions)	9.2	9.3	10.0	11.7	14.0
% population	15.7	15.5	16.4	19.2	23.2
All 75+ (millions)	4.0	4.4	4.5	5.2	6.4
% population	7.0	7.4	7.5	8.5	10.6
All 85+ (millions)	1.0	1.2	1.3	1.4	1.8
% population	1.7	2.0	2.1	2.3	2.9

Source:
Making a Difference, 2000

While the statistics shown in Table 10.1 demonstrate significant changes in the size of the older population, there are other associated changes. The growth in the population has not occurred evenly across the age groups. Particularly relevant is the change in the composition of the under-sixteen age group. In mid 1971, they constituted 25 per cent of the population. By mid-2004, under-16s accounted for 19 per cent of the total population (Office for National Statistics, 2005). This has future implications for the ratio of working age to non-working age people if the current policy of compulsory retirement and pension provision continues to operate.

The P. D. James novel *The Children of Men* (now released as a film) offers a frightening futuristic world where no one has been born for eighteen years. Older people, once, they become dependent, are shipped out to sea and drowned. While futuristic, the book reflects demographic debate and discussion around an increasingly ageing population.

Exercise

Have old people become more visible throughout all aspects of society?

Look at the situations below. How visible are older people when you are:

1. out for a drink
2. at the pictures
3. on public transport
4. in the post office
5. at university

Another significant change has been in the increased longevity of the population. Not only has there been an increase in the number of people reaching retirement age, but there has been a concomitant massive change in the number of people living into their eighties and beyond. In mid-1971, 7 per cent of the total population was aged 85 and over. By mid-2004 this had risen to 12 per cent of the

Anne Llewellyn's grandmother on her 101st birthday.

total population (Office for National Statistics, 2005). This can be further demonstrated in an examination of the numbers of people living to 100 and beyond. In 1951, only 300 people in the UK reached age 100, compared to a projected 36,000 in 2030 (Debate of the Age, 1998).

The age at which one becomes eligible for pensions has become widely accepted as the definition of when old age begins and is reflected in institutional practices. Social service departments are structured around provisions for under 65s and over 65s and mental health services are structured around people of working age and over 65s. The impact of this has been to see the over 65s as a distinct category of the population, with different needs to other groups within the population. This has also resulted in the perpetuation of ageist practices in terms of discrimination and allocation of resources, with a tendency to see the over 65-age group as an

Homogenous a group of ◄ homogenous group with similar needs, leading to a one-size-fits-all
individuals or systems model of service provision.
that are seen as being
unified and sharing
common characteristics.

Social disadvantage and old age

Poverty and social exclusion

There are persistent and significant inequalities in older age (Phillipson, 1998), based on social stratification processes, such as occupational history, gender and ethnicity. There are 1.3 million pensioners totally reliant on the state pension and benefit system, although 20–30 per cent do not claim the means tested benefits to which they are entitled. Deacon and Bradshaw (1983) suggest that this is because of issues such as the stigmatisation of selective benefits.

> Pensioners make up a disproportionate share of those with the lowest incomes. Although pensioners on average enjoy better incomes than they have in the past, the rising average conceals a large minority dominated by older single women who have no additional resources other than the state retirement pension and means-tested benefit.
>
> (Social Exclusion Report, 2004: 62)

Older people occupy a significant proportion of sub-standard housing in the UK, which is more likely to be poorly insulated, contributing to problems of fuel poverty and an excess of winter deaths related to hypothermia. The Social Exclusion Report (1999) estimated that 20,000 to 45,000 people over the age of 65 die in winter months (depending on the harshness of winter conditions) and twice as many people living in energy-inefficient houses are from lower income groups. There is a higher incidence of ill-health and disability associated with older people, with two thirds of all disabled people being over the age of 60 (Age Concern, 1998). However, the incidence of disability and life-limiting illnesses are not evenly distributed across occupational groups, with men from manual occupations having a higher incidence of self-reported illness than men from non-manual occupational groups. Anxiety and depression are also significant contributors to morbidity in the 60 to 69 age group, possibly associated with dislocation from work roles, bereavement and other losses (Paul et al., 2006)

Exercise

- Go to the Help the Aged or Age Concern website (www.helptheaged.org.uk; www.ageconcern.org.uk).
- List three ways in which older people can become socially disadvantaged.

Social gerontology

Social gerontology is a relatively new discipline and adopts a multidisciplinary approach, drawing on theories from the social sciences, the arts and the humanities. The sociology of old age is concerned with:

1. people over their life course
2. age-related social structures and institutions
3. the dynamic interplay between people and structures, as they both influence each other.

(Riley and Riley, 1999)

However, Riley and Riley (1999) have argued that there has been a tendency in social gerontology to focus on individuals rather than the structural context within which old age is experienced, and there has been a tendency to treat older people as an *homogenous* group. They expose two fallacies in these approaches to the understanding of old age. Firstly, there is a life-course fallacy, which interprets age differences as the process of ageing, and secondly there is the fallacy of *cohort-centrism*, assuming common experiences among population cohorts.

Cohort-centrism the view that all people born in the same historical period will have common experiences.

> . . . the variability of the ageing process is one of the few truly universal social principles

(Riley and Riley, 1999: 125)

Old age as a social problem

Traditional theories of ageing have focused on old age as a problem at both a *micro* and a *macro* level. At a micro level, the focus is on the individual who experiences problems associated with the processes of ageing, while at a macro level, the focus is on the problem that society experiences due to an ageing population. The issue of power is implicit within this approach, as problem identification often reflects dominant values and ideas. There are two approaches here, the humanistic approach, which explores old age as a problem for individuals, and the organisational approach, which explores old age as a problem for society. Humanistic gerontology operates at the micro-level and has a relatively long tradition in social gerontology. Some research in this tradition has focused on identifying disadvantaged groups and describing their circumstances (e.g. Booth's study of poverty in the late nineteenth century in London, which identified older people as a group likely to experience poverty. This research was influential in the subsequent development of old age pensions, categorising older people as a group, distinct from other adults – see Jones, 1991). Other studies have focused on describing the circumstances of individuals, exploring issues such as loneliness and isolation (Tunstall, 1963), rather than the processes of ageing and the structural and institutional practices that shape older people's experiences.

The organisational approach, on the other hand focuses on macro-level issues, examining how the growing numbers of older people contribute to problems for societies and institutions. The burden of dependency thesis (Phillipson and Walker, 1986) presupposed that structural and institutional processes led to categorisation of older people as dependent (e.g. the construction of an age of retirement) with people becoming increasingly reliant on welfare provision to meet these culturally created needs (e.g. state pensions). Within this perspective, the state has three important functions:

- The allocation of scarce resources.
- Mediation between different groups in society.
- Addressing the conditions that threaten social order.

(Estes, 2001)

As the population aged and increasing numbers of people became dependent on welfare provision, older people came to be viewed as a problem for the welfare state. The growing numbers of older people who were dependent on welfare provision came to be seen as a burden due to the rising costs of sustaining this provision, leading to the widespread view that there was an economic crisis within the welfare state, and that the apocalyptic demography of an ageing population was largely responsible for this.

Furthermore, the burden of dependency thesis may lead to inter-generational conflict, as groups become segregated and compete against each other for resources. In particular, concerns have been raised about the relationship between workers and pensioners and the priorities for different groups (Phillipson, 1998).

Exercise

- Look at political party manifestoes.
- Is there evidence that services and provisions for younger people are seen as higher priority?
- Does the language change when talking about older people's provision (reflecting the notions of burden and crisis)?

Burden of dependency thesis the theory that older people are dependent on the state and this creates a burden on the welfare system.

Stereotypes ideas held about membership of particular groups, based primarily on membership of that group. They may be positive or negative.

Although there have been criticisms of this *burden of dependency thesis*, as it fails to take account of the positive contributions that older people can make to society, notions of crisis in funding statutory provision for older people continue to underpin policy debates in relation to income maintenance and health and social care provision (Victor, 2005). Criticisms of the *burden of dependency thesis* also emanate from a social model of disability perspective (see Chapter 11), which argues that disability does not necessarily create dependency, but the environment (physical and social) contributes to degrees of dependency. In the context of older age, the economic environment in terms of culturally created dependency through policies of compulsory retirement is important, but so too is the social and cultural environment which stereotypes older people and contributes to ageist practices.

The understanding of old age as a social problem derives from a biological model of ageing, which views old age as a period of inevitable physical decline and increasing dependency. There is an assumption that these processes are universal and occur in a uniform way as we age. These theories are reductionist and tend to homogenise older people, failing to acknowledge diversity and the impact of social, environmental and psychological factors on the processes and experiences of ageing. The focus on ageing as a problem fails to account for 'normal' or non-problematic ageing. The generalisation of deviance in old age has contributed to the negative stereotyping of older people.

- What stereotypes of older people are evident in the photograph opposite?
- What other stereotypes of older people can you think of?
- Think of other forms of popular culture (birthday cards, fairy tales, TV programmes – soap operas, sitcoms).
- Are there similar stereotypes portrayed within these different forms of popular culture?

Hazan (2000) has identified a number of stereotypes in old age, such as the assumption of the inextricable link between ageing and dependency, inflexible attitudes, conservative outlook and senility.

Stereotypes of older people.

> A *stereotype is presumed universally applicable, without regard to interpersonal differences.*
>
> (Hazan, 2000: 15)

This assumption of generality and universality in old age has led to particular forms of welfare provision for older people, based on assumptions of increasing dependency. Hugman (1994) has argued that health and social care services became medicalised, based on these assumptions of universal dependency, with an emphasis on secondary and tertiary care services and professional expertise. This welfarist model led to a form of health and social care provision, with the emphasis very much on health care needs and needs being met through a service-led agenda. Social care needs were seen as a lesser priority and there was failure to acknowledge a diversity of needs and abilities among older people.

While to some extent it is true that as people age there is a higher possibility of ill health and disability (Kings Fund Report, 2002), the assumption of inevitability has been challenged (Wilson, 2000). A purely biological focus on the process of ageing provides little insight into the impact of social and psychological processes that affect the individual.

Functionalist theory

Functionalist theories are generally concerned with social roles and how individuals adapt their roles. Underpinning these theories are notions of social value, normative expectations, equilibrium, integration and harmony. Disengagement theory, activity theory and age stratification theory all fall under the umbrella of functionalist theory.

Disengagement theory older people disengage from society and other people disengage from older people. This is seen as mutually beneficial.

◄ Disengagement theory

Within a broad theory of chronological age, Cumming and Henry (1963) proposed a disengagement theory, whereby older people are seen to disengage from society and society is seen to disengage from older people. This is seen as mutually beneficial in facilitating the acceptance of role changes associated with chronological changes and developments. However, it has been criticised as it sees old age in a negative light of reduced economic productivity, and is based on the normative premise that it is natural for older people to leave the labour market at a given age. This is in fact a social construction, which is based on the capitalist need for human resource management. A fixed retirement age suggests some rigidity in the labour market, but the reality is that retirement is used as a way of managing the labour market. There was, for example, a growing trend towards early retirement in the latter quarter of the twentieth century (Hill, 1996) linked to mass unemployment, the decline in semi-skilled and unskilled jobs and the concomitant growth in financial provision in old age. Chronological age is a poor indicator of ability to work, and negative stereotypes are used as justification for the exclusion of older people from the labour market (Phillipson, 1998). Furthermore, disengagement is not universal, with some

Gerontocracy a society or ◄ institution ruled by older people.

occupational groups being dominated by a *gerontocracy*.

Disengagement theory also fails to account for some of the other roles that older people may take on when they leave paid employment, e.g. grandparenting and volunteering. Volunteering can help people to adjust to other losses in life, giving them a sense of purpose and fulfilment (Baldock, 1999) and is becoming an important part of a mixed economy of welfare, which relies on the voluntary sector to provide important health and social care services to various client groups. Thompson (1999) has argued that grandparents are increasingly playing a part in the care of pre-school children and in after-school care of older children. This is supported by government policies, which stress the importance of the grand-parenting role in the light of other demographic changes such as the increase in the number of single-parent families and increased female participation in the paid labour market. In terms of social work practice, it is also important to note that grandparents play a significant role in caring for children who no longer live with parents due to abuse, neglect or other child protection issues.

Activity theory the view that the ageing process is delayed and quality of life is enhanced when old people remain socially active.

Activity theory

A counter-theory to the disengagement theory is *activity theory* (Havighurst, 1963), which posits that, rather than older people being seen as increasingly inactive, old age is a period of activity and engagement in different pursuits. However, this too has been criticised as it is seen as prescriptive and normative, and fails to acknowledge social divisions and social circumstances (poverty and poor health, for example), which may impact on an individual's ability to participate in activities. Thus the notion of a prescribed norm of activity as proposed by this theory is in danger of *pathologising* and victim-blaming those who are unable or unwilling to participate.

Exercise

- Go to your local leisure centre. What sort of activities are aimed specifically at older people?
- Why is it necessary to direct activities at this age group?
- Why might sociologists be critical of this approach?

Age stratification theory

Age stratification theory assumes that people can be grouped together, with the assumption that people of a similar age will have similar experiences and age-related abilities. Three basic themes are relevant in this theory:

1. The meaning of ageing and the position of older people within a particular social context.
2. Transitions within the lifecycle are related to social definitions of ageing. Thus, as was discussed earlier, retirement as a particular social construction defines the experiences of age-related cohorts.
3. Processes for the allocation of resources between different groups are related to social definition.

The allocation of age-related roles and the assumption of age-related abilities leads to homogenisation of older people, assuming common experiences and circumstances. However, this theory is also useful for exploring the power that underpins social definitions, and helps to explain the relative value of different social groups within a socially differentiated society. Evaluation of each group is based on dominant social values, and the marginalisation of certain groups can therefore be seen to reflect the relative power that different groups hold.

Fisher (1978) delineated four distinct historical periods of attitudes towards older people in the United States of America (although there are clear comparisons within other western industrialised nations).

1. A period of veneration and respect, which resulted in a *gerontocratic* society. This period ran approximately from the early 1600s to 1820 and the process of industrialisation.
2. A period characterised by revolutionary attitudes spreading across Europe and USA, associated with developments in industrial capitalism – societies became much more supportive of youth and older people became increasingly denigrated. During this time, pejorative terms for older people (such as 'old fogey') emerged.
3. 1800–1970. There remained an increasing emphasis on the values and virtues of youth in terms of productivity in the capitalist economy, but also, increasingly, in terms of identity, the body and health. (It could be argued that this continues today.)
4. 1970s onwards is characterised by older people being increasingly seen as a burden on society and as a social problem, requiring welfare intervention (see above the burden of dependency thesis).

Exercise

- Think of terms which are used to describe older people.
- Is the language about older people mainly pejorative?
- Why would sociologists argue that the elderly is an inadequate term for describing older people and their experiences?

What these theories fail to take account of is the impact of political and economic processes on the experiences of ageing and analysis of class, gender and ethnicity as variables that contribute to differential experiences of ageing are largely absent. Conflict theories, on the other hand, are concerned with the macro-level analysis of the political and economic context of ageing and can be seen to derive from Marxist and Weberian sociological perspectives.

Conflict theories

Political economy theory

Political economy theory challenges the biomedical and individualistic approach to ageing and argues that experiences of ageing are structured within a given political and economic context.

In advanced capitalist societies, old age is seen within the context of the division of labour and the inequalities that are structured through this. Thus, rather than being a time of harmony and homogeneity, older age is characterised by divisions, which are based on class, gender and ethnicity. Walker (1981) identified the *social creation of dependency* in old age, based on the notion of forced retirement and the pensions system. From the same perspective, Townsend (1981) referred to the *structured dependency of old people*. This draws on Titmuss' notion of the social division of welfare (1958) in which he argues that dependencies are either naturally occurring (childhood, for example) or are culturally created (old age), with state intervention through the welfare system providing some form of assistance. However, he goes on to argue that this leads to social divisions as there is a social division of welfare related to the social division of labour.

Estes (1979) identifies a *structural lag*; which is created by age barriers and reflects the mismatch between the abilities and resources of older people and the opportunities that they are afforded within the capitalist society. In addition she referred to the *ageing enterprise* of capitalist society, where older people become processed and treated as a commodity. Policies segregate older people from other adults, leading to social divisions and stigmatisation. Thus social policies, rather than ameliorating social problems, may contribute to continuing social divisions and inequalities.

This perspective has been criticised for the over-emphasis on class as the basis for divisions and inequalities. The theories of the 1970s and 1980s

> ended up reproducing a framework which emphasised the primacy of class. For a period, such class reductionism inhibited analyses between the relationship between class, race, gender, sexuality, or other markers of social differentiation.
>
> (Brah, 1994: 811)

Furthermore, political economic theories have been criticised for failing to explore the experiences of older age for individuals, and their meanings, interpretations and interactions within society. In response to this, a critical gerontology has developed, which integrates macro-level and micro-level theories to provide a more comprehensive analysis of old age (Phillipson, 1998). This offers opportunities for exploring the multiple roots of oppression and disempowerment in old age, but at the same time explores how old age can have meaning or lack meaning for older people and can offer opportunities for empowerment. Estes (2001) has developed an approach to understanding old age, which integrates structural factors in post-modernity, the role of the state, the intersection of multiple roots of oppression (class, gender, ethnicity) with notions of citizenship and the ageing enterprise.

Positive ageing

In the field of gerontology, a number of theories have developed since the 1970s that have challenged the negative view of older age, and have explored the diversity of experience and offered more positive conceptualisations of older people. Laslett (1989) was one of the first theorists to offer a more positive perspective of ageing in his theory of the Third Age. According to Laslett, old age is not a period of social and physical inactivity, but with the increasing longevity of the population, an increasing number of people are able to enjoy an extended period of fulfilment in retirement. For Laslett, the lifecycle is made up of four stages:

1. A first age of dependency, socialisation and education. This is usually (although not exclusively) associated with periods of childhood and adolescence.
2. A second age of maturity, independence, familial and social responsibility. This stage is usually associated with adulthood, child rearing and engagement in paid employment.
3. A third age of personal achievement and fulfilment (similar to Maslow's psychological theory of self-actualisation). Although this might coincide with the second age, Laslett argues that it often occurs once people have been divested of family and work responsibilities and are able to pursue goals of personal fulfilment.
4. A fourth age of dependence and decrepitude. This he sees as a fairly short period of time before death.

The third age concept has been subjected to a number of criticisms, not least that it fails to take account of social divisions based on political and economic factors and health status. Many have argued that Laslett offers a halcyon account of old age, which does not reflect the reality of people's experiences based on structural and ideological divisions. Nevertheless, the theory has some value in that it provides a counter-view to the prevailing view of inevitable dependence in old age, and questions the assumption that older people cannot/do not make a useful contribution to society.

Vincent (1995) has argued that consumption is a dominant way in post-modern society in which people are integrated into the political economic structure. Although there is evidence of ageist practices within the consumer market, with advertisers either focusing on a youth market or promoting products to defy the ageing process, increasing attention is being paid to older people as active consumers, e.g. through travel companies, car manufacturers, insurance companies, the clothing and fashion industry, acknowledging the importance of the grey market in capitalist society.

Life course and biographical approaches

In developing gerontological theory, there is growing emphasis on a life-course perspective, which sees old age within the context of the whole life journey (Binstock and George, 2001). Life-course perspectives integrate the micro worlds of individuals and the macro patterns of institutional organisation and social change. Thus the experience of old age is, in part, dependent on other experiences throughout the life course. Experiences of racism, sexism or other forms of discrimination may affect people's perceptions and experiences in old age, as well as social stratification processes, contributing to people's income and health status in older age. Thus old age is a period of heterogeneity, with people having very different experiences.

> People's location in the social system, the historical period in which they live and their unique personal biography shape the experience of old age.
> (Stoller and Gibson, 1994: xxiii)

Exercise

- Write down the things that have affected the patterns of your individual lives.
- Now divide these into macro-level societal changes and individual micro-level factors.

The macro-level factors may be factors, which unite you with other members of an age cohort, but the micro-level factors are unique to you and shape the experiences that you have had and the way that you have responded to them.

Ruth and Kenyon (1996) have identified three benefits of using a biographical approach to the study of old age.

1. They contribute to the development of theories of adult development and old age.
2. They provide a focus on the public and personal way that people develop.
3. They provide an important understanding as to how individuals believe that life can be enhanced.

Biographical approaches shape the way that people age from within, and people's narratives are important for understanding the richness and complexities of lived experiences. Featherstone and Hepworth (1991) refer to the mask of ageing, which relates to the observable physical processes associated with ageing (wrinkles, greying or thinning of hair, loss of physical stature, decline in sensory perceptions). Seeing beyond this mask, through a phenomenological understanding of the meaning of ageing to individuals helps us to see beyond the negative experiences and engage with individuals as unique human beings.

The new critical gerontology that is emerging helps us to understand the plurality of experiences that older people have and the impact of other variables such as gender and ethnicity in the biography of the individual.

Gender and old age

Old age is gendered (Arber and Ginn, 1995), with an intersection between ageing and gender. On average, women outlive men and outnumber men in older age groups. Over the age of 75, women outnumber men by two to one, by four to one in the 85+ age group and by seven to one living to 100 and beyond (Bernard and Phillips, 1998). Men are more likely to suffer from life-threatening illnesses such as coronary heart disease (CHD) and strokes, leading to a higher premature mortality rate, whilst women are more likely to suffer from life-limiting illnesses such as diabetes, arthritis etc. There is some evidence that this pattern will change with changing lifestyles and work practices, meaning that the differentials will become less marked in the future (Annandale, 1998). Nevertheless, the experiences of ageing may be very different for men and women. Two thirds of men receive non-state pensions, whereas three quarters of women do not. This is significant as non-state pensions offer a better income than state pensions, so the incidence of poverty and social exclusion amongst older women is much higher.

The sexualisation of women's value also leads to women's and men's differential experiences of ageing (Ginn and Arber, 1993). Once past the age of reproductive capacity, women's contribution to society becomes devalued as women are judged in terms of physical appearance. Men's physical appearance is less important, as they are valued for their continuing contribution to economic productivity. For women, age-related appropriate behaviours are constructed, particularly in terms of the body and fashion. The *mutton dressed as lamb* simile is a good indication of the age-related expectations in society. This emphasis on appearance becomes commodified through the availability of cosmetic surgery and anti-ageing products (Annandale, 1998). This dual standard of ageing is not just about appearance, but further contributes to oppressive practices in respect of older women.

> structures, policies and ideology of western capitalist society are a major cause of women's relative social and economic powerlessness. In societies such as ours that are systematically . . . at times sexist, racist and ageist . . . it is hardly surprising that amongst the myriad disadvantaged groups, older women feature particularly strongly.
>
> (Bernard and Meade, 1993: 2)

This picture of an older couple reflects a demographic trend, as the age structure of BME groups changes, leading to a much higher percentage of ethnic elders. (Cliff Parnell)

Ethnicity and old age

There are also significant trends in relation to minority ethnic groups and the ageing population. Ahmad and Walker (1997) have argued that there is a paucity of literature about ethnic elders (although, there is now a growing body of research and literature – see, for example, Blakemore and Boneham, 1994), and one of the explanations for this is that ethnic elders constitute a very small percentage of the total aged population and of the total minority ethnic population. However, this is projected to change, as patterns of migration of the 1950s and 1960s result in significant population change as minority ethnic groups age. Thus minority ethnic elders constitute one of the fastest growing groups within the older population.

The experiences of minority ethnic elders also have to be understood in the context of wider social practices and ideologies, in

Table 10.2 People over the age of 65 by ethnic group (%)

	(%)
Black-Caribbean	9
Black-African	2
Indian	6
Pakistani	4
Bangladeshi	3
Chinese	5

Source:
2001 Census

relation to the structural position of minority ethnic populations and the impact of direct, indirect and institutional racism (see Chapter 5). There needs to be a more complex theoretical underpinning to understand the diverse range of experiences that ethnic elders may have, based on racism and ageism, and acknowledging the importance of understanding difference within difference (not all older people from minority ethnic backgrounds will have the same experiences, and it is important not to conflate ethnic categories). This is important for social work practice. Social workers face significant issues in engaging and working with minority ethnic elders. The issue may be more to do with available translation services and social work organisations' willingness and ability to engage with differing needs relating to cultural and familial lifestyles.

Older people from black and minority ethnic groups may be particularly disadvantaged and are more likely to suffer discrimination in accessing services according to the King's Fund Report (2002). Norman (1985) refers to the triple jeopardy for ethnic elders of ageism and racism and the perception of a lack of access to appropriate services. There may also be a fourth jeopardising factor of not having English as a first language, thus further reducing the accessibility of the services. The one-size-fits-all approach can disadvantage ethnic elders, and take-up tends to be low, reflecting a level of unmet need and a lack of awareness of needs amongst service providers. The King's Fund Report (2002) concludes that most black elders would prefer to access mainstream services rather than specialist service provision, but may have difficulties because of a lack of awareness amongst service commissioners and providers.

Ageism

What is ageism? Ageism involves discrimination against people on the basis of age. While it can affect any age group, the concern here is with the way that older people are discriminated against on the basis of stereotypes that are universally applied to particular groups within the life course. Older people may frequently be subjected to ageist practices at an individual as well as an institutional level, based on stereotypical assumptions and values.

> In particular, ageism legitimates the use of chronological age to mark out classes of people who are systematically denied resources and opportunities that others enjoy, and who suffer the consequences of such denigration, ranging from well-meaning patronage to unambiguous vilification.
> (Bytheway and Johnson, 1990, cited in Bytheway, 1995: 14)

Ageism is widespread in advanced capitalist societies as demonstrated in the Report by Age Concern in 2005. More people reported suffering age discrimination than any other form of discrimination and was particularly experienced by people over the age of fifty-five. The report also identified the perception that age discrimination is not only getting worse, but that demographic factors will exacerbate this.

Age discrimination may be either direct or indirect and both are seen as widespread in health and social care. The King's Fund Report (2002) identified a number of areas in health and social care where older people are either directly discriminated against through policies such as breast screening, based on explicit age criteria, or more indirectly through referral and commissioning processes.

The King's Fund Report (2002) also highlighted widespread discrimination against older workers within health and social care employment. It has been argued that the composition of a workforce should reflect the composition of the community it serves and within which it operates. Not only might a paucity of older workers within the institutional structures impact on the direction of policies, but also services may be seen to be unrepresentative by service users.

The Kings' Fund Report (2002) also found that there is underdevelopment of user-involvement in policy formulation of services, despite Government policies stressing the importance of user perspectives and patient and public involvement in health and social care (NHS Plan, 2000; Your Health, Your Care, Your Say, 2006 – available at www.dh.gov.uk). Furthermore, three quarters of senior managers in health and social care believed that age discrimination operated in local services and that ageism is endemic in health and social care employment and service provision.

Risk

A further manifestation of ageism and stereotypical assumptions informing practice with older people is in the way that risk is managed. Risk is an unavoidable feature of post-modern life, yet stereotypical assumptions about the physical and mental capacity of older people, as well as the historical approach to older people's needs based on notions of dependency may impact on the way that risk is managed and people's ability to be independent. Recent policies in relation to older people have stressed the importance of maximising independence through person-centred and anti-discriminatory approaches (NSF for Older People, 2001; Choosing Health White Paper, 2004 – www.dh.gov.uk). Yet, the focus on risk management can inhibit this independence and the value and self-esteem of older people.

As we move towards an agenda of legal protection for vulnerable adults, the need to promote positive risk-taking as part of risk management becomes increasingly important. A number of authors have stressed the importance of positive risk-taking. Positive risk-taking asks the question as to why risk is always negative and associated with danger, harm and injury. Rather, health and social care professionals should be working to enable people to try and explore new activities. Elements of risk in this approach need to be explored in partnership with users and carers. However, O Sullivan (2002) discusses how positive risk-taking models are somewhat vague in detail. This is an area that needs exploring in relation to work with older people (and other groups). As the adult protection agenda develops, it is important that we do not over-protect people, while supporting their vulnerability. The Social Care Institute of Excellence has produced a good practice guide on managing the mental health needs of older people, which supports positive practice in this area (SCIE, 2006 – www.scie.org.uk).

Questions to consider

- Do we allow older people to take risks in the same way as other social groups?
- Is there evidence of unnecessary hospital or care home admissions because of family or professional reluctance to accept risks among older people?

Scenario 1

Violet is an eighty-three-year-old woman with dementia who lives in warden-assisted accommodation. Recently, she has become increasingly forgetful and has left food burning on her stove, causing the smoke alarms to go off. She has also been wandering around at night, asking her neighbours the time and for items of food. Her daughter and the warden tell you that they cannot manage the situation. You discuss the risks for Violet and your manager suggests that you start to look at care home options.

Scenario 2

You go to see Violet to discuss the above risks and concerns. Her daughter says her mother cannot cope with having a conversation about these concerns. However, after some time chatting generally to Violet, it transpires that she keeps buying food and then forgetting where it is. She shows a burn on her arm where she dropped a boiling pan. She often feels hungry in the night, as she is not managing to cook. You suggest a memory prompting system concerning where basic food items are and ask Violet if she could manage to use a microwave. Although the warden and her daughter are reluctant to try this approach, they agree to give it a go for two weeks. You obtain funding for someone to pop in during the day to see if Violet has eaten, and the warden agrees to look in on Violet in the evening. Two weeks later and all report that Violet has been much calmer and her appetite has improved. While she still occasionally wanders at night, she can be prompted to find items she has forgotten. You agree to review things again in a few weeks.

Of course, there are some real causes of risk for older people, neglect of which may compromise their health status and ability to participate independently in society. For example, it is important that older people (like other people) are adequately nourished and hydrated in order to maintain health and functionality; older people have the highest incidence of falls (apart from the under fives) and there is increased risk of serious damage associated with the falls (Standard 5 of the NSF focuses specifically on falls prevention and management); risk of abuse from care-givers (see below). However, frequently, management of risk is focused on individual capacity, and diverts attention away from the social and environmental context of risks. Much of the work on falls prevention for example, has focused on providing equipment and education to older people, and assistive technologies so that they can summon help. Whilst this may be effective, it needs to be provided in conjunction with wider preventative measures, such as:

- improving pavements and pedestrianised areas
- improving quality of living accommodation, to remove environmental hazards within the home
- reducing fuel poverty and other structural factors that contribute to morbidity and mortality among vulnerable older people.

Risk and abuse

There are a number of reasons why the issue of elder abuse has not received the same societal or policy attention as child abuse:

- Older people may not come into contact with external agencies as often as children, making detection more difficult.
- There may be a lack of attention focused on elder abuse compared to child abuse within professional education programmes, reflecting cultural and professional priorities.
- Cultural ideologies about the protection of vulnerable children tend to get greater attention, reflecting the emphasis on the values and virtues of youth in western societies and the ageist attitudes to older people.

Biggs (1996) argues that the acknowledgement of domiciliary elder abuse presents a paradox to governments, as they promote the family as a unit of caring within community care policies. It is, however, important to understand the nature and incidence of abuse (in both domiciliary and institutional settings), as the impact of abuse can not only disempower older people, but also compromises their rights to citizenship.

In recent years, the problem of elder abuse has become much more prominent in both the mass media and in policy formulation. Comic Relief has drawn attention to the abuse of vulnerable older people and a number of TV documentaries have exposed both domestic and institutional abusive practices. Dad, a screenplay with Richard Briers showed a fictional account of elder abuse, which

Exercise

- Ask colleagues/friends if they have heard of Margaret Panting.
- Now ask if they have heard of Victoria Climbié.
- Is there a difference in the responses?

Victoria Climbié was an 8-year-old girl who was systematically abused by her care-givers, her aunt and her aunt's boyfriend, which eventually resulted in her death. The death was widely reported in the news media. Both caregivers were charged under the CJS and there was a public enquiry to investigate why statutory services of social care, health care and the police service had failed to protect the child.

Margaret Panting was a seventy-eight-year-old lady who was taken out of a care home to be cared for by family. Within one month she was dead, and on investigating her death the pathologist found over one hundred injuries on her body, including cigarette burns and lacerations. Her son-in-law and his sons were arrested on suspicion of her murder, but the Crown Prosecution Service decided that there was insufficient evidence to bring charges against them. This death largely escaped the attention of the mass media, and there was no public enquiry to investigate what lessons may be learned from this case (Action on Elder Abuse. www.elderabuse.org.uk).

Questions to consider

1. Why do you think there is such a difference between the public and statutory responses to these two incidences of abuse and death?
2. Does this reflect an ageist attitude and lack of public concern about older people compared to younger people?
3. Does society perceive children as more vulnerable than older people, and therefore in need of a greater amount of protection?

highlighted the tensions and conflicts between parents and children that can lead to adult abuse. As a dominant form of information and social attitude formation (see Chapter 2), the media play an important role in raising awareness about elder abuse.

In policy terms, *No Secrets* (DH, 2000b) clarifies the role of Social Service Departments and Social Workers within a multi-agency framework, based on principles of collaborative working, empowerment of service users, supporting their rights (the issue of capacity is crucial here) and acknowledging that in the right to self-determination, older people have the right to take risks, providing there is proper understanding of the risks involved. Health and social care professionals need to address risk in partnership with service users to promote independence, rather than dependence (a clear theme identified by the adult social care paper *Independence, Well Being and Choice*, DH, 2005). There is ongoing debate about the efficacy of the quasi-legal framework to protect vulnerable adults and it is likely that further legislation will be proposed in this area. An Adult Protection Bill has been passed in Scotland (2006) (www.scottish.parliament.uk/business/bills/62-adultSupport), and there has been a recent Private Members' bill on the protection of older people. It is important that there is ongoing debate on this issue, so that we do not move from negligence to over-protection.

Older people may also be disempowered through institutional practices and community care policies. Long-term care needs of older people with varying degrees of dependency have historically been provided for through a system of nursing and residential care homes (Means and Smith, 2003). While there is evidence of much good and innovative practice within this care sector, there is also evidence of institutionalisation and a lack of individual care or autonomy, as the following quote illustrates.

> Nothing quite prepared me for the shock of entering residential care. Most of the staff are incredibly patient and kind – and I appreciate their help – but it is the constant bustle and ringing of bells from which one cannot escape . . . and the limited choice about food, activities or even companionship, which I find so hard to take. Then I am not allowed to do anything considered the least bit risky, one understands it is to keep one safe . . . but it's pretty galling at my age, after a life of independence, to find oneself so powerless and constrained.
>
> (cited in McClymont, 1999)

Institutionalisation may lead to loss of liberty, stigmatisation, lack of autonomy, poor material resources and loss of dignity. In addition, institutionalisation is often associated with a medicalised or welfarist model of care, with power being concentrated in the hands of professionals. A good example of this is in the care of the dying, which has become increasingly, medicalised and sequestered from society. While it is not just older people who die, the rise in longevity and chronic illness means that, increasingly, dying has come to be associated with old age.

Exercise

Look at an obituary page in a local newspaper.

- What does it tell us about the ages at which the majority of people die?
- Does it tell us anything about the location of most people's deaths?

Most people die in some form of institution, although increasingly people are expressing preferences for a home death. Death in an

Social death a concept that describes the way that people are viewed prior to their biological death. Used by Sudnow in his critique of the social organisation of death.

institution can lead to social isolation and may impact on the quality of the dying experience. Komaromy (2000) identified the objectification of the deceased within nursing and residential homes and referred to the concept of *social death* in which institutional practices may lead to people being treated as though dead, before the actual biological death has occurred. The medicalisation of death and dying also leads to a number of issues in relation to power and control. Information processes are important in terms of control, and within a medicalised model of care professionals are seen as the experts and therefore have power over information. People may not be informed about their impending death for a number of reasons, but Davey (2001) argues that ageist practices also contribute to medical decisions about information sharing in relation to end-of-life care.

> In April 2000 Age Concern England publicized an account of a do-not-resuscitate (DNR) decision written in the hospital notes of an older patient without her knowledge, and the British media claimed doctors 'let older patients die' who could have been resuscitated
>
> (Davey, 2001: 247)

Age Concern (1999) has also raised concerns about older people being denied adequate fluids and nutrition in hospital settings, although the medical profession have disputed this claim (*The Independent*, 7 December 1992).

In late modernity, topics such as euthanasia, assisted suicide and advanced directives have featured more highly on both the pubic and the political agenda (Blank and Merrick, 2005). However, the pluralist nature of late modern societies means that there is no single source of moral authority (Turner, 1992). Secularisation has led to a reduction in the role of religion in guiding moral decisions, while at the same time medical and legal decisions have become more omnipresent. Individuals may find their autonomy and ability to be self-determinate in decisions around end-of-life care compromised within this context. There is an important role for social workers here. Social work interest and involvement in palliative care and end-of-life care is increasing, and Croft et al. (2005) point to the important role for social workers in advocacy and information-sharing at the end of life, which can help to improve the quality of the dying experience.

Much of the discussion above seems to paint a rather negative picture of older age. However, recent policy imperatives have sought to promote positive ageing, working in partnership with older people to enable and empower them and maximise independence (e.g. NSF for Older People, 2001). The Single Assessment Process (SAP), implemented in June 2002 as part of Standard 2 of the NSF is concerned with collaborative working between professionals to provide person-centred, effective and coordinated care. Older people are central to this process, as the care is about and for them and they are the experts in their own care needs. Thus the principles of SAP focus on the strengths and resources of older people, rather than service-led provision. Although there have been a number of criticisms of the practical operation of SAP (e.g. Glasby, 2004), it does provide the potential for a more enabling approach to the care of older people. Social workers are ideally placed to engage in this enabling approach.

> Social workers have expertise and experience in working with older people who are experiencing health and social care difficulties. They often have to understand these difficulties in the wider context of the older person's family, social, financial, housing and other circumstances. Social workers also play an important role in contributing to, or coordinating, assessment and care planning where a number of agencies are involved. The single assessment process guidance builds on these strengths.
>
> (www.dh.gov.uk)

Conclusion

Although the evidence throughout this chapter has shown that ageism and discrimination are widespread within contemporary western democracies, current gerontological theory offers a different way of conceptualising older people as a diverse group of individuals with multiple stories to tell. This is increasingly informing policies, which aim to provide greater flexibility of service provision for older people, combating discrimination and valuing and empowering older people, hearing their voices and respecting their rights as active citizens.

Social work practice with older people needs to be seen within the context of these wider changes. Social workers are distinguished from other professional groups and practitioners through their value base of anti-oppressive practice, and respect for the rights of individuals and social workers can play an important role in promoting anti-ageist practice and positive experiences for older people. A number of social work theories lend themselves to working with older people. For example, the systems-based approach promotes a view of service users within a broader family and social context, allowing for a more comprehensive understanding of the individual within their social context. This is very much in keeping with the notion of person-centred and individualised care. In addition, a systems approach can help to focus on the different organisational sources of support that may be available to individuals, helping to remove some of the barriers that have developed around health and social care provision (Lymbery, 2005).

Although social work with older people may have been constrained by organisational boundaries, priorities and funding issues, an understanding of gerontological theory and the diverse needs and experiences of older people can help to develop a more emancipatory approach to working with older people. Social workers are ideally placed to witness the inequities and oppressions that people experience and to challenge existing political and economic structures that may shape those experiences in order to truly empower older people. Within the radical social work movement, there has been relatively little attention in relation to older people's services, but demographies and changing ideological contexts make this an area where social workers can really make a difference to people's experiences.

Summary points

- Chronological age is the most commonly used definition of old age and is often used in service provision and social policies.
- Sociological perspectives help us to understand the social construction of ageing as a distinct category of adulthood.
- Structural perspectives locate ageing and the experiences of ageing within the social, political and economic structures of society.
- Social action perspectives help us to understand the experience of ageing from the perspective of the individuals who experience it.
- Experiences of old age are wide and varied, but a significant minority of older people are vulnerable and socially disadvantaged.
- Institutional practices may contribute to the disempowerment and marginalisation of older people.
- The concept of positive ageing is important in helping older people to be empowered and valued.

Questions for discussion

- How do the sociological perspectives of old age help us to understand the marginalisation of older people in contemporary capitalist societies?
- Is ageing biological or social? How can the structures and institutions of society shape the experience of ageing?
- How can sociological perspectives help us to develop an understanding of ageism and inform anti-oppressive social work practice?
- Have a look at the voluntary sector websites. What services and projects are available to enhance quality of life in old age?

Further reading

Arber, S. and Ginn, J. (eds) (1995) *Connecting Gender and Ageing: A Sociological Approach*. Buckingham: Open University Press. Although rather dated, this is a useful text for exploration of the intersection between gender and ageing.

Blakemore, K. and Boneham, M. (1994) *Age, Race and Ethnicity*. Buckingham: Open University Press. Although rather dated, this book is useful as it explores the relationship between ageing and ethnicity and provides a useful discussion of the importance of understanding culture in relation to the experience of ageing.

Bowling, A. (2005) *Ageing Well: Quality of Life in Old Age*. Buckingham: Open University Press. This book embraces the positive aspects of ageing and explores ways in which professionals can work with older people to enhance their quality of life.

Lymbery, M. (2005) *Social Work with Older People: Context, Policy and Practice*. London: Sage. Although, as the title suggests, this is a book about social work practice with older people, it is useful for understanding the context of practice with older people and the development of a specific policy agenda.

Phillipson, C. (1998) *Reconstructing Old Age*. London: Sage. This book explores theories of old age in an accessible way, and engages with contemporary debates in social gerontology as well as how theory can help us to understand and address some of the challenges in relation to an ageing population.

Victor, C. (2005) *The Social Context of Ageing: A Textbook of Gerontology*. London: Routledge. This provides a good overview of the theorising of old age within social gerontology, and also explores issues, such as material resources in old age, family and caring networks which are relevant for social work practice with older people.

Walker, A. and Hennessy, C. (2004) *Growing Older: Quality of Life in Old Age*. Buckingham: Open University Press. This text is based on material from an ESRC funded project, which explores issues of quality of life, and focuses on ways in which these can be enhanced.

11

Health and Disability

Sociological interest in health and illness is a relatively new sub-discipline of sociology, although it has gathered momentum since the 1970s. Historically, mainstream sociology has largely ignored disability, with sociological perspectives focusing on health and chronic illness. However, more recently sociological perspectives have been influenced by the emergence of disability studies, which have informed the development of 'medical' and 'social' models of disability and are relevant to health and social care policies in this area. Throughout this chapter, debates and discussions about these models will be explored, particularly focusing on disability to exemplify these arguments. This chapter is concerned with looking at people with a range of disabling conditions, whether these are congenital (born with a condition) or acquired (through illness or accident). References and examples will be made to people with physical, learning and sensory (hearing/vision) disabilities.

The key issues that will be explored in this chapter are:

- The meaning of disability and different theoretical models to explain disability.
- Historical perspectives on disability and the development of sociological thinking on health and illness.
- The emergence of the social model of disability and post-modern sociological perspectives.
- Criticisms of the social model.
- The application of the social model of disability and contemporary issues in social work practice.

By the end of this chapter, you should be able to:

- Demonstrate an understanding of the different models of disability.

- Discuss the nature of social disadvantage and disempowerment experienced by people with disabilities.
- Understand the sociology of the body theory and its relevance within health and disability studies.
- Discuss the relationship between risk and disability.

Approaches to health, illness and disability

Biomedical model the theory that the basis of disease, including mental illness, is physical in origin. Illness can be identified objectively through signs and symptoms and treated scientifically with technology, e.g. drugs and surgical interventions. The body can be likened to a machine that can be broken down into its component parts.

Historically the biomedical model has heavily influenced studies of health, illness and disability. Within this perspective, the organisation of health and illness has been seen to be very much concerned with treatment and improving function. Kleinman's (1988) model of the three overlapping sectors of health care (the professional sector, the folk sector and the popular sector) is useful for understanding the organisation of health and illness. The folk sector includes alternative and complementary forms of health care provision that sit outside the professional biomedical sector. The popular sector is the lay sector of health care, which includes individuals, families, communities and peer influences (Nettleton, 2006). The popular sector is important in terms of socialisation of health and illness behaviours as well as providing informal care. However, in western society, the professional sector has historically had the most power and influence in determining policy, deciding what is illness and how to treat it, and in managing the nation's health. The professional sector is dominated by the medical or individual model of illness and disability. In this model acute infectious diseases were the major causes of morbidity and mortality and dominated the health and social care sector until the present day.

Functionalism and illness

From a functionalist perspective, professionals 'manage' illness and health problems, supporting a stable society. Talcott Parsons (1951) was one of the first sociologists to look at health and illness. He developed the idea of a *sick role* for people with disabilities from a functionalist perspective (see Chapter 2). His emphasis was on people taking responsibility for their sickness/treatment and getting better, as illness prevented them from carrying out the 'normal' functions in society (e.g. employment, contributing to their community). Hence, their role was to get well and commit to this process. This process was very much seen as medically orientated, requiring ongoing treatment from health professionals. This continual process of assessment and revision can be seen within twentieth century social policies relating to illness. For example, medical practitioners are engaged in on-going review of eligibility for incapacity benefit and, more recently, there has been a drive towards returning incapacity benefit recipients to work. This would seem to echo the view that illness is related to work ability and societal obligations and responsibilities (Nettleton, 2006).

A number of criticisms has been levelled at this analysis. Many chronically ill or disabled people would not see themselves as sick and it does not take account of impairment as opposed to sickness (Oliver, 1993). Many disabled people are not sick, but have ongoing impairments that do not present as daily health problems. For example, a person who is blind or deaf is probably not going to need or be in receipt of ongoing treatment. Also, some people are not going to recover from long-term health problems or disabilities. How would their place in society fit into Parsons' model of the sick role?

Another major concern is that by focusing on the 'sick' role, much of the solution is in the hands of health professionals to help people get well. This creates a label and a *stigma* associated with sickness, and reinforces a strong power dynamic between doctor and patient.

Additionally, it does not seem to take account of other ways in which people obtain help and support. Bilton et al. (2002) discuss how there is an assumption that individuals will seek the support of their doctor. In fact, studies show that other avenues of support are explored prior going to the doctor (Scambler, 1997). Increasingly, people are turning to new alternative and complementary methods of support with illness. Parsons analysis does seem simplistic, although Radley (1993) has argued that the sick role may still have relevance for people with chronic conditions, who may have periods of exacerbation of symptoms where they require acute medical care.

However, Parsons' contribution was that for the first time 'sick' people were acknowledged as having a role or function within society and sociological theory. This was a significant step in the development of the sociology of health and illness.

Stigma severe social disapproval of personal characteristics or beliefs that are against cultural norms. Goffman describes how stigma can manifest itself and the damaging effects it can have on individual members of society.

The impact of a medical approach on disabled people

In helping us to understand history, language is important. Health and social care professionals use different language to talk about people with disabilities, which to a degree reflects different theoretical perspectives. Social services and social care academics talk about people with disabilities and adult social care services. Health services and health academics talk about people with chronic illnesses and/or long-term conditions. The sociology of disability, the sociology of the body and the sociology of health and illness are all sub-disciplines of sociology, which are relevant to an understanding of health and disability. There is considerable debate between these sociological perspectives and how they relate to biomedical and social models of health, illness and disability. There has been a tendency to present these models as polarised and juxtaposed, but the two models can be

Holism the idea that a system cannot be explained or determined by its component parts but through an understanding of how the system operates in total or as a whole.

complementary, using different aspects of expertise appropriately to provide holistic care.

Defining disability

Historically, the following World Health Organisation (1980) definition has been widely used:

International classifications of impairments, disabilities and handicaps

Impairments (I) Abnormalities of the body structure and appearance and of organ system function, resulting from any cause; in principle 'impairments' means impairments at the organ level.

Disabilities (D) The consequences of impairment in terms of the functional performance and activity of the individual; disabilities thus represent disturbances at the level of the person.

Handicap (H) The disadvantages experienced by the individuals as a result of impairments and disabilities; handicaps reflect interaction with and adaptation to the individual's surroundings.

Source: Wood (1980: 14)

Discussion points

- How useful do you find this definition of disability?
- Thinking sociologically about the way in which language classifies people (see discussion of Foucault in Chapter 1), what does this say about disability?

According to this definition, disability is very much concerned with how the body functions and can be treated and has been the subject of criticism from the disability rights movement. As a result, the World Health Organisation amended the above definition in 2002 to include the impact of personal and environmental factors.

The usefulness of the World Health Organisation's redefinition of disability in 2002 is contested. Sociologists such as Bury (1997) have argued that the redefined ICIDH classification of disability helped assess the needs of disabled people within both a biomedical and social model framework. In his view, it does take account of social and environmental issues which impact upon people with disabilities. These needs are supported by functional assessment (what people can/cannot do without support), rehabilitation and counselling. However, Oliver (2006) sees the above classification as focusing predominantly on the functional aspects of the individual's impairment, rather than the reaction of society to impairment, and it is still too closely

The focus of professional intervention with disabled people is often around adaptations or equipment. Thus disabled people 'adapt' to their environment. (Joe Tamassy)

connected with medical model perspectives. The principal focus of this model is on rehabilitative assessment, with social and environmental factors being seen as secondary to this issue.

The historical context of disability

Barnes (1991) discusses how the fear of the abnormal contributed towards the enforced dependency, institutionalisation and segregation of disabled people. Capitalist modes of production led to changes in societal structures, systems and relationships and disabled people struggled to compete economically, leading to institutionalisation (Oliver, 1993). Goble (2004) sees this as leading to disability being classified and professionalised, leading to institutional care. Essentially, those who were viewed as the 'village idiot' were removed to large institutions and segregated from others. While disabled people were not necessarily independent in pre-industrialised society, industrialisation exacerbated exclusion and social disadvantage.

Discussion points

- How do you view disabled people?
- Thinking sociologically, what were the historical consequences of segregation for disabled people?
- Can you think of a positive portrayal in the media of someone with a disability?

Historical perspectives on cure, research and treatment have heavily influenced how disabled people are viewed and treated within society. Industrialisation led to the study and classification of 'normal' and 'abnormal' bodies, in a similar way to sexual behaviour. This has led to divisions between medical professionals and sociologists that are apparent today and the focus on illness can be seen in the language of policy until very recently. 'Handicapped', 'spastic' and 'retarded' are all terms that were used in policy and medical procedures throughout the nineteenth and twentieth centuries. Indeed, it was only in the mid-1990s that the voluntary organisation the Spastics Society changed its name to Scope. Barton (1996) discusses how the terms themselves imply lack of function and therefore lack of worth.

Historically, there also appears to have been a difference between those with intellectual and physical difficulties. Race (2002) discusses the way in which people with learning disabilities were colonised and shut away from society. At the end of the nineteenth century, there was a real concern that people with learning disabilities would impact upon birth demographics. This was part of a wider concern about population growth and the growth of poverty and at the beginning of the twentieth century there was much support for the theory of eugenics. Eugenics theory can certainly be seen to have contributed towards 'shutting disabled people away', leading to asylum or colony care that continued until the 1960s. People with disabilities lived in self-contained communities, where opportunities for independence and empowerment were virtually non-existent and standards of care and support were variable.

The eugenics debate about 'imperfect genes' is still relevant today. As science advances, there are possibilities for cloning certain characteristics and 'abnormalities' can be more accurately detected earlier in pregnancy. There is, therefore, still a debate about the 'value' of people with learning (and other disabilities).

Exercise

Find out where your local learning disabilities hospital/asylum was sited. Some of the buildings may be associated with people with learning disabilities to this day. It may also be possible to view archive photos of the hospital through your local town or city photographic records.

- From a sociological perspective, think about how disabled people might be controlled and disempowered by asylum care.

Writers such as Williams (1996) chronicle the impact of illness on daily life. However, as Watson (2005) points out, all people have to deal with issues such as changing jobs/ending relationships. For Bury there is a period of disruption and adaptation due to chronic illness and impairment. This connects with Kubler-Ross's stages of loss model (Kubler-Ross, 1969). Kubler-Ross argues that people go through the following five stages when grieving or adjusting to loss:

- denial
- anger
- bargaining
- depression
- acceptance

Having an illness is seen as similar to bereavement as individuals go through a period of grieving for the loss of a particular function, which may be followed by adjustment. For example, a person who needs to have a catheter goes through a period of loss of function. Within this model, counselling and psychological intervention would support loss and adjustment and the individual would be supported to be able to cope with using a catheter. Indeed, this is very much how disability is viewed within health services at the current time.

This approach focuses on the individual managing their condition and becoming the 'expert'. This kind of approach has informed the Expert Patient (DH, 2001) programme, where patients learn ways of coping better with their condition. From this perspective, it is seen as empowering, as the patient learns to navigate the medical system to their advantage. The power of the professional sector is seen as being limited by the patient/service user 'taking control', although the onus is still on the individual being able to deal with a complex health and social care system.

From this perspective, disability is still seen very much within the individual or medical model and links with Parsons' perspective, in that managing and dealing with disability is like a full-time job. Negotiating the medical system, appointments, seeking advice and coping with functional loss would not appear to leave much time for other activities! It is still very much based on seeing disabled people as having 'sickness status'.

The biomedical model does seem often to ignore the nature of many disabling conditions and sidesteps a debate about how society reinforces barriers for disabled people in society. The debates about whether biomedical and social constructionist perspectives on health and disability can be coterminous or are separate continue. There is therefore a debate between those who are seen to focus on impairment and those who reject impairment as the key issue for disabled people (Thomas, 2004). It is this debate which has led to the emergence of the social model of disability.

Previously, we have talked about gender, sexuality and hierarchies of power (Connell 1987 and 1995). If we take it that white, able-bodied and heterosexual men are at the 'top of the power tree' then disabled people feature near the bottom. Historically, disabled people have had very little power for many years, and indeed it is only recently that change has occurred. Issues of power are therefore fundamental within disability sociology.

The emergence of the social model of disability

Many writers have been critical of the medical model because it implies some kind of 'personal tragedy' (Oliver, 1990), contributing to assumptions about the 'tragedy' of illness and disability by non-disabled people. Disabled writers have also been critical of the voluntary sector, which they saw as reinforcing dependency and the 'personal tragedy' model. By the 1960s a plethora of charitable groups and organisations were in existence. Disabled writers saw them as being very much tied to the medical model, and being preoccupied with research, cure and treatments. They were also seen as being concerned with fundraising and 'doing for' people. They were critical of charities for not campaigning on social care, transport and other environmental barriers. As such, they were part of the structures that segregated and isolated disabled people.

In the 1960s the disability rights movement began to emerge, partly as a response to criticisms of asylum care (Goffman, 1961). An inquiry into poor patient care at Ely Hospital in the 1960s received widespread publicity (Race, 2002). In this same period disabled people themselves were beginning to question models of colony and asylum care. Questions and challenges to the way in which disabled people were being treated also arose academically.

The central premise of this challenge was to the individual or medical model of disability. It is argued that the focus should be on social, political and economic constructs and not on the individual and their illness. From this perspective, it is society and its structures that are seen as a more significant problem than the illness or disability itself. From a structuralist perspective disabled people are excluded from key political and economic organisations and are not generally visible within the media or popular culture. They are excluded in areas such as housing, employment and transport, predominantly because of access issues. It is these barriers to participation in society that are the problem rather than being sick or ill.

Unlike lesbians and gay men (see Chapter 7), there have been more visible signs of people with disabilities throughout history. Indeed, derogatory terms to describe disabled people have been used for many centuries. Terms such as 'cripple', 'half wit', 'mute' and 'village idiot' have passed into common parlance. Disabled people were seen as freaks, exhibited in circus shows and in lunatic asylums and were seen as a threat to the social norms of the day due to our fear of the unknown and abnormal (Barnes, 1991). The films *Hunchback of Notre Dame* and *The Elephant Man*, for example, show how disabled people were treated with repulsion and fear. More recently, disabled people played a number of the 'villains' in the film *The Da Vinci Code*, seeming to indicate that these attitudes continue to permeate society. The media is a powerful institution, shaping social attitudes and continues to portray disabled people negatively. For Barnes (1992) this has contributed to structural inequalities for disabled people, who are portrayed in the media as the passive recipients of charity in need of extensive help and support or as objects of pity/fear. Advertisements, TV programmes and films continue to amplify these notions.

Exercise

- Can you think of a contemporary film/drama where this a positive image of disability?
- Now think about blockbuster films such as Spiderman. How many times are 'villains' in such films disabled?

The emerging movement in America in the 1960s for independent living and civil rights challenged these perspectives. At the same time, disabled people in Britain began to argue that they were experiencing social oppression. These ideas became conceptualised as *the social model of disability*. There has been some debate about whether the social model is a theory or an approach (Oliver, 2004; Thomas, 2004), but it has offered a new sociological perspective on health and disability. The social model of disability rejected the medical model and argued that it is society that causes disability not impairment. As outlined above, disabled people face a number of barriers within society (Swain et al., 1993). This causes exclusion from the main arenas of society (home, employment, socialisation etc.). If these barriers are removed, then disabled people can participate in society. For the proponents of the social model, economics are important.

This debate can be related to Marxist perspectives on sociology. The process of industrialisation led to a key relationship between those who owned the means of production (capitalists) and those who worked for them (labour force). As society is about the relationship between capital and labour, the disabled person is of no use or value and is removed from the means of production (Oliver and Sapey, 2006). Impairment meant that the disabled person could not easily work and, as stated earlier, this led to institutionalisation and exclusion.

There are obvious barriers here for people with impaired mobility. Reflect on how this may contribute to their social exclusion from mainstream society. (Mark Jensen)

Discussion points

Discuss the following institutions/structures.
From a social model perspective, what might be the barriers to disabled people actively participating in these areas?

- media
- city of London financial institutions
- armed forces
- social services
- education

From a social model perspective, it is society that needs to adjust to accommodate disabled people and this needs to occur in all social, political and economic institutions.

There is now a comprehensive range of literature on the social model of disability. The position of a number of disabled sociologists has also sparked considerable debate (see, for example, Oliver, 2004). However, the use of the term 'social model' can be heard frequently in discussions with care professionals about how they work with disabled people and is also referred to extensively in government documents.

Weeks (2003) discusses the role of social movements at times of flux in society. The disability rights movement has had such an impact on society, in a similar way to the development of the lesbian and gay movement or the feminist movement. Since the 1960s there have been significant changes to how disabled people are viewed in society:

- There have been changes to the law about how disabled people should be treated at work and should have access to all public buildings (Disability Discrimination Act 2005 – www.opsi.gov.uk/ACTS/acts2005/20050013.htm).
- The Independent Living Fund and the Community Care (Direct Payments) Act (1996) aim to help disabled people to control and organise their own personal care (www.opsi.gov.uk/acts/acts1996/1996030.htm). This process is being continued with the piloting of individual budgets (DOH 2007b).
- Disabled people are, to a degree, more visible in the media and on TV.
- Disabled people have become politicised and have campaigned for change. For example, the Disability Rights Commission advocates for a right to independent living.

These are a few examples of how a social movement has affected how disabled people are perceived in society and also reflects the impact of new theories and ideas from disabled writers.

As we discussed in relation to the sociology of health and illness, both biomedical and social model perspectives can contribute to our understanding and, for some, the social model is seen as too generic and not relevant to all disabled people.

Criticisms of the social model

Some disabled writers have criticised the social model as being based on a white middle-class perspective and not taking account of the particular needs of disabled women or disabled people from an ethnic minority background. Writers such as Fawcett (2000) and Thomas (1999) have sought to focus on the needs of disabled women. Ideas from both the sociology of disability and the sociology of gender are relevant and of particular concern are issues around sexuality and childbearing and motherhood. Abortion and birth control, for example, can be seen as divisive issues. Although many feminist writers have broadly welcomed testing during pregnancy, giving women control over reproduction (Sheldon, 2004) disabled women writers have been critical of antenatal screening, seeing this as new eugenics. Writers have commented that these debates have become polarised, and that more discussion needs to take place.

There is also criticism of the social model for generally not taking account of difference. Writers such as Crow and French feel that personal experience of disability (and impairment) is important (Crow, 1996; French, 1993). This in turn has been criticised as 'turning back the clock' to a focus on the individual rather than the wider social and political constructs for disabled people.

More recently, Banton and Singh (2004) writing about race and disability, argue that the social model has begun to take account of social divisions and the number of factors that need to be taken into account as well as the disability. Variables such as class, race, gender, sexual orientation and age create different experiences for disabled people from particular groups. For example, Asian disabled people using community care services may have a particular experience. For example, there may be evidence that Asian people do not access community care services in a particular area. The needs of disabled Asian people therefore need to be seen in the context of broader social and economic divisions.

Exercise

- Find out about services for disabled people in your local area.
- Are these services organised for or with the service users?
- Do they take account of cultural issues?
- How do services take account of social division relating to ethnicity generally?

Deal (2003) also found in his research that a 'hierarchy of impairment' existed among disabled people themselves. Certain conditions were seen as worse than others. This would seem to indicate that attitudes towards disability and its effects exist between disabled people.

Oliver (2004) summarises this debate, arguing that there is a need to adapt the social model ideas, rather than the social model itself being flawed. He is critical of the ongoing debate about whether the social model can accommodate social divisions and believes time would be better spent on adapting the social model to these ideas. Oliver also argues that the debate about whether impairment is a factor is also divisive.

Discussion points

- How do you think social divisions and social disadvantage relate to disabled people?
- Relate this to one or more of the following:
  - class
  - ethnicity
  - gender
  - sexuality
  - age

Sociology and the body: medical and social perspectives?

Generally, the body has become the focus of increased sociological theorising and there has been an emerging discussion about how the body relates to experience of disability within society. While agreeing that structuralist perspectives are important, there has been a debate about how the body, impairment and sickness are viewed in society. Shakespeare and Watson (2001) argue that the sociology of disability needs to include an understanding of the sociology of the body. Impairment is not just biological and aspects of medical and social perspectives can be complementary as stated earlier.

Our bodies are the subject of much discussion across the media and on TV, with advice on how to look, lose weight and be fit. Thus perspectives on body are influenced by social structures and the prevailing norms of the day. This process influences the view of the disabled body and this image and perception of the body is an issue for disabled people (Shakespeare and Watson, 2001). Writers do not dispute the impact of social oppression, but also believe that cultural and stereotypical factors influence how disabled people are perceived. There was considerable debate and criticism when a statue of the disabled artist, Alison Lapper, was exhibited in Trafalgar Square. It was argued that this was because disabled people are perceived with fear and seen as abnormal (Barnes, 1991).

The body and its functions impact upon the lived experiences of disabled people. For example, being in constant pain will have an impact on how people cope with daily living. It is argued that the issues are therefore wider than structural oppression. Ideas about our bodies, impairment and pain all impact upon the disabled person.

So there has been debate about how the social model treats disabled people as one homogeneous group. What this appears to point to is that there are variations amongst disabled people and disabled writers about how they view the sociology of disability. Ideas around the sociology of the body, argue for a *social relational* understanding of disability as well as *social oppression*.

Discussion points

- Do you think impairment impacts upon how disabled people lead their daily lives?
- From a sociological perspective, is this more or less important than structural barriers in society (e.g. employment, transport).

We have examined a complex debate between traditional medical perspectives on disability and the social model of disability. More recently, there have been calls for a debate between these two perspectives. Thomas (2004) discusses how some writers see both social oppression and impairment as issues for disabled people. Thomas and Woods (2003) discuss the importance of working with health professionals to support people with learning disabilities in obtaining appropriate treatment. They see this as enabling and allowing people to access resources in society and that this process is different from working to a medical model perspective.

However, currently, there is no single sociology of disability or health and illness. Rather, professionals working in the field tend to be influenced predominantly by the individual or medical model of disability or the social model of disability. This is important for social workers, who work closely with a range of professionals, often in inter-professional teams. Social work has been criticised for being too heavily influenced by the medical model (Oliver and Sapey, 2006; Morris, 2004). Far from empowering disabled people, social workers are seen as encouraging dependency.

Social disadvantage, social exclusion and disability

The context of social work practice with disabled people is seen as reinforcing dependency and limiting choices for disabled people. Oliver and Sapey (2006) have written about applying the social model of disability to social work practice. In their view, the profession has predominantly used the individual model of disability. This is set against the background of institutional practices and community care and perhaps explains why the profile of social work is low within disability studies.

From the 1960s the segregation of disabled people in asylums gave way to community care. Notions of community care were first introduced in the 1959 Mental Health Act with the argument that it was better to care for people with enduring mental illness outside institutions. Arguments for the de-institutionalisation of a number of care groups (older people, people with mental illnesses, people with disabilities) gathered momentum through the 1970s and 1980s, culminating in the 1988 Griffiths Report, advocating care in the community to maximise independence and to increase service user choice. However, it can also be argued that community care was cheaper than care within institutions (McDonald, 2006).

Ideologically, the increased attention about care in the community in the late 1980s reflects the Thatcherite notion of rolling back the frontiers of the nanny state. Institutional care was seen as creating dependency. The ideal of community care is seen to provide maximum independence to individuals and choice over the range of services that they may access. The question of choice relates to the normalisation debate and work of theorists such as Wolfensberger (1972) was key to the idea that people with learning disabilities should lead 'normal' and valued lives in the community. Institutional care was seen to limit choices. Oliver and Sapey (2006) discuss the lack of choice and the care regime in homes for physically disabled people in the 1970s.

The advent of the 1990 NHS and Community Care Act was therefore intended to reduce dependency and reduce segregation within society. This principle of community care has continued under the New Labour Government since 1997 (NHS Plan, 2000; Independence, Well-Being and Choice, 2005; Your Health, Your Care, Your Say, 2006).

However, community care policies have been heavily criticised by the disability rights movement. One of the key issues here is the development of the care management role within the community care framework. Priestley (1999) sees care management as oppressive in the way that it defines the needs of disabled people. The links with gate-keeping resources, assessing needs and providing support within eligibility criteria are seen as reinforcing exclusion for disabled people. Packages of care provide a limited range of support, focused at home, and limiting community involvement and participation.

So, community care does not necessarily provide choices. The economic imperatives around community care limit the true availability of a range of 'products' for disabled people to choose from. Sharkey (2006) discusses the notion that community care is perceived as 'picking' your product off the supermarket shelf. This is not the case, with resource constraints leading to restricted choices.

Disability and social work practice

In recent years, there has been little specific literature on social work with disabled people. Indeed, there has only been one text in the last twenty years that has dealt specifically with the social work role with physically disabled people (Oliver and Sapey, 2006), although there is an emerging body of literature exploring the social work role with people who have learning disabilities (see, for example, Williams, 2006). This may reflect the fact that social work with disabled people has historically been seen as a 'cinderella' service in comparison with other areas of funding. There are wide variations in how social work support to disabled people is organised between local authorities. However, from a social model perspective, social workers should:

- work alongside service users to empower and support them to take control of their own lives
- be aware of social divisions and inequalities
- be aware of both micro and macro environments, in that wider social, political and economic issues should be taken into account during assessment (for example, lack of employment and inadequate housing).

Risk management and adult protection

With the pressure on resources and social work being geared towards people with high dependency, risk assessment and adult protection have become a key part of the social work role with disabled people. Ross and Waterson (1996) have argued that the focus on management of risk appears disproportionate and risk assessment often appears to be in conflict with a social model perspective. Part of looking at function, assessment and adjustment is concerned with the risks to a person, which may include risk of falling, risk of abuse or risk of self-neglect. The disabled person may also be vulnerable to abuse from family or friends (see Chapters 5 and 10) or from the workers who are supposedly there to support them. The enquiry about learning disabilities services in Cornwall in 2006 highlighted poor practice and risk issues for people with disabilities (Health Care Commission, 2006). Hunt (1998) discusses the ongoing nature of abuse and scandal within social care settings. According to social model theorists, risk issues are often related to resources, poor training and to workers with negative attitudes to disability (Oliver and Sapey, 2006). As care is often provided by a variety of agencies, part of the social workers' job is to ensure appropriate support. Challenging negative attitudes towards disability and abusive practice should be a central part of the social worker role. However, it is significant that the Health Care Commission reported that social workers did not feel able to challenge health care professionals within the NHS in Cornwall (Health Care Commission 2006 – www.healthcarecommission.org.uk). Does this reflect the power balance between the social and the medical models and difficulties in working in partnership?

There have been recent debates related to the need for appropriate adult protection procedures. The DH 'No Secrets' guidance (DH, 2000) highlighted the need for professionals to be aware of a duty to protect vulnerable people and writers such as Pritchard (2001) have discussed the need for more specific legislation on protecting vulnerable adults. Empowering practice could be seen as a feature of this process in supporting service users to deal with abuse (see Chapter 10).

More recently, the idea of positive risk-taking has been discussed. Rather than seeing what disabled people cannot do, the focus should be on enabling people to be independent. This very much fits with a social model perspective of working in partnership with people to overcome barriers. Ross and Waterson (1996) discuss how social work intervention is often about negative risk-taking, rather than supporting disabled people to change or eliminate barriers in their lives.

Risk assessment and adult protection work poses a key ethical dilemma for social workers in applying social model and social relational perspectives. There is no one answer to this issue, but it is about balancing rights, positive risks and negative risks. Balancing risk and protection and empowerment can be problematic as social workers are often working within inter-professional teams and health professionals may be operating to different risk criteria than social care professionals.

Case study

You are a hospital social worker in a multi-disciplinary team meeting to discuss Connor, a thirty-five-year-old man with multiple sclerosis. Connor wishes to return home after a period in hospital where he had a catheter fitted. Several medical staff are concerned about Connor's ability to cope at home, feeling that he has not adjusted to using the catheter. They think he would benefit from going to a local rehabilitation unit.

Connor says he wants to go home and will manage. He is happy to have more support, although seems confused about his finances. He tells you that another social worker had told him that there was not sufficient money to pay for extra support.

- What would be your key actions in this scenario?
- How would sociological perspectives help you to assess risk in this situation?
- How would you apply a social model perspective? Does it conflict with a medical model perspective?

Empowering practice – working with the social model of disability

The notion of citizenship is important in empowering social work and relates to enabling and supporting disabled people to achieve equal rights and status within society. Writers such as Barnes,

Finkelstein, Morris and Oliver argue that this should be the focus for social workers, as the role would directly challenge the social and political constructs that impact upon disabled people. This has been made complex due to the following:

- Social workers are part of organisations which can be seen as oppressive.
- Resources often mean that Social Services have become more involved in 'gate-keeping' resources, rather than supporting people's rights. Services tend to be focused on those with higher levels of dependency.
- The disabled people's movement has argued increasingly that social workers are more preoccupied with risk and resources than enabling disabled people to challenge social oppression.
- Services often appear to be designed around doing things for people, rather than with them. This appears to be more related to an individual model of disability than a social model of disability. This was a recent criticism of the Green Paper 'Independence Well Being and Choice' (DH, 2005).
- There has been an emphasis on professionalism above working alongside disabled people.
- Many disabled people are still seen as being forced into institutional care due to a lack of appropriate alternative services.

Reading through this list, it would appear that social work is more influenced by the medical model than a social model. Function, assessment of needs and resources govern the services that disabled people receive. Risk management, as in other areas of social work, appears to be a preoccupation. Risk assessments with disabled people appear to be focused on negative rather than positive risk-taking, in that disabled people are not encouraged to explore new options and risks. The focus in assessment is seen as related to needs and risks, which the Government appears to have recognised with the publication of a new guide to empowering practice in this area (DH, 2007a).

Morris (2004) and Priestley (1999) discuss how the focus on care management within social work has created an agenda that is about care needs rather than rights. Budget restrictions have led to local authorities creating set criteria for eligibility for services. From this perspective, if your needs are unmet then you do not receive a service and therefore the structural oppression of many disabled person has not changed.

The above presents a rather gloomy picture for social work interaction with disabled people. However, there are a number of ways in which the social model of disability can be used within contemporary social work practice. The recent review of adult social care in the Green Paper 'Independence, Well Being and Choice' (DH, 2005) and the White Paper 'Our Health, Our Say' (DH, 2006) discusses the need for services to enhance independence, give disabled people control and promote empowerment. A recent report has looked at the pace of change in modernising adult social care services (DH, 2007b).

Morris (2004) argues that a focus on rights would have a greater impact on quality of life. For example, a right to independent living would mean that community care services would have to be provided to support this. Priestley (1999) discusses the benefits of user-led services where disabled people are in control of budgets and services.

Empowerment can be defined as:

> A process in which individuals, groups or communities become able to take control of their circumstances and achieve their own goals, thereby being able to work towards maximising the quality of their lives.
>
> (Adams, 1996: 43)

This is further developed by Braye and Preston-Shoot (1995) who identify the following features of empowerment:

- Extending one's ability to take effective decisions.
- Individuals, groups and/or communities taking control of their circumstances and achieving their own goals, thereby being able to work towards maximising the quality of their lives.
- Enabling people who are disempowered to have more control over their lives and to have a greater voice in the institutions, services and situations, which affect them.

Central to this is the notion of power, where people have the power to make decisions and are not just the recipients of exercised power. Brager and Sprecht (1973) use the concept of a ladder of participation in decision-making to reflect the degree of power that people may have, ranging from high participation, where users and carers are actively involved in the decision to low participation and are informed of decisions that have been made.

Both the GSCC Codes of Practice and writing around anti-oppressive practice would appear to echo the need for social work intervention that is from an empowering social model perspective (e.g. Thompson, 2005). Involving service users and carers has also been advocated within social work degree programmes. Thus, there does appear to be a commitment to empowering practice from a social model perspective.

Direct payments and individual budgets

> Disabled people campaigning for direct payments argue that the resourcing by the state of their effective demand for personal assistants constitutes genuine empowerment through the extension to them of their contractual rights, in contrast to the purely rhetorical empowerment underwritten through procedural rights, where the

gatekeepers to care resources remain social workers and health care professionals.

(Morris, 1993 in Ungerson, 1997)

The issues relating to empowering practice seem clearer in this area. Direct payments are widely seen by the disabled people's movement as a means by which disabled people can control, organise and manage their own care packages. This challenges social oppression, as disabled people are able to access services and support as they wish. In social model terms, it means that one of the barriers to full participation in society is removed. By controlling the money for their care, disabled people are in control of what Morris (2004) calls their 'additional care requirements'. For example, a disabled person can employ his or her own carers so as to have their lifestyle requirements accommodated. Many care packages are organised around shift systems where the disabled person is 'put to bed' at a set time, but direct payments gives control and flexibility.

Disabled organisations have campaigned extensively for direct payments. Research has highlighted the importance of social services collaborating with disabled people concerning how direct payment schemes work (Hasler et al., 2000). Research has also shown that direct payments give control to disabled people themselves and are empowering (Stainton and Boyce, 2004). There are currently a number of pilot projects looking at simplifying the process through the use of individual budgets (DH, 2007b).

The Labour Government has been keen to promote the use of direct payments to a variety of user groups. In reality, there appears to be an issue about take-up, particularly for older people and people with learning disabilities. The 2001 White Paper 'Valuing People' (www.dh.gov.uk) on services for people with learning disabilities, highlighted how few people with learning disabilities were in receipt of direct payments. A review of the above White Paper discussed how significant progress still needed to be made in this area. In addition, there are regional variations in the availability of direct payments.

Social workers and care managers through community care assessment can promote the take up of direct payments. However, direct payments themselves may be subject to resource constraints. Fruin (2000) points to the variations between local authorities in implementing direct payments.

Person-centred planning

Person-centred planning applies particularly to work with people with learning disabilities. The way in which learning-disabled people have not been consulted or given choices has been well documented (Race, 2002; Thomas and Woods, 2003; Williams, 2006). The 2001 White Paper, 'Valuing People' (DOH, 2001) advocated the use of person-centred planning by care professionals. Rather than services being organised for people, services are organised with people. From a social model perspective, people's rights and choices are discussed.

There are however, drawbacks. Although learning disability day services are being re-organised, there are issues about funding. Many staff have not received training around person-centred planning and lack of appropriate and independent advocacy services means that people, particularly with severe learning disabilities, may not receive the appropriate support to make their wishes and opinions known (Oliver and Sapey, 2006).

However, person-centred planning is a positive mechanism by which social workers can work from a social model perspective.

Advocacy

Disabled people and their families have viewed advocacy positively. Advocacy helps disabled people to challenge structural oppression and to access services and supports. Increasingly, with the pressures on resources, social workers have been less directly involved in providing advocacy services, but signposting people to and working positively with advocates is one way of putting social model ideas into practice.

Oliver and Sapey (2006) discuss the lack of advocacy services. This is also something that has been picked up by organisations such as MENCAP (www.mencap.org.uk). Thomas and Woods (2003) discuss how advocacy can enable learning-disabled people to participate in society. Particularly with this group, it is a positive way of challenging social exclusion, which all too often exists for people with learning disabilities. Organisations such as People First (www.peoplefirst.org.uk) provide opportunities for people with learning disabilities to self-advocate or advocate on behalf of others.

One of the tensions for social workers is being able to advocate for service users, where resource constraints and other pressures may conflict with this role. There is no easy answer to this ethical dilemma, but it is important that you are aware of local advocacy services and can signpost service users and carers to these services. Thus (particularly where there are conflicts), social workers can facilitate access to the appropriate support. Being informed about this kind of debate is seen as necessary to reflecting and considering such ethical dilemmas (McDonald, 2006).

Working alongside disabled people and disabled organisations challenges oppressive organisations. Disabled organisations can be seen as controlled by disabled people themselves, relating to the ladder of participation, where such levels of control give a higher level of empowerment. Payne (2000) has discussed the importance of community social work and the recent agenda in involving users and carers in service organisations is a positive way that social services can work from a social model perspective. However, too often involving service users and carers can be seen as tokenistic.

There are now degree programmes where people with disabilities are actively involved and equal partners in training courses, degrees and indeed running courses for social care staff and others (Race, 2002). Social work degree programmes are actively seeking to involve users and carers in social work education, which is a positive way of working alongside people with disabilities.

There is a further issue about disabled students within social work education itself. While this has been advocated, Crawshaw (2002) discusses how the number of disabled students is low. A positive way of challenging professional images of people with disabilities would be by a positive programme of recruiting disabled social work students. A Best Practice Guide concerning disabled students has been produced (University of Hull, 2005).

Conclusion

This chapter has explored sociological perspectives on disability and in particular the relevance of the social model of disability to social work practice. We have seen how this creates ethical dilemmas for social work practice and examined how this impacts upon contemporary policy and services. A recent DH Report comments on the tensions for social care services between the 'choice' agenda (e.g. individual budgets) and the 'protection' agenda (e.g. risk management and adult protection) (DH, 2007b). There is not always an answer to these ethical dilemmas, but it is important to understand the challenges in working in the area of health and disability and how sociological perspectives can help develop our understanding. It often appears that it is not possible for social workers to challenge structural inequalities, but the discussion in this chapter shows that it is possible. It is always important to examine our own values and attitudes, as it may be this that it is holding us back more than any other reason.

Summary

- There are a range of post-modern sociological perspectives on health and disability. Different language can be used by health, social care and disability studies commentators to describe these perspectives.
- There are two key models, the social model and the individual or medical model of disability. The two are frequently seen as polarized.
- Social workers are seen as too often following the medical model and encouraging the dependency of disabled people.

- Social workers can promote empowerment for disabled people through initiatives such as direct payments.
- This often conflicts with the need for resource management and risk management and protection processes.

Other areas of discussion

- Following on from the exercise about disabled people in the media, do you think there have been significant changes in how disabled people are treated within society?
- Do you think disabled people need social workers?
- Given the current pattern of resource constraints, assessments and eligibility criteria, do you think empowering practice with disabled people is possible?
- Individually, the next time you undertake a social outing (e.g. to the shops, bank, pub, cinema, etc.), think about the physical and social barriers facing people with impairments. List these barriers and reflect critically on the disabling society.

Further reading

Barnes, C. (1991) *Disabled People in Britain and Discrimination: A Case for Anti-Discrimination Legislation*. London: Hurst and Co. This book provides a good overview of historical and social perspectives concerning disability.

Nettleton, S. (2006) *The Sociology of Health and Illness*. 2nd edn. Cambridge: Polity. This is a very accessible book which provides a comprehensive discussion of the sociological debates in relation to health and illness.

Oliver, M. and Sapey, B. (2006) *Social Work with Disabled People*, London: Palgrave. Discusses in detail the issues relating to whether social work can work in an empowering way with disabled people in the current climate.

Swain, J. et al. (2004) *Disabling Barriers – Enabling Environments*. London: Sage. This book provides an overview of the key issues within disability studies and disability sociology.

Williams, P. (2006) *Social Work with People Who Have Learning Difficulties*. Exeter: Learning Matters. This book summarises the main issues in contemporary learning disability practice.

12

Mental Health

Given the prevalence of mental health problems, it is likely that all social workers will come across people with mental health problems whatever the setting in which they are working. In this chapter, we will examine how the current role of social work within mental health legislation is historically linked to psychological and sociological perspectives, which are often seen as secondary to the biomedical model. There is currently a dichotomy in mental health policy and practice between a biomedical model and social and psychological perspectives. Issues of power, risk and social disadvantage are central to this debate. Social workers need to be fully aware of these perspectives. As student social workers, you also need to be aware of current challenges for social work role within mental health policy and practice. This will inform practice and ensure that support is available to a variety of service user and carer groups. Golightley (2006) details the complexities of working across user groups and the consequent difficulties this causes for service users.

This chapter will address the following key issues:

- definitions of mental illness and mental disorder
- biomedical approaches and asylum care
- sociological perspectives on mental illness
- issues of social disadvantage, social exclusion and mental illness
- contemporary perspectives; recovery model versus risk management; power, control and risk issues
- social work practice and mental health problems; empowerment and advocacy in a contemporary context.

By the end of this chapter, you should be able to:

- Demonstrate an understanding of the biomedical approach to mental illness and its relevance in the historical development of mental health services.

- Discuss a number of social models and the way in which they explain mental illness and mental health problems.
- Demonstrate an understanding of a range of social variables in relation to mental health problems (class, ethnicity, gender).
- Discuss the concept of stigma, and understand the importance of stigmatisation in people's experiences of mental illness.
- Understand the relationship between mental illness and social exclusion.
- Discuss ways in which a sociological understanding of mental illness can inform social work practice.

Mental health, sociology and social work

Mental health problems are widespread within society, and adults with mental health problems represent one of the most disadvantaged and disabled groups within modern Britain. Although severe and enduring mental illnesses are relatively rare (less than one in 200 adults is affected by symptoms of schizophrenia each year), the impact on service users and carers is enormous. Mental health problems such as depression and anxiety are much more widespread, with an estimated 1 in 6 people experiencing them at any one time (NSF for Mental Health, 1999). There is a higher incidence of diagnosis of mental illness in areas of multiple deprivation, as well as differential rates based on gender, ethnicity and sexuality.

Mental health (and sociological perspectives) are core to social work practice. Frequently, social workers may be working with service users, where users or carers are also at specific 'risk' of developing significant mental health problems.

Discussion points

- Which service user and carer groups might be most at 'risk' of developing mental health problems?
- Thinking sociologically, what social factors may contribute to this? See how you did when you have finished reading the chapter.

Definitions of mental illness

Mental illness and mental disorder are wide and ill-defined areas, which makes definition problematic. Taylor and Field (2007) argue that we can distinguish between three different types of overlapping populations who may access mental health services:

- Those suffering from impaired bodily function – e.g. people with learning disabilities, people with forms of senile mental confusion.
- People with behavioural problems such as alcohol misuse, eating disorders.
- People with what are termed mental illnesses – e.g. schizophrenia, bipolar disorders and depression.

While these different categories demonstrate the complexity of defining mental disorder and the wide range of populations who engage with mental health services, they are not very helpful in terms of providing an objective definition of mental illness.

A crude distinction can be drawn between biological and social approaches to defining mental illness, although the two approaches are not mutually exclusive. The biological approach formed the basis of much of the early psychiatric approach to mental illness (and retains relevance in contemporary psychiatric approaches). It is also important to understand the dominant psychiatric approach in understanding the social processes that have impacted on the treatment of mental illnesses as well as the experiences of service users and their carers.

This also relates to current issues about the social work role within mental health legislation. Authors such as Golightley (2006) have argued that social workers are there as a check to the dominant psychiatric approach. Changes within mental health legislation coupled with the restructuring of mental health social care and health services have been seen as weakening the social work role and thus psycho-social perspectives on mental health.

Exercise

- Do a search on services for people with mental health problems in your area.
- Discuss with a colleague.
- Is there a range of services? Are they divided into 'social' and 'medical' services?

Biological approaches

Biological approaches to mental illness (psychiatry) developed during the Enlightenment, with the focus on scientific knowledge. This heralded a change in thinking from one focused on description of symptoms and holistic treatment to one that focused on attempts to understand the functioning and anatomical structures of the brain. Causes of mental illnesses increasingly came to be seen as the result of genetics and chemical dysfunction within the brain. Genetic approaches were particularly prevalent, and can be seen as part of the ideological context of the late nineteenth century, based on Darwin's theory of evolution. Genetic malfunctions were believed to be passed down through the generations, worsening with time. This can be related to the development of the eugenics movement and selective out-breeding (see Chapter 11). Biological approaches therefore focused on individual abnormality, with surgical and pharmacological treatments.

Early psychological theories of mental disorder also focused on individual malfunctioning, particularly in terms of personality development and stabilisation. For example, from a Freudian

Psychoanalytical the treatment and study of psychological problems and disorders, developed initially by Freud.

◄ *psychoanalytical* standpoint, it was believed that personality stabilisation could be achieved through progression through a series of sequential and developmental stages, and that interruption or regression of these stages led to mental abnormality. There is some evidence of this theoretical standpoint in contemporary explanations of eating disorders (Bruch, 1973).

Biomedical models of mental illness have been highly influential in the development of psychiatric treatments. The belief that mental illness/disorder could be treated at an individual level and the

Physiology study and science of functions (of bodies/organisms).

◄ acceleration of research into brain anatomy and *physiology* led to the growth of the asylum system.

> The establishment of a comprehensive asylum system provided both a rationale for the confinement of lunatics in one place and an opportunity for the close scientific scrutiny of odd behaviour, delusions and delinquencies necessary for the development of a conceptual framework.
>
> (Rogers and Pilgrim, 2001: 46)

Social control and asylum care

The growth of the asylum system can be traced back to the 1860s and can be related to a wider context about social control and deviance that applied to other societal groups. Jones (1960) has argued that mental health asylums initially developed as humanitarian retreats located in the countryside. However, the growth of asylums has been particularly associated with developments in industrial capitalism and the need to contain deviance and promote the protestant work ethic and notions of individual responsibility.

> there is a clear relationship between prevailing social structures, dominant ideology and the way society handles its deviants.
>
> (Abbott and Sapsford, 1987: 7)

Thus the real growth in the asylum model can be seen alongside developments in the Poor Law and as part of the drive to maintain social control. As with learning disabilities, asylums became colonies for people with mental health problems. Self contained, they allowed for people with mental health problems to be virtually invisible within their local community.

Project work

- Use the internet to find out where your local asylum was situated. Part of it may still be in use for current mental health services.
- Pay a visit or do some research. How was social control exerted? Can you see any evidence of empowering practice?

Foucault (1979) has argued that the asylum system reflected the post-Enlightenment approach to power and control. Behaviour could be controlled through biomedical surveillance of the population, with the medical profession (and psychiatry in particular) having legitimate authority to determine what was illness and how to treat it. From Weberian perspectives (see Chapter 2), if medical practitioners are given the legitimate authority to diagnose and treat illness, then that deviance can be controlled and compliance is enforced through medical treatments.

These structural power relations are reinforced by the feelings of helplessness that many mental health service users report. Indeed, people who self harm or who have eating disorders will often discuss how in the face of authority this was their way of achieving a measure of control. So in these terms, mental distress could be seen as a reaction to powerlessness, whether from institutions, families or communities. Thus mental distress can be experienced as an internalised oppression.

Control and surveillance is also manifest through the design of the asylums and the inter-relationships between staff and patients, demonstrating hierarchical patterns of organisation. Geographical layout was important, based on the Foucauldian model of the panopticon, where the asylum was built around a central watchtower so that inmates could be potentially observed all the time (like prisons). Individual wards also reflected this panopticon design (see Chapter 1).

Exercise

- Find a film about asylum care (e.g. *One Flew Over the Cuckoo's Nest*).
- How do you think asylum design reinforces power and control?

This psychiatric and asylum model of care-dominated mental health service provision up until the final quarter of the twentieth century, when it came under increasing scrutiny from diverse groups, including service users and their carers.

> The complaint that mental health services are too coercive, too narrowly focused on medication and do not offer the kind of support that people want is widespread among people with mental problems. They see a service focused on containment, with little regard for people's individual experiences, few resources devoted to talking therapies and an emphasis on crisis management rather than preventative care.
>
> (Laurance, 2003: 4)

The adoption of a biomedical approach to mental illness has been criticised, particularly from a sociological perspective. Although there may be an organic basis to some mental disorders (e.g. senile mental confusion, Down's syndrome) abnormal behaviour cannot be measured objectively, but is dependent on the social constructions of normality and abnormality. These social constructions are often a product of social and political circumstances and reflect dominant social processes and structures. Medical practitioners are able to decide what is illness and how to treat it and thus their influence extends increasingly into other areas of social life.

Medicalisation

Medicalisation can be defined as a process whereby processes and experiences that were previously seen as normal have increasingly come under the control of medical practitioners, to be diagnosed, investigated and treated (a classic example of this is childbirth – a normal physiological process, in many instances, that has come to be controlled through the specialisms of obstetrics and midwifery). Medicalisation has particular relevance in the arena of mental health problems, as behaviours can be labelled and subject to treatments, acting as a powerful tool of social control. In addition, it is argued that the biomedical approach to the treatment of mental illness not only reduces the importance of structural factors, but also diverts policy attention away from them.

Sociological perspectives on mental illness

In the latter part of the twentieth century, social approaches to the understanding of mental illness and mental health started to emerge, which are much more akin to the philosophy and values of social work practice. It is for this reason that the approved social worker role has been part of mental health legislation, to provide a balanced approach with other key medical professionals and ensure that social and environmental factors are taken into account when considering compulsory detention for people with mental health problems.

Therefore, the social work role has been closely aligned to developing social approaches.

Social stress theory

This perspective is concerned with the adaptive responses of individuals to stressful life events, which are located within individual's social and cultural contexts.

> in all social classes, the greater the number of life events, both positive and negative, then the greater the probability of psychiatric symptoms appearing.
>
> (Myers, 1974 cited in Pilgrim and Rogers, 2005)

However, this is rather simplistic and does not account for the higher prevalence amongst people lower down the social scale, as well as the presence of other variables that may mediate people's ability to manage the life events. Social integration is linked to good mental and physical health and lower mortality rates (Repper and Perkins, 2003). In addition the presence or perception of having emotional support from others improves mental and physical health and acts as a buffer on the impact of major life events. Intimate and confiding relationships provide the most powerful basis for emotional support. Thus it is argued that the breakdown of kinship networks and traditional communities (see Chapter 8) has led to more dislocated people within society without these buffers of emotional support.

Case study

You are asked to see Patrick, a fifty-eight-year-old man, following a referral from a neighbour. The neighbour has heard shouting from his house and that local children have been shouting obscenities to Patrick through the letterbox. She has not seen him for several days. When you go to see Patrick he is reluctant to let you in the house, but eventually, he lets you in. Patrick looks undernourished and unkempt and the house is in considerable chaos and is quite dirty. Patrick tells you that his mother died a month ago and that she 'had always looked after him'. He doesn't have any other relatives and says he is scared to go out as the local children make fun of him and threaten him. Until recently, he worked in a local factory, but says he cannot cope with going to work when his mum is not there to help him in the morning.

- What social stresses is Patrick under?
- Discuss ways in which Patrick's kinship network and local community have contributed to his experiences.

Social stress and vulnerability therefore can be seen as affecting marginalised groups within society. For example, one of the key criticisms of community care has been that it has led to isolation within the community as opposed to isolation in an asylum. Social stress can also be a key issue for asylum seekers and refugees, who experience displacement, discrimination, hostility and violence within local communities.

Discussion points

- How might social stress lead to social exclusion?
- What can social workers do to address this?

Two classic studies that have looked at stress and depression and coping mechanisms have been the studies by Gove and Tudor (1973) and Brown and Harris (1978). Gove and Tudor (1973) explored the apparent prevalence of depression in housewives and offered a number of explanations, related to the housewife role. They concluded that the stress of the female role in the traditional male breadwinner family was related to depression. Housework was often unstructured and monotonous, not time limited and with long hours, leading to frustration. This was compounded by fact that the skills required for the housework tasks are often not commensurate with women's qualifications or educational ability. Furthermore, the unitary role of housework offered no opportunity for compensation in other roles to manage the stressors. Ironically, more recent research (Annandale and Hunt, 2000) has shown that as more and more women have entered the paid labour market (see Chapter 5) they have taken on multiple roles, leading to higher incidences of stress and depression; the traditional roles within the domestic division of labour (housework, childcare and more recently informal care of other dependants) have continued alongside paid labour, leading to role overload, feelings of inadequacy and dissatisfaction.

Brown and Harris (1978) argued that the ability to manage stress was mediated through social factors. In a study of post-natal depression (PND), they concluded that women were more likely to suffer from post-natal depression if they had a combination of high vulnerability factors and high provoking agents. Vulnerability factors included low intimacy with husband or partner, loss of mother or poor relationship with mother, previous episode of PND, a previous loss (death or separation) and a lack of employment outside the home. Provoking agents included factors such as loss or threat of loss and long-term difficulties (e.g. poverty and social exclusion), domestic violence and marital breakdown. In addition, Brown and Harris saw personality characteristics as important, based on childhood experiences and low self-esteem.

The social stress theory can also be used to explain the rising incidence of suicide. Suicide is the second most important cause of death for younger men, with concerns over the previous two decades about the growing incidence of suicide amongst this group. In addition, the unemployed, prisoners, people with life-threatening physical illnesses, or who are being treated for mental illness, the recently divorced and separated, farmers and health professionals have a higher than average incidence of suicide. Mental health policy in recent years has sought to address this, particularly in relation to a high prevalence of suicide amongst young males (National Suicide Prevention Strategy, 2002 – www.dh.gov.uk).

Structural perspectives – social disadvantage and mental illness

This theory argues that the causes of mental illness can be located within the structural inequalities of society, and that there is a relationship between processes of stratification and the presence of mental illness. This is particularly important for social workers, as their current role within mental health legislation is to consider environmental and social factors impacting upon mental ill-health and to look at other solutions rather than hospitalisation. The following are all examples of structural inequalities within society.

Social class

There is a clear social class gradient within the diagnosis of mental illness. In poorer areas of society, there are higher rates of schizophrenia, alcoholism and psychosis. In a survey of General Practice consultations, it was found that for all psychiatric disorders, consultation rates were higher for people from Social Class V (www. statistics.gov.uk). The causes for this are debated. Some have questioned whether it is the poverty that leads to the mental health problem or whether it is the other way round, and mental health problems lead to social exclusion from the labour market, and thus **Social drift hypothesis** the theory that people who are disadvantaged drift down the social scale. This is related to social exclusion. lead to poverty. This is known as the *social drift hypothesis* (Blane et al., 1993). A number of studies have pointed to the importance of relative deprivation as a precipitating factor in the causation of mental illness. This seems to be related to notions of citizenship and social inclusion (see Chapter 3).

> *Relative deprivation has a greater impact on morbidity and GP consultation for stress-related conditions such as depression, anxiety and headache/migraine . . . Relative deprivation is also associated with poorer mental health for . . . mothers of young children.*
>
> (Barker and Taylor, 1997)

Employment and material conditions

There is a clear relationship between labour market impoverishment and increased mental illness (Fryer, 1995). The stress of poverty is an important contributory factor, but so is loss of status in a society that values doing over being. This can also help to explain the increasing morbidity from mental health problems in retirement, as older people become dislocated from economic and social roles (see Chapter 10). Loss of employment can lead to a loss of sense of self, reducing social worth and self-esteem, which may also impact on roles and relationships. Fagin and Little's (1984) research explores the impact of male unemployment and roles within a traditional family structure and concludes that these changes in family dynamics and roles and relationships causes stress and the potential for mental health problems among both genders. Furthermore, there is a triangular relationship between material conditions and physical and mental health problems. Those who suffer material deprivation are more likely to suffer from both poor physical and mental health.

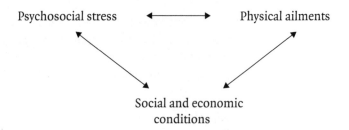

Figure 12.1 Physical and mental health and material deprivation.

There is clearly a relationship between unemployment and mental illness, but also a relationship between work and mental health problems. Role overload, thwarted ambition, bullying and the target-driven economy can all lead to stress in the workplace and alienation (to use Marxist terminology). Recent changes within mental health organisations have been linked to higher levels of stress for mental health social workers. Research by Carpenter et al. (2003) showed that social workers were struggling with their changing roles within community mental health trusts.

Housing

Poor housing conditions and poor layout and design of dwellings have been linked with a higher incidence of physical and psychological problems. Littlewood and Tinker (1981) concluded from their research that mothers living in high-rise flats were more likely to experience stress due to the physical conditions of the accommodation. Significant factors included no play areas for children, difficulties in carrying prams and other equipment up flights of stairs and social isolation due to the inability to get out.

Noise and harassment are also seen as contributory factors. The policy to house homeless families in bed and breakfast accommodation has been linked to a higher incidence of stress-related problems, not just because of poor quality living space, but also due to the effects on intimate partner relationships if there is a lack of defined adult space (Davies, 1994).

Recently, problems with poor housing and local communities have been highlighted by policies connected to social exclusion. Correlations between crime, poor housing and problem neighbours have featured strongly in the media in recent years (Goodey, 2004). There is evidence to suggest that such fears can impact upon mental health and there have been policy attempts to deal with community fears about security and harassment (see chapter 4).

Women may experience the hopelessness and isolation depicted in this picture for a number of reasons. (Sheryl Griffin)

Gender and patriarchy

Most of the sociological discussion about gender in relation to mental health has been about women, although there is a growing body of research about men's mental health. More women than men either suffer from mental health problems or are diagnosed and labelled as such, although men predominate in categories of mental illness that seem to be indicative of the outward display of emotions, such as schizophrenia, alcoholism and psychoses. This may be related to processes of primary socialisation, which encourage boys to be more overt in displays of anger, and girls to internalise.

Various theories have been put forward to explain the gender disparities in mental health, including social causation theories and social constructionist approaches. Women's material position in society, in particular, has been explored, with female material deprivation being related to the hegemony of breadwinner society, and horizontal and vertical segregation in the paid labour market (see chapter 5).

Women are also generally responsible for caring for sick or disabled relatives and there may be financial implications of caring (Carers National Association, 2000). Taking time away from your own career can have personal stress and financial implications (Evandrou and Glaser, 2003) and caring can restrict personal freedom and lifestyle. As social workers, you may be working with carers of people with mental or physical health problems who themselves are becoming unwell.

Sex-role stereotyping and gender socialisation are also seen as important factors in the explanations of gender inequalities in mental health. Women are socialised to be passive and to direct anger internally and are therefore more likely to be diagnosed with depression and neurotic conditions.

> men's conduct has been more associated with public anti-social acts, violent and sexual offences, drunken aggressive behaviour etc., whereas women's behaviour has been associated more with private self-damaging acts, where aggression is directed at self rather than others, depression, parasuicide, eating disorders, self-mutilation etc. Men are more likely to indulge in behaviour that is anti-social, and to be labelled as criminally deviant than women. This is then reflected within psychiatry, in that men are more likely to have labels which refer to and incorporate the threat of their behaviour.
>
> (Pilgrim and Rogers, 2005: 57)

Research has also focused on men and their dislocation from traditional roles and the relationship to increased mental health problems.

Exercise

Look at these two scenarios. How might labelling and stereotyping affect how professionals act?

1. Jurgen arrives in casualty late one Saturday night. He is drunk and abusive to reception staff and appears to be covered in blood on his right arm, but says he will only see a doctor. When he is asked to wait to see a doctor, he becomes abusive and picks up a chair and throws it at a wall. The police are called and Jurgen is removed from the building.

2. Jurgen arrives in casualty late one Saturday night. He is drunk and abusive to reception staff and appears to be covered in blood on his right arm, but says he will only see a doctor. He becomes agitated when he is asked to wait and picks up a chair and throws it at the wall. A member of the self-harm team is called. who talks to Jurgen and persuades him to sit down and talk to her. Jurgen begins to weep uncontrollably and says that he has been cutting himself because he has split up from his partner and lost his job and sees no point in going on with his life.

There may also be gender differences in obtaining help. Women are generally more likely to consult with GPs (Sandman et al., 2000) and are more likely to engage with health promotion and preventative health strategies (White, 2001) that may impact on earlier detection and/or prevention of serious health problems.

Ethnicity and mental health

Ethnicity is now seen as a key determinant of mental health. Whilst there is limited research into the areas of race and mental health, a number of studies (Brown, 1997) have concluded that overall rates of diagnosis of mental illness are higher among African-Caribbeans and some groups of Asians and, in particular, severe mental illness such as schizophrenia. In a study in 1987, McGovern and Cope reported that schizophrenia was diagnosed between four and twelve times more in African-Caribbean immigrants and seven to eighteen times more often in British-born people of African-Caribbean descent than amongst the British white population. Black people are 44 per cent more likely than average to be detained under the Mental Health Act and black Caribbean men are 29 per cent more likely to experience physical restraint (Inside Outside Report, 2003 – available at www.dh.gov.uk). Furthermore, people from African-Caribbean backgrounds are more likely to be detained by the police under Section 136 of the Mental Health Act, even though there is no significant ethnic difference in the use of violent or threatening behaviour (Smaje, 1995). The evidence about incidence and diagnosis of mental illnesses among people of Asian descent is less conclusive. Some studies have found a slightly higher incidence of hospitalisation for mental health problems among Indian and Pakistani immigrants than white English men (Dean et al., 1981), while others have found a lower incidence (Cochrane, 1977). However, Raleigh (1996) suggests that cultural and language differences may lead to an under-reporting of mental health problems among people of Asian background. However, there is evidence to suggest that both Asian and African Caribbean people are more likely to receive medicalised rather than psychological treatments (Fernando, 2002).

Social-class positioning, racism, disadvantage and social stress (for example, from migration) are all factors affecting ethnic minority groups. Stereotypical images influence assessment and the services provided. Consequently, people from ethnic minority groups can be seen to avoid service input, until a specific crisis is reached. This then reinforces the control aspect of mental health services.

The relationship between race, ethnicity and mental health has been of particular debate in Britain since the 1970s. The nature of this debate has changed from a preoccupation with so-called race differences, ethnic and cultural dispositions to particular forms of mental illness to considering ethnic inequalities in service experience and outcomes linked to the poor experiences of BME groups in British society and its institutions. The Macpherson Report (1999) into the death of Stephen Lawrence in 1999 defined institutional racism as

> the collective failure of an organisation to provide an appropriate and professional service to people because of their colour, culture or ethnic origin.

Facilitated by an amendment to the Race Relations Act (2000), institutional racism has become a focus for intervention for public organisations and recognition of the manifestation of racism has been highlighted by a number of high profile cases in mental health care. The death of David Bennett led to recognition that widespread stereotyping, cultural ignorance, institutional discrimination and the stigma and anxiety associated with mental health often combine to undermine the ways in which mental health services recognise, assess and respond to the needs of BME communities (*Breaking the Circles of Fear*, 2002).

> Further, if a patient's cultural, social and religious needs are not scrupulously considered, these will inevitably affect his reactions and may exacerbate his symptoms. It is essential that every patient is treated according to his needs.
> (The Independent Inquiry into the Death of David Bennett, 2003: 23 – available at www.nscstha.nhs.uk)

Breaking the Circles of Fear (2002) research found that, on the one hand, service users feared using mental health services which were seen as a part of a coercive 'system' akin to the criminal justice system in terms of regulation, while on the other hand professionals, fuelled by misconceptions and stereotypes, feared intervention with black people. There continues to be a debate about ethnicity and mental health as part of the amendments to the 1983 Mental Health Act. *Mind* reports that concern has been expressed by organisations about the impact of some aspects of proposed legislation on BME communities (www. mind.org.uk/News+ policy+and+campaigns/Press/MHA030707.htm).

Discussion points

- With a colleague, discuss what you think about the above research?
- Thinking about social justice, how can social workers engage with the effects of racism in the mental health system?

Social reaction theory: social exclusion and mental illness

This theory argues that mental illness is not an objective category, but the labelling of mental illness stems from the reaction of others to deviant behaviour. Thus, it is argued, states of normality and deviance are socially constructed within societies. This can be observed within common parlance. Terms such as 'loony', 'nutter' and 'fruitcake' are widely used as terms of abuse for people who are seen as 'different' from others.

All societies have a dominant set of norms and values, which Scheff (1966) calls the residual rules of the society. He argues that societies have two sets of rules and norms – those that are regulated through the legal framework and those that reflect the dominant value systems and expected codes of behaviour within society. Scheff refers to these as the residual rules and these rules differ between and within societies and over historical periods. They are constructed through the ruling majority. People are seen as deviant when they break these residual rules, although this is not an objective category. Whether someone is labelled as mentally ill for residual rule breaking depends on a number of factors:

- Degree of marginality of the residual rule-breaker
- Perceived seriousness of the rule-breaking
- Social distance between the labeller and labelled
- Tolerance of the society to contain the deviant behaviour.

Thus labelling is seen as important within the social constructionist approach to mental illness. This can be particularly well demonstrated through the Rosenham study of 1977. A number of people who had not actually been diagnosed with mental illness were admitted to mental institutions throughout the United States. The only person within the hospitals who was aware that these were not real patients was the medical Director. The brief of these *pseudo patients* was to get themselves discharged from hospital. Throughout the period of the study, not one of the pseudo-patients was discharged. In fact all of their behaviour came to be seen within the context of the label – e.g. one of the pseudo-patients was taking notes of his experiences, and written in his medical notes was the fact that he displayed excessive writing behaviour indicative of his schizophrenic diagnosis.

Social constructionism is seen as important for the containment of deviance. A number of case studies demonstrate how dominant social norms have been legitimated through the construction of psychiatric diagnoses and the labelling of *deviant* and *abnormal* behaviour in relation to, for example, homosexuality (see Chapter 7). Drapetomania was another psychiatric classification of the late nineteenth century; this was a diagnostic label placed on Negro slaves in the nineteenth century, the symptoms of which were characterised by slaves repeatedly attempting to escape from their masters. Drapetomania and the legitimation of the diagnosis are indicative of the dominant ideologies of the time which were based on Darwinian theory of social evolution: African and African-Caribbean populations were seen to be inferior to whites and therefore it was OK to use them as slaves. Failure to comply with this accepted ideological norm therefore constituted deviance and needed to be managed.

A more contemporary example of social constructionist approaches can be seen through the examination of Attention Deficit Hyperactive Disorder (ADHD), the incidence of which Rogers and Pilgrim (2005) have argued has dramatically increased over the last couple of decades. However, Cooper (2005) has questioned whether there is a real rise in the incidence of ADHD, or whether there is a rise in labelling of this question. In particular, he points to the role of schools and teachers in referring children who are seen as deviant, and questions whether this is more about classroom management and social control than a manifestation of a greater incidence of pathology.

Discussion points

- What do you think of these labelling examples?
- How might social workers challenge these stereotypes?

Thus social perspectives have questioned the biomedical (psychiatric) approach to mental illness and have focused on the social context of mental illness. In addition, social perspectives tend to be critical of the objectification of the medicalised approach, as they ignore the lived experience of individuals and the importance of agency and social interactions. Social scientists (and this is increasingly reflected in policy and policies) have particularly focused on the concept of stigma in relation to mental illness and the consequences of stigmatisation for service users and their carers.

Stigma

The term stigma was originally used by the ancient Greeks to denote someone who was different. Stigma (or stigmata) referred to the outer bodily signs that indicated deviance (e.g. branding of the skin in the case of criminals). In contemporary western society, a number of clinical conditions are said to be stigmatised or stigmatising and mark the individual out as different from other members of the population. Goffman (1968) defines stigma as the relationship between people's actual and perceived social identity. Stigmatising conditions may be based on discreditable attributes (those that are not immediately visible – e.g. in the case of the mental illness, where it is the label that often marks someone out as being different) or discrediting attributes which are immediately visible (e.g. someone with a facial disfigurement). People with stigmatised conditions come to be seen as inferior or culturally unacceptable (Williams, 1987) and there are negative moral connotations associated with them.

Labelling is an important aspect of stigmatisation in mental illness, and is not necessarily based on objective criteria, but reflects the dominant stereotypes of society. These stereotypes become reinforced through a number of agencies, such as the criminal justice system, the education system and the medical system. The media also have an important role to play in the stereotyping and continued stigmatisation of people with mental health problems, often depicting people as dangerous axe-wielding maniacs who are out of control and who harass and threaten the rest of society. The label of mental illness is often seen as people's primary defining characteristic in newspaper stories – e.g. schizophrenic patient murders after being released from hospital and pejorative language is deployed to perpetuate the negative image of people with mental health problems.

Stigmatisation can have a profound effect on people's social identity and social relationships, and people with mental health problems, not only have to manage the symptoms that they experience, but also have to manage societal reactions. The following quote from the Department of Health ShiFT document, *Action on Stigma* (2006), illustrates the attitudes and discrimination faced by people who have been diagnosed with a mental illness.

When I applied for a job as a cleaner at a care home, the manager called me and wanted to know more about my disability, which I'd declared. She pressed me so I said 'I'll be absolutely open with you. I've got a schizo-affective disorder and I hear the voices of people I know.' There was complete silence on the phone. She didn't say a word. So I said 'Hello, are you still there?' All she said was 'I'll be in touch.' Anyway, a few days later, lo and behold, I received a rejection letter. To me, her silence spoke volumes and I felt very discriminated against.

(www.shift.org.uk)

Not only does the stigmatisation have an impact on the societal view of mental illness, but also affects people's sense of self when they have been diagnosed with mental illness. Through the process of secondary deviance, people may come to see themselves within the context of their label of primary deviance, affecting their self-image and self-esteem. Thus they internalise the dominant stereotype of society, which affects their sense of self-worth and self-belief, with implications for social interaction, as well as help-seeking behaviours.

Stigmatisation and social exclusion

Due to a combination of stereotyping, stigmatisation and discrimination, adults with mental health problems are one of the most socially excluded groups within contemporary British society. Although many people with enduring mental illness say that meaningful employment would make a significant difference to their lives, less than a quarter (21 per cent) have any form of work, and even fewer are in well-paid employment (Social Exclusion Unit Report, 2004). The report further concludes that the cost to the economy in terms of missed employment opportunities is £23 billion per year and the summary costs of care, premature death and economic loss amount to £77 billion per year. The discrimination in employment against people with mental illness is evident in the fact that less than 50 per cent of people who are signed off sick for six months or more with mental illness will ever work again. Thus long-term unemployment and the attendant problems of material disadvantage, social exclusion and low self-worth are a particular issue. People who had been diagnosed with a psychotic illness were three times more likely than the rest of the population to have debt problems, to be in social housing provision and to be separated or divorced from their partner (http://archive.cabinetoffice.gov.uk/seu).

So we are perceived as a social burden. We lose sight of our potential, and when we try to move on, discrimination and stigma prevent us getting jobs that use our skills and experience and push us out of housing and education. The jobs we do get are poorly paid, and don't utilise our skills and experience. And there are practical considerations – we stand to lose our financial security, whether state benefits or private insurance, when we attempt to rebuild our lives. We also stand to lose the health and social services that we find helpful, so that at the time when we most need support, our coping mechanisms are undermined. Moving back into society becomes a risky business.

(Mental Health and Social Exclusion, 2004)

Contemporary perspectives and the social work contribution

Many commentators (e.g. Tew, 2005) would argue that social work is in a good position to understand issues of social exclusion, disadvantage, power and risk that are closely associated with mental health. Yet, social workers are a minority occupational group within mental health. However the role of social workers in working with users and carers is a vital one and, whilst there has always been ambiguity about the role of approved social workers and their use of compulsory powers under mental health legislation, the role of social work in mental health is facing increasing uncertainty. The realignment of professional lines into hybrid workers is seen as a particular threat to social work, as the title of 'approved social worker' is due to be replaced at this time of writing to 'approved mental health worker'.

> Social work does bring something distinctive to the mental health arena. The strong support offered to the social work role by service users at the consultation conference is testimony to that. Articulating it is more difficult and the NWW group will be attempting to do that in a succinct way. It is a constellation of values, commitment to social justice, partnership with users and carers, the ability to see the social context of individuals and how this influences both behaviours and recovery, and a commitment to the worth of each individual which meant social workers practised social inclusion before the term had been invented. Above all it stands as a challenge to the traditional medical model of diagnosis, prescription and treatment, which does not fully acknowledge the mental health service user as best, informed about their needs.
>
> (Terry Bamford, for NIMHE, National Institute for Mental Health Excellence, 2006, www.nimhe.csip.org.uk)

Whatever the outcome of changes to mental health legislation, you need to be aware of the debate between psycho-social perspectives on mental health and the dominant psychiatric model. This debate has been crucial in shaping mental health policy in recent years, and has led to many changes in services. New service models such as crisis resolution and primary mental health care teams are community based and seek to engage and work with people in local communities. One of the key issues to consider is where social exclusion is mirrored in service exclusion. Organisations such as Rethink and the Zito Trust point to how people with complex and severe mental health needs often pass from pillar to post.

Policy has attempted to address this. The National Service Framework for Mental Health published in 1999 set targets and standards to tackle mental health problems in five key areas: health promotion and stigma, primary care and access to specialist services, the needs of those with severe and enduring mental illness, carers' needs and suicide reduction. The review of progress within the NSF in 2004 set further objectives in working with people who have a dual diagnosis, tackling issues of social exclusion, the needs of people from ethnic minority groups, provision of psychological therapies and in patient care.

The policy agenda would therefore appear to recognise many of the social issues for people with mental health problems (poverty, unemployment, homelessness, exclusion). However, policy also points to critical issues with service delivery, which is highly relevant to social workers. Tew (2005) summarises the debate well. Psychiatric models appear to provide a clear and coherent framework within which to conceptualise and 'treat' mental health problems, but work with people with mental health problems is often confusing, uncertain and no solution is readily available.

Sociological perspectives enhance our understanding of these dilemmas and uncertainties. As Tew states:

> It is important to develop a repertoire of concepts and models that may help us beyond the territory of just treating symptoms, and may be useful in giving meaning to experience, and in enabling and supporting recovery.
>
> (Tew, 2005: 9)

It is this more pluralistic model that led to the formation of the Social Perspectives Network, which aims to create debate around social and psychological theories relating to mental health. Social work with a focus on anti-oppressive practice (see Chapter 1) is a key contributor to this debate and we would argue that social workers have much to offer in the new partnerships in mental health practice.

Recovery movement

The recovery movement has been closely linked to the development of mental health user networks. Ideas from this movement can be linked to the social model of disability. Mental health problems lead to stigma and social exclusion and thus the person with mental health problems has to contend with many barriers in employment, housing and relationships. Essentially, people with mental health problems should be supported and enabled to value their own strategies for coping with mental illness. This takes account of the barriers within society that prevents this. Rather than focusing on 'cure' and symptom management, recovery perspectives propose that mental health users have the capacity to find their own solutions. A person may not stop hearing voices, but might be helped to live with them. Recovery perspectives therefore support enabling practice, rather than seeking to manage people and create dependence. A recovery model stresses the importance of hope and personal resilience and there is a growing interest in how people's spiritual beliefs can be a source of personal strength (Barker and Buchanan-Barker, 2003).

Wallcraft (2002) discusses some of the factors that support a recovery perspective. For example, financial security and living environment are highlighted. Social workers are often working with people who have severe mental health problems, who may need more support with these issues as a prerequisite for recovery.

User involvement and survivor experiences

Beresford and others have written extensively about the development of mental health user organisations and services. The mental health user movement has challenged the predominance of a medical and individualised model of mental illness, arguing that issues of power, control, stigma and labelling are seen as essential to understanding and working with people who have mental health difficulties.

Many health and social care professionals are now required to work with mental health users, as this has become a policy imperative. If you walk into a psychiatric unit you will generally see the minutes of User Involvement Committees or other groups displayed on notice boards. User networks and organisations are now common within mental health services. User organisations have been highly critical of mental health policy and practice, which is exemplified by ongoing debate and discussion around changes to mental health legislation.

Values and empowerment

At the heart of social perspectives is the recognition of people's experiences within society, as significantly contributing to the development of mental health problems. Working to empower service users requires professionals to be open and able to embrace new ideas and models. Tew (2005) discusses the importance of not being 'fixed' to a particular model. Whittington (2002) echoes this in research findings concerning what service users expect from social workers. Communication skills and an open attitude are vital, and are seen as central to social work training. Rogers, Pilgrim and Lacey (1993) highlight how mental health service users wish to have contact with professionals on their own terms. Anti-oppressive practice is at the heart of this process, recognising how structural inequalities have impacted upon people with mental health problems. Social workers should work to listen, empathise and connect with mental health service users and carers. This may require us to step outside of the 'us and them' divide.

Discussion points

You may want to do this privately.

- Think about the issues discussed in this chapter.
- Have you or someone you know experienced a mental health problem?
- Was professional help sought? What approaches and help (if any) did professionals offer?

Mental health social work and the future

Sociological perspectives in mental health have a powerful resonance with the value base of social work practice. On the one hand, the role of social factors in mental ill-health has been given credence in a plethora of social initiatives, services, policy and good practice guides. At the same time, recent debates around mental health legislation show that power and control issues in mental health are highly relevant. Public concern about managing risk and media portrayals of people with severe mental health problems has led to proposed policies of containment.

Social work is influenced by this dichotomy. Many social workers are now generally based within community mental health teams, and tend to work with people with severe mental health problems. Preventative mental health social work is seen as difficult in this current climate. Social work recruitment to mental health services has been difficult, as workers have faced uncertainty about their futures within mental health services.

However, there are positive changes within mental health practice. There is a rich vein of sociological perspectives on mental health, which can help greatly with understanding and working with people who have mental health difficulties. Many health professionals have argued that they are working from a 'holistic' model of mental health (Tew, 2005). Therefore, seeing all health professionals as working from a psychiatric approach can be reductionist. Indeed, even amongst psychiatrists, there is a critical psychiatric movement that sees social factors as more of an imperative than biomedical models. The Critical Psychiatry Movement is influenced by ideas from what is known as the 'anti psychiatry' movement, encapsulated by the work of R. D. Laing in the 1960s. This challenged methods used in psychiatry (i.e. ECT treatment). Additionally, there have been many different models of mental health services that have formed in the last twenty years. These are provided by statutory, voluntary and user-led organisations. It is therefore simplistic to see services as polarised between medical (health) and social (social care) perspectives.

It is important that social workers engage and work with new perspectives and ideas. Social workers do and can make a positive contribution to practice with people who have mental health difficulties. Moving away from the 'us and them' debate to working alongside service users sits well with empowering practice.

Summary points

- A biomedical model of mental illness has dominated treatment and support since the 1860s.
- Sociological perspectives on social reaction theory, stigma and labelling are important for understanding the social context of mental health problems.
- Structural inequalities influence mental illness, leading to social exclusion and disadvantage.
- Sociological perspectives have become increasingly important in challenging biomedical treatments and are exemplified in recovery and empowerment models.
- Social work has a key role to play in this debate and in contributing to positive practice in partnership with service users, carers and other professionals.

Questions for discussion

- Are the biomedical model and the social model of mental illness mutually exclusive, or can they be used in conjunction with each other to empower and enable people?
- Is the role of the social worker in mental health under threat? If so, what might be the implications of this?
- Is mental illness real, or a social construction, based on dominant ideas of normality and abnormality?

Further reading

Busfield, J. (2001) *Rethinking the Sociology of Mental Illness?* Oxford: Blackwell. This book provides a critical discussion of key issues in mental health policy and the social understanding of mental health practices.

Fernando, S. (2002) *Mental Health, Race and Culture.* 2nd edn. Basingstoke: Palgrave. This provides a comprehensive discussion of issues related to ethnicity and culture in both diagnosis and treatment of people from minority ethnic backgrounds.

Laurance, J. (2003) *Pure Madness: How Fear Drives the Mental Health System*. London: Routledge. This book is very critical of the nature of mental health services, and provides a good critical commentary of the sources of oppression for people with mental health problems.

Pilgrim, D. and Rogers, A. (2005) *A Sociology of Mental Health and Illness*. 3rd edn. Buckingham: Open University Press. This is an easy-to-read book, which provides a comprehensive discussion of social theories of mental illness.

Tew, J. (ed.) (2005) *Social Perspectives in Mental Health: Developing Social Models to Understand and Work with Mental Distress*. 2nd edn. London: Jessica Kingsley. This is a very accessible text, which brings together a range of different perspectives that help us to explore mental health issues. There is comprehensive coverage of the context of mental health problems and policies for a range of different service user groups.

Conclusion

Throughout this book, there has been an attempt to stimulate what has been called the sociological imagination. Social workers are constantly involved in situations where an understanding of the immediate is not always the whole picture. As with all human interactions, there may be an emotional or moral response to the presenting concern. However, sociology helps us to think 'outside the box' and to consider many different social factors that impact upon the service users and carers that social work is involved with. Through applying 'sociological imagination', commonalities with service users and carers can become apparent. All of us interact with society and its structures and different characteristics affect those relationships. Social workers may share particular attributes with service users, such as class, race and sexuality.

Additionally, this book has explored how contemporary society can leave the people we work with excluded and 'shut out' from power, resources, help and access to services. A key aim of this text has been to explore how sociology can help you to see the bigger picture, by using the case studies and examples as a method of using sociological thought to see how service users and carers are often subject to national policy, national issues and structural issues with oppression and power.

The other key aim of this book has been to support empowering and emancipatory social work practice using sociological perspectives. Adams (1996:2) has argued that empowerment 'could be, if it has not already become, the central emerging feature of social work'. Professional and policy guidelines frequently stress the role of social workers in empowering and enabling service users, which can occur at both micro and macro levels. At the micro level, users are empowered to be self-determinate and to make their own decisions, whilst macro level approaches focus on challenging the structural processes that oppress and disempower individuals. The discussions throughout this book have focused on the nature of power and social disadvantage and have explored ways in which sociological theories can not only help us to understand and explain these factors and their impact on individuals, but how they can also help to inform social work theory and practice to provide more emancipatory ways to working with individuals, groups and communities.

Marsh (2005) has argued that the pursuit of social justice has formed the basis of traditional social work, but also remains an important principle of social work in addressing the challenges of the twenty-first century. Sociological theories can help to inform social workers, so that they can challenge social injustices and the structural and institutional oppressions that service users (and social workers themselves) may face.

Institutional oppression ◄ the systematic mistreatment of people within a social identity group, supported and enforced by the society and its institutions, solely based on the person's membership in the social identity group.

Academic debates have reflected that there are opportunities for positive practice, despite challenges connected with the social work role and task (McDonald, 2006; Healy, 2005). While fully aware of many of the professional issues in social work (resource management, job pressures and organisational constraints to name a few), it is our view that sociological perspectives can support emancipatory practice in the following ways:

- Assessment and care planning – the understanding of a situation will be enhanced by applying sociological perspectives. This supports positive practice by allowing social workers to not label or stigmatise service users and carers, but consider how exclusion and marginalisation has contributed to their current situation.
- Supporting positive inter-professional working, by offering informed perspectives on the situations that professionals face. Sociological knowledge can be used to explore perspectives that others may not have considered.
- Sociology enables us to see the wider political, economic and social context. You may not have the resources or personal power to solve all these problems, but such an understanding can help to advocate for service users to access services and receive appropriate support.

Finally, we would like to hope that this book has begun a life-long interest in sociology and sociological theory. As stated in Chapter 1, sociology has always been part of the social work curriculum, and this book is intended to continue to support that. As stated above, there is not always an answer to the complex issues and situations social workers find themselves in, but sociology is seen as enhancing understanding and therefore practice.

This is illustrated by the following quotes about how young people view their social workers.

'The good thing about my social worker is she helps me when I'm upset and she gives me advice. I do lots of things with her, like playing games.'

'My perfect social worker would be happy, easy to talk to, and really helpful.'

'My worker's made a difference to my life by helping me be good. I trust her because she's good at keeping a secret and I believe she would keep confidential any information on me.'

(Children's professionals: what I really think of my . . . Social worker
Children's Express, 2005)

Sociology enables us to understand the world around us, and an informed social worker can make a positive difference.

Useful resources

Databases

AgeInfo – database from the Centre for Policy on Ageing at
    www.cpa.org.uk/ ageinfo/ageinfo2.html
Intute at www.intute.ac.uk/socialsciences/lost.htm
www.scie-socialcareonline.org.uk
Social Trends at www.statistics.gov.uk
SWAP Subject Centre News at www.swap.ac.uk/news/news.asp/

Government bodies

Commission for Social Care Inspection at www.csci.org.uk
Department of Health at www.dh.gov.uk – the Government
    Department responsible for health and social care
Department for Education and Skills at www.dfes.gov.uk – the
    Government Department responsible for children, family and
    school policy
Every Child Matters at www.everychildmatters.gov.uk – covers a whole
    range of issues in relation to family and child policy
General Social Care Council at www.gscc.org.uk – Details codes of
    practice and conduct for social work
Northern Ireland Social Care Council (NISCC) at www.niscc.info/
Northern Ireland Executive: Department for Health, Social Services
    and Public Safety at www.dhsspsni.gov.uk/
Scottish Executive, Health Department at
    www.scotland.gov.uk/Departments/HD
The Scottish Social Services Council at www.sssc.uk.com/
The Welsh Assembly Government: Department for Health and Social
    Services at www.wales.gov.uk

Websites

Age Concern at www.ageconcern.org.uk/ – addresses current issues
    about older people's services and needs
Albert Kennedy Trust at www.akt.org.uk – a site which offers advice
    and support to lesbians, gays and bisexuals
Alcohol Concern at www.alcoholconcern.org.uk – advice, support and
    information on the impact of addiction

Barefoot Social Work at www.radical.org.uk/barefoot – the voice for radical social work in Britain

Barnardo's at www.barnardos.org.uk – addresses issues about children's needs and services

British Association of Social Work at www.basw.co.uk – site of association representing social work

Carers organisation at www.carers.org – provides information for carers

Child Poverty Action Group at www.cpag.org.uk – includes useful statistics and publications on child poverty

Commission for Racial Equality at www.cre.gov.uk – includes useful statistics and publications on race and ethnicity

Community Care at www.communitycare.org.uk – features articles as well as other information about contemporary social work

Disability Alliance at www.disabilityalliance.org – campaigning umbrella organisation, particularly focused on benefits and living conditions

Disability Rights Commission at www.drc.gb.org – promotes equality and citizenship for disabled people

www.gcal.ac.uk/heatherbank/index.htm – provides information about the founding mothers of social work

Help the Aged at www.helptheaged.org.uk/ – addresses current issues about older people's services and needs

Institute for Public Policy Research at www.ippr.org.uk – independent think-tank, exploring policy responses and promote social justice and democratic participation

Joseph Rowntree Foundation at www.jrf.org.uk/ – includes publications on a range of social issues

Law Society at www.lawsociety.org.uk – useful for legal aspects of family policy

Make poverty history campaign at www.makepovertyhistory.org – provides facts and details of campaigns to tackle poverty globally

MENCAP at www.mencap.org.uk – offers a range of advice for people with learning difficulties

MIND at www.mind.org.uk – campaigns on issues for people with mental health problems

www.nacro.org.uk – a useful website which explores issues about rehabilitation

National Childrens Home at www.nch.org.uk

National Institute for Mental Health in England at www.nimhe.org.uk – organisation which supports positive change in mental health

National Society for Prevention of Cruelty to Children at www.nspcc.org.uk

Radical social work at www.radical.org.uk/barefootcasecon.htm – provides discussions and papers from a Marxist social work perspective

Sainsbury Centre for Mental Health at www.scmh.org.uk – includes publications and briefing papers to improve quality of life for people with mental health problems

Stonewall provides clear information about citizenship rights for lesbians and gay men at www.stonewall.org.uk/

Selected journals

Ageing and Society
Body and Society
British Journal of Social Work
Child and Family Social Work
Children and Society
Community Care
Disability and Society
Journal of Children and Poverty
Journal of Gender Studies
Journal of Mental Health
Journal of Poverty and Social Justice
Race and Class
Social Identities
Social Work Education
Sociology
Sociology of Health and Illness

References

Abbott, P. and Sapsford, R. (1987) *Community Care for Mentally Handicapped Children*. Milton Keynes: Open University Press

Abbott, P., Wallace, C. and Tyler, M. (2005) *An Introduction to Sociology: Feminist Perspectives*. London: Routledge

Abel-Smith, B. and Townsend, P. (1965) *The Poor and the Poorest*. London: Bell and Sons

Abercrombie, N. et al. (1988) *Contemporary British Society*. Cambridge: Polity

Abrams, M. (1978) *Beyond Three Score Years and Ten*. Mitcham: Age Concern

Acheson, D. (1998) *Independent Inquiry into Inequalities in Health: Report*. London: HMSO

Action on Elder Abuse (2006) *Adult Protection Data Monitoring*. London: Action on Elder Abuse

Action on Elder Abuse and Better Government for Older People (2004) *Placing Elder Abuse within the Context of Citizenship: A Policy Discussion Paper*. September. London: Action on Elder Abuse

Adams, R. (1996) *Social Work and Empowerment*. Basingstoke: Macmillan

Adams, R., Dominelli, L. and Payne, M. (ed.) (2002a) *Critical Practice in Social Work*. Basingstoke: Palgrave

Adams, R., Dominelli, L. and Payne, M. (eds) (2002b) *Social Work: Themes, Issues and Critical Debates*. Basingstoke: Palgrave

Adoption and Children Act (2002) London: HMSO

Agnew, R. (1992) Foundations for a general strain theory of crime and delinquency, *Criminology* 30(1) 47–87

Ahmad, W.I. and Walker, R. (1997) Asian older people: housing, health and access to services. *Ageing and Society*. 17(2) 141–66

Ahmed, B. (1990) *Black Perspectives in Social Work*. Birmingham: Venture Press

Alcock, P. (1997) *Understanding Poverty*. 2nd edn. Basingstoke: Macmillan

Alcohol Concern (2006) *Young People's Drinking*. Alcohol Concern's Quarterly Information and Research Bulletin

Alcohol Concern (2004) *Women and Alcohol*. Factsheet 2

Allen, R. (2006) *From Punishment to Problem Solving: A New Approach to Children in Trouble*. Centre for Crime and Justice studies: King's College London

Alsop, R. Fitzsimons A. Lennon K. (2002) *Theorizing Gender: An Introduction*. Cambridge: Polity Press

Annandale, E. (1998) *The Sociology of Health and Medicine: A Critical Introduction*. Cambridge: Polity Press

Annandale, E. and Hunt, K. (eds) (2000) *Gender Inequalities in Health*. Buckingham: Open University Press

Anthias, F. and Yuval-Davis, N. (1998) *Women – Nation – State*. Basingstoke: Macmillan

Arber, S. and Ginn, J. (1995) *Connecting Gender and Ageing: A Sociological Approach*. Buckingham: Open University Press

Aries, P. (1962) *Centuries of Childhood*, London: Jonathan Cape

Armstrong, D. (1995) The rise of surveillance medicine. *Sociology of Health and Illness* 17(3) 393–404

Asquith, S., Clark, C., Waterhouse, L. (2005) *The Role of the Social Worker in the 21st Century: A Literature Review*. University of Edinburgh

Audit Commission (2000) *Another Country: Implementing Dispersal Under the Immigration and Asylum Act, 1999*. 1 June

Baldock, C.V. (1999) Seniors as volunteers: an international perspective on policy. *Ageing and Society*. 19(5) 581–602

Baldwin, S. and Falkingham, J. (eds.) (1994) *Social Security and Social Change: New Challenges to the Beveridge Model*. London: Harvester Wheatsheaf

Banton M. and Singh G. (2004) 'Race, disability and oppression' in Swain, J., Finkelstein V., French, S. and Oliver, M. (eds.) (1993) *Disabling Barriers – Enabling Environments*. London: Sage

Barclay Committee (1982) *Social Workers: The Roles and Tasks*. London: National Institute for Social Work/ Bedford Square Press

Barker, D. and Taylor, H. (1997) Inequalities in health and health service use for mothers of young children. *Journal of Epidemiology and Community Health*. 51. 74–9

Barker, M. and Petley J. (eds) (2001) *Ill Effects: The Media/Violence Debate. Communication and Society*. London: Routledge

Barker, P. and Buchanan-Barker, P. (2003) *Spirituality and Mental Health: Breakthrough*. London: Whurr

Barnes, C. (1991) *Disabled People in Britain and Discrimination*. London: Hurst

Barnes C. (1992) *Disabling Imagery and the Media; an Exploration of the Principles for Media Representations of Disabled People*. Halifax: British Council of Organisations of Disabled People/Ryburn Publishing Ltd

Barrett, M. and McIntosh, M. (1982) *The Anti-Social Family*. London: Verso

Barron, C. and Lacombe, D. (2005) Moral panics and the nasty girl. *Canadian Review of Sociology and Anthropology*. 42(1) 51–69

Barron, R. D. and Norris, G. M. (1976) Sexual divisions and the dual labour market in D. L. Barker and S. Allen (eds) *Dependence and Exploitation in Work and Marriage*, London: Longman

Barton, L. (ed) (1996) *Disability and Society: Emerging Issues and Insights.* Harlow: Addison Wesley Longman Ltd

Baudrillard, J. (1994) *Simulacra and Simulations.* Ann Arbor, MI: University of Michigan Press

Bebbington, A. and Miles, J. (1989) The background of children who enter local authority care. *British Journal of Social Work.* 19(5)

Beck, U. (1992) *Risk Society: Towards a New Modernity.* London: Sage

Beck, U. and Beck-Gernsheim, E. (1995) *The Normal Chaos of Love.* Cambridge: Polity

Becker, H. (1963) *Outsiders: Studies in the Sociology of Deviance.* Free Press: New York

Beckett, C. (2006) *Essential Theory for Social Work Practice.* London: Sage

Beechey, V. (1982) The sexual division of labour and the labour process: a critical assessment of Braverman. In S. Wood (ed.) *The Degradation of Work? Skill, Deskilling and the Labour Process.* London: Hutchinson

Ben-Ari, A.T. (2001) Homosexuality and heterosexism: views from academics in the helping professions. *British Journal of Social Work.* 31. 119–131

Benedict, R. (1995) *Patterns of Culture. Reissue Edition.* Boston: Houghton Mifflin

Benjamin, O. and Sullivan, O. (1999) Relational resources, gender consciousness and possibilities of change in marital relationships. *Sociological Review.* 47(4) 794–820

Benston, M. (1972) The political economy of women's liberation. In Glazer-Malbin, N. and Waehrer, H. Y. (eds) *Woman in a Man-Made World.* Chicago: Rand McNally.

Beresford, P. and Croft, S. (1993) *Getting Involved: A Practical Guide.* Joseph Rowntree Foundation

Berger, P. (1966) *Invitation to Sociology.* Harmondsworth: Penguin

Bernard, M. and Meade, K. (eds) (1993) *Women Come of Age: Perspectives on the lives of Older Women.* London: Edward Arnold

Bernard, M. and Phillips, J. (eds) (1998) *The Social Policy of Old Age.* New Romney: CPA

Bernstein, B. (1975) *Class, Codes and Control.* London: Routledge and Kegan Paul

Best, S. (2005) *Understanding Social Divisions.* London: Sage

Best Practice Guide (2005) *Disabled Social Work Students and Placements.* University of Hull: British Association of Social Workers

Beveridge, W. (1942) *Social Insurance and Allied Services.* Cmnd 6404. London: HMSO

Bhavani, K. and Coulson, M. (1986) Transforming Socialist-feminism: The challenge of racism. *Feminist Review.* 23. 81–92

Biemann, U. (2002) Remotely sensed: a topography of the global sex trade. *Feminist Review,* 70. 75–88

Biggs, S. (1996) A family concern: elder abuse in British social policy. *Critical Social Policy.* 16(2) 62–83

Bilton, T., Bonnett, K., Jones, P., Stanworth, M., Sheard, K. and Webster, A. (2002) *Introductory Sociology. 4th edition.* Basingstoke: MacMillan

Bindman, J. and Doezema, J. (1997) *Redefining Prostitution as Sex Work on the International Agenda. Anti-Slavery International and the Network of Sex Projects* – available at www.walnet.org/csis/papers/redefining.html

Binstock, R. and George, L. (eds) (2001) *Handbook of Ageing and Social Sciences.* San Diego: Academic Press

Blakemore, K. and Boneham, M. (1994) *Age, Race and Ethnicity.* Buckingham: Open University Press

Blane, D. et al. (1993) Social selection: what does it contribute to social class differences in health. *Sociology of Health and Illness.* 15(1)

Blank, R.H. and Merrick, J.C. (2005) *End-of-Life Decision Making: A Cross-National Study.* Massachusetts: MIT Press

Blaxter, M. (1976) *The Meaning of Disability.* London: Heinemann

Blewett, J., Lewis, J. and Tunstill, J. (2007) *The changing roles and tasks of social work, A literature informed discussion paper,* January, London: Synergy Research and Consulting

Bochel, H., Bochel, C., Page, R. and Sykes, R. (2005) *Social Policy: Issues and Developments.* London: Prentice Hall

Boden, S. (2006) Dedicated followers of fashion? The influence of popular culture on children's social identities. *Media, Culture and Society.* 28; 289–98

Bonnie, S. (2004) Disabled people, disability and sexuality in Swain, J., French, S., Barnes, C. and Thomas, C. (eds) *Disabling Barriers-Enabling Environments.* London: Sage

Bottoms, A. (1995) *The Philosophy and Politics of Punishment and Sentencing* in Clark and Morgan (eds)

Bourdieu, P. (1986) *Distinction: A Social Critique of Judgements of Taste.* London: Routledge and Kegan Paul

Bourdieu, P. (1988) *Language and Symbolic Power.* Cambridge: Polity

Bovenkerk, F. (1984) The rehabilitation of the rabble: how and why Marx and Engels wrongly depicted the lumpen-proletariat as a reactionary force. *The Netherlands Journal of Sociology (Sociologica Neerlandica)* 20(1) 13–42 cited in Mann, K. (1992) *The Making of an English Underclass? The Social Divisions of Labour and Welfare.* Buckingham: Open University Press

Bradshaw, J. and Millar, J. (1991) *Lone Parent Families in the UK.* Department of Social Security Report, No. 6. London: HMSO

Brandon, M., Thoburn, J., Lewis, A. and Way, A. (1999) *Safeguarding Children with the Children Act, 1989.* London: The Stationery Office

Brager, G. and Sprecht, H. (1973) *Community Organizing.* New York; Columbia University Press

Brah, A. (1994) 'Race' and 'Culture' in the Gendering of Labour Markets', in Maynard, M. and Purvis, J. (eds) *Researching Women's*

Lives from a Feminist Perspective. London and Bristol, PA: Taylor and Francis

Bramlett, M.D. and Blumberg, S.J. (2007) Family structure and children's physical and mental health. *Health Affairs.* 26(2) 549–58

Braye, S. and Preston-Shoot, M. (1995) *Empowering Practice in Social Care.* Buckingham: Open University Press

Brewer, C. and Lait, J. (1980) *Can Social Work Survive?* London: Temple Smith

Bronfenbrenner, U. (1979) *The Ecology of Human Development: Experiments by Nature and Design.* Cambridge, Mass., and London: Harvard University Press

Brown, B., Burman M. and Jamieson, L. (1993) *Sex Crimes on Trial: The Use of Sexual Evidence in Scottish Courts.* Edinburgh: Edinburgh University Press

Brown, D. (1997) *Black People and Sectioning: The Black Experiences of Detention under the Civil Sections of the Mental Health Act.* London: Little Rock Publishing

Brown, H.C. (1998) *Social Work and Sexuality: Working with Lesbians and Gay Men.* Basingstoke: Palgrave Macmillan

Brown, G.W. and Harris, T. (1978) *Social Origins of Depression: A Study of Psychiatric Disorder in Women.* London: Tavistock

Bruch, H. (1973) *Eating Disorders.* Houston: Basic Books

Bulmer, M. and Solomos, J. (1998) Introduction: re-thinking ethnic and racial studies. *Ethnic and Racial Studies.* 21(5). 819–37

Bury, M. (1997) *Health and Illness in a Changing Society.* London: Routledge

Busfield, J. (2001) *Rethinking the Sociology of Mental Illness.* Oxford: Blackwell

Butler, J. (1990) *Gender Trouble: Feminism and the Subversion of the Identity.* London: Routledge

Bytheway, B. and Johnson, J. (1990) On defining ageism. *Critical Social Policy.* 27. 27–39

Callender, C. (1992) *Redundancy, Unemployment and Poverty.* In Glendinning, C. and Millar, J. (eds) *Women and Poverty in Britain: the 1990s.* London: Harvester Wheatsheaf

Cameron, D. and Fraser, E. (1987) *The Lust to Kill: A Feminist Investigation of Sexual Murder,* Cambridge: Polity Press

Carpenter, J., Schneider, J., Brandon,T. and Wooff, D. (2003) Working in multidisciplinary teams: the impact on social workers and health professionals of integrated mental health care. *British Journal of Social Work.* 33, 101–3

Carter, J. (2003) *Ethnicity, Exclusion and the Workplace.* Basingstoke: Palgrave

Cartwright, A. and O'Brien, M. (1976) *Social Class Variations in Health Care.* In Stacey, M. (ed.) *The Sociology of the NHS.* Sociological Review Monograph 22

Case Con Manifesto at www.radical.org.uk/barefoot/casecon.htm

Castells, M. (1997) *The Power of Identity*. Oxford: Blackwell

Cavanagh, K. and Cree, V. (eds) (1996) 'Why do men care? In *Working with Men: Feminism and Social Work*. London: Routledge

Central Council for the Education and Training of Social Work (CCETSW) The Rules and Requirements for the Diploma in Social Work, 1991

Centre for Contemporary Cultural Studies (1982) *The Empire Strikes Back*. London: Hutchinson

Chand, A. and Keay, L. (2003) *Child Protection and its Impact for Black Families Living in the UK: Research into Practice*. Conference Report

Chawla-Duggan, R. (2006) Exploring the role of father development workers in supporting early years learning. *Early Years*. 26(1) 93–109

Cheal, D. (1988) *The Gift Economy*. London: Routledge

Cheurprakobkit, S. and Johnston, W. (2007). Inappropriate internet sites: Citizens' attitudes about their computer skills and the need for training. *International Journal of Police Science and Management*, 9(1) 1–13

Children Act (1989) Cmnd 41. London: HMSO

Children (Leaving Care) Act (2000) London: HMSO

Chouhan, K. and Lusane, C. (2004) *Black Voluntary and Community Sector Funding: Its Impact on Civic Engagement and Capacity Building*, York: Joseph Rowntree Foundation

Clark, C. and Morgan, R. (eds) (1995) *The Politics of Sentencing Reform*. Oxford: Clarendon Press

Clarke, A. (2001) *The Sociology of Health Care*. London: Prentice Hall.

Cleaver, F. in 'Do men matter?' New horizons in gender and development. *Insights* Issue 35, December 2001

Cline, S. (1995) *Lifting the Taboo: Women, Death and Dying*. London: Abacus

Civil Partnerships Act (2004) London: HMSO

Cochrane, R. (1977) Mental illness in immigrants to England and Wales: an analysis of mental hospital admissions 1971. *Social Psychiatry*. 12. 2–35

Cohen, A. (1954) *Delinquent Boys: The Culture of The Gang*, New York: Free Press

Cohen, A. (1985) *The Symbolic Construction of Community*. London: Routledge

Cohen, S. (1972) *Folk Devils and Moral Panics*. London: Paladin

Commission For Racial Equality (1997) *The Irish In Britain*. London

Community Care (2007) 'Social workers should refuse to co-operate with "unethical" removals of asylum-seeking children in care, British Association of Social Workers says', 8 May 2007 - www.communitycare.co.uk

Comstock, G. (1991) *Violence against Lesbians and Gay Men*. New York: Columbia University Press

Connell, R. W. (1987) *Gender and Power: Society, the Person and Sexual Politics*. Cambridge: Polity Press

Connell, R.W. (1995a) *Masculinities*. Cambridge: Polity

Connell, R.W. (1995b) *Gender and Power*. Cambridge: Polity

Cooper, P.W. (2005) Specialist pedagogy for ADHD. In A. Lewis and B. Norwich (eds) *Special Teaching for Special Children*. Maidenhead: Open University Press

Corsaro, W. (2005) *The Sociology of Childhood* 2nd edition. London: Pine Forge Press

Cox, O. (1970) *Caste, Class and Race: A Study in Social Dynamics*. New York: Monthly Review

Council of Europe (1996) European Convention on the Exercise of Children's Rights Strasbourg, 25.1.1996

Crawshaw, M. (2002) Disabled People's Access to Social Work Education – Ways and Means of Promoting Environmental Change. *Social Work Education* 21 (5), 503–14

Cree, V. (2000) *Sociology for Social Workers and Probation Officers*. London: Routledge

Cree, V. (2003) *Becoming a Social Worker*. London: Routledge

Cree, V. and Wallace, S. (2002) *Risk and Protection in Social Work Futures: Crossing Boundaries, Transforming Practice*. In Adams, R., Dominelli, L. and Payne, M. (eds).

Cree, W. and O'Corra, S. (2006) Core training standards for sexual orientation. www.pfc.org.uk/files/making_series_more_inclusive_for_pgb_people.pdf

Croft, S., Beresford, P. and Adshead, L. (2005) *What service users want from specialist palliative care social work – findings from a participatory research project*. In J. Parker (ed.) *Aspects of Social Work and Palliative Care*. Wiltshire: Quay Books

Crompton, R. (1998) *Class and Stratification: An Introduction to Current Debates*. 2nd edn. Cambridge: Polity

Crow, L (1996) Including all our lives: renewing the social model of disability, in C Barnes and Mercer G (eds) *Exploring the Divide: Illness and Disability*. Leeds: The Disability Press

Cumming, E. and Henry, W.E. (1961) *Growing Old*. New York: Basic Books

Dahrendorf, R. (1959) *Class and Class Conflict in an Industrial Society*. London: Routledge

Dalley, G. (1988) *Ideologies of Caring: Rethinking Community and Collectivism*. Basingstoke: Macmillan

Davey, B. (2001) Do-not-resuscitate decisions: too many, too few, too late? *Mortality*. 6 (3) 247–64

Davie, G. (2000) Religion in modern Britain: changing sociological assumptions. *Sociology* 34; 113–28

Davies, D. and Neal, C. (eds) (1996) *Pink Therapy: A Guide for Counsellors and Therapists Working with Lesbians, Gay and Bisexual Clients*. Buckingham: Open University Press

Davies, M. (1994) *The Essential Social Worker*. 3rd edn. Aldershot: Arena

Deacon, A. and Bradshaw, J. (1983) *Reserved for the Poor: The Means Test in British Social Policy*. Oxford: Blackwell

Deal, M. (2003) Disabled people's attitudes towards other impairment groups: a hierarchy of impairments. *Disability and Society*. 18 (7) 897–910

Dean, G., Walsh, D., Downing, H. and Shelley, P. (1981) First admission of native-born and immigrants to psychiatric hospitals in South East England 1976. *British Journal of Psychiatry*. 139. 506–12

Denny, E. and Earle, S. (eds) (2005) *Sociology for Nurses*. Cambridge: Polity Press

Denzin, N.K. (1987) Postmodern children. *Society*. 24(3) 32–5

Department for Education and Skills (2005) *Education and Training Statistics for the UK*, 2005 edn

Department for Education and Skills (2004) *Every Child Matters*. London, HMSO

Department for Education and Skills (2002) *Bullying – Don't Suffer in Silence*. London: HMSO

Department of Health (2007a) *Independence, Choice and Risk: A Guide to Best Practice in Supported Decision-Making*. London: HMSO

Department of Health (2007b) *Modernising Adult Social Care – What's Working*. London: HMSO

Department of Health (2005) *Independence, Well Being and Choice*, Green Paper, London: HMSO

Department of Health (2004) *National Service Framework for Children, Young People and Maternity Services*. London: HMSO

Department of Health (2002a) *Meeting the Religious and Spiritual Needs of Patients and Staff*. HSG (92)2, Health Service Guidelines. London: NHS Management Executive

Department of Health (2002b) *Requirements for Social Work Training*. London: HMSO

Department of Health (2001a) *The Expert Patient: A New Approach to Chronic Disease Management for the 21st Century*, London: Department of Health

Department of Health (2001b) *Valuing People: A New Strategy for Learning Disability for the 21st Century*, White Paper, London: HMSO

Department of Health (2001c) *The National Service Framework for Older People*. London, HMSO

Department of Heath (2001d) *Seeking Consent: Working with Children*. London: HMSO

Department of Health (2000a) *The NHS Plan*. London: HMSO

Department of Health (2000b) *No Secrets: Guidance on Developing and Implementing Multi-Agency Policies and Procedures to Protect Vulnerable Adults from Abuse*. London: Department of Health

Department of Health (1999a) *Making a Difference*. London: HMSO

Department of Health (1999b) *The National Service Framework for Mental Health*. London: HMSO

Department of Health (1998) *Modernising Social Services: Promoting Independence, Improving Protection, Raising Standards*. Cm. 4169. London: HMSO

Department of Health (1993) *Sometimes I think I can't go on anymore.* London: HMSO

Department of Health (1990) *National Health Service and Community Care Act.* London: HMSO

Department of Health and Home Office (2003) *The Victoria Climbié Inquiry: Report of an Inquiry by Lord Laming.* London: HMSO

Dex, S. (1985) *The Sexual Division of Work: Conceptual Revolutions in the Social Sciences.* Brighton: Harvester Wheatsheaf

Dillon, T. (2004), Looking straight at gay parents, USA Today, September 2004, www.usatoday.com

Dobash, R. and Dobash, R. (1979) *Violence Against Wives.* New York: Free Press

Dominelli, L. (2002) *Feminist Social Work: Theory and Practice.* Basingstoke: Palgrave Macmillan

Dominelli, L. (1997) *Sociology for Social Work.* Basingstoke: MacMillan

Dominelli, L. (1998) *Anti Racist Social Work.* Basingstoke: Palgrave

Donald, J. and Rattansi, A. (eds) (1992) *Race, Culture and Difference.* London: Sage

Donzelot, J. (1980) *The Policing of Families.* London: Hutchinson

Douglas, M. (1992) *Risk and Blame: Essays in Cultural Theory.* London: Routledge

Douglas, R.M. (2002) Anglo-Saxons and the Attacoti: the racialisation of Irishness in Britain between the world wars. *Ethnic and Racial Studies.* 25. 40–63

Dreaden, C. and Becker, S. (2004) *Young Carers Report in the UK.* The Children's Society

Duncombe, J. and Marsden, D. (1993) Love and intimacy: the gender division of emotion and 'emotion work': a neglected aspect of sociological discussion of heterosexual relationships. *Sociology*, 27

Dunleavy, P. (1986) The growth of sectoral cleavages and the stabilization of state expenditures. *Environment and Planning.* 4, pp. 129–44.

Durkheim, E. (1952) *Suicide: A Study in Sociology.* London: Routledge and Kegan Paul.

Dworkin, A. (1981) *Pornography: Men Possessing Women.* London: Women's Press.

Edgell, S. (2006) *The Sociology of Work: Continuity and Change in Paid and Unpaid Work.* London: Sage

Ehrenreich, B. and English, D. (1978) *For Her Own Good: 150 Years of the Experts' Advice to Women.* London: Pluto Press

Ellis, H. (1946) *The Psychology of Sex.* London: William Heinemann

Engels, F. (1902) *The Origin of the Family, Private Property and the State.* Chicago: Charles H. Kerr and Company

Engler, S. (2006) Sweating over sweatshops. *New Internationalist.* November

EOC (2006) *Sex and Power: Who Runs Britain?*

Elliott, F. R. (1996) *Gender, Family and Society.* Basingstoke: Macmillan.

Estes, C. (2001) *Social Policy and Aging*. London: Sage

Estes, C. (1979) *The Aging Enterprise*. San Francisco: Jossey-Bass

Evandrou, M. and Glaser, K. (2003) Combining work and family life: the pension penalty of caring. *Ageing and Society*, 23(5) 583–603

Evans, G. and Mills, C. (1998) Identifying class structure. A latent class analysis of the criterion-related and construct validity of the Goldthorpe class system. *European Sociological Review*. 14. 87–106

Evers, A., Pijls, M. and Ungerson, C. (eds) (1994) *Payments for Care: A Comparative Over View*. Aldershot: Avebury

Eysenck, H.J. (1971) *Race, Education and Intelligence*. London: Maurice Temple Smith

Fagin, L. and Little, M. (1984) *The Forsaken Families*. Harmondsworth: Penguin

Fairburn, C. and Brownell, K.D. (eds) (2002) *Eating Disorders and Obesity*. 2nd edn. New York, Guildford Press

Fanon, F. (1952) *Black Skin White Masks*, New York : Grove Press

Faulks, S. (2006) *Human Traces*. London: Vintage

Fawcett, B. (2000) *Feminist Perspectives on Disability*. Harlow: Prentice Hall

Featherstone, M. (1991) *Consumer Culture and Postmodernism*. London: Sage

Featherstone, M. and Hepworth, M. (1991) *The Mask of Ageing and the Postmodern Life Course* in M. Featherstone, M. Hepworth and B. S. Turner (eds) *The Body, Social Process and Cultural Theory*. London: Sage

Felson, M. (1998) *Crime and Everyday Life*. 2nd edn. Pine Forge Press, California

Fenton, S. (1999) *Ethnicity: Racism Class and Culture*. Basingstoke: Palgrave Macmillan

Fernando, S. (2002) *Mental Health, Race and Culture*. 2nd edn. Basingstoke: Palgrave

Field, J. (1993) Coming out of two closets. *Canadian Woman Studies*. 13 (4) 18–19

Finch, J. and Groves, D. (1983) *A Labour of Love: Women, Work and Caring*. London: Routledge and Kegan Paul

Finch, J. and Mason, J. (1993) *Negotiating Family Responsibilities*. London: Routledge

Finch, N. (2004) Family policy in the UK. 3rd report. *Welfare Policy and Employment in the Context of Family Change*

Firestone, S. (1971) *The Dialectic of Sex*. London: Jonathan Cape

Fisher, D.H. (1978) *Growing Old in America*. New York: Oxford University Press

Fitzpatrick, T. (2005) *New Theories of Welfare*. Basingstoke: Palgrave

Fook, J. (2002) *Social Work: A Critical Introduction*. London: Sage

Forgacs, D. (ed.) (1999) *A Gramsci Reader: Selected Writings 1916–1935*. London: Lawrence and Wishart

Forster E. M. (1971) *Maurice*. London: Penguin

Foucault, M. (1979a) *The History of Sexuality, Vol 1, An Introduction*. trans. Robert Hurley. London: Allen Lane

Foucault, M. (1979b) *Discipline and Punish*. Harmondsworth: Penguin

Fraser, D. (1984) *The Evolution of the British Welfare State*. 2nd edn. London: Macmillan

Freire, P. (1972), *Pedagogy of the Oppressed*. Harmondsworth: Penguin

French, S. (1993) Disability, impairment or something in between? in Swain, J., Finkelstein V., French, S. and Oliver, M. (eds.) (1993) *Disabling Barriers – Enabling Environments*. London: Sage

Freud, S. (1975) *The Psychopathology of Everyday Life*. Harmondsworth, Penguin

Frones, I. (1994) Dimensions of childhood in J. Qvortrup, M. Bardy, S. Sgritta, and Wintersberger (eds) *Childhood Matters: Social Theory, Practice and Politics*. Aldershot: Avebury

Fruin, D. (2000) *New Directions for Independent Living: Inspection of Independent Living Arrangements for Younger Disabled People*. London: Department of Health

Fryer, D. (1995) Labour Market disadvantage: deprivation and mental health. *The Psychologist*. 8(6) 265–72

Furedi, F. (2002) *Paranoid Parenting: Why Ignoring the Experts May be Best For Your Child*. Chicago: Chicago Review Press

Garland, D. (2001) *The Culture of Control: Crime and Social Order in Contemporary Society*. Oxford: Oxford University Press

Garrett, P.M. (2002) Social work and the just society: diversity, difference and the sequestration of poverty. *Journal of Social Work*. 2(2) 187–210

Garside, R. (2006) Criminality and social justice: challenging the assumptions, *Social Justice: Criminal Justice*. Smith Institute

General Social Care Council. (2002) *Codes of Practice for Social Workers and Employers*. London: GSCC

Gewirtz, S. (2001) Cloning the Blairs: New Labour's programme for the re-socialization of working class parents. *Journal of Educational Policy*. 16(4) 365–78

Giddens, A. (2006) *Sociology*. 5th edn. Cambridge: Polity Press

Giddens, A. (1997) *The Consequences of Modernity*. Cambridge: Polity

Giddens, A. (1991) *Modernity and Self-Identity: Self and Society in the Late Modern Age*. Cambridge: Polity

Gillies, V. (2005) 'Raising the meritocracy': parenting and the individualization of social class. *Sociology*. 39. 835–53

Gilroy, P. (1982) The myth of black criminality. *Socialist Register*. 47–56

Gilroy, P. (1997) *There Ain't No Black in the Union Jack*. London: Hutchinson

Gilmore, D. (1990) *Manhood in the Making: Cultural Concepts of Masculinity*. New Haven, Conn.: Yale University Press.

Ginn, J. and Arber, S. (1993) *Ageing and Cultural Stereotypes of Older Women*. In J. Johnson and R. Slater (eds) *Ageing and Later Life*. London: Sage

Glasby, J. (2004) The single issue. *Nursing Older People*. 16(3)

Goble G. (2004) Dependence, independence and normality in Swain, J., French, S., Barnes, C. and Thomas, C. (eds) *Disabling Barriers– Enabling Environments*. London: Sage

Goffman, E. (1961) *Asylums*. Harmondsworth: Penguin

Goffman, E. (1968) *Stigma: Notes on the Management of Spoiled Identity*. Harmondsworth: Penguin

Goldberg, A. (1999) *Sex, Religion and the Making of Modern Madness*. New York: Open University Press

Golding, J. (1997) *Without Prejudice: Mind Lesbian Gay and Bisexual Mental Health Awareness Research*. London: Mind Publications

Goldson, B. (1997) Children in trouble: state responses to juvenile crime, in P. Straton (ed.) *Childhood in Crisis*. London: UCL Press

Goldthorpe, J.H. et al. (1968) *The Affluent Worker in the Class Structure*. Cambridge: Cambridge University Press

Golightley, M. (2006) *Social Work and Mental Health*. 2nd edn. Glasgow: Learning Matters

Goode, E. and Ben-Yehuda, N. (1994) *Moral Panics: The Social Construction of Deviance*. Oxford: Blackwell

Goodey, J. (2004) *Victims and Victimology: Research, Policy and Practice*. London: Longman

Gove, W. and Tudor, J. (1973) Adult sex roles and mental illness. *American Journal of Sociology*. 78. 812–35

Grady, P.(2004) Social work responses to accompanied asylum- seeking children in Hayes, D. and Humphries, B. *Social Work, Immigration and Asylum*. London: Jessica Kingsley Publishers

Graham, H. (1983) Caring: A Labour of Love. In Finch, J. and Groves, D. (eds) *A Labour of Love: Women, Work and Caring*. London: Routledge and Kegan Paul.

Graham, H. (1987) Women's smoking and family health. *Social Science and Medicine*. 25

Gramsci, A. (1971) *Selections From the Prison Notebooks*. London: New Left Books

Grant, G., Goward P., Richardson M. and Ramcharan, P. (eds) (2005) *Learning Disability: A Life Cycle Approach to Valuing People*. Buckingham: Open University Press

Green, L. (2005) Theorizing sexuality, sexual abuse and residential children's homes: adding gender to the equation. *British Journal of Social Work* 35. 453–81

Greenstreet, W. (2006) *Integrating Spirituality in Health and Social Care: Perspectives and Practical Approaches*. Oxford: Radcliffe Publishing

Griffiths, R. (1988) *Community Care: Agenda for Action*. London: HMSO

Gunaratnam, Y. (1997) *Culture is not enough: a critique of multiculturalism in palliative care*. In D. Field, J. Hockey and N. Small. (eds.) *Death, Gender and Ethnicity*. London: Routledge

Habermas, J. (1989) *The Structural Transformation of the Public Sphere: An Inquiry into a Category of Bourgeois Society*. Cambridge: Polity

Hakim, C. (1996) *Key Issues in Women's Work: Female Heterogeneity and the Polarization of Women's Employment.* London: Athlone

Hall, S. (1992) New ethnicities in Donald, J. and Rattansi, J. (eds.) *Race, Culture and Difference.* London: Sage

Hall, S. (1996) *Representation: Cultural Representations and Signifying Practices.* London: Sage/Open University

Hall, S., Critchter, C., Jefferson, T., Clarke, J. and Roberts, B. (1978) *Policing the Crisis: Mugging, the State and Law and Order.* London: Macmillan

Hall, S. and Jefferson, T. (eds) (1976) *Resistance Through Rituals.* London: Hutchinson

Hallsworth, S. (2005) *Street Crime.* Cullompton: Willan Publishing

Halsley, A.H. Heath, A. and Ridge, J. (1980) *Origins and Destinations.* Oxford: Clarendon Press

Haralambos, M. and Holborn, M. (2004) *Sociology: Themes and Perspectives.* 6th edn. London: Collins

Harris Interactive (2002) Press release: fewer than half of all lesbian, gay, bisexual and transgender adults surveyed say they have disclosed their sexual orientation to their health care provider www.harrisintractive.com/news/ allnewsbydate.asp?NewsID=555

Hasler, F., Zarb, G. and Campbell, J. (2000) *Key Issues for Local Authority Implementation of Direct Payments.* London: Policy Studies Institute

Havighurst, R. (1963) *Successful Aging.* in Williams, R.H. et al. *Processes of Aging.* vol 1. Chicago: University of Chicago Press

Hazan, H. (2000) *The Cultural Trap: The Language of Images.* In Gubrium, J. and Holstein, J. (eds.) *Aging and Everyday Life.* Oxford: Blackwell

Healthcare Commission (2006) *Joint Investigation into Services for People with Learning difficulties at Cornwall Partnership NHS Trust.* London: Healthcare Commission

Healy, K. (2000) *Social Work Practices: Contemporary Perspectives on Change.* London: Sage

Healy, K. (2005) *Social Work Theories in Context: Creating Frameworks for Practice.* London: Palgrave Macmillan

Hearn, J. (1996) Is masculinity dead? A critique of the concept of masculinity/masculinities, in M. Mac an Ghiall (ed.) *Understanding Masculinities.* Buckingham: Open University Press

Hearn, J. and Parkin, W. (2001) *Gender, Sexuality and Violence in Organisations: The Unspoken Forces of Organization Violations.* London: Sage

Hehir, B. (2005) Looking for someone to blame. *Nursing Standard.* 20(7) 32–3

Heidensohn, F. (1985) *Women and Crime,* London: Macmillan

Hendrick, H. (1992) Children and Childhood. *Refresh* 15: Autumn

Herbert, H. (1994) Counselling gay men and lesbians with alcohol problems, *Journal of Rehabilitation*

Herdt, G. (1981) *Guardian of the Flutes.* New York: McGraw-Hill

Herrnstein, R. J. and Murray, C. (1994) *The Bell Curve: Intelligence and Class Structure in American Life*. New York: The Free Press

Hetherington, K. (2000) *New Age Travellers: Vanloads of Uproarious Humanity*. London: Cassell

Hickman, M. (1995) *Religion, Class and Identity: the State, the Catholic Church and the Education of the Irish in Britain*, Aldershot: Avebury

Hicks, S. (2005) Sexuality: social work theories and practice, in Adams, R., Dominelli, L. and Payne, M. (eds) *Social Work Futures: Crossing Boundaries, Transforming Practice*. Basingstoke: Palgrave Macmillan

Hicks, S. (2006) Genealogy's desire: practices of kinship amongst lesbians and gay foster-carers and adopters. *British Journal of Social Work*. 36, 761–76

Hill, A. (2003) A Lost Generation Trapped on Our Forgotten Estates. *Observer*, Sunday 30 November 2003

Hill, M. (1996) *Social Policy: A Comparative Analysis*. Hemel Hempstead: Prentice Hall

Hill Collins, P. H. (2000). *Black Feminist Thought: Knowledge, Consciousness and the Politics of Empowerment*. 2nd edn. New York: Routledge

Himmelweit, S. (1995). The discovery of 'unpaid work': the social consequences of the expansion of 'work.' *Feminist Economics* 1 (2) 1–19

Hobcraft, J. (1998). *Intergenerational and Life-Course Transmission of Social Exclusion: Influences of Child Poverty, Family Disruption, and Contact with the Police*. CASE paper 15, London School of Economics: ESRC Centre for the Analysis of Social Exclusion

Hockey, J. (1997) *Women in Grief: Cultural Representation and Social Practice*. In D. Field, J. Hockey and N. Small. (eds) *Death, Gender and Ethnicity*. London: Routledge

Hogan, R. (1980) Nursing and human sexuality. *Nursing Times*. 76. 1299–1300

Holman, R. (1978) *Poverty: Explanation of Social Deprivation*. Oxford: Martin Robertson

Home Office (2002) *Respect and Responsibility: Taking a Stand Against Anti-Social Behaviour*. Cm.5778, London: HMSO

Hooks, B. (1986) *Ain't I a Black Woman? Black Women and Feminism*. London: Pluto

Hooks, B. (1991) *Yearning: Race, Gender and Cultural Politics*. Turnaround

Horner, N. (2006) *What is Social Work: Context and Perspectives*. 3rd edn. Maidstone: Learning Matters

Howarth, C., Kenway, P., Palmer, G. and Miorelli, R. (1999) *Monitoring Poverty and Social Exclusion*. Joseph Rowntree Foundation

Hugman, R. (1994) *Ageing and the Care of Older People in Europe*. Basingstoke: Macmillan

Humphries, B. (2004) Refugees, asylum-seekers and social work in Hayes, D and Humphries, B. *Social work, Immigration and Asylum*. London: Jessica Kinglsey

Hunt, G. (1998) *Whistleblowing in the Social Services*. London: Arnold

Hutton, W. (1995) *The State We're In*. London: Jonathan Cape

Ignatieff, M. (1997) The meaning of Diana. *Prospect*. October 6–7

Isay, R. (1989) *Being Homosexual: Gay Men and Their Development*. London: Penguin

Jackson, C. and Tinkler, P. (2007) 'Ladettes' and 'modern girls': 'troublesome' young feminininities. *Sociological Review*. 55(2) 251–72

Jackson, S. and Rahman, M. (1997) Up against nature: sociological thoughts on sexuality in Gubbay, J., Middleton, C. and Ballard, C. (eds) *The Students Companion to Sociology*. Oxford: Blackwell

James, A. and Prout, A. (1990) *Constructing and Reconstructing Childhood: Contemporary Issues in the Sociological Study of Childhood*. London: Falmer Press

Jewson, N. (1975) The disappearance of the sick man from medical cosmology, 1770–1870. *Sociology* 10(2) 225–44

Johnson, T. (1972) *Professions and Power*. London: Macmillan

Jones, C. (2002) Social Work and Society. In Adams, R., Dominelli, L. and Payne, M. (eds) *Social Work: Themes, Issues and Critical Debates*. Basingstoke: Palgrave

Jones, K. (1960) *Mental Health and Social Policy 1845–1959*. London: Routledge and Kegan Paul

Jones, K. (1991) *The Making of Social Policy in Britain 1830–1990*. London: Athlone Press

Jones, S. (1994) *The Language of Genes*. London: Flamimgo.

Joseph, S. (2005) *Social Work Practice and Men who have Sex with Men*. New Delhi: Sage

Kendall, J. (1992) Fighting back: promoting emancipatory nursing actions. *Advances in Nursing Science*. 15(2) 1–15

Keith, M. (1993) From punishment to discipline? Racism, racialisation and social control. In M. Cross and M. Keith (eds) *Racism, The City and the State*. London: Routledge

Kenen, S. (1997) Who counts when you're counting homosexuals? Hormones and homosexuality in mid twentieth century America, in V. Rosario (ed). *Science and Homosexualities*. London: Routledge

King, M. and McKeown E. (2003) Mental health and social well being of gay men, lesbians and bisexuals in England and Wales. Joint Project between University College London and MIND

King's Fund Report (2002) *Age Discrimination in Health and Social Care*. London: Kings Fund

Kinsey, A., Wardell, B. P. and Clyde, M. (1948) *Sexual Behavior in the Human Male*. Philadelphia: W. B. Saunders

Kinsey, A., Wardell, B. P., Clyde, M. and Gebhard, P. H. (1953) *Sexual Behavior in the Human Female*. Philadelphia: WB Saunders

Kleinman, A. (1988) *The Illness Narratives: Suffering, Healing and the Human Condition*. New York: Basic Books

Kline, S. (2005) Countering children's sedentary lifestyles: An evaluative study of a media-risk education approach. *Childhood* 12; 239

Komaromy, C. (2000) The sight and sound of death: the management of dead bodies in residential and nursing homes for older people. *Mortality.* 5(3) 299–315

Koutrolikou, P. (2005) *Negotiating 'Common Grounds' Through Local Government and Urban Regeneration Policies and Initiatives; The Case of Hackney.* London

Kubler-Ross, E. (1969) *On Death and Dying.* New York: Macmillan

Laing, R. D. (1967) *The Politics of Experience and the Bird of Paradise.* Harmondsworth: Penguin

Lansdown, G.(2001) Children's welfare and children's rights in Foley, P., Roche, J. and Tucker S. (eds) *Children in Society: contemporary Theory, Policy and Practice.* London: Palgrave / The Open University

Laslett, P. (1989) *A Fresh Map of Life: The Emergence of the Third Age.* London: Weidenfeld and Nicolson

Laurance, J. (2003) *Pure Madness: How Fear Drives the Mental Health System.* London: Routledge

Le Grand, J. (1982) *The Strategy of Equality.* London: Allen and Unwin

Lea, J. and Young, J. (1984) *What is to be Done about Law and Order?* Harmondsworth: Penguin

Leavitt, R. and Power, M. (1989) Emotional socialization in the post modern era. *Social Psychology Quarterly.* 52. 35–43

Lee, N. (2001) *Childhood and Society: Growing up in an Age of Uncertainty.* Buckingham: Open University Press

Lee, D. and Newby, H. (1983) *The Problem of Sociology.* London: Unwin Hyman

Lees, S. (1993) Judicial rape. *Women's Studies International Forum.* 16 (1)

LeVay, S. (1993) *The Sexual Brain.* Cambridge, MA: Massachusetts Institute of Technology Press

Levitas, R. (1998) *The Inclusive Society: Social Exclusion and New Labour.* Basingstoke: Macmillan

Lewis, G. (ed.) (1998) *Forming Nation, Framing Welfare.* London: Routledge in association with Open University Press

Lipsky, S. (1987) *Internalized Racism.* Seattle: Rational Island Publishers

Lipton, G. (ed.) (2004) *Gay Men Living with Chronic Illnesses and Disabilities: From Crisis to Crossroads.* Canada: Haworth Press

Littlewood, J. and Tinker, A. (1981) *Families in Flats.* London: HMSO.

Lonsdale, S. (1990) *Women and Disability: The Experience of Physical Disability among Women.* London, Macmillan.

Lorde, A. (1984) *Sister Outsider.* Freedom CA: The Crossing Press

Lymbery, M. (2005) *Social Work with Older People.* London: Sage

Lyotard, J. F. (1984) *The Post-Modern Condition.* Manchester: Manchester University Press

Mac and Ghiall (ed.) (1996) *Understanding Masculinities.* Buckingham: Open University Press

McClure, G. (2001) Suicide in children and adolescents in England and Wales 1970–1998. Br J Psych. 2001; 198. 469–74

McClymont, M. (1999) Hearing Older Voices. Elderly Care. 11(6) 8–12

McDonald, A. (2006) Understanding Community Care. London: Palgrave Macmillan

McGovern, D. and Cope, R. (1987) The compulsory detention of males of different ethnic groups with special reference to offender patients. British Journal of Psychiatry. 150. 505–12

McKinlay, J. B. (1995) The everyday impacts of providing informal care to dependent elders and their consequences for the care recipients. Journal of Aging and Health. Nov. 7(4) 497–528

Mackie, M. (1987) Constructing men and women: gender socialisation in Cree, V. (2000) Sociology For Social Workers and Probation Officers. London: Routledge

Macionis, J. and Plummer, K. (2005) Sociology: A Global Introduction. 3rd edn. Harlow: Prentice Hall

Mack, J. and Lansley, S. (1985) Poor Britain. London: George Allen and Unwin

MacNicol, J. (1987) In pursuit of the underclass. Journal of Social Policy. 16(3)

Macpherson, W. (1999) The Stephen Lawrence Inquiry London, The Stationery Office

Malik, K. (1996) The Meaning of Race: Race, History and Culture in Western Society. London: Macmillan

Malik, K. (2005) Islamophobia myth. Prospect. February 2005

Manthorpe, J. (2003) Nearest and dearest? The neglect of lesbians in caring relationships. British Journal of Social Work. 33; 753–68

Marsh, J.C. (2005) Social Justice: Social Work's Organising Value. NASW.

Martin, T.L. and Doka, K.J. (2000) Men Don't Cry . . . Women Do: Transcending Gender Stereotypes of Grief. Philadelphia: Brinner/Matzel

Mason, D. (1995) Race and Ethnicity in Modern Britain. Oxford: Oxford University Press

Matter of the Inquiry into the Legality of the Use of Force by the United Kingdom against Iraq, 11 October 2002, chaired by Professor Colin Warbrick, London

Matthews, R. and Young, J. (eds) (1986) Issues in Realist Criminology. London: Sage Publications

Matza, D. (1964) Delinquency and Drift. New York: Wiley

Meade, M., Florin, J. and Gesler, W. (1988) Medical Geography. New York, Guilford

Means, R. and Smith, R. (2003) Community Care: Policy and Practice. 3rd edn. Bristol: Policy Press

Merrin, W. (1999) Crash, bang, wallop! What a picture! The death of Diana and the media. Mortality. 4(1) 41–62

Merton, R. (1938) Social structure and anomie. American Sociological Review. 3 (October) 672–82

Messerschmidt, J. (1993) *Masculinities and Crime*, Rowman and Littlefield: Lanham

Miles, R. (1982) *Racism and Migrant Labour*. London: Routledge and Kegan Paul

Miles, R. (1989) *Racism*, London: Routledge

Millet, K. (1970) *Sexual Politics*. New York, Doubleday

Mohanty, C.T. (1992) Feminist encounters: locating the politics of experience. In M. Barrett and A. Phillips (eds) *Destabilizing Theory: Contemporary Feminist Debates*. Cambridge: Polity

Morgan, D. (1996) *Family Connections: An Introduction to Family Studies*. Cambridge: Polity

Morgan, S. (2000) Risk making or risk taking? *Open Mind*. 101, Jan/Feb.

Morris J. (2004) Independent living and community care: a disempowering framework. *Disability and Society*. 19 (5) 427–43

Mullaly, R. (1993) *Structural Social Work: Ideology, Theory and Practice*. Toronto: McClelland and Stewart

Murdock, G.P. (1949) *Social Structure*. New York: Palgrave Macmillan

Murray, C. (1994) *Underclass: The Crisis Deepens*. London: IEA

Myers, J. (1974) Social class, life events and psychiatric symptoms: a longitudinal study. In B.S. Dohrenwend and B.P. Dohrenwend (eds) *Stressful life events: Their Nature and Effect*. New York: Wiley

Mythen, G. (2004) *Ulrich Beck: A Critical Introduction to the Risk Society*. London: Pluto

Navarro, V. (1976) *Medicine Under Capitalism*. London: Croom Helm

Nettleton, S. (2006) *The Sociology of Health and Illness*. Cambridge: Polity Press

NICE/SCIE (2006) Practice guide: Dementia: supporting people with dementia and their carers in health and social care (NICE clinical guide 42)

Nicolson, L. (ed.) (1990) *Feminism/Postmodernism*. London: Routledge

Norman, A. (1985) *Triple Jeopardy: Growing Old in a Second Homeland*. Centre for Policy on Ageing

Norton, R. (1992) *Mother Clap's Molly House: The Gay Subculture in England, 1700–1830*. London: GMP Publishers

Nott, J. and Gliddon, G. (1854) Types of mankind in Haralambos, M., Heald, R.M. and Holborn, M. (eds) (2004) *Sociology Themes and Perspectives*. London: Collins

Oakley, A. (1974) *The Sociology of Housework*. Oxford: Martin Robertson

O'Connor, P. (2006) Young people's constructions of the self: late modern elements and gender differences. *Sociology* 40. 107–24

Office for National Statistics (2000) *Individuals in the Top and Bottom Quintile Groups of Household Disposable Income; By selected Risk Factors*. London: HMSO

Office for National Statistics. (2004) *Labour Force Survey*, Spring 1996 and 2004, London: HMSO

Office for National Statistics (2005) *Labour Force Survey*, Spring 2005 dataset. London: HMSO

Office for National Statistics (2005) *Annual Survey of Hours and Earnings 2005*, revised December 2005. London: HMSO

Office for National Statistics (2005) *UK Time Use Survey*, London: HMSO

Ó'Gráda, C. (2005) *The Great Irish Famine*. Cambridge: Cambridge University Press

Oliver, M. (1990) *The Politics of Disablement*. London: Macmillan

Oliver, M. (1993) Disability and dependency: a creation of industrial societies? In J. Swain, V. Finkelstein, S. French and M. Oliver (eds) *Disabling Barrier – Enabling Environments* London: Sage

Oliver, M. (1996) *Understanding Disability: From Theory to Practice*. London: Palgrave Macmillan

Oliver, M. (2004) If I had a hammer: the social model in action in Swain, French, and Finkelstein (eds) *Disabling Barriers – Enabling Environments*. London: Sage

Oliver, M. and Sapey, B. (2006) *Social Work with Disabled People*. Basingstoke: Palgrave Macmillan

Orchard, H. (ed.) (2001) *Spirituality in Health Care Contexts*. London: Jessica Kingsley

Ormerod, P. (2005) The impact of sure start. *Political Quarterly Publishing Co.*

O'Sullivan, T. (2002) '*Managing Risk in Decision Making*' in Adams, R., Dominelli, L. and Payne, M (eds) *Critical Practice in Social Work*. London: Palgrave

Owusu-Bempah, J. (1993) Toeing the white line in Clarke, J (ed.) *A Crisis in Care? Challenges to Social Work*. London: Sage /The Open University

Parekh, B. (2000) *The Future of Multi-Ethnic Britain*. London: Profile Books Ltd

Parkin, F. (1979) *Marxism and Class Theory; A Bourgeois Critique*. Cambridge: Cambridge University Press

Parsloe, P. (ed.) (1999) *Risk Assessment in Social Care*. London: Jessica Kingsley

Parsons, T. (1951) *The Social System*. London: Routledge and Kegan Paul

Parsons, T. and Bales, R.F. (1955) *Family Socialization and Interaction Process*. Glencoe, IL: The Free Press

Parton, N. and Franklin, F. (eds) (1991) *Social Work, the Media and Public Relations*. London: Routledge

Pascall, G. (1997) *Social Policy: A New Feminist Analysis*. London: Routledge

Paul, C., Ayis, S. and Ebrahim, S. (2006) Psychological distress, loneliness and disability in old age. *Psychology, Health and Medicine*. 11(2) 221–32

Payne, M. (2005) *Modern Social Work Theory: A Critical Introduction*. 2nd edn. London: Palgrave Macmillan

Payne, M. (2000) *Anti-Bureaucratic Social Work*. Birmingham: Venture

Pease, B. and Pringle, K. (eds) (2001) *A Man's World? Changing Men's Practices in a Globalized World*. London, Zed.

Pew Research Center (2006) *Europe's Muslims More Moderate The Great Divide: How Westerners and Muslims View Each Other*. 13-Nation Pew Global Attitudes Survey

Phillipson, C. (1998a) *Reconstructing Old Age*. London: Sage

Phillipson, C. (1998b) Changing work and retirement: older workers, discrimination and the labour market. In Bernard, M. and Phillips, J. (eds) *The Social Policy of Old Age*. New Romney: CPA

Phillipson, C. and Walker, A. (eds) (1986) *Ageing and Social Policy: A Critical Assessment*. Aldershot: Gower

Phoenix, A. (1991) *Young Mothers?* Cambridge: Polity

Pickard, S. (1995) *Living on the Front Line*. Aldershot: Avebury

Pierson, J. (2002) *Tackling Social Exclusion*. London: Routledge

Pilgrim, D. and Rogers, A. (2005) *A Sociology of Mental Health and Illness*. 3rd edn. Buckingham: Open University Press

Pilkington, A. (2003) *Racial Disadvantage and Ethnic Diversity in Britain*. London: Palgrave Macmillan

Polack, R. J. (2004) Social justice and the global economy: new challenges for social work in the 21st century. *Social Work* 49(2) 281–90

Policy Research Institute for Ageing and Ethnicity (2003) *Minority Elderly Care in Europe*

Polivy, J. and Herman, C.P. (2002) Causes of eating disorders. *Annual Review of Psychology*. 53. 187–213

Power, C. (2004) *Room to Roam England's Irish Travellers*. Report of Research Funded by the Community Fund, June 2004

Priestley, M. (1999) *Disability Politics and Community Care*. London: Jessica Kingsley

Pritchard J. (2001) *Good Practice with Vulnerable Adults*. London: Jessica Kingsley

Quam, J.K. (1997) The story of Carrie and Annie. *Journal of Gay and Lesbian Social Services*. 6 (1) pp. 97–9

Quershi, H. and Walker, A. (1989) *The Caring Relationship*. London: Macmillan.

Race, D. (2002) *Learning Disability – A Social Approach*. London: Routledge

Radley A. (ed.) (1993) *Worlds of Illness: Biographical and Cultural Perspectives on Health and Disease*. London: Routledge

Raleigh, V. (1996) Suicide patterns and trends in people of Indian subcontinent and Caribbean origin in England and Wales. *Ethnicity and Health*. 1. 55–63

Rattansi, R. (1992) Changing the subject? Racism, culture and education, in Donald, James and Ali Rattansi (eds) (1992) *'Race', Culture and Difference*. London: Sage

Refugee Council (2006) *UK Country Report for 2005 for European Council on Refugee and Exiles*

Repper, J. and Perkins, R. (2003) *Social Inclusion and Recovery: A Model for Mental Health Practice*. Edinburgh: Bailliere Tindall

Revans, L. (2007) Children Make their mark. *Community Care*, 12 July. 20–21

Rex, J. and Tomlinson, S. (1970) *Colonial immigrants in a British City: A Class Analysis*. London: Routledge and Kegan Paul

Rich, A. (1980) Compulsory heterosexual and lesbian existence. *Signs* (54) 631–60

Richardson, D. (1998) Sexuality and citizenship. *Sociology* 32 (1) 83–100

Richmond, M. (1917) *Social Diagnosis*. New York: Russell Sage Foundation

Riley, M.W. and Riley, J.W. (1999) Sociological research on age: legacy and challenge. *Ageing and Society*. 19(1) 123–33

Rivers, I. (1995) Mental health issues among young lesbians and gay men bullied in school. *Health and Social care in the Community*. 3 (6) 380–388

Roach, S.M. (2004) Sexual behaviour of nursing home residents: staff perceptions and responses. *Journal of Advanced Nursing*. 48(4) 371–9

Robinson, K. (2005) Childhood and sexuality: adult constructions and silenced children in Mason, J. and Fattore, T. *Children Taken Seriously: In Theory, Policy and Practice*. London: Jessica Kingsley

Rogers, A. and Pilgrim, D. (2001) *Mental Health Policy in Britain*. 2nd edn. Basingstoke: Palgrave

Rogers, A., Pilgrim, D. and Lacey, R. (1993) *Experiencing Psychiatry: Users' Views of Services*. London: Macmillan

Rose, H. (1981) Rereading Titmuss: the sexual division of labour. *Journal of Social Policy*. 10(4) 477–502

Rosenham, D. E. (1996) Being sane in insane places. In Heller, T. et al. (eds) *Mental Health Matters*. Buckingham: Open University Press

Ross, L. and Waterson, J. (1996) Risk for whom? Social work and people with physical disabilities in Kemshall, H. and Pritchard, J. (eds) *Good Practice in Risk Assessment and Risk Management 1*. London: Jessica Kingsley

Rowntree, B. S. (1901) *Poverty: A Study of Town Life*. London: Macmillan.

Rowson, M. (2000) Blueprint for an unequal world. *Health Matters*. 41. 10–11

Runnymede (1997) *Islamophobia: A Challenge for Us All*. Report of the Commission on British Muslims and Islamophobia, chaired by Gordon Conway. London: The Runnymede Trust

Ruth, J.E. and Kenyon, G. (1996) Biography in adult development and aging in J.E. Birren, G.M. Kenyon, J.E. Ruth, J.J.F. Schroots and T. Svensson (eds) *Aging and Biography: Explorations in Adult Development*. New York: Springer

Rybash, J.M., Roodin, P.A. and Hoyer, W.J. (1995) *Adult Development and Aging*. 3rd edn. Dubuque: Brown and Benchmark

Said, E. (1997) *Orientalism*. London: Harmondsworth

Sainsbury Centre for Mental Health (2002) *Breaking the Circles of Fear: A Review of the Relationship between Mental Health Services and African and Caribbean Communities*. London: SCMH

Sandman, D. et al. (2000) *Out of touch: American men and the health care system*. New York: The Commonwealth Fund

Sarup, D. (1996) *Marxism, Structuralism, Education*. London: Falmer Press

Sashidharan, A. (1989) in Clarke, J. (ed.) *A Crisis in Care? Challenges to Social Work*. London: Sage /The Open University

Savage, M. and Warde, A. (1993) *Urban Sociology, Capitalism and Modernity*. Basingstoke: Macmillan.

Scambler A., Scambler G. and Craig, D. (1981), Kinship and Friendship Networks and Women's Demands for Primary Care. *Journal of the Royal College of General Practitioners*. 26, 746–50.

Scambler, G. (1997) *Sociology as Applied to Medicine*. 4th edn. London: Bailliere Tindall.

SCIE Research Briefing (2005) *Being a Father to a Child with Disabilities: Issues and What Helps*. 18 October

SCIE (2005) *Managing Risk and Minimising Mistakes in Services to Children and Families*.

Scott, H. (1984) *Working Your Way to the Bottom: The Feminization of Poverty*. London: Pandora Press

Scraton, P. (ed.) (1987) *Law, Order and the Authoritarian State*. Milton Keynes: Open University Press

Seebohm Report (1968) *Report of the Committee on Local Authority and Allied Personal Social Services*. Cm 3703. London: HMSO

Selwyn, J., Frazer, L. and Fitzgerald, A. (2004) *Finding adoptive families for black, Asian and black mixed-parentage children: agency policy and practice*. Executive summary and Best practice guide; NCH

Shakespeare, T. and Watson, N. (2001) The social model of disability: an outdated ideology? *Research and Social Sciences and Disability*, vol. 2, 9–28

Shakespeare, T., Gillespie-Sells, K. and Davies, D. (1996) The sexual politics of disability: untold desires. *Journal of Royal College of General Practitioners*. 26: 746–50

Sharkey, P. (2006) *The Essentials of Community Care*. Basingstoke: Palgrave Macmillan

Shavit, Y. and Blossfeld, H. (eds) (1993) *Persistent Inequality: Changing Educational Attainment in Thirteen Countries*. Boulder, Colorado: Westview Press

Sheldon, A. (2004) Women and disability in Swain J., French, S., Finkelstein, V. (eds) *Disabling Barriers – Enabling Environments*. London: Sage

Shersey, M. J. (1973) *The Nature and Evolution of Female Sex*. New York: Random House

Shilling, C. (1993) *The Body and Social Theory*. London: Sage.

Showalter, E. (1987) *The Female Malady: Women, Madness and English Culture 1830–1980*. Harmondsworth: Penguin

Simon, A., Owen, C., Moss, P. and Cameron, C. (2003) Mapping the Care Workforce: Supporting Joined Up Thinking. Secondary Analysis of the Labour Force Survey for Childcare and Social Work. Research Report, Thomas Coran Research Unit, Institute of Education, University of London. April, 2003

Simon, B. (1984) Breaking school rules. *Marxism Today*. September. 19–25

Sinfield, A. (1978) Analyses in the social division of welfare. *Journal of Social Policy*. 7(2) 129–56

Singh, G. (1992) *Race and Social Work: From Black Pathology to Black*. Race Relations Unit, University of Bradford

Sivanandan, A. (2001) *Poverty is the New Black*. Institute of Race Relations

Skeggs, B. (2005) The making of class and gender through visualizing moral subject formation. *Sociology*. 39: 965–82

Smaje, C. (1995) *Health, 'Race' and Ethnicity: Making Sense of the Evidence*. London: Kings Fund Institute

Smart, C. (1977) *Women, Crime and Criminology*. London: Routledge and Kegan Paul

Social Exclusion Unit Report (2004) *Mental Health and Social Exclusion*. London: The Stationery Office

Smith, A. (1986) *The Ethnic Origins of Nations*. Oxford: Blackwell

Smith-Battle, L. (2000) The vulnerabilities of teenage mothers. *Advances in Nursing Science*. September. 29–40

Solomos, J. and Back, S. (2000) *Theories of Race and Racism: A Reader*. London: Routledge

Stainton, T. and Boyce, S. (2004) I have got my life back; users experience of direct payments. *Disability and Society*. 19 (5) 443–54

Stedman-Jones, G. (1984) *Outcast London*. Oxford: Oxford University Press

Stice, E. (2002). Risk and maintenance factors for eating pathology: A meta-analytic review. *Psychological Bulletin*, 128, 825–48

Stoller, E. and Gibson, R.C. *Worlds of Difference: Inequality and the Aging Experience*. Thousand Oaks, CA: Pine Ferge Press

Swain, J., Finkelstein V., French, S. and Oliver, M. (eds) (1993) *Disabling Barriers – Enabling Environments*, London: Sage

Swann Report (1985) *Education For All*. London: HMSO

Tanyi, R. A. (2002). Towards clarification of the meaning of spirituality. *Journal of Advanced Nursing*. 39 (5), 500–9

Tarleton, B., Ward, L. and Howarth, J. (2006) *Finding the Right Support? A Review of issues and Positive Practice in Supporting Parents with Learning Difficulties and their Children*. London: Baring Foundation

Taylor, D. and Field, S. (2007) *Sociology of Health and Health Care*. 4th edn. Oxford: Blackwell

Taylor, I., Walton, P. and Young, J. (1973) *The New Criminology: For a Social Theory of Deviance*, London: Routledge and Kegan Paul

Terry, J. (1997) *The seductive power of science in the making of deviant subjectivities.* in V. Rosario (ed.) *Science and Homosexualities.* New York: Routledge

Tew, J. (ed.) (2005) *Social Perspectives in Mental Health: Developing Social Models to Understand and Work with Mental Distress.* 2nd edn. London: Jessica Kingsley Publishers

Thoburn, J., Wilding, J. and Watson, J. (2000) *Family Support in Cases of Emotional Maltreatement and Neglect.* London: Stationery Office

Thomas, C. (1999) *Female Forms: Experiencing and Understanding Disability.* Buckingham: Open University Press

Thomas, C. (2004) How is disability understood? An examination of sociological approaches. *Disability and Society.* 19 (6) 569–83

Thomas, D. and Woods, H. (2003) *Working with People with Learning Disabilities: Theory to Practice.* London: Jessica Kingsley Publishers

Thomas, N. (2005) *Social Work with Young People in Care.* London: Palgrave Macmillan

Thompson, N. (1998) *Promoting Equality – Challenging Discrimination and Oppression in the Human Services.* Basingstoke: Macmillan

Thompson, N. (2005) *Understanding Social Work: Preparing for Practice.* 2nd edn. Basingstoke: Palgrave

Thompson, P. (1999) The role of grandparents when parents part or die: some reflections on the mythical decline of the extended family. *Ageing and Society.* 19(4) 471–503

Thoburn, J., Lewis, A. and Shemmings, D. (1995) *Paternalism or Partnership? Family Involvement in the Child Protection Process.* London: HMSO

Thorogood, N. (1987) Race, class and gender. The politics of housework. In J. Brannen and G. Wilson (eds) *Give and Take in Families.* London: Allen and Unwin

Titmuss, R.M. (1958) *Essays on the Welfare State.* London: Allen and Unwin

Titterton, M. (2005) *Risk and Risk Taking in Health and Welfare*

Tomlin, C. (2002), *Samuel Pepys; the Unequalled Self.* London: Penguin

Toennies, F. (1963) *Community and Society.* New York: Harper and Row

Townsend, P. (1979) *Poverty in the United Kingdom: A Survey of Household Resources and Standards of Living.* Harmondsworth: Penguin

Townsend, P. (1981) The structured dependency of the elderly: the creation of social policy in the twentieth century. *Ageing and Society.* 1(1) 5–28

Toynbee, P. (2004) We can break the vice of the great unmentionable: Language cements a child's class destiny into place in its first three years. *Guardian.* Friday 2 January

Trotter, J. (2000) Lesbian and gay issues in social work with young people: resilience and success through confronting, conforming and escaping. *British Journal of Social Work.* 30, 115–23

Trotter, J. and Hafford-Letchfield, T. (2006) Promoting best practice in dealing with Sexual orientation issues. *Community Care.* 9/11/06

Tunstall, J. (1963) *Old and Alone.* London: Routledge

Turner, B.S. (1992) *Regulating Bodies: Essays in Medical Sociology*, London: Routledge

Ungerson, C. (1997) Social Politics and the Commodification of Care. *Social Politics*. 4: 362–81

UNHCR (2003) *Refugees: Myths and Facts*, Information and Briefing. www.unhcr. org.uk

UNICEF UK (2003) *Child Trafficking Information Sheet*. January 2003

UNICEF (2006) *Child Protection Information Sheet: What is Child Protection?*

United Nations Convention on the Rights of the Child. Resolution 44/25, 20 November 1989

United Nations (2006) Population Division of the Department of Economic and Social Affairs of the United Nations Secretariat (2005) (World Population Prospects: The 2004 Revision. Highlights. New York: United Nations)

United Nations Standard Minimum Rules for the Administration of Juvenile Justice (the Beijing Rules) 1985

US Department of State Trafficking in Persons Report, 2005

Van Gennep, A. (1960) *The Rites of Passage*. London: Routledge and Kegan Paul

Victor, C. (2005) *The Social Context of Ageing: A Textbook of Gerontology*. London: Routledge

Vincent, J. (1995) *Inequality and Old Age*. London: UCL Press

Vogel, E. and Bell, N. (1968) The emotionally disturbed child as the family scapegoat. in Bell, N. and Vogel, E. (eds) *A Modern Introduction to the Family*. New York: The Free Press.

Vosler, N. R. (1996) *New Approaches to Family Practice: Confronting Economic Stress*. Thousand Oaks, CA: Sage

Wally, S. (1990) *Theorising Patriarchy*. Oxford: Blackwell.

Walker, A. (1981) Towards a political economy of old age. *Ageing and Society*. 1(1) 73–94

Walklate, S. (1995) *Gender and Crime*. Hemel Hempstead: Harvester Wheatsheaf

Wallcraft, J. (2002) Turning Towards Recovery? A Study of Personal Narratives of Mental Health Crisis and Breakdown. Unpublished Ph.D. thesis. London South Bank University cited in Tew, J. (ed.) 2005

Walter, T. (1999) (ed.) *The Mourning for Diana*. Oxford: Berg

Walter, T., Littlewood, J. and Pickering, M. (1995) Death in the news: the public invigilation of private emotion. *Sociology*. 3(4) 579–96

Walther, L. (1979) The invention of childhood in Victorian autobiography, in Gittens, D. (1998) *The Child in Question*. Basingstoke: Macmillan

Warner, M. (1993) *Fear of a Queer Planet: Queer Politics and Social Theory*. Minneapolis: University of Minnesota Press

Watson, N. (2005) Chronic illness, disabling barriers, discrimination and prejudice in Denny E and Earle S (eds) *Sociology for Nurses*. Cambridge: Polity

Weber, M. (1976) *The Protestant Ethic and the Spirit of Capitalism*. London: Allen and Unwin

Weeks, J. (2003) *Sexuality*. London: Routledge

Weiss, I. (2005) *Is there a Global Common Core to Social Work. A Cross-National Comparative Study of BSW Graduate Students*. NASW

Wentzel, K.R. (1994) Family functioning and academic achievement in middle school: A socio emotional perspective. *Journal of Early Adolescence*. 14 (2), 268–91

White, A. (2001) How men respond to illness. *Men's Health Journal*. 1(1) 18–19

White, K. (2002) *An Introduction to the Sociology of Health and Illness*. London: Sage

Widgery, D. (1991) *Not Going Gently*. Cited by Cline, S. (1995)

Wigfall, V. (2006) Bringing back community: family support from the bottom up. *Children and Society*. 20. 17–29

Wilfrey, D.E. and Saelens, B.E. (2002) *Epidemiology and Causes of Obesity in Children*

Williams, F. (1996) Postmodernism, feminism and the question of difference. In Parton, N. (ed.) *Social Theory, Social Change and Social Work*. London: Routledge

Williams, L. and Germov, J. (1999) *The thin ideal: women, food and dieting*. In J. Germov and L. Williams (eds) *A Sociology of Food and Nutrition: The Social Appetite*. Oxford: Oxford University Press

Williams, P. (2006) *Social Work with People with Learning Difficulties*. Exeter: Learning Matters

Williams, S. (1987) Goffman, interactionism and the management of stigma in everyday life. in G. Scambler (ed.) *Sociological Theory and Medical Sociology*. London: Tavistock

Williams, S. (2000) *Medicine and the Body*. London: Sage

Wilson, A. N. (2006) *After the Victorians*. London: Arrow

Wilson, G. (2000) *Understanding Old Age*. London: Sage

Wilson, J. Q. and Kelling, G. (1982) Broken Windows. *Atlantic Monthly*. March: 29–38

Wilton, T. (2000) *Sexualities in Health and Social Care*. Buckingham: Open University Press

Wolfensberger, W. (1972) *The Principle of Normalisation in Human Services*, Toronto: National Institute on Mental Retardation

Wood, P. (1980) *International Classifications of Impairments, Disabilities and Handicaps*. Geneva: World Health Organisation

World Health Organisation (2002) *Towards a Common Language for Functioning, Disability and Health: ICF*, Geneva: WHO

Wright, E.O. (1978) *Class, Crisis and the State*. London: New Left Books

Wright, E.O. (1997) *Class Counts: Comparative Studies in Class Analysis*. Cambridge: Cambridge University Press

Wyness, M. (2006) *Childhood and Society: An Introduction to the Sociology of Childhood*, Basingstoke: Palgrave

Young, J. (1971) *The Drug Takers*. London: Paladin

Young, J. (1986) *Ten Points of Realism*, in Matthews and Young (eds.)

Young, J. (1999) *The Exclusive Society: Social Exclusion, Crime and Difference in Late Modernity*. London: Sage

Young, M. (1958) *The Rise of the Meritocracy*. Harmondsworth: Penguin

Young, M. and Wilmott, P. (1973) *The Symmetrical Family: A Study of Work and Leisure in the London Region*. London: Routledge and Kegan Paul

Index